Tax Cheating

Tax Cheating

Illegal–But Is It Immoral?

Donald Morris

excelsior editions

Published by State University of New York Press, Albany

For information, contact State University of New York Press, Albany, NY
www.sunypress.edu

Excelsior Editions is an imprint of State University of New York Press

Production by Ryan Morris
Marketing by Fran Keneston

Library of Congress Cataloging-in-Publication Data

Morris, Donald, 1945–
   Tax cheating : illegal—but is it immoral? / Donald Morris.
       p.   cm.
   Includes bibliographical references and index.
   ISBN 978-1-4384-4270-9 (pbk. : alk. paper) — ISBN 978-1-4384-4271-6
   (hbk. : alk. paper)   1. Tax evasion—Moral and ethical aspects—United
   States.   2. Income tax—Moral and ethical aspects—United States.
   3. Taxation—Moral and ethical aspects—United States.   I. Title.
   HJ4653.E75M67 2012172'.1—dc23
                                                                                2011031099

10   9   8   7   6   5   4   3   2   1

[W]hat more is necessary to make us a happy and a prosperous people?—
A wise and frugal Government, which shall restrain men from injuring one
another, shall leave them otherwise free to regulate their own pursuits of
industry and improvement, and shall not take from the mouth of labor the
bread it has earned.

—Thomas Jefferson (Inaugural Address, March 4, 1801)

CONTENTS

PREFACE

The goal of writing about the ethical dimensions of tax cheating grew out of my reaction to a public opinion poll I read in 1999. According to the poll, 87 percent of Americans believe that tax cheating is always wrong. That level of agreement among Americans led me to wonder what forces were at work—was it a high level of patriotism, a belief that the government employs its scarce resources wisely, or an acknowledgment of the value of the tangible and intangible benefits we receive in return for our tax dollars? I wondered how such a distasteful process as filling out a tax return and writing a check to the treasury could possibly strike such a powerful moral chord in that many people.

After ruminating on the question for a number of years, puzzling about where to begin to look for an answer, it occurred to me that there is simply a lot of confusion about taxes and about the origins of moral duties. Perhaps, I realized, I could attempt a clarification and exploration of the question that 87 percent of my fellow citizens apparently agree on—but with which I do not—to see where it led. In so doing I would need to define cheating in general and tax cheating in particular. I would also need to address the difference between a *general* moral obligation to obey the law versus a *specific* moral duty to pay the exact amount of income tax determined to be a person's share by the elaborate machinations of the Internal Revenue Code.

Tax evasion has been the subject of research in law, criminology, accounting, psychology, and economics for many years. It is a crime with well-defined characteristics. More than one writer has addressed the ethics of tax evasion, some defending occasions when evading taxes is the morally proper thing to do. Unlike tax evasion, however, tax cheating is largely undefined and has been all but ignored by researchers. When mention is made of tax cheating in the literature or by politicians or the news media, it is either assumed that its meaning is commonly known and needs no explanation, or that it has the same meaning as tax evasion. The definition of tax cheating developed here, however, is considerably broader and more complex than the relatively well-defined concept of tax evasion. I argue that what constitutes tax cheating is every bit as complex as the tax laws being cheated.

Clarifying what activities are encompassed by *tax cheating* requires looking at the income tax system as a whole and evaluating the respective roles played by taxpayers, the IRS, the Internal Revenue Code, Congress, the courts, the economic and political ideologies that influence congressional thinking, and those who are paid to influence the legislative process. Understanding the moral quality of tax cheating requires an understanding of the contribution each of these elements makes to the system. A first step in addressing the problems of our current Tax Code involves understanding that the moral quality of cheating is determined by the moral quality of the rules being cheated. To the extent the current Code lacks any moral foundation, cheating its rules—while certainly illegal—cannot be immoral. To adequately comprehend the meaning of tax cheating in this way, it is necessary to evaluate the moral quality of our income tax system employing insights from law, economics, accounting, psychology, criminology, sociology, and philosophy.

After several years of seemingly unproductive reading and thinking about tax cheating, during the summer of 2007 I finally began to manipulate the parts of the answer I was looking for, gradually finding a place for each within the puzzle. During the next three years I arranged and rearranged the pieces to form a reasonably coherent argument about the lack of a moral foundation for paying income taxes under the current system. In so doing I concluded that it is not complexity itself that results in the Code's lack of moral grounding, but unharnessed complexity beholden to no guiding principle or moral intuition; the parts of the Code have simply metastasized.

Since the 1930s there have been complaints in Congress that the Tax Code is too complex. But even if it were somehow possible to simplify the current Tax Code—getting back to the constitutional mandate to raise revenue for defense and the general welfare—continuing to ignore the systemic problems (most notably the self-assessment model) that encourage and enable tax cheating, would mean that we had come no closer to producing a Code that allowed us to judge for ourselves what share of the tax burden we are paying and, also—just as important— whether it is our fair share.

ACKNOWLEDGMENTS

I would like to express appreciation to my brother Jim for his encouragement in the initial stages of this project as well as his assistance at the end in reading and commenting on certain topics treated in the book. His knack for recognizing an idea's potential for resonating with the public has been honed through his many years in advertising. My lifelong friend and fellow CPA Tim Bogan was kind enough to read early drafts of a number of chapters, providing valuable feedback. His perspective as a practitioner of both tax and common sense gave me encouragement that I was on the right track.

In the spring of 2010 the University of Illinois Springfield reduced my teaching load to allow additional time for me to complete this project, which I began to formulate in 2000; for that much-needed time I would like to thank my dean Ron McNeil and my department chair Leonard Branson. The outside reviewers for SUNY Press provided helpful suggestions and comments for which I am grateful and which improved the final product. Andrew Kenyon of SUNY Press has also been most helpful in guiding the manuscript through the necessary processes while offering encouragement along the way. Also from SUNY Press, I want to thank Alan V. Hewat for his editorial assistance and Ryan Morris for her production expertise.

I received invaluable editorial assistance from Katherine McCracken, whose eye for detail is truly amazing. Her wide-ranging knowledge and vast experience saved me from many an embarrassing mistake. I cannot thank her enough. The clerks in the Supreme Court libraries both in Santa Fe, New Mexico, and Springfield, Illinois, were of great help in locating a number of the legal materials cited in the book. My teaching colleague at the UIS Center for Teaching and Learning, Brian Jackson, read a number of chapters and offered insightful comments and suggestions. In spite of the excellence of my editorial help, there will remain errors in this book,

and these are of my own making. I anticipate that some of these errors are
the result of my treading into certain subject areas—especially economics,
law, psychology, criminology, and sociology—where my knowledge and
experience are only those of an interested outsider. I gladly accepted the
risk of these errors in exchange for the opportunity to pursue an interdis-
ciplinary study of tax cheating.

In their responses to my requests for feedback, a number of public
officials, mostly U.S. Senators and Congressmen, as well as the Internal
Revenue Service Oversight Board and employees of the U.S. Justice
Department engaged in the Tax Defier Initiative, were instructive. Jen
E. Ihlo, National Director of the Tax Defier Initiative, upon receiving
portions of this manuscript for comment, informed me that the "Tax
Division's mission is to enforce the nation's tax laws fully, fairly, and
consistently, through both criminal and civil litigation, in order to
promote compliance with the tax laws and maintain confidence in the
integrity of the tax system." The Division's mission, she explained, "does
not include reviewing books or other similar materials." I found this
response disappointing for two reasons. First, in my letter I had not asked
for a book review but rather for Ihlo's professional opinion on whether a
book such as this crossed the line and qualified me as a Tax Defier
(something I was hoping to avoid). Second, it was disappointing because
the specific focus of this book includes exploring reasons for (1) problems with the enforcement of the nation's tax laws, fully, fairly, and
consistently; (2) problems with compliance with the tax laws; and,
most of all, (3) problems in maintaining confidence in the integrity of
the tax system. As such, the out-of-hand dismissal of research on the
very topics of interest to her organization—though perhaps on a more
philosophical level than her organization's direct responsibility—seemed
unfortunate.

Others I would like to thank include the following political leaders
who have, on occasion, expressed an interest in, or concern for,
reforming the Internal Revenue Code. To each I mailed information
on the purpose and content of the book as well as sample chapters.
I anticipated using any feedback to make suggested improvements
in the book. In no particular order they include Congressman Steve
King (R-IA), Senator Kit Bond (R-MO), Senator Harry Reid (D-NV),
Congressman Dennis Kucinich (D-OH), Senator Susan M. Collins
(R-ME), Senator Tom Coburn (R-OK), Congressman Spencer Bachus
(R-AL), Congressman Brad Ellsworth (D-IA), Senator Sam Brownback
(R-KS), Senator Barbara Boxer (D-CA), Senator Charles Schumer (D-NY),

Senator Jim Bunning (R-KY), Congressman Mike Thompson,(D-CA), Congressman Earl Pomeroy (D-ND), Congressman Jason Altmire (D-PA), Congressman Lloyd Doggett (D-TX), Congressman John Linder (R-GA), Senator Jon Kyl (R-AZ), Senator Richard C. Shelby (R-AL), Congressman Bob Goodlatte (R-VA), Congressman Ron Paul (R-TX), Congressman Charles B. Rangel (D-NY), Senator Richard J. Durbin (D-IL), Senator Saxby Chambliss (R-GA), Congressman Bob Woodall (R-GA),Treasury Secretary Timothy F. Geithner, Lawrence H. Summers, Director of the White House National Economic Council for President Barack Obama, Nina E. Olson, National Taxpayer Advocate, the IRS Oversight Board, and Congressman Patrick J. Tiberi (R-OH). Representative Tiberi wrote back that he was honored that I asked him to comment on the book but that his current schedule did not allow time to participate in such an endeavor. The lack of any response from any of the rest of these public officials was instructive to me in understanding the difficulties faced by anyone hoping to promote a rational public dialogue on tax reform and problems with the current tax régime in the marketplace of ideas.

Some of the ideas exposed here I have worked out in more limited contexts and they have appeared previously in journal articles. Though these contexts have been noted in the book, I would like specifically to acknowledge the journals and the articles. "Tax Penalties and Deterrence: Determining Effectiveness and Taxpayer Perceptions," *The CPA Journal* (Sept. 2010); "Assessing Professional Tax Advice and Taxpayer Sophistication," *The Tax Adviser* (Dec. 2009); and "Tainted Money and Charity: Do 501(c)(3)s Have a Right to Refuse a Gift?" *Nonprofit and Voluntary Sector Quarterly*, (2008, vol. 38, no. 4).

And, although many years have passed since they first impressed me with the cogency of their ideas, I would like to thank my professors— John Hospers (Cal. State University, LA), Father Francis H. Eterovich (DePaul University), S. Morris Eames (Southern Illinois University, Carbondale), and William F. Marutzky (DePaul University)—for their lasting impact and inspiration.

For the *New Yorker* cartoon by Mike Twohy, appearing in chapter 1, I would like to thank The Cartoon Bank (New York, NY, permission granted). For the Rube Goldberg cartoons appearing in chapters 3 (Pencil Sharpener) and 6 (Simplified Income Tax Return), I would like to thank Rube Goldberg, Inc. (Westport, CT, permission granted). Finally, I would like to express my fond appreciation to Theresa McCracken for her cartoons (especially No. 7323, chapter 5, permission granted), and those she fashioned to the specific topics addressed in the book (chapter 2, No. 8546; chapter 3, No. 8460; chapter 4, No. 8462; chapter 7, No. 8534; chapter 8, Nos. 8474 and 8463, permission granted). The resulting cartoons were always superior to my clumsy suggestions. I hope the reader will see that in this age of word inflation, a good picture is now probably worth much more than a thousand words.

ONE

TAX CHEATING—THE PROBLEM

Our revenue laws as a body might well be entitled, "Acts to promote the corruption of public officials, to suppress honesty and encourage fraud, to set a premium upon perjury and the subornation of perjury, and to divorce the idea of law from the idea of justice."

—Henry George (1839–1897), *Progress and Poverty*

Introduction

Emma, an eighty-seven-year-old woman in a wheelchair, is escorted by her daughter Zoe into an Indian tribal casino near Green Bay, Wisconsin. The older woman puts a $20 bill into a quarter slot machine and plays for ten minutes until she wins a $160 jackpot. She cashes in her winnings and the mother and daughter leave to celebrate with a lunch out. The $160 is never reported on the mother's tax return as required by law. This is one end of the tax cheating continuum. It is the end calling for reform of our laws, however, rather than for heaping moral blame on our citizens. As Justice Oliver Wendell Holmes Jr. observed, "a law which punished conduct which would not be blameworthy in the average member of the community would be too severe for that community to bear."[1] Agreeing with this assessment, Richard Posner writes, "A law is unjust if it is so contrary to dominant public opinion that virtually no one will either obey or enforce it, or if it is so incomprehensible that no one can obey it, or if it is enforced so rarely that people forget about it and it becomes a trap for the unwary."[2] These characteristics describe significant portions of the Tax Code; and, as a result, many casual gamblers like Emma would be surprised to learn they are tax cheaters.

At the other end of the tax cheating continuum are cases involving the infamous, the wealthy, the legendary, and the celebrated. Actor Wesley

1

Snipes, former Mets pitcher Jerry Koosman,[3] golfer Jim Thorpe,[4] *Survivor* winner Richard Hatch, country singer Willie Nelson,[5] Leona Helmsley, Spiro Agnew, and Al Capone are examples. Tax cheating is practiced by business leaders as well. On May 7, 2009, for example, the U.S. Department of Justice reported that a jury had convicted four former partners of the international accounting firm of Ernst & Young for promoting highly lucrative but fraudulent tax shelters. The partners were charged with tax evasion, conspiracy, and other crimes relating to these schemes. The tax shelters were designed to help individuals with annual taxable income in excess of $10 million to reduce their income tax bills.[6] The sophistication and intricacy of the devices required the expertise of some of the brightest CPAs and tax attorneys in the country. Acknowledged crime figures have also failed to learn from Al Capone's mistakes. In 2008 Chicago mob boss Michael "Mickey" Marcello, business associate of Joey "the Clown" Lombardo, was sentenced to 102 months in prison and ordered to pay $65,000 for conspiracy to commit tax fraud.[7]

The serious end of the tax cheating continuum includes ordinary citizens as well. During 2009 the Tax Division of the Department of Justice began prosecuting clients of UBS, one of the world's leading financial firms, who were aided in hiding their wealth in Swiss bank accounts and failing to disclose this information or to report the resulting income to the IRS. As part of an agreement with the United States government, UBS consented to provide the United States with "the identities of, and account information for, certain U.S. customers of UBS's cross-border business. UBS also admitted in the agreement, in great detail, how it had conspired to defraud the United States by impeding the IRS."[8] In this connection, the Tax Division filed a petition in court to enforce an IRS summons issued to UBS to obtain additional names and account information for about fifty-two thousand U.S. taxpayers.[9] In the wake of this news the IRS offered a partial amnesty program (reduced penalties) for tax cheaters who had not reported the income from their offshore accounts. As a result almost fifteen thousand taxpayers turned themselves in during 2009. The success of this program led the IRS in 2011 to offer a "New Offshore Voluntary Disclosure Initiative" for hidden offshore accounts.[10]

Tax Cheating

In *Cheating the Government,* Frank Cowell refers to tax cheating as "an intrinsically interesting economic problem with profound implications for the fiscal relationship between government and the citizen."[11] Tax cheating is not a new problem. The Bible chronicles the disdain felt for tax collectors. Among the ancients, Aristotle offers the following admonition that, while addressed to the law generally, applies as well to a discussion of tax cheating. "In all well-attempered governments there is nothing which should be more jealously maintained than the spirit of obedience to law, more especially in small matters; for transgression creeps in unperceived and at last ruins the state."[12] Ruining the state, in the context of tax cheating, implies an economic dimension that may exceed Aristotle's original meaning. But tax cheating, whatever it is ultimately determined to include, is certainly a transgression that may creep in unperceived. More than twenty percent of the nation's income currently goes unreported, untaxed, or uncollected and the problem has been growing during recent decades.[13]

Tax cheating is not a legal term with a well-defined meaning. It is a popular term used by taxpayers, the news media, politicians, and occasionally an IRS commissioner. In 1984 IRS Commissioner Roscoe Egger asked, "Can we afford any longer a tax system whose very unfairness and complexity invite tax cheating?"[14] Tax cheating is frequently equated with tax evasion, but that is not how I characterize the problem.[15] Tax cheating is broader and includes what the Tax Code and IRS Regulations refer to as "erroneous items."[16] In this book, I employ tax cheating as an umbrella concept of which tax evasion is one component. The definition of cheating developed here is morally neutral.[17] This neutrality is important because if we are to distinguish instances where cheating is a serious moral infraction from those where cheating is trivial, the definition of cheating should not prejudice the case by smuggling in a moral bias. A similar problem is encountered with many definitions. To allow for both good art and bad art, for example, a definition of art must not itself contain elements of valuation. Likewise, a definition of cheating must allow for a spectrum of moral disapprobation; the moral quality of the cheating will depend ultimately on the moral status of the enterprise being cheated.

The scope of this book is limited to the morality of tax cheating in the context of the current U.S. Internal Revenue Code.[18] It focuses primarily on individual taxpayers, who supply 70 percent of tax revenue to the treasury. While small business and small business corporations are discussed in chapter 2, the topic of tax cheating by large corporations is not addressed, nor the related issue of corporations as responsible moral agents, nor questions about corporate governance. This also is not an economic or political discussion of the ideal form of taxation, though alternatives are mentioned. While these are worthy topics of debate, the scope of this work is more limited. It is a discussion of the moral duty to comply with the current income tax laws or to disobey these tax laws, or the absence of a moral duty either way. Finally, it is not a treatise of the legitimacy of government or its right to impose taxes.[19]

Discussions of tax cheating are frequently framed in terms of a distinction between tax avoidance and tax evasion. One economist tells us, "It would be a mistake to blur the boundary between 'evasion' and 'avoidance.'"[20] Tax avoidance includes measures undertaken to pay as little tax as *legally* possible. It involves "changing your behavior so as to reduce your tax liability."[21] Investing in tax-exempt municipal bonds rather than taxable corporate bonds is an example. An often cited defense of tax avoidance is the statement of Justice Learned Hand in his dissenting opinion in *Newman,* a U.S. Court of Appeals case.

> Over and over again courts have said that there is nothing sinister in so arranging one's affairs as to keep taxes as low as possible. Everybody does so, rich or poor; and all do right, for nobody owes any public duty to pay more than the law demands: taxes are enforced extractions, not voluntary contributions. To demand more in the name of morals is mere cant.[22]

To draw attention to the open-ended nature of some tax cheating, I have not framed the problem of tax cheating by employing the distinction between tax avoidance and tax evasion. It may not be, and sometimes is not, clear ahead of time whether a particular transaction, or its characterization on a tax return, is legal or not. For example, ostensibly legal transactions undertaken primarily for tax reasons—meaning there is no independent economic motive except for saving taxes—may be questioned by the IRS and the courts, and labeled *tax avoidance schemes* or purely tax-motivated transactions.[23] When such transactions occur in business they are said to serve no business purpose.[24] In such cases, tax avoidance that embraces only the letter of the law and ignores its spirit, may still be illegal and therefore constitute tax cheating. Thus, the complexities of the law and the nuances of interpretation can blur the line between avoidance and evasion. As Goethe observed, "You can't tell a thief in the dark, when all the cows are black and all the cats are gray."[25]

Tax evasion refers to the *illegal* steps taken to accomplish the goal of minimizing taxes. It is "failing to pay legally due taxes,"[26] and is generally associated with fraud and subterfuge. In cases of tax fraud considerations of intention are critical while for negligence (and most tax avoidance) they are not. In distinguishing tax avoidance from tax evasion a taxpayer's intent may also run afoul of the result achieved. John Dewey generalized this condition in *The Quest for Certainty*. "Judging, planning, choice, no matter how thoroughly conducted, and action no matter how prudently executed, never are the sole determinants of any outcome."[27] So, to begin this inquiry by accepting the topic under investigation as bifurcated into tax avoidance (legal) and tax evasion (illegal) would be to miss the opportunity to address a central issue in a discussion of tax cheating—the adjoining ground. As Dewey also observed, "To see that a situation requires inquiry is the initial step in inquiry."[28]

Sociologist Edward Schur observes, "For most individuals, and even for major corporations with high-powered legal and accountancy staffs and advisors, the borderline between legitimate minimizing and illegal manipulation is extremely hazy."[29] Though there are clear cases of tax avoidance as well as of tax evasion, the fact that there is also a gray battleground of contention in between means that treating the distinction as if it added clarity to the problem of tax cheating is to cut off our chance for refining our understanding from the outset. In *Newman*, the fact that Justice Hand's above-quoted defense of tax avoidance put him on the losing side of the case—it was his dissenting opinion—shows the importance of addressing the issue of the middle ground.

Tax Cheating and Morals

The question of a moral duty to comply with the income tax laws has practical significance for the Treasury and Congress because the decision to obey or disobey a law often comes down to incentives. Penalties, fines, and imprisonment may be disincentives to breaking the law but so may a belief that what the law requires has an ethical foundation. As Benno Torgler points out, "Experiments that consider the interaction between subjects indicate that moral constraint works as a disincentive to evade taxes."[30] Other researchers tell us, "The identification of underlying moral beliefs and social influences related to [tax] compliance behavior should help policy-makers to create strategies to modify or address these factors."[31]

Thus, from a public policy perspective, if compliance with the income tax laws is a growing problem, it is important to consider all the available tools for promoting obedience to the Tax Code. If ethical considerations are an incentive for complying with the tax law, the design and implementation of the Internal Revenue Code should take account of how best to harness this force. Reporting the results of a survey of public opinion on tax evasion, academic researchers found that "individual moral beliefs are highly significant in tax compliance decisions. When tax evasion is seen as a moral issue, individuals are less likely to evade taxes regardless of the tax situation."[32] This should not be surprising given the fact that most people feel a moral obligation to obey the law.[33]

Morality provides a system of constraints on conduct. John Mackie explains,

> It works by modifying an agent's view of possible actions, by attaching to them a moral characterization, favourable or adverse, which has prescriptive entailments. . . . It thus brings pressure to bear upon intentions, but in a peculiarly direct way. Moral wrongness is a bit like a penalty, but moral sense . . . attaches it more tightly than any penalty to the wrong act, and discourages such acts more directly than by way of deterrence.[34]

Though not conclusive, there is evidence in the literature on deterrence that "conscience appeals can be more effective than sanction threats."[35] Abandoning this ally of tax compliance—the dimension encouraged by moral influences—is cutting off one leg of the stool; but this has been Congress's unwitting strategy since the income tax was introduced in 1913.

The force and authority of conscience, Adam Smith declared, "is, upon all occasions, very great; and it is only by consulting this judge within, that we can ever see what relates to ourselves in its proper shape and dimensions; or that we can ever make any proper comparison between our own interests and those of other people."[36] The ability of lawmakers to rely on help from the consciences of taxpayers to encourage compliance with the law means less need for direct, and often intrusive, deterrence measures. To the extent that Congress continues to ignore this aspect of tax policy, they do so at their own peril. Social psychologist Tom Tyler in *Why People Obey the Law* explains that "law breaking is viewed both as morally wrong and as a violation of an obligation owed to authorities. . . . If authorities can tap into such feelings, their decisions will be more widely followed."[37] But when legislators are preoccupied with ideological squabbles, amassing campaign reelection funds, and demagoguery, it diminishes the force of obligation felt toward their authority and reduces respect for their laws.

Cheating and Being Cheated

"If you are cheated out of a single dollar by your neighbor," Henry David Thoreau observed, "you do not rest satisfied with knowing you are cheated, or with saying that you are cheated, or even with petitioning him to pay you your due; but you take effectual steps at once to obtain the full amount, and see to it that you are never cheated again."[38] The IRS assumes a similar stance: the amount you owe the treasury does not eclipse the fact that you do owe the treasury. While the IRS certainly puts greater effort into collecting larger tax debts, even very small amounts owed to the treasury are taken seriously and actively pursued.

Part of the dynamic inherent in tax cheating results from the fact that, while taxpayers are cheating the tax system of what the law says is its due, many taxpayers also feel they are cheated by the government that takes their money and spends it in ways that often seem hard to justify, or beyond justification. When tax cheating becomes an issue of financial revenge—an eye for an eye—the moral dimension of the problem is clearly exposed.

Tackling any problem is harder when we cannot define the problem's parameters or even what the terms used to name the problem mean. Tax cheating suffers from such a lack of definition. Although the term *cheating* is not clearly defined, we know it generally has to do with fairness, with rules—whether stated or implied—with deception and intention, and is often associated with competition and engaged in to garner an advantage. It also is usually taken for granted that cheating means doing something wrong; but, as I argue in chapter 5, this is not necessarily the case.

Tax Fairness

In taxation there are at least two levels of fairness. A 2002 IRS fact sheet discussing its National Research Program states that one of the program's goals is, "to more effectively catch tax cheating and help ensure everybody pays a fair share."[39] The dimension of fairness the IRS speaks of in wanting everyone to "pay a fair share" is from its perspective as enforcer of the law. Based on the law's determination of how much each person should pay, the assessment and collection of tax should be administered fairly and uniformly. The law should be administered without regard to a taxpayer's race, gender, religious affiliation, sexual orientation, sphere of political influence, relative wealth, and so on. In speaking of tax policy, this was one of John Stuart Mill's points when he wrote: "For what reason ought equality to be the rule in matters of taxation? For the reason that it ought to be so in all affairs of government. A government ought to make no distinction of persons or classes in the strength of their claims on it."[40]

Mill's other point relates to the nature or substance of the laws. For example, the authors of *The Flat Tax* argue: "The substantial revenue the government would derive from the flat business tax is the key to the fairness of our tax system."[41] In such cases, the law's fairness is questioned in terms of what groups or entities should pay taxes and at what tax rates; that is, consideration is given to factors of distributive justice including the redistribution of wealth, progressive tax rates, fiscal incentives, and the influence of special-interest groups.[42] Designing the underlying system to be fair may result in tax justice at this more basic level. But the "fair share" notion raised at this more fundamental level—that of social philosophy and public policy—though critical, is not the focus of this book, except insofar as the current Internal Revenue Code fails to define *our fair share* in any articulable way. This failure impacts the administration of the tax, in turn, by undermining the Code's moral authority. This issue is addressed more fully in chapter 3.

As Mill's statement illustrates, these two contexts of fairness are distinct and yet easily blended in thought, thereby blurring their identities. It is important to add clarity to discussions of tax policy by seeking a definition of *tax cheating* as it relates to administration or compliance and by making distinctions explicit about which kind of fairness is under discussion and by drawing out the logical consequences of alternative positions.

The Meaning of Cheating in Tax

According to the U.S. Tax Court, in determining the ordinary usage of words when employed in tax matters, it is appropriate to consult a dictionary.[43] Dictionary definitions are lexical definitions, and while important as historical references, they are only one of numerous kinds of definitions.[44] In the case of *cheating*, dictionary definitions include the characteristics fraud and deception. *Black's Law Dictionary* says cheating necessarily implies a fraudulent intent.[45] If so, without fraudulent intent, an act cannot be cheating. However, as the opening discussion of recreational gambling indicates, this is a more restrictive conception of cheating than intended by the IRS or, in many instances, by the public.

As *cheating* is a term with potential ethical rather than legal import, its ethical dimension must be extracted and examined. In *Moral Thinking*, R.M. Hare says,

> The first step that the moral philosopher has to take, in order to help us think better (that is more rationally) about moral questions, is to get to understand the meanings of the words used in asking them; and the second step, which follows directly from the first, is to give an account of the logical properties of the words, and thus of the canons of rational thinking about moral questions.[46]

Some users of the word *cheating* connect it with trickery, fraud, or deception while others take a broader view. In *Lying, Cheating, and Stealing*, for example, Stuart Green specifically excludes deception and covertness from his definition of cheating.[47] A great deal of tax cheating—referred to as "playing the audit-selection lottery"—requires no attempt to cover one's tracks but relies on the scant chance of an IRS examination. Just as speeding is widespread among drivers because there are not enough police to catch the majority of offenders, income tax cheating often involves no more than hoping to be among the 99 percent of taxpayers who are not audited. This is why one commentator writes, "To hide unreported income from auditors, taxpayers in some settings must affirmatively falsify routine records, keep multiple sets of books, misclassify transactions, create false documents, and the like. In other situations, taxpayers may be able to simply 'forget' to record 'naturally' less visible income-generating transactions."[48] This indicates that there is a broad spectrum of activity qualifying for the label tax cheating.

In an early tax case heard by the Supreme Court, Justice Holmes said, "A word is not a crystal, transparent and unchanged, it is the skin of a living thought and may vary greatly in color and content according to the circumstances and the time in which it is used."[49] Definitions that move us past the dictionary are an attempt to point our thinking in a new direction and are called stipulative.[50] When a dictionary definition is insufficient to capture emerging shades of meaning, as is the case with tax cheating, forging a stipulative definition is appropriate and often helpful. Doing so functions like proposing a new hypothesis to solve a problem in science. The new definition, like the new hypothesis, is tested for adequacy or effectiveness against experience. If the new definition allows us to think more clearly about a problem—making our decisions more grounded—its relative effectiveness is established. Stipulative definitions are used by reformers and moral entrepreneurs to help mold changes in public thinking.

But the importance of defining tax cheating goes beyond clarity and understanding. Sociologist Howard Becker tells us that authority is maintained by controlling definitions. "Superordinate groups," he claims, "maintain their power as much by controlling how people define the world, its components, and its possibilities, as by the use of more primitive forms of control."[51] Specifically, Becker reports, "control based on the manipulation of definitions and labels works more smoothly and costs less" than more primitive means.[52] "We control people," says Becker, "by accusing people of deviant acts."[53] The government's manipulation of definitions—doublethink in George Orwell's *1984*—is an example of this process. Thus, if those responsible for taxing and collecting taxes can get the upper hand by defining tax cheating in a negative, stigmatizing moral sense—as a form of deviance—their job is made easier. So whether tax cheating is defined as morally indifferent behavior or as an act of moral deviance is more than a matter of semantic quibbling, it has practical consequences for the treasury.

But to effectively utilize the strategy of stigmatizing tax cheaters, current legal restrictions on privacy would have to be loosened, allowing public disclosure of who has cheated, how, and how much.[54] It is unlikely, however, that taxpayers would favor a public registry of tax cheaters as there is, for example, for sex offenders who prey on children.[55] The tension between taxation and privacy is important and is addressed further in chapters 3 and 6. The resolution of this tension may only come from increasing transparency for both the Tax Code and taxpayers.

The wide range of activities combined under the heading of tax cheating makes it difficult, initially, to attack the problem. Former IRS Commissioner Egger said, "Tax cheating is generally regarded [by the public] as a minor infraction, not something shameful or the least bit embarrassing. In some sense, it's becoming the taxpayer's revenge against an unfair system."[56] There is research supporting this view as well as opposing it. One study finds that polls and "current research indicate that Americans no longer value nor feel an ethical duty towards paying their taxes."[57] These findings contrast sharply with others. In an article entitled "Moral Majority: Most People Disapprove of Any Tax Cheating" the *Wall Street Journal* reported that 87 percent of one thousand people polled in 1999 believed that tax cheating is always wrong.[58] Prior research reported similar results.[59]

At the core of this apparent divergence may be confusion or disagreement regarding the meaning of tax cheating. Like the terms *expedient*, *ambitious* and *opportunistic, cheating* is frequently used to express moral disapproval; on other occasions, however, its use is morally neutral. In baseball, for example, a shortstop playing out of position in anticipation of the batter's tendency to hit the ball to his left is said to be cheating toward second base, but there is no moral import to this use of the term *cheating*.

Regardless of this uncertainty about the meaning of *cheating*, what is clear is that its use to express ethical disapproval is appropriate only in situations where intention is involved and not in situations of inadvertency. For an activity to qualify as cheating, in the morally significant sense, it must be intentional. In the context of taxes, fraud is the most obvious example; a person cannot commit fraud unintentionally. However, at least some, and perhaps most, of what is popularly referred to as tax cheating is either unintentional—often the result of ignorance or confusion—or the taxpayer's intentions are irrelevant, as when errors are the result of negligence. Tax negligence encompasses errors and omissions caused by not taking the time and effort to fully study, understand, and comply with the tax law.

Difficulties in pinning down the meaning of tax cheating arise in areas where the failure to pay taxes or report income is not strictly intentional, but is the consequence of misunderstanding the requirements of the law or interpreting the law in one's own favor, though this may involve stretching its spirit. However, as one court explained, "Were simple misreading of the Tax Code a valid defense to tax liability . . . we have no doubt that incompetency in providing accounting services would carry a premium."[60]

Tax Fraud

In Dante's *Inferno* the deepest reaches of hell are reserved for those who commit fraud, and immersion in ice (rather than fire) is their eternal torture. "Since fraud belongs exclusively to man," Dante writes, "God hates it more and, therefore, far below, the fraudulent are placed and suffer most."[61] Fraud is broadly understood to include deceptions in many forms. Tax fraud is the most serious form of tax cheating. British philosopher H. L. A. Hart writes, "At any given moment the life of any society which lives by rules, legal or not, is likely to consist in a tension between those who, on the one hand, accept and voluntarily co-operate in maintaining the rules, and so see their own and other persons' behaviour in terms of the rules, and those who, on the other hand, reject the rules and attend to them only from the external point of view as a sign of possible punishment."[62] Research by psychologists provides evidence that most people feel an obligation to obey the law and that the key determinants of this feeling are personal morality and the legitimacy of the law or legal authority.[63] For the rest, attending to the tax law only from an external point of view may lead to tax cheating and in some cases to tax fraud.

While most violent crimes are committed at night by young males, tax crimes are associated with a somewhat older and more diverse demographic, operating in the light of day.[64] Jeremy Bentham, in *Of Laws in General,* wrote that "if it be once determined to place the act in the catalogue of offences it may be necessary to make the punishment which is employed to combat it a severe one: owing for example to the powerfulness of the seducing motive. Instances of this sort are most frequent among offenses against revenue."[65] In some sense enforcing the tax laws is paramount to enforcing all laws, as the second must be financed by the first.

Enforcing the tax laws is most frequently accomplished through a series of penalties. Most tax penalties are civil and not criminal. Even the significant 75 percent fraud penalty is for a civil offense.[66] Criminal tax fraud is described in the Internal Revenue Code thus:

> Any person [including corporations] who willfully attempts in any manner to evade or defeat any tax imposed by this title or the payment thereof shall, in addition to other penalties provided by the law, be guilty of a felony and, upon conviction thereof, shall be fined not more than $100,000 ($500,000 in the case of a corporation), or imprisoned for not more than five years, or both, together with the costs of prosecution.[67]

Though fraud is a general category of tax cheating, specific activities tracked by the IRS include abusive tax schemes, bankruptcy fraud, corporate fraud, employment tax evasion, financial institution fraud, gaming fraud, health care fraud, insurance fraud, money laundering, tax evasion uncovered in narcotics enforcement, public corruption crimes, questionable refunds, telemarketing fraud, and abusive tax return preparation.[68] The Internal Revenue Code also contains sections describing specific criminal offenses including (1) the willful attempt in any manner to evade or defeat any tax,[69] (2) the willful failure to file a return or pay the tax,[70] (3) perjury and false statements,[71] as well as (4) the willful aiding or assisting in the preparation of a false return.[72] Prison inmates have recently been singled out as perpetrators of tax fraud.[73] Even the nonprofit sector has not been immune from questionable tax activities.[74]

In the overall scheme of tax enforcement, the IRS reports only a limited number of criminal tax fraud convictions, due in part to the difficulty of proving a taxpayer's willful intent. According to the Supreme Court, willfulness means the "voluntary, intentional violation of a known legal duty."[75] Numerous defenses are available to deflect the government's charge of willfulness, including the law's complexity.[76] "It is settled," according to one federal court, that when the law is "vague or highly debatable," a defendant lacks the requisite intent to violate it.[77] We will return to the problem of tax complexity in chapter 3.

Total criminal tax fraud investigations initiated for FY2010 were 4,706, with 2,184 convictions and 2,172 taxpayers sentenced. The incarceration rate was 81.5 percent.[78] Based on these figures—in a country with 300 million citizens and 140 million tax returns filed—we might conclude either that

- not much tax fraud is occurring,
- it is difficult to prove willfulness,
- the IRS is seriously understaffed, or
- the deterrent effect of IRS penalties and the threat of prison time are quite powerful.

Hans Sherrer observes, "In any given year the odds of someone's being murdered is *twenty times* greater than that they will be prosecuted and convicted of a tax law violation by the federal government."[79] In its publication *War Tax Resistance,* the War Resistors League offers comfort to its supporters: "War tax resistance involves little risk of jail. Since World War II, only about 30 people have been jailed."[80] War tax resistance consists of attempting to pay taxes for all governmental functions except defense. In spite of the meager quantity of cases, the Criminal Investigation Division of the IRS is apparently quite adept at seeking out the bigger fish to investigate. A study of almost six hundred criminal prosecutions by the IRS between 2000 and 2004 revealed that the average case involved a misstatement of income—understating income or overstating deductions—of almost $2 million, with almost 90 percent of the cases involving at least $100,000 in misstatements.[81]

For 2010 the IRS reported 401 criminal investigations initiated against taxpayers who failed to file a tax return. Of that number, 247 were sentenced to federal prison or other modes of incarceration. The incarceration rate was 78.9 percent and the average prison sentence was forty-three months.[82] At a 1993 hearing before the Congressional House Ways and Means Committee, IRS Commissioner Richardson was interrogated by a member of the committee about the scant number of criminal prosecutions for failing to file. The congressman quipped, "If we only have 700 cases completed or being worked on the criminal side and there are 10 million nonfilers, odds are pretty good for a nonfiler."[83] Not mentioned was the fact that the IRS's statistics on nonfilers includes taxpayers not required to file because their taxable income is below the threshold but also excludes many taxpayers who should file but operate in the cash or shadow economy or otherwise avoid third-party tax reporting such as W-2s and 1099s.[84]

Penalties and Deterrence

"The importance of deterrence," Margaret Levi writes, "is that it persuades taxpayers that *others* are being compelled to pay their fair share."[85] Congress has devised a wide array of tax penalties to aid the IRS in its attempts to control how taxpayers behave. This model for encouraging tax compliance is based on simple assumptions about human behavior, rationality, and how people make decisions. In weighting their tax compliance choices, lawmakers presume that taxpayers put various factors on either side of a mental-balance scales, noting the overall impact on the arrow's position—and deciding whether compliance is outweighed by the interests on the other side of the scales. The amount of a potential tax penalty is assumed to be one of these factors. Overlooked in this legalistic-economic model is the effect of the butcher with the golden thumb. Weighing alternatives is not accomplished in a vacuum but under the influence of a wide range of psychological decision-altering distortions.[86] Dating back to a seminal study of why people in flood-prone regions of the country don't buy flood insurance,[87] researchers in psychology and economics have addressed numerous flaws in the simplistic view of decision making as purely rational evaluation of alternatives. Most of us do not think like Mr. Spock. Some psychologists claim that "the influence of deterrence on compliance may be overrated."[88] The study of flood insurance disclosed that "if the chances of an event are sufficiently low, people do not even reflect on its consequences."[89] For a decade (2001–10)

"It's funny how two intelligent people can have such opposite interpretations of the tax code!"

the average IRS audit rate stood below 1 percent—for many people, not sufficient to prompt reflection on the consequences of tax cheating.

Psychological research on the extrarational influences on our decision processes has burgeoned and its effects now impact thinking in many areas. In this book, for example, several topics relating to these influences are touched on, including availability and subjective probability (chap. 1), intertemporal choice (chap. 3), prospect theory (chap. 6), and adaptation (chap. 8). In spite of this progress in understanding how people make decisions, lawmakers, the majority with legal rather than psychological training, cling to the traditional model of folk psychology, "based mostly on the common perception of unaided intuition."[90]

It is possible that Congress's willingness to abandon the moral dimension of tax policy as an ally can be explained by a belief (even if unfounded) in the powerful deterrence force of tax penalties or the threat of prison time, leaving no need to rely on the conscience of taxpayers. But one moral philosopher tells us, "We see a legal penalty as just, as immediately morally appropriate, only if the act to which it is attached is morally wrong."[91] Thus, if the tax law itself is seen as lacking a supporting moral foundation—as I argue here—penalties employed to enforce the Tax Code are also forced to accomplish their deterrent effects without the benefit of an ethical dimension.

In a book on IRS practice and procedure, Michael Saltzman reports, "Sanctions for noncompliance [with tax laws] . . . are forms of retribution, of varying degrees of severity ranging from small fines to heavy prison sentences, the threat of which contributes to maintaining compliance with the revenue laws at high levels."[92] Most tax penalties—small fines—are assessed for minor infractions of the law (late filing, late paying); but then general crime statistics reveal that nearly all crimes are "mundane, simple, trivial, easy acts aimed at satisfying desires of the moment."[93] In *Spies v. United States,* the Supreme Court emphasized the importance of tax penalties:

> The United States has relied for the collection of its income tax largely upon the taxpayer's own disclosures. . . . This system can function successfully only if those within and near taxable income keep and render true accounts. In many ways, taxpayers' neglect or deceit may prejudice the orderly and punctual administration of the system as well as revenues themselves. Congress has imposed a variety of sanctions for the protection of the system and the revenue.[94]

Deterrence Theory

Penalties raise revenue but they are also sanctions assumed to act as deterrents, and their deterrent effect has been the subject of study. Researchers discovered that taxpayers are aware of some penalties and their deterrent effect is evidenced by the fact that taxpayers sometimes diversify their tax cheating—a little here, a little there—to minimize the imposition of penalties. In particular, one study found "marked variations in compliance levels across line items [on a tax return] which appear to be systematically related to the difficulty of establishing noncompliance and the penalties for detected noncompliance."[95] It was also found that reminding taxpayers about potential legal sanctions shortly before they file their tax returns results in an increase in the amount of income reported compared to a control group where no such reminder was given.[96] And an increase in the number of criminal investigations leading to the incarceration of tax cheaters has also been shown to have a significant effect on voluntary tax compliance.[97] These results are consistent with the findings of deterrence theory, indicating that people avoid illegal behavior because of a fear of social disapproval, the perceived threat of legal punishment, and a moral commitment to the law.[98]

Sociologist Stephen Pfohl reports that "[f]or deterrence to function effectively as a means of social control, there must be some guarantee that a high percentage of offenders either really will be punished or at least believe that they will be punished."[99] In *The Psychology of Taxation,* Alan Lewis explains, "The probability of detection, the size of the fine and tax rates may well prove to be among the most important determinants of tax evasion, but even if this is so, the decision to evade tax is based on an individual's perception of the chance of being caught, the size of the fine and tax rates, not on what they actually are."[100] Here the IRS may benefit from taxpayers' subjective miscalculations of their chances of being audited or put in prison, based on the psychological distortion known as *availability.*

"Availability provides a mechanism by which occurrences of extreme utility (or disutility) may appear more likely than they actually are."[101] Research concludes that people are poor judges of the relative chances of particular kinds of events happening to them. Psychologist Barry Schwartz observes, the availability of news stories on homicide, for example, makes it appear more likely than it is.[102] Because of this, people believe their chances of being murdered equal their chances of dying from a stroke, when in fact death by stroke is eleven times more likely.[103] The more available the kind of event is to a person's calculation process—the more recent or more vivid the experience—the more likely the event appears. Psychologists Tversky and Kahneman explain, "The impact of seeing a house burning on the subjective probability of such accidents is probably greater than the impact of reading about a fire in the local newspapers. Furthermore, recent occurrences are likely to be relatively more available than earlier occurrences."[104] In general, "A person is said to employ the availability heuristic whenever he estimates frequency or probability by the ease with which instances or associations could be brought to mind."[105]

Because of this distortion, a doubling of the audit rate, for example, should result in more than doubling taxpayers' anxiety, as each audited individual regales family, friends and coworkers with stories of ruthless interrogation, garnished wages, frozen bank accounts, and unrelenting humiliation, producing a rippling effect of consternation. The aversion many people express for an IRS audit may thus distort their perception of its likelihood and increase their compliance. This has been documented in what is referred to as the *spillover effect,* where taxpayers report more of their income as the perceived likelihood of an audit increases.[106] One outcome of this effect is that "providing taxpayers with an accurate perception of risks (which is less than they currently fear) could actually increase cheating."[107] Another researcher concurs, explaining that because "taxpayers tend to overestimate their risk of audit, publicity about very low audit rates may cause an individual taxpayer to maintain a false belief that she is unlikely to be audited."[108]

We also know that some deterrents can be too threatening, resulting in resistance and even countermeasures. In *Sanctions and Social Deviance,* criminologist Charles Tittle wrote, "There may be threshold levels as well as levels of diminishing returns for sanction severity and these may vary from person to person and from population to population."[109] In addition, some penalties (or at least their payment) may even produce the opposite of their intended deterrent effect. Research in *trust theory* has shown that requiring the payment of fines can release individuals from moral norms otherwise constraining their conduct.[110] Based on this finding, a taxpayer who pays a tax penalty one year may subsequently feel entitled to cheat on his or her next year's tax return.

Economic Deterrence

As noted, tax penalties are assumed to act as economic deterrents, thereby discouraging tax cheating. But even if we grant the deductive argument that all taxes (including tax penalties) are disincentives, all disincentives are deterrents, and so all taxes are deterrents, this does not answer the question of how effective is a given tax penalty. The Internal Revenue Code contains roughly fifty different income tax–related penalties, ranging from one-half percent interest a month to 100 percent of the tax due. Most of these penalties are unknown to the majority of taxpayers, calling into question their possible deterrent effect.[111] One of the reasons for the emphasis on deductive reasoning in economic debates is the frequent impossibility of conducting relevant large-scale controlled experiments in a functioning economy. This does not mean economists can't or don't conduct experiments—they do. However, as Samuelson points out, "It is more difficult to perform experiments in economics than in the laboratory sciences. . . . Economists cannot measure economic variables with the precision that physical scientists can . . . [because] it is difficult to replicate the real economy in a laboratory."[112] This limitation applies to answering questions about a tax penalty's power to deter specific kinds of tax cheating. One study indicated that very high penalty rates, such as 900 percent, do have a marked deterrent effect.[113] This finding, however, offers little potential benefit for the real world or even for lawmakers. Another study concluded that, "Nonevaders do not need deterrence to keep them from evading" and that for "habitual evaders . . . deterrence does not seem to have any effect."[114]

"Unlike physical scientists," an economics text tells us, "economists rarely have the chance to conduct controlled experiments to validate their models. Instead, economists most often test hypotheses by looking at actual experiences in markets."[115] But finding a market reflecting all the complexities of the income tax system is a challenge. The IRS knows there is a problem here. It admits, "Some penalties may be too low under current law to change behavior. Other penalties may be so high that examiners have been unable or unwilling to assert them, particularly when they believe that taxpayers have made inadvertent errors."[116] With little empirical evidence to rely on, the amounts set for various tax penalties are arbitrary, simply the outcome of a political process, and often based on the need for revenue as much as for compliance. Here the members of Congress must balance their need to raise revenue against their "need" to get reelected.[117]

An especially mysterious example of this arbitrariness is the $10,000 penalty imposed on taxpayers who renounce their U.S. citizenship for purposes of avoiding the income and estate tax and then fail to comply with the IRS requirement to file Form 8854 "Expatriation Information Statement."[118] While $10,000 may seem significant to the average taxpayer, the deterrent effect of this penalty is aimed at the actions of individuals with more than $2 million net worth who are moving to a tax haven country and turning in their U.S. passports. In light of its dubious deterrent force, we can only hope that the expected revenue gain from this penalty was not earmarked to fund a program of any importance.

Limiting the Need for Formal Sanctions

Investigation of the effects of particular deterrents on lawbreaking is notoriously difficult, in part because there is no universal agreement on the causes of crime. One well-known study of crime claims that the supposed causes of illegal behavior—and by implication, therefore, the projected effects of deterrents—are often dependent on the background of the researchers providing the answers. This is an instance of the syndrome: "For a man with a hammer, every problem is a nail." In their

General Theory of Crime, Gottfredson and Hirschi observe that "for the sociologist, crime is social behavior (when in fact it is the contrary); for the psychologist, crime is learned behavior (when in fact no learning is required); for the biologist, crime is an inherited trait (when in fact crime, like accidents, cannot be inherited); finally, for the economist, crime is economic behavior or labor force participation (when in fact it is uneconomical behavior outside the labor force)."[119] On this score Carroll observes, "Attempts to deter noncompliance without understanding the sources and processes of noncompliance are unlikely to provide a satisfactory answer to the problem."[120] Thus, before there can be a sapient answer about the effectiveness of tax penalties as deterrents, we would need an objective, multidisciplinary, empirical investigation, which I have yet to locate.

While the existence of tax penalties may point to areas of tax-cheating concern, the relative effectiveness of these penalties as deterrents remains unknown. Danshera Cords argues that "[m]ore important in deterring tax noncompliance [than penalties] are a taxpayer's internalized norms regarding the importance of tax compliance."[121] The leg of the enforcement stool represented by the moral belief that tax cheating is wrong—which Congress has chosen to cut off—may therefore be more important to a system requiring self-assessment than penalties and other formal deterrents. But, as I illustrate throughout this book, Congress has inexplicably abandoned the idea that there should be any moral duty to obey the income tax laws.

Tax Penalties—Is the IRS Making it Worse?

Although I will ultimately lay the blame for most tax cheating at the feet of Congress, the IRS contributes in certain ways to aggravating the problem through fomenting a lack of confidence in its ability to do its job well. Public perceptions of the IRS, for example, have been cited as a source of noncompliance. One survey finds that only 58 percent of the public agree that the IRS and its staff are "experienced/knowledgeable," while 37 percent do not. The findings are the same for perceived trustworthiness (59 percent versus 38 percent). Commenting on these results the author concludes, "There seems to be a problem with a tax system that the majority of the public consider as complicated and unfair."[122] Part of this perception may be related to an uneven handling of tax penalties. Here we find evidence that the IRS is apparently contributing to the kind of unfairness it is primarily charged with enforcing.

The IRS data on civil penalties for 2009 shows that 14 percent of the number (but 53 percent of the amount) of these penalties were abated.[123] This disparity implies that penalties of larger dollar amounts are more likely to be abated than penalties of smaller dollar amounts. For individuals writing bad checks to the treasury 6 percent of the number but 36 percent of the amount was abated, indicating larger bad checks are more likely to be forgiven than smaller ones.[124]

In the context of tax cheating, the apparent inequitable enforcement of the law with regard to abating penalties—larger dollar assessments receiving more favorable treatment in terms of abatement than smaller dollar assessments—raises questions of fairness. This questioning assumes that incurring a larger penalty is a proxy for the relative resources available for paying the penalty. Are larger corporations or wealthier individuals—those capable of triggering larger penalties—really favored in IRS penalty abatements as the numbers seem to imply?[125]

The general rule on abating penalties ("liabilities in respect of a tax") gives the IRS authority to abate a penalty if it is (1) excessive in amount (2), is assessed after the statute of limitations for collections has expired, or (3) is erroneously or illegally assessed.[126] The bias in favor of abating larger penalties may have different explanations. Perhaps the larger the penalty the more likely the taxpayer is to request abatement. But presumably even a small penalty is a big deal to an impoverished taxpayer. It may also be a matter of who is asking the IRS to back off; that is, the taxpayer with the larger penalty may be politically connected. The question of why the IRS first assesses and then abates the majority of these penalty dollars remains open. If size matters, the affect on the morale of the average taxpayer should not be ignored. And if the abatements are granted for any of the three reasons cited by the Code (excessive amount, assessed too late, or assessed erroneously or illegally) this invites the question of IRS competence and why these larger penalties get assessed in the first place.

According to the author of *Tax Compliance and Tax Morality*, "The timely filling out of the tax form and the timely paying of the taxes are ... important compliance determinants for a tax administration."[127] The majority of IRS tax penalties—more than 50 percent of civil penalty dollars—are assessed against individuals for paying taxes late, failure to make estimated tax payments, or filing returns late,[128] all requirements fundamental to a voluntary tax system. Tellingly, these most frequently assessed penalties are imposed for actions that are the most difficult for a taxpayer to disguise and for which deceit is of little help. Here banking on the audit-selection lottery is of no assistance either. The date of receipt for a tax payment or a tax return is objectively verifiable either by the postmark or receipt by the IRS, and the IRS tracks 100 percent of these items.[129]

Since the most common penalties appear to have little to do with tax cheating, though they represent half the civil penalty dollars, their usefulness as a framework for analyzing tax cheating may be limited, though the remainder of the IRS's arsenal of tax penalties may still serve this purpose. Among the latter the most significant for an understanding of tax cheating may be penalties for negligence and disregard of the rules, a topic addressed in chapter 6.

Cheating—Specific Characteristics

A central thread of this book involves reviewing possible meanings of cheating in general, and of tax cheating in particular. In *Lying, Cheating, and Stealing,* Green writes, "Cheating consists of breaking an equitable and fairly enforced rule with the intent to obtain an advantage over some party with whom the rule-breaker is in a cooperative rule-governed relationship."[130] He then questions the equitable and fairly enforced criteria in the light of the Internal Revenue Code, and says, "Whether such rules are sufficiently just, however, to allow us to refer to their violation as a form of cheating is a question that cannot be resolved here."[131]

Other studies have addressed the ethical status of tax cheating without specifically tackling the underlying concept of cheating. Most have addressed the broader questions of the ethical responsibility to obey the law or more limited questions such as the morality of tax evasion.[132] Leo Martinez, for example, believes that tax evasion is not morally wrong and therefore that any lesser form of tax cheating cannot be immoral either. He concludes that, "As long as taxpayers otherwise intend to obey the law, tax evasion is a morally neutral economic proposition."[133]

An Oxford law professor writing early in the last century observed, "Many a rascal takes his way through life without being made to answer for his sins if he takes care not to infringe the prescriptions of the law."[134] In coming to understand the meaning of tax cheating it will be necessary to determine whether infringing the prescriptions of the law includes only instances of breaking the strict requirements of the law or whether following the letter but flouting the spirit of the law also qualifies as cheating. As K. D. Deane notes, "To adhere to the letter of the law and to ignore its spirit is often taken as a sign of moral turpitude equal to (if not worse than) that of the straightforward law-breaker."[135]

Similar threshold questions include: (1) Are the taxpayer's intentions or motives in breaking the law significant in making a determination about tax cheating? (2) Can cheating be unintentional? (3) What about situations in which a taxpayer consciously tries to comply with the law but because of its complexity, fails? In such cases, the IRS may still impose a penalty for negligence, as this does not require establishing the taxpayer's intentions.[136] We also need to determine whether the term *cheating*, which typically carries a moral residue, has meaning or significance outside the moral sphere. Can we cheat without violating any moral rules and, alternatively, when we do violate moral rules, is the term *cheating* always applicable? A better understanding of what constitutes tax cheating will open the way to more effective ways of dealing with the problem—or deciding if it is in fact a problem and not, as some believe, a solution to a larger problem.

In the chapters to follow, little else will be said about the IRS's role in promoting or deterring tax cheating, as the IRS is primarily the messenger. Instead, the other players will be scrutinized: the taxpayers, the courts, and the Internal Revenue Code. I will defend the position that it is the Tax Code itself—or rather its author, the Congress—that is most responsible for tax cheating, as it sets the rules. In the process I will refine what is meant by tax cheating and ultimately explain why tax cheating—under the current system—is not a proper target of moral disapproval.

TWO

THE TAX GAP, TAX PROTESTORS, AND SMALL BUSINESS

All too often, IRS aims its powerful enforcement weapons on the
easy targets, those taxpayers attempting to comply with the tax
laws instead of those thumbing their noses at it.
—U.S. Representative J. J. Pickle (D-TX) (1913–2005)

The Voluntary Tax System

In a book disclosing the dark side of international finance, the author
reports that tax compliance in the United States has traditionally
been high. "Whether because of patriotism, a sense of fairness, the
need to finance the functions of government generally approved
of, or fear of criminal or civil prosecution, Americans have on the
whole paid a significantly higher share of taxes legally owed than the
citizens of most other countries."[1] The implication of this assessment
is ironic, as the U.S. income tax system is referred to as voluntary;
so perhaps we are fortunate our system engenders only as much
cheating as it does, which is apparently less cheating than in other
parts of the world. But the notion of the system's voluntariness is often
misconstrued.

That a taxpayer must file a tax return and pay the tax due is not voluntary in the usual sense. If you don't file an income tax return, one can be
filed for you.[2] The IRS tells us, "The word 'voluntary' as used in by the
courts[3] and in IRS publications, refers to our system of allowing taxpayers
to determine the correct amount of tax and complete the appropriate
returns, rather than have the government determine the tax for them."[4]
The contrast is with a real estate tax, for example, where the government
assesses the tax and sends a bill.

But rights imply duties, and the right voluntarily to determine our own income is constrained by a duty to know and understand the rules. As one commentator reminds us, "One of the special characteristics of tax laws in comparison to criminal laws is that they do not simply prohibit a particular conduct. Instead, they impose affirmative obligations to become informed about tax rules, to keep records, to report income and expenses, all in a timely fashion."[5] These obligations frame the question of a moral duty not to cheat in a different light. A moral obligation not to cheat implies a moral duty to educate oneself about the rules. And while the right to drive a car also imposes a duty to know the rules of the road, knowing the Tax Code, IRS Regulations, and myriad court rulings poses a much greater burden of education and compliance. John Stuart Mill (1806–1873) warned that "the strongest objection . . . to raising the whole or the greater part of a large revenue by direct taxes, is the impossibility of assessing them fairly without a conscientious cooperation on the part of the contributors, not to be hoped for in the present low state of public morality."[6] Researchers in this area advise that "[a] taxing system relying on self reporting requires responsible taxpayers with compliant behavior."[7] However, Slemrod and Bakija tell us—from an economist's perspective—it is "not in any one individual's interest to contribute voluntarily to the government's coffers. Each citizen has a very strong incentive to ride free on the contributions of others, since one's own individual contribution is just a drop in the bucket and doesn't materially affect what one gets back from the government."[8] Such a voluntary system is therefore ethically flawed, as it incentivizes irresponsibility and noncompliance. Perhaps voluntarily assessing and paying our taxes is supererogatory and thereby worthy of praise, but does not amount to exercising a moral duty to pay income tax.

It is my contention that in the context of the present U.S. income tax system a sense of duty is misplaced. I argue that the Tax Code is structured in a fashion precluding its serving as a source of moral allegiance. The expression of a knee-jerk moral duty to pay taxes should therefore be questioned, as it either evinces a more general civic duty or ethical loyalty to the law, or expresses another more fundamental moral duty believed to apply to paying income taxes as well.[9] An example of the latter might be acceptance of the moral principle that no one should aim to be a financial burden on someone else. The Tax Code's inability to inspire a moral obligation, I argue, is a function of its design, most particularly its system of self-assessment, leading to a moral dilemma, discussed in the next chapter.

The World of Tax Protestors

A survey by the IRS Oversight Board reveals that 4 percent of taxpayers believe it is acceptable to cheat as much as possible on their income taxes.[10] Tax cheating in the United States is most easily identified in those who opt out of filing and paying income taxes, often citing the voluntary nature of the income tax as their justification. The IRS and the courts call them tax protestors. Some tax protestors object to the existence or substance of the law. Others believe the law's jurisdiction does not extend to them or their income. Some protestors claim their wages and salaries are exempt from taxation. This argument is based on questioning the federal government's taxing jurisdiction or on the dollar's removal from the gold standard in 1933, or on an exchange theory of labor in which a person's efforts are exchanged in the marketplace for pay of an equal amount, resulting in no gain.[11] However, as the court in *Connor* stated, "Every court which has ever considered the issue has unequivocally rejected the argument that wages are not income."[12]

While some tax protestors simply don't file, others file a return but fill in only zeros in the spaces for income. In 2009, a District of Columbia police officer was sentenced to fourteen months in prison for putting a zero on the line for wages on his 2002 return although his W-2 showed he had earned $155,211.[13] In *Cibirac*, the Tax Court observed, "The majority of courts, including this Court, have held that, generally, a return that contains only zeros is not a valid return."[14] This was clarified in *Moore*, where the court explained that a tax might conceivably be calculated on the basis of the zero entries, but "there must also be an honest and reasonable intent to supply the information required by the tax code."[15]

The IRS reports the following example, illustrating typical characteristics of tax protestors:

On July 15, 2009, in Oklahoma City, Oklahoma, George Edward Boyd, of Stillwater, Oklahoma, was sentenced to 33 months in prison, followed by three years of supervised release, and ordered to pay $51,309 in restitution. Boyd retired from the United States Air Force in 1993 and has worked as an international cargo pilot for Atlas Air, Inc., since December 1998. Trial evidence showed that Boyd had openly contested the legal authority of the federal government to assess, levy, and collect certain personal income taxes since 1996 and that he failed to file personal income tax returns for the calendar years 1996 through 2000. . . . Boyd signed federal income tax returns for the years

2001 through 2007 in which he reported that he had zero wages. He earned between $80,000 and $115,000 in wages from Atlas Air in each of those years. On each of these seven returns, Boyd claimed a tax refund which totaled over $163,700 for the seven years. The refunds Boyd claimed were calculated by Boyd by adding the Medicare and Social Security withholding to his federal income tax withheld. According to the jury's verdict, Boyd knew that these seven refund claims were false because they were based on false information about his wages and the amount of federal income tax withheld from his wages. He signed several returns after IRS Criminal Investigation special agents told him that his legal theories were incorrect and after he knew his case had been recommended for criminal prosecution.[16]

Some tax protestors question the government's authority to levy the income tax and the constitutionality of the income tax. They question whether the income tax has a proper birth certificate; but in 1916 the Supreme Court settled this question in *Brushaber*.[17] According to the Court, in light of the Sixteenth Amendment, taxation of income, "from whatever source derived," is constitutional.[18]

Tax protestors approach the issue of constitutionality from various angles. Some have argued that the Sixteenth Amendment, which provides that "Congress shall have the power to lay and collect taxes on income, from whatever source derived, without apportionment among the several states and without regard to any census or enumeration," was not properly ratified. They have claimed, for example, that there were defects in the states' ratification of the Amendment. This has been argued from diverse perspectives, including: "(i) versions of the Amendment ratified by the states contained defects in spelling, punctuation, wording, or capitalization; (ii) state legislatures did not follow proper procedures in ratifying the amendment; (iii) state governors did not sign the Amendment; (iv) one or more of the states that ratified the Amendment was not legally a state; and (v) the Amendment does not contain an enabling clause."[19] Regarding these alleged flaws in the ratification process of the Sixteenth Amendment, the court in *Knoblauch* affirmed that "every court that has considered this argument has rejected it."[20]

The Fifth Amendment

Two alternate protestor arguments involve the Fifth Amendment. One holds that the income tax is a violation of the Fifth Amendment's due process requirement, which prevents the federal government from taking property without due process of law. Due process includes a right to notice and an opportunity to be heard. But it does not require, as protestors allege, a hearing before the tax has to be paid or can be withheld from wages. In *Phillips,* the Supreme Court found that the procedures contained in the Internal Revenue Code fully satisfy the due process rights of taxpayers.[21] Rubbing salt in the tax protestors' wounds, courts have even held that the imposition of retroactive taxes does not offend the due process clause.[22]

A second Fifth Amendment claim involves asserting the right against self-incrimination. On the basis of this strategy some tax protestors have argued that the Fifth Amendment protects them against having to file a tax return. In *Stillhammer,* the court stated: "The Fifth Amendment does not serve as a defense for failing to make any tax return, and a return containing no information but a general objection based on the Fifth Amendment does not constitute a return as required by The Code."[23] This Fifth Amendment rule applies to criminal prosecutions and stipulates that a person may not be compelled to bear witness against him or herself. Courts have routinely held that reporting income on a tax return does not fall under this protection.[24]

Further, even if the income reported on the tax return is derived from illegal pursuits—which might appear incriminating—it is still subject to income tax and requires filing a tax return. According to the court in *Sullivan,* "It would be an extreme if not an extravagant application of the Fifth Amendment to say that it authorized a man to refuse to state the amount of his income because it had been made in crime."[25]

Protestors have also claimed that the income tax is a form of enslavement, making taxpayers work for the government without compensation and without their consent. As such, they argue, it is a violation of the Thirteenth Amendment, which prohibits slavery and involuntary servitude except as punishment for a crime. However, the IRS points out, "The federal income tax only requires payment of taxes on a person's income. It does not force a person to labor involuntarily, or to labor at all."[26] In *Abney,* the court ruled that the income tax is not a constitutional violation of the Thirteenth Amendment.[27] According to the court, "The specification, that the [income tax] act violates the Thirteenth Amendment by imposing involuntary servitude . . . seems to us far-fetched, indeed frivolous." And in *Drefke,* the court held that a prison sentence for failing to file a federal income tax return does not constitute the imposition of slavery as prohibited by the Thirteenth Amendment.[28]

Jurisdictional Questions

Another angle tested by tax protestors involves the federal government's taxing jurisdiction. In *Cracking the Code,* Peter Eric Hendrickson argues that this jurisdiction applies only to the District of Columbia, military bases (forts), and other federal lands ceded by the individual states to the federal government. "All other areas within the union are under the exclusive jurisdiction of one of the several states, and are thus insulated from federal authority."[29] In *Ward,* the taxpayer claimed that the IRS has jurisdiction only over individuals in "Washington D.C. . . . [and] federal enclaves within the states, and territories and possessions of the United States" because the 1913 Tax Act says its reach includes these regions. Here "includes" is interpreted by the taxpayer—but not the courts—to mean "includes only" these regions and thus it *excludes* individuals residing in the fifty states outside the "federal enclaves" within those states.[30] Ward's attorney and engineer of the arguments, Lowell H. Becraft Jr., later found himself in trouble for continuing to bring such arguments before the court involving what the judge called, "revisionist historical theories that have absolutely no basis in law."[31]

Using similar reasoning some protestors have argued that the U.S. government lacks the jurisdiction to tax them because they are only citizens of one of the fifty states. This involves the possibility that a taxpayer could be a citizen of one of the states without being a citizen of the United States. In 2008, a dentist was sentenced to thirty months in prison and ordered to pay $155,683 after conviction on three counts of willful failure to file tax returns. The dentist claimed to have renounced his U.S. citizenship and was now only a citizen of the Republic of Louisiana.[32] In *O'Driscoll,* the court stated: "Despite [the taxpayer's] linguistic gymnastics, he is a citizen of both the United States and Pennsylvania, and liable for federal income taxes."[33] Other cases employing this approach involve citizens of the Republics of Minnesota,[34] Illinois, and Wisconsin.[35] In reference to a scheme for excluding income earned outside the District of Columbia in one of the fifty states—as foreign earned income—the IRS admits it is aware that "some promoters may be marketing a package, kit, or other materials that claim to show taxpayers how they can avoid paying income taxes based on this and other meritless arguments."[36]

Tax Defier Initiative

In 2008 the Tax Division of the Justice Department embarked on a "Tax Defier Initiative" ("TAXDEF") that "targets persons who attempt to undermine our entire tax system." The defier cases generally involve individuals who, the Justice Department reports, "spout rhetoric denying the fundamental validity of the tax laws as an excuse for not paying taxes, while also availing themselves of the benefits and rights that the United States provides to its citizens and residents."[37] In light of the inquisitional tone of its mission, I wondered why it was not called the Tax Defiler Initiative. Actor Wesley Snipes received a three-year sentence under this program.[38] Considering the First Amendment right to free speech—and what Justice Holmes called the marketplace of ideas—it is presumably not the "spouting rhetoric" that gets taxpayers in trouble but the failure to pay taxes or file returns.[39]

The allure of tax protesting has spawned a cottage industry—peddling kits, materials, books, Web sites, and seminars—marketing its wares to taxpayers seeking a way out of the income tax.[40] The court in *Sloan* remarked, "Like moths to a flame, some people find themselves irresistibly drawn to the tax protester movement's illusory claim that there is no legal requirement to pay federal income tax. And, like moths, these people sometimes get burned."[41]

The promoters of tax protest materials include tax return preparers, who advise clients to take what the courts and the IRS consider frivolous positions on their tax returns, by employing one of the techniques above.[42] In *Murphy,* an accounting firm "calling itself Anderson's Ark & Associates (AAA) . . . offered no legitimate services; it instead specialized in international-scale tax fraud. Murphy . . . turned to AAA in 1997 in an effort to dramatically lower his past and future income tax liability. AAA obliged, helping Murphy set up a sham, zero-income partnership that took on huge, predetermined losses in sums perfectly tailored to eliminate Murphy's present and past tax liability. AAA also served as a conduit for Murphy to direct money to offshore bank accounts under the guise of advertising expenses."[43]

According to Danshera Cords, "Tax protestors impose significant, unwarranted costs on tax administration, and tax protestors are neither adequately deterred nor sufficiently punished under the current framework of civil and criminal penalties."[44] But, the same writer warns, "even a tax protestor can raise a legitimate claim that the law was misapplied in a particular instance." So, she concludes, "if the courts and the Service dismiss all tax protestor claims without any consideration, some legitimate claims will be missed, which may reduce the public confidence in the fairness of the overall tax system eventually reducing tax compliance."[45]

If, as I am contending, the current income tax is not a proper object of moral attention, then tax protestors, while legally on the wrong side of the law, are doing nothing morally wrong and some may be acting on the basis of an opposing moral belief, a form of conscientious objection or civil disobedience. I discuss these topics, including conscientious objectors who oppose paying taxes used for war, in chapter 8.

The Gaping Tax Gap

Some tax protestors are scofflaws testing the IRS's ability to enforce the law. Add to these taxpayers who claim to have earned less than they did and those who pay less than what they owe and we have the major sources of what the Internal Revenue Service calls the *tax gap*. The tax gap is "the difference between what taxpayers should pay and what they actually pay on a timely basis."[46] Before it was called the tax gap, there were estimates of underreported income taxes. In 1973 the tax shortfall by one estimate was $93 billion.[47] An Internal Revenue Service report estimated the tax

gap for 1985 at between $68.9 and $70.4 billion.[48] For 1988 the same report estimated the tax gap at between $79.3 and $80.9 billion; and by 1992 the range had increased to between $93.2 and $95.3 billion. According to one source, "The extent of tax evasion for the major income and consumption taxes in the U.S. is substantial, more than 20 percent for the federal income taxes."[49] The IRS's most recent estimate of the tax gap was for 2001. The amount of tax paid for that year was $1.767 trillion. For 2001, the IRS projected the tax gap at more than $345 billion, 20 percent of the amount of taxes actually paid.[50]

In *The Great American Tax Dodge,* the authors report that if tax cheating were a business, it would be the nation's largest corporation.[51] Others have pointed out that the amount of unpaid taxes equals the amount the federal government pays each year for Medicare or the amount of the 2005 budget deficit.[52] Former IRS Commissioner Lawrence Gibbs claimed, "There will always be a gap—some would say an ever-widening gap—between the compliance level that the law requires of taxpayers and the level of compliance that the IRS can obtain through its compliance and taxpayer assistance programs."[53]

The estimated tax gap is based on nonfiling, underreporting, and underpaying, however, and does not include unpaid taxes on illegal income (embezzling or other forms of fraud, illegal drugs, prostitution, Ponzi schemes, illegal Internet and sports gambling, shoplifting,[54] loan sharking, and so on) or whatever additional tax might be due from the undocumented cash or underground economies, making a comprehensive estimate of unpaid taxes surely larger but incalculable.

In its 2007 *Reducing the Federal Tax Gap,* the IRS reports that "estimates of the tax gap are associated with the legal sector of the economy only. . . . Although they are related, the tax gap is not synonymous with the 'underground economy.' Definitions of the 'underground economy' vary widely." However, according to the IRS, most people characterize the underground (or shadow) economy in terms of the value of goods and services that elude official measurement. The IRS admits that some elements of the underground economy do not contribute to the tax gap—for instance, taxes due on income from illegal sources—and that some contributions to the tax gap are excluded from the "underground economy." "The greatest area of overlap between these two concepts," the IRS reports, "is sometimes called the 'cash economy,' in which income (usually business in nature) is received in cash, helping to hide it from taxation."[55] Not surprisingly, the major cause of the underground economy, according to Ingo Walter, is taxation.[56] The same writer tells us that "as many as 43 percent of Americans do not pay the full amount of tax they owe."[57] Part of the problem, according to one study, is that "evaders and participants in the underground economy perceive a lower probability of detection than others."[58]

At a congressional hearing on the tax gap, Congressman John Linder (R-GA) asked then IRS Commissioner Mark Everson about the size of the underground economy: "Would you be shocked if I said it was over $2 Trillion?"[59] Though estimating either the underground economy or the criminal economy is not easy, the authors of *Chasing Dirty Money,* after reviewing differing estimates, allow that the "underground economy, and even the criminal economy, probably amount to hundreds of billions of dollars each in the United States."[60]

Dwarfing the tax gap and apparently also escaping measurement, according to a former IRS commissioner, is money transferred offshore. Asked whether or not he knew the offshore economy could be as large as $10 trillion, and growing by $800 billion a year, Commissioner Mark Everson admitted that he had "seen large numbers like that." He explained: "The international disguising of flows of funds offshore, particularly by individuals, is very hard to track, especially if it goes through tax havens or countries that have secrecy laws."[61] In *Tax Havens: How Globalization Really Works,* the authors cite three estimates of the total of U.S. financial assets held offshore in the range of $9 to $10 trillion. The missing annual tax revenue from these offshore investments is estimated at $62.5 billion, none of which is included in the official tax gap figure.[62]

For 2009 the Association of Certified Fraud Examiners estimates that fraud in the United States costs businesses approximately 5 percent of their annual revenue.[63] The proceeds represent one element of the illegal economy. How to project the amount of tax cheating resulting from this fraud poses an interesting problem. A crude measure might start with gross domestic product (GDP). For 2009 the U.S. GDP was estimated by the Bureau of Economic Analysis at $14.256 trillion. Five percent of this amount is $713 billion. Assuming the fraud proceeds go unreported on the fraudsters' income tax returns—and at an effective tax rate of 25 percent—an additional $178 billion of tax revenue went missing that was not included in the official tax gap figure. While economists may criticize these rough estimates of the cash and underground economies and the amounts escaping taxation through tax haven investments and fraud, the purpose of this exercise was to point out that the 2001 official U.S. tax gap estimate of $345 billion is based only on people "in the system"—those who are known to the IRS or subject to information reporting—and is seriously understated and out of date.

The IRS's own estimate of the tax gap may be skewed either on the low side to underplay its ineffectiveness in dealing with noncompliance or on the high side to support an argument for greater funding and increased workforce. In any case, the IRS reports that voluntary compliance with the tax laws as measured by the tax gap is 83.7 percent.[64] The voluntary compliance rate is "the amount of tax for a given year that is paid voluntarily and timely, expressed as a percentage of the corresponding amount of tax that the IRS estimates should have been paid. It reflects taxpayers' compliance with their filing, reporting, and payment obligations."[65] This rate of compliance, as noted, does not include either the tax missing on illegal activities or that due from some portion of the cash economy (to the extent that these are separate categories) or on tax haven income. The true compliance with the Tax Code is therefore certainly less than 83.7 percent but how much less is unknown, and its full measure defines the problem of tax cheating.

There are many explanations for the growing tax gap. They include the law's complexity, belief that the system is unfair, the perception that the value of goods and services received from the government is less than taxes paid, the growing national income disparity, financial strain on lower-income taxpayers,[66] and the advantages available to small businesses for underreporting and overdeducting.

It is well accepted that one of the most powerful tools for encouraging tax compliance, keeping the gap from growing even larger, has been the IRS document matching and tax withholding programs. Withholding on employee wages and its reporting on Form W-2 as well as other payments reported on Form 1099 have induced most taxpayers to report at least the items they know the IRS already knows about. For fiscal year 2010 the IRS reported receiving 2.7 billion such documents, or an average of about nineteen documents for each taxpayer.[67] Of course, the number of nonfilers, noted earlier, indicates that not all taxpayers concern themselves with this issue, or they avoid earnings that trigger reporting to the IRS. Over and over, those responsible for trying to close the tax gap have advised that income reporting by third parties, IRS document matching, and withholding taxes on income should be expanded.[68]

At the same time, however, the amount of income for which IRS reporting (matching) is not required has more than doubled in recent decades, from 8.7 percent in 1980 to 18.4 percent in 2000.[69] Reporting and matching are thus moving in the wrong direction to solve the problem.

In *The Cheating Culture,* David Callahan pinpoints one aspect of the problem: "Enforcement priorities should be determined by whose cheating is most costly, as opposed to who the easiest targets are."[70] This echoes Representative Pickle's remark quoted at the opening of this chapter. The Government Accountability Office (GAO) concurs, stating that the "IRS generally does not design its major enforcement programs to specifically pursue components of the tax gap."[71] Unfortunately, the practical advice, "follow the money" is apparently replaced by the IRS with the bureaucratic advice, "follow the matching documents," focusing its attention on compliant and semicompliant taxpayers rather than those outside the system's web.

Small Business and the Tax Gap

In the U.S. individuals pay the majority of the income tax, so it is not surprising that the lion's share of the IRS's $345 billion tax gap estimate is generated by individual taxpayers as well. Specifically, $245 billion (71 percent) of the total gap is attributed to individuals who either failed to file ($25 billion), filed but underreported their income ($197 billion), or filed but failed to pay the amount owed ($23 billion).These are annual figures and again, exclude the undocumented criminal, cash, or underground economies or income generated in tax haven accounts. Were the federal government required to report the cumulative annual tax gap on its balance sheet—as a receivable due from the taxpayers—its current balance when compared to the national debt would be staggering, even to the most jaded elected officials.

The most telling breakdown of the IRS data indicates individuals operating small businesses account for the single largest slice of the tax gap at $195 billion (80 percent of the individual gap and 56.5 percent of the total).[72] This is not a new phenomenon; field research from the 1960s showed differences between the income-reporting propensities of the self-employed and those of employees.[73] According to the IRS, understated income, not overstated deductions, produces more than 80 percent of individual underreporting, while business activities, not wages or investment income, generated most of the understated individual income.[74] Capital gains, in particular, are one of the easiest sources of income to underreport, and also one requiring greater compliance costs to detect.[75] Research on tax compliance finds that the complexity of the law and the particular circumstances of the taxpayer have increased the variety of opportunities available for tax evasion.[76]

Given this analysis of the tax gap, the 31.9 million small businesses—favored by the Code with numerous tax breaks and credited with serving as the greatest engine of new job and wealth creation—are also the single biggest source of tax cheating.[77] Walter reports that those with the greatest opportunity to cheat—professionals, the self-employed, and small business owners—report an average of only 47 percent of their taxable income to the IRS.[78] This group includes small corporations, about which another researcher observes: "The vast majority of the so-called small corporations differ from the popular concept of corporate businesses: they are primarily professional practices and small businesses that incorporate for tax reasons and whose fictitious corporate entity cannot be distinguished from the persons of its officers."[79]

A study of criminal investigations of tax fraud reveals that 68 percent of the IRS investigations focus on small business.[80] It is widely acknowledged that the middle class is highly tax compliant because most income is from wages and subject to IRS reporting and tax withholding. By contrast taxpayers in the upper economic strata—which includes many small-business owners—enjoy greater potential for tax cheating because more of their income is immune from third-party reporting. *Transaction visibility* is the term used by economists to describe this difference. The economic advantage to higher-income taxpayers in transaction invisibility is growing. Between 1980 and 2000, Kim Bloomquist an IRS economist reports, "[t]he top five percent of taxpayers saw their non-matchable income grow from 19.1 percent of total AGI ... to 37.9 percent" (a 98 percent increase).[81] This represents "over 77 percent of the increase in non-matchable income."[82] "Much of the erosion in share of matchable income," Bloomquist continues, is "due to the growth in small business income."[83] For the other 95 percent of taxpayers, during the same twenty year period, the percent of non-matchable income increased from 5.8 percent to 8.5 percent (a 47 percent increase).[84] So while the percent of non-matchable income increased for all taxpayers between 1980 and 2000, the increase for the top 5 percent of taxpayers was double the increase for everyone else (and double a number that was already three times greater than everyone else). The end result in 2000 was that the top 5 percent had achieved a potential for tax cheating that was four and one-half times the other 95 percent. One consequence, according to Joel Slemrod, is that "what is apparently a highly progressive tax rate structure may in fact, be proportional, or even regressive, if taxes levied on the wealthy are not collected."[85] This problem is not unique to the United States; in France, one observer tells us, the "tax system actually contains concessions for ordinary wage-earners to compensate for their poor evasion opportunities when compared with the self-employed."[86]

The term *small business* is, of course, vague, and its meaning depends on the context. The Tax Code contains numerous unrelated definitions of a small business, including (1) not more than 100 shareholders,[87] (2) initial capitalization of not more than $1 million,[88] (3) less than $50 million in assets,[89] (4) $5 million or less in annual revenue,[90] and (5) fewer than 25 employees.[91] In my accounting practice, which specialized in small businesses, I serviced clients ranging from a one-man computer programmer to an auto parts supplier with annual sales of $35 million to a national subsidiary of a public company. The small business tax cheating problem is not limited to sole proprietorships or the corner mom and pop pizza restaurant. In a study of small corporations—those with assets of between $1 million to $5 million—66.7 percent failed to report part of their income.[92] For corporations with assets in the range of $5 million and $10 million—68.0 percent were cheating. To give perspective on how small these businesses are, their average work force was 125 employees.[93] In addition, according to Eric Rice "more profitable corporations are relatively less compliant" than less profitable corporations.[94] Since these figures are based on IRS examinations (audits), it is estimated that they may be catching only half the aggregate corporate noncompliance and only one-third of individual small business noncompliance.[95] In the same article, Rice admits that "actual tax evasion may simply be untraceable, because it is either too far outside the law or completely 'off the books.'" Compounding the problem of business tax cheating is the fact that many businesses do not even file tax returns. In a 2010 report, The GAO advises that "the Internal Revenue Service (IRS) does not know how many businesses failed to file required returns, nor does it have an estimate of the associated lost tax revenue—the business nonfiling tax gap."[96]

"Borrowing from the treasury by cheating on one's tax return," one commentator reports, is attractive because, "unlike other creditors, the government requires no loan application, makes no credit checks, and allows repayment to be delayed,"[97] often indefinitely. It is perhaps this unconventional nondebt-nonequity source of financing—employing tax dollars due but effectively embezzled from the treasury—that fosters the storied ability of these symbols of free enterprise to create new jobs while producing new wealth for their owners. This is not an antibusiness or anticapitalist smear; rather, it is a call for leveling the playing field small businesses compete on. I owned and operated a small business for ten years, adhering to the classical view of competition, abiding by the law.

But in so doing I was disadvantaged by competing against other small businesses employing the government as a silent (but unwitting) partner, supplying them cheap (or sometimes free) capital. As one economist notes, "In the case of an income tax, the evader may pay little or no income tax and maintain a pricing advantage over competitors."[98] If a significant sector of small business relies on this informal system of government welfare for its germination, incubation, and growth, we should ask why the unacknowledged taxpayer subsidy of these important economic engines cannot be identified as such, and help be offered to this important sector directly and in the light of day rather than as an "unplanned national subsidy."[99] One response—bordering on a conspiracy theory—is that "society is well served by allowing tax evaders to continue evading taxes because such activity is wealth-generating and stimulates the economy."[100] I assume a society is also well served if its laws are enforced uniformly rather than selectively. "Taxes, unlike death, are not inevitable," Robert Kagan tells us, but "cheating is inevitable. It is difficult to see, however, why the government should not try to make it equally hard for all citizens to cheat."[101]

The IRS's 2007 study *Reducing the Federal Tax Gap* recommends few new strategies that could effectively address this specific issue. The most promising techniques recommended for countering tax cheating—which include expanding third-party reporting, expanding IRS access to the National Directory of New Hires, and strengthening tax penalties—are also those promising little effect in the small business setting.[102] About penalties, Montesquieu warned, continuing to strengthen them—making them more and more severe—has the effect of lessening the impact of milder penalties,[103] and it is the latter that most tax cheating is subject to.

According to former IRS Commissioner Mark Everson, there is a "50 percent or so noncompliance rate where there is no reporting or withholding."[104] Because it is well known that third-party reporting and withholding accounts for the insignificant portion of the tax gap contributed by employees—who have 99 percent compliance in reporting their wages[105]—recent legislation has extended additional reporting to many small businesses—those accepting credit card payments. The law requires banks to report credit card transaction totals from their business customers to the IRS.[106] The small business community was naturally opposed to such bank reporting and, therefore, congressional measures to implement this change have taken time to win sufficient votes; and continuing efforts are afoot to have it repealed. Businesses in the cash-only or barter economies will be unaffected by such reporting in any event, and the number of these businesses will be likely to swell.

Small businesses hold so many advantages over the tax compliance process that, aside from the IRS's ability to instill fear, the government is overmatched. "For many people," Graetz reports, "the fear of an audit is the only effective stimulus to comply with the tax law."[107] But this fear has a double edge, as Jeremy Bentham pointed out: "When a man is conscious beyond a doubt that the act he is about to commit is within the prohibition of the law, that accordingly it is of the number of those acts which are marked out for punishment, his ingenuity will of course be set to work to escape detection."[108] Presently, only 39 percent of taxpayers report that the fear of an IRS audit greatly influences their compliance behavior, while 36 percent say it has little or no influence on their compliance.[109]

Summarizing the problem of small business tax cheating, one authority tells us, "Though they agree with the general rationale of government taxing and spending, many people still try to escape as much of the tax bite as they can. They may engage in barter. They may work for less if they are paid in cash and no record is kept."[110] The simplest and most potent tools small businesses use in cheating include skimming revenue off the top and failing to report exchanges of goods and services. It is commonplace for small business owners to pay personal expenses through the business. From using the company's vehicles (cars, limos, airplanes, boats) and other assets for personal use, to paying for travel, country club dues, household help, and even nannies and tutors for their children, the business owners' imaginations are the only limit. In the tax jargon, any measurable economic benefit conveyed by a corporation to a shareholder can be construed as a taxable dividend to the shareholder (and the cost nondeductible by the corporation). Called *constructive dividends,* these benefits are rarely taxed unless the corporation is audited by the IRS.[111] Such self-directed economic benefits are viewed by many small business owners as one of the rights or privileges of ownership.

Other strategies involve nonworking spouses of owners placed on the payroll to receive 401(k) or profit-sharing contributions. Tradespeople— painters, plumbers, gardeners, roofers—who do legitimate work for the small business are called upon to do similar tasks at the owners' homes, and the invoices for this work are paid out of the business accounts as well. Personal legal and tax work also finds its way into a company's books, camouflaged among business-related counterparts. Corporate employees, such as mechanics or janitors, are required to perform work on the shareholders' personal assets (cars, homes) while being paid by the corporation. Shareholder-owned assets are leased or rented to their controlled corporations at rental rates far in excess of what an outside party (or "hardheaded business person")[112] would be willing to pay. Interest-free loans are frequently made from the corporation to the share-holder of a small business. The foregone interest is legally income to the corporation, but the frequency of its actual inclusion on the corporation's tax return is another matter.[113] If the loan itself lacks the characteristics of a commercial loan, the IRS will say it is unreported dividend income.

Many small businesses brazenly set their own tax rates by asking themselves how much tax they are willing to pay. The U.S. Government Accountability Office (GAO) reports that self-employed business owners operating on a cash basis report only 11 percent of their income.[114] For cash-intensive businesses, arriving at the palpable amount of income to report is child's play. The central cause of this problem was obvious to John Stuart Mill more than a century ago. "The objection to [the income tax], in the present low state of public morality," Mill reported, is "the impossibility of ascertaining the real incomes of the contributors."[115] While the tax gap is often blamed on the complexity of the tax law, former IRS Commissioner Everson asked, "What is so hard to understand if you have $100,000 in revenues that you have to report $100,000 in revenues? That is not necessarily a confusion issue."[116] Focusing on small business independent contractors in particular, Malamud and Parry ask: "Does anyone believe that the complexity of the Internal Revenue Code is the cause of the tax gap for contractors."[117]

Here I would like to cite but one example from my CPA practice, to illustrate how small businesses are fatally placed on the honor system by the current tax régime. The client was one of a number of real estate developers for whom I did accounting and tax work. The client's home-building business targeted upscale home buyers, many operating or retired from operating their own small businesses. In the sales discussion between the builder and the potential customer, the benefits of putting down a cash deposit on the new home were mentioned. If roughly 10 to 15 percent of the home's price were paid up front in cash (folding money), it was suggested, the purchase price, as stated on the real estate closing statement and at the county tax assessor's office, would be 10 to 15 percent lower. This apparent price reduction, the sales pitch continued, would save the homeowner real estate taxes for years to come. The unspoken other side of the equation was that the cash received would be skimmed by the developer and never appear in the business records or in any bank account. The 10 to 15 percent represented the average profit on a home, resulting in the appearance that some homes were sold at breakeven. The breakeven strategy was explained by the fact that the real profit on the home had already been made on the lot sale and that the construction business supported the salaries of family members employed in the business, thereby ensuring an economic, though not an accounting, profit for the builder. Unfortunately this tactic was hidden not only from the IRS but also from the outside CPA. Skimming leaves no trail on a company's books. Not until after I had sold my accounting practice was I informed that this tax cheating scheme had gone on under my nose; I can only hope it was an infrequent occurrence.

A more sophisticated tax cheating technique, employed by many small businesses, is the formation of multiple taxpaying entities—C corporations, S Corporations, LLCs, limited partnerships, trusts—through which to control essentially one business. This allows transferring income and expenses from one entity to another, thereby lowering or avoiding taxation.[118] One such scheme, which recently resulted in IRS criminal prosecutions, involved the deduction of $55.7 million for "'billing' and 'management fees' to related corporations over a three year period, where the related corporations did not report the income."[119] While the IRS is empowered to use its X-ray vision to see through such schemes, there are only so many auditors and so many hours in the day.

None of this is meant to imply that all small business owners are dishonest in their dealings with the government. But if we consider that there are 23.1 million sole proprietorships and 4 million small business corporations (S Corporations), 1.9 million closely held C corporations (taxpaying), and 3.1 million partnerships, even a modest percentage skimmed from their revenues or otherwise diverted from taxable income adds meaningfully to the tax gap.[120] The statement attributed to former Senator Everett Dirksen (R-IL), "A billion here, a billion there, and pretty soon you're talking real money," may be applicable here. Studies show that certain sources of income, including self-employment income, cause greater expenditure of time and money on tax compliance than others.[121]

In addition, the IRS reports that small business is one of the sectors in which tax compliance is deteriorating, especially in the areas of gross receipts, bad debts, and vehicle expense.[122] This is also why I am skeptical of economically persuasive models of tax reform, such as the flat tax, that proclaim as an advantage the "more reliable principle of taxing business income at the source, rather than hoping to catch the income at the destination."[123] In Hall and Rabushka's version of a flat tax, for example, the 23 million unincorporated businesses—not always known for their record-keeping prowess—would be a primary source of their business tax, a key to the flat tax. As one critic tells us, "The move to a flat rate would not by itself reduce the aggregate cost of compliance by very much."[124] And a flat tax system perpetuating the current sources of the tax gap would offer little benefit.[125] The locus of control is still with the taxpayer—the small business—and is carried on through self-assessment. Of the flat tax, Lawrence Summers said, "I think a flat tax is a bad idea whose time should never come."[126]

The Broken Window of Opportunity

Robert Kagan warns, "Widely observed but unpunished tax evasion has the potential to escalate."[127] Small business owners talk to each other. They know the system is badly broken and that Congress is not trying too hard to fix it. The fox is firmly in charge of the henhouse. This phenomenon was identified thirty years ago in a different context by criminologists James Q. Wilson and George L. Kelling, employing the analogy of a broken window. In their research a link was found between criminal behavior and the existence of a broken window. "At the community level, disorder and crime are usually inextricably linked, in a kind of developmental sequence. Social psychologists and police officers tend to agree that if a window in a building is broken and is left unrepaired, all the rest of the windows will soon be broken."[128] "Passersby observing it will conclude that no one cares or no one is in charge."[129] A broken window is a catalyst. "An unrepaired broken window signals would-be criminals that no effective policing exists in a community; in effect, the physical breakdown and disorganization of a community may tell criminals that committing crime carries few costs."[130] Since the publication of Wilson and Kelling's findings in 1982, other researchers have questioned the connection between minor acts of vandalism such as window breaking and inferences with wider implications.[131] But in the broader context of crimes of opportunity, even if a broken window is meant only as a metaphor for a lack of external regulation and enforcement, there is strong reason to associate wrongdoing with perceived opportunity, or at least opportunism.[132]

As the burgeoning literature on fraud and fraud investigation indicates, opportunity is one corner of the "fraud triangle," the other two being financial pressure and rationalization.[133] The intensity of any one of the three elements reduces the amount of the other two required to push someone over the line. If there is a broken window now signaling to small businesses, it is the knowledge that, with its current detection and audit methods and miniscule audit rates, the IRS is no match for the ingenuity of those bent on the creation of new wealth. As Machiavelli warned us, "There cannot exist good laws where there are no good armies."[134]

For political reasons, Congress has lacked the will to confront the problem of small business tax cheating. "The structure of the policy process is biased against enforcement techniques," according to John Scholz, "partly because groups adversely affected by proposed enforcement techniques lobby against them while few groups lobby to support them, and partly because influential administrative and congressional policymakers are more concerned with other aspects of tax policy."[135] This may be an example of *regulatory capture theory,* wherein those who are subject to regulation gain control of their regulators.[136]

Small business is characterized inside the Beltway as monolithic, and put on a pedestal in recognition of its good deeds, while its misdeeds with respect to tax cheating are largely ignored. Proposed solutions to its tax cheating ways have been scarce and piecemeal. On at least one occasion, for example, a bill has been introduced in Congress to deal with unreported cash. It would have required a universal exchange of existing U.S. dollars for new dollars. President Roosevelt used a similar approach with Executive Order 6102, requiring the surrender of all gold coins, gold bullion, and gold certificates to the government by May 1, 1933, in exchange for their assigned value in U.S. dollars. The exchange strategy has been used in other countries to flush out cash hoards with the intent of discovering their source. The process involves printing a new series of dollar bills, recognizably distinct from the current dollars, which will then expire. The old cash must be turned in to receive a dollar-for-dollar exchange for the new bills. Presumably, taxpayers holding large quantities of folding money would be called upon to account for its source. This is a crude instrument and its effects would only be temporary. It would not affect cash already deposited to a bank account, as there are presently other controls on these transactions.[137] But even such proposals have never gained much support in Congress, indicating that those affected and the amounts involved must be worth protecting. Rather than calling tax cheaters on the carpet, the decision is often made to sweep the problem under the carpet. "Justice," as Nietzsche saw it, "which began by setting a price on everything and making everyone strictly accountable, ends by blinking at the defaulter and letting him go scot free."[138]

Another anti-cheating proposal that has surfaced periodically is the requirement of tax withholding on payments from government agencies to business service providers. The need for this appears obvious: If a company wants to perform work for the government it should be required to pay tax on its profits. A version of this proposal was passed by Congress in 2005 and signed into law, though its implementation has been consistently delayed by Congress.[139] It requires only a 3 percent withholding rate and only on payments greater than $10,000 to government contractors.[140]

If a small business knows not only that the revenue it has received was reported to the IRS, but also that its account has been credited with some part of the tax on that income, there is a powerful incentive for filing a tax return and reporting the income. But even if a business fails to respond to this incentive, the IRS would have received the 3 percent tax and the reported revenue could be used to assess the total tax due, and more accurately determine the tax gap. However, following this law's enactment in 2005, lobbying efforts by contractor trade associations[141]—seeking the repeal of the withholding rule—initially pushed back the rule's effective starting date. And even though it finally became a requirement in 2011, the IRS regulations implementing the change called for another two-year delay, buying more time for the trade associations to work with their sympathetic lawmakers for the repeal of the withholding rule.

The 2009 legislation that forestalled implementation of this 2005 government contractor reporting and withholding rule means that the government's tax revenue during this period has been reduced and its need to borrow increased (or its need to raise taxes elsewhere on compliant taxpayers). One trade association reported the additional revenue gain to the treasury from this withholding at $11 billion.[142] Effectively, this lost tax revenue increases the price the government (and hence taxpayers) pays to these contractors without a corresponding benefit. This single example of special interest intervention in the tax process is nothing new nor is it unique, but the wider implications of this growing practice were set forth as a forewarning by former IRS Commissioner Charles Rossotti in 2005: "Tax revenue called for by the tax code will be paid by a smaller and smaller fraction of taxpayers and the revenue shortfalls will add to the already huge budget-deficit projections."[143]

So rather than requiring government contractors to report their income and pay tax on their profits, as a long-overdue condition of doing business with the government, congressional leaders have responded by leaving this item on the table for negotiation—as a dangling stick seeking to attract more carrots. As if these developments were not already bad news for average taxpayers, even the IRS was recently found guilty of awarding contracts to contractors owing back taxes to the IRS.[144]

In an ominous warning about our national tax policy, one writer explains the path we are flirting with. As the government's need for revenue grows, it takes on more employees and new tasks.

> The defense establishment increases in size, or welfare programs expand beyond what they were when taxation was publicly discussed and established. The ordinary taxpayers may not be attentive at first to the effects of these changes on the return they receive for their revenue, but at some point they are likely to come alive to any deteriorations in their situation and to government expenditures of which they strongly disapprove. It is then that noncompliance should increase, thus setting the stage for a renegotiation of the tax contract.[145]

What form this renegotiation will take and when it will occur are unknown. But as compliant taxpayers come to understand the extent of the growing official tax gap as well as the hidden and unmeasured tax gaps fostered by the cash, underground, and illegal economies—exacerbated by tax haven warehousing of untaxed income, and as they witness Congress's feeble efforts to deal with these problems—they will ultimately recognize their own role as unwitting enablers. To the residents living near a dam, a small leak in the dam is not just a small leak; it is a warning sign of impending disaster. Whether Congress continues to believe that the annual loss of 20 percent or more of anticipated tax revenue is only a small leak will determine the ultimate nature of taxpayer response. When it comes to tax cheating, Congress appears indecisive, short on ideas, and lacking the will to effect significant change. In the next chapter, I offer suggestions for addressing these problems.

THREE

TAX COMPLEXITY

> Inasmuch as all persons and property within the jurisdiction of a sovereignty are subject to taxation, and since the property cannot speak and the persons have no direct voice in wording the tax laws, it is a fundamental duty of the law-givers to make the scope of a tax law definite and its meaning clear; and therefore all doubts respecting scope and meaning are to be resolved in favor of the taxpayer.
>
> —*First Trust & Saving Bank v. Smietanka,* 268 F. 230 (1920)

The Complexity Problem

"The creation of the initial revenue policy," we are told, "is usually a quite public event, accompanied by a high degree of negotiation from a wide range of potential taxpayers."[1] When the income tax was enacted in 1913, it was intended to apply to a minority of citizens, and tax rates were modest. Complexity was not a problem and the self-assessing process was not perceived as burdensome. With the advent of the income tax, the Congressional Committee Reports for the *Revenue Act of October 1913* proclaimed: "In view of the many valuable governmental purposes to be subserved, those citizens required to do so can well afford to devote a brief time during some one day in each year to the making out of a personal return of income for purposes of taxation." Much has changed since those simpler times when Congress believed that "all good citizens...will willingly and cheerfully support and sustain this, the fairest and cheapest of all taxes."[2]

By 1936 members of Congress were already complaining that "our existing income-tax law is concededly complicated, and the need for its simplification has long been recognized."[3] In 1939 less than 6 percent of

Americans owed income tax, however, and so the problem was contained. But by the end of World War II more than 75 percent of Americans had an income tax liability,[4] making complexity a problem for most taxpayers. A century after the birth of the income tax, Ingo Walter writes, "The growing complexity of tax codes and their use for a broad range of political purposes other than raising revenue has added further to the impression of unfairness, gradually undermining tax morality and stimulating the search for escape even among otherwise law-abiding people."[5] IRS Taxpayer Advocate Nina Olson adds, "Complexity engenders ill will toward the IRS and a willingness to fudge."[6]

The transition from simply raising revenue—for defense and the general welfare—to advancing political and social ideals has been gradual but steady. "As if managing nursery plants," writes Fox, "Congress sprinkled income exclusions and deductions throughout the garden of tax laws to help ensure that each of us grew in the right direction."[7] According to Kaplow, these "rules that consciously deviate from tax principles in order to subsidize certain activities and groups" are one source of tax complexity.[8] Referred to inside the Beltway as "tax expenditures"[9] (and addressed more fully in chapter 8) these shadow subsidies for countless kinds of taxpayers and activities—yet with no discernable guiding principle reining in their proliferation—present taxpayers with an insurmountable obstacle to grasping what their fair share of the tax burden should look like. Thus the Tax Code, and its current level of complexity, is seen by some as strangling itself as taxpayers throw up their hands. A system that started by requiring "a brief time during some one day each year" has exploded into a multibillion dollar industry with its own lobbyists and standard industrial classification.[10] With the passage of each new tax bill, tax attorneys and CPAs joke among themselves, calling it their latest permanent employment act. Complexity not only leads to noncompliance—it helps taxpayers justify noncompliance.

Of particular relevance to this discussion is the IRS's confession that the tax gap has "one critical unknown piece. The data do not reveal how much of the gap is attributable to willful non-compliance or carelessness and how much is the result of a lack of understanding of [the taxpayer's] full tax obligation."[11] This question has practical significance, for as Torgler tells us, "Complexity may result in unintentional non-compliance if taxpayers have problems in filling out the tax form. It can [also] reduce the moral costs of evading taxes,"[12] making such actions easier to rationalize. Even the keenest conscience requires a certain degree of clarity to guide its vision, which the present tax miasma fails to supply.

Thus, the question of how much of the tax gap is the result of tax cheating reinforces the importance of the question posed earlier: Does tax cheating encompass only willful noncompliance, or does it also include failures due to negligence, ignorance, confusion, or misunderstanding? This question is addressed again in chapter 6.

Though it is of their own making, members of Congress frequently criticize the complexity they have created. Congressman Steny Hoyer (D-MD) reported, "The Internal Revenue Code is a Kafkaesque maze of complexity that confounds millions of Americans every single year. Our tax system is an embarrassment that treats many taxpayers unfairly. And at the very same time, it creates an opportunity—and some would argue an incentive—for those who would exploit its complexity to avoid compliance."[13] To dramatize the complexity problem, elected officials have

"Even trees shouldn't die in vain."

employed various techniques, including estimates of the number of pages (or words) comprising the Code. To make their point, some have reported that the Code is considerably longer than *War and Peace* or the Bible.[14]

A search of the Internet will turn up estimates of the Code's length ranging from 2,500 pages to 2,5000,000 pages. Former IRS Commissioner Charles Rossotti reports that in preparing for a congressional hearing, he asked his experts for the number of pages in the Tax Code. "Weeks later," he writes, "they came back somewhat sheepishly and advised me against citing any particular number of pages," for fear that other experts would take issue.[15] The nonprofit educational Tax Foundation calculates that the Internal Revenue Code contains 2,139,000 words and the Regulations explaining the Code another 6,958,000.[16] Though I do not subscribe to the theory that complexity and numbers of words or pages are necessarily correlated, I decided to have a look for myself. The Code is officially *Title 26 of the United States Code*. The edition published by the U.S. Government Printing Office fills two volumes, each three inches thick. The total pages in these two volumes are 2,327. Other editions contain more or fewer pages, depending on various factors of publication. West Publishing, for example, offers a twenty-seven-volume edition, *United States Code Annotated,* which references court cases and other sources to the various sections and subsections of the Code.

Another measure of tax complexity is the number of sections comprising the Internal Revenue Code. In 1954 the Code contained 103 sections. In 2005 the Code contained 736 sections, more than a 600 percent increase in fifty years. One of the reasons for the increasing number of sections and hence the increasing pace of tax complexity is the growing number of lobbyists. In 2000 the number of registered lobbyists in Washington, D.C., was 16,342. But this number more than doubled to 34,750 by 2005.[17] The growing number of lobbyists is an index of their effectiveness in getting special provisions favorable to their clients added to, removed from, or modified in the Internal Revenue Code; 83 percent of the Code now applies to only 29 percent of the taxpayers.

Legal complexity is nothing new. In his 1836 *A Treatise on Political Economy,* French economist Jean-Baptiste Say warned that, "the intricacy of law...holds out a great encouragement to fraud, by multiplying the chances of evasion."[18] One measure of the Code's intricacy is its inability to deal simply with simple matters. Whether one taxpayer is a dependent of another is an example. In 2005, in an effort to bring unity to the tax definition of a child, Congress complicated the process by introducing a new term: *qualifying child.* Unfortunately, in any given year, more than one taxpayer may qualify as supporting a qualifying child; under the prior rules this was not possible. To remedy this potential problem the law contains family tie-breaking rules based on blood and money.[19]

In the case of a child of divorced parents, where joint custody requires the child to stay one-half the time with one parent and the other half with the other, the number of nights of a child's stay must be counted by each parent to determine where the child slept the most nights. The IRS Regulations even specify that a night beginning in one year and ending in another (could they just say New Year's Eve?) will count toward the year in which the night began.[20] Other special cases are addressed as well, including which divorced parent claims a child on sleepover nights, what happens when the parent who is supposed to have custody cannot, because of illness or military service, which parent claims a child who goes to summer camp, and so on. The Code provides a tiebreaking rule in the event that two parents appear to qualify equally (during a leap year?); in that case the parent with the higher income trumps the other.[21] This is the kind of drudging specificity we need if we are truly to become a nation of bookkeepers.[22]

Richard Posner says that "the purposes of a law are defeated if compliance is impossible, and this futility is felt as injustice when the violation of the law carries with it heavy sanctions; for then law seems all costs and no benefits."[23] While compliance is not yet impossible, Herrnstein and Murray, authors of *The Bell Curve,* report the tax law's complexity is a source of growing concern. "As of the end of the twentieth century," they write, "the United States is run by rules that are congenial to people with high IQs and that make life more difficult for everyone else. This is true in the areas of criminal justice, marriage and divorce, welfare and tax policy." Among the rules that make everyday life more difficult, according to the authors, is the Tax Code: "The 1040 income tax form is such an easy target that it need only be mentioned to make the point."[24] This brings us back to former IRS Commissioner Egger's rhetorical question, "Can we afford any longer a tax system whose very unfairness and complexity invite tax cheating?"[25]

Is Complexity to Blame?

Goethe wrote, "If you really have something to say, do you have to hunt for words and phrases to say it?"[26] Commenting on the Tax Code, K. D. Deane notes that "Vague and ill-defined law is in principle objectionable, and although 'vague and ill-defined' might well describe the common law (at least in its historical development), taxation is entirely a creature of statute: in theory, therefore, it should be possible to present a clear and precise code to the taxpaying public."[27]

Though speaking of English law two hundred years ago, and not of our Internal Revenue Code, Jeremy Bentham's description of the problems resulting from legal complexity have a contemporary ring. "At present such is the entanglement [of laws], that when a new statute is applied it is next to impossible to follow it through and discern the limits of its influence. As the laws amidst which it falls are not to be distinguished from one another, there is no saying which of them it repeals or qualifies, nor which of them it leaves untouched: it is like water poured into the sea."[28] Echoing this complaint—but speaking of our current Tax Code—Sheldon Pollack observes, "Old policies are seldom repealed by the 'incremental' policymaking that prevails in the tax arena; new policies (very often at cross-purposes to the old) are simply grafted onto the tax code."[29] As a result, the tax laws have become "increasingly unstable, incoherent, and excessively complex."[30]

One reason we have, in addition to the income tax, excise taxes, sales taxes, gift taxes, real estate taxes, use taxes, estate taxes and the rest of the list is, according to Webber and Wildavsky, the fact that "a multiplicity of tax sources provides a far-reaching redundancy into the nooks and crannies of income otherwise hard to reach. Where income may be hidden it is found by multiple probes from different vantage points."[31] This approach sounds strangely like a military tactic employed in the mountains of Afghanistan.

Some believe that simplifying the income tax system, rendering it more equitable and lowering the tax rates will help "reinstate a higher degree of tax morality."[32] Given the underlying premise of self-reporting our income, I find this wishful thinking, akin to the notion that we can bring back "traditional family values" through moral exhortation or legislation. The horses have left the gate. As the complexities of income generation, recognition, transmission, and concealment have increased, the government's ability to employ its citizens as reliable agents of their own tax assessment has not kept pace and is now trailing the taxpayers' charge.

Fair Share and Complexity

The moral sea change is due in part to the inability of any taxpayer to know with any assurance that what he or she is paying represents a fair share of the national tax burden. With a real estate tax, for example, we understand generally how our house is valued and also that if our house is smaller than our neighbor's we should be paying a smaller tax; the same rate is applied to all. But our income tax allows two people (or ten or a hundred) with the same spendable (or economic) income—but different taxable income—to pay different amounts of tax.[33] An individual who collects Social Security and invests in municipal bonds, for example, may have the same number of dollars coming in as her neighbor who works a full-time job for $12 an hour. Yet the first may pay no tax and the second may pay 15 percent or pay nothing and receive the Earned Income Tax Credit. In this limited example, each component (limiting the tax on Social Security, exempting municipal bond interest from taxation, graduated tax rates, and the Earned Income Tax Credit) may have been introduced originally to ensure that each taxpayer pay his or her fair share. But in combination with one another—and multiplied by the vast array of other special provisions, each also designed to make some aspect more fair to some constituency—anyone's intuitive ability to look at his or her own tax return and say "That's my fair share" is denied.

In 2000, IRS Commissioner Charles Rossotti stated, "Few issues have generated as much discussion in recent years as tax-code complexity." This complexity becomes "even more burdensome" to taxpayers and the IRS, according to Rossotti, "when there are frequent changes, or when changes are made effective shortly in the future or retroactively."[34] In a telling statement regarding its increasingly frustrating position as enforcer of the Internal Revenue Code, the IRS made the following eye-opening admission.

> The complexity of the Tax Code makes it difficult for taxpayers to understand their tax obligations and for the IRS to administer the tax law. Special rules, subtle distinctions in the tax law and complicated computations add to this complexity and foster a sense of unfairness in our tax system which ultimately discourages compliance. Notwithstanding an increasing awareness of the discrepancy in taxes due and taxes paid, the tax law continues to move in a direction of increasing complexity, which frustrates efforts to reduce the tax gap. In 2006 alone, Congress passed six items of legislation that affected the tax law. Within these bills, 223 provisions required over 1,200 actions by the IRS to implement the new requirements. These changes to the tax law further increased complexity and, therefore, lessened the IRS's ability to increase voluntary compliance. Simplification may require a paradigm shift.[35]

Paradigm Shift

Calling for a paradigm shift has unfortunately turned into a cliché. But the writer credited with coining the term, Thomas Kuhn, presented the concept as a yardstick for recognizing significant change as a fundamental shift in how a problem is perceived. Kuhn analyzed scientific explanations or achievements that were "sufficiently unprecedented to attract an enduring group of adherents away from competing modes of scientific activity."[36] A paradigm is a body of accepted theory (including underlying assumptions or principles) that forms the basis for communication and research for mainstream practitioners at a particular time. "To be accepted as a paradigm, a theory must seem better than its competitors, but it need not, and in fact never does, explain all the facts with which it can be confronted."[37] Further, he explains, "Paradigms gain their status because they are more successful than their competitors in solving a few problems that the group of practitioners has come to recognize as acute."[38] Applied to the current income tax system, experts and policymakers are certainly faced with a few acute problems, not the least of which are complexity, tax cheating, and the growing tax gap.

The most commonly proposed alternatives to the current Tax Code are a flat income tax, a European-style value added tax, or national sales tax. But a true paradigm shift in this context would require a move away from the traditional voluntary compliance model. Voluntary compliance when practiced only by some necessarily leads to resentment by others and loss of faith that the system can be fair. This lubricates the slippery slope of tax cheating. The proponents of a flat tax believe that compliance will be higher if the tax is perceived as fair.[39] As a general proposition their claim is beyond question. But those who now benefit from the progressive tax rates—and countless deductions and credits that would be abandoned with a flat tax—may not agree that the removal of these items is fair.

Advocates of a value-added tax (VAT) or a national sales tax may believe such a tax is less conducive to cheating than an income tax—because fewer taxpayers would be involved in self-assessment and administration. However, there is evidence that tax cheating would be just as great a problem, and this solution also fails to solve the problem of the underground economy.[40] Both reforms may be an improvement over the current Code, but if there is an additional alternative that promises to eliminate tax cheating—by eliminating self-reporting—the better may not be the enemy of the good. Economist Joel Slemrod reports: "There is wide agreement that voluntary taxes are bad policy,"[41] and both a flat tax and a national sales tax require voluntary compliance in the same sense as the current income tax. The same small businesses, for example, that flout the current income tax will lead the way in flouting a national sales tax or a flat tax with the same results—a growing tax gap and diminishing respect for the law.

About voluntary tax systems, John Stuart Mill (1806–1873) observed, "The main reliance must be placed, and always has been placed, on the returns made by the person himself. The tax, therefore, on whatever principles of equality it may be imposed, is in practice unequal in one of the worst ways, falling heaviest on the most conscientious."[42] Similarly, in Plato's *Republic*, Socrates's adversary Thrasymachus argues that "in their relations with the state, if there are direct taxes or contributions to be paid, the just man contributes more [than his share] from an equal estate" and the unjust man less than his share.[43] According to these criticisms, those most concerned with paying their fair share will invariably end up paying more than they should, resulting in an unfortunate paradox. This result has helped erode the ethical force of the ideal of each taxpayer paying his or her fair share. As Andy Rooney observed on CBS's *60 Minutes*, "Generally speaking I think Americans are willing to pay their income taxes. They just want to be damn sure they paid their share—not their share and part of someone else's."[44]

According to the IRS, "A wide range of factors influence voluntary compliance, although there is little empirical confirmation as to the most important of these factors or their magnitudes."[45] Among the assumed factors, the IRS lists the economy, demographics, and sociopolitical factors such as swings in patriotic sentiment. It does not mention the Code's lack of a moral underpinning. As to the IRS's own level of influence, it admits, "It is very difficult to determine the impact that any IRS activity has on voluntary compliance."[46] I would assert that fear and intimidation are currently its greatest weapons.[47]

Economic Insights

Economists have also supplied insights into the voluntary tax system. One of the most basic involves the calculation by taxpayers of the utility of reporting their income. In a typical example an individual taxpayer "makes his decision by comparing the marginal costs and benefits of cheating....The marginal benefit (MB) for each dollar not reported is t, the amount of taxes saved. The expected marginal cost (MC) is the amount by which the penalty goes up for each dollar of cheating (the marginal penalty) times the probability of detection [the audit rate]."[48] This standard economic model that predicts taxpayers' behavior according to their marginal tax rates and the cost and probability of an audit predicts significantly greater tax evasion than occurs. We are told, for example, that "empirical and experimental findings in the tax compliance literature has shown that the standard [economic] model of tax evasion based on an expected utility-maximization approach, predicts a higher degree of tax evasion than observed. Thus the tax compliance puzzle is why people pay taxes."[49] "Given the low penalty for tax evasion and the audit rate," Eric Posner reports, "tax evasion should be widespread."[50] And other researchers concur: "Based on the current audit and penalty rates, compliance is much higher than traditional economic models of compliance would predict."[51]

Given these findings it has been hypothesized that other forces must be affecting taxpayers' decisions; among these, ethical values has been suggested. "One important reason why the conventional expected utility model of tax compliance overpredicts the prevalence and extent of tax evasion," according to researchers, "is that compliance behavior is assumed to be motivated solely by financial considerations, whereas in reality many taxpayers are influenced by a variety of other feelings, which we call moral sentiments."[52]

Another economic insight concerns the impact Congress can have on taxpayers' compliance decisions by (on the one hand) lowering or (on the other hand) raising tax rates. According to the standard economic understanding, "Cheating increases when marginal tax rates go up."[53] During the last 30 years, however, while the tax gap has increased, tax rates have decreased, indicating the problem is not as simple as some have assumed. And recent work by other economists predicts the opposite effect. "One of the most interesting results in the tax evasion literature is that an increase in the income tax rate would counterintuitively increase tax compliance."[54] Hence, President Truman's request for a one-handed economist.

The Moral Dilemma

Cicero, in *On Obligations,* wrote: "This is the aim and purpose of laws, to keep intact the unifying bonds between citizens."[55] The growing problem of tax cheating represents the severing of these bonds. David Callahan, author of *The Cheating Culture,* reports, "Scholars who have examined 'the psychology of taxation' say that a tax system is in big trouble if it lacks legitimacy. Distrust in a society also spells trouble for tax collectors. Research across nations has found that tax evasion is higher in societies with lower levels of trust between people. People must want to pay taxes at some level, believing not only that their tax bill is fair, but that their destiny is bound up with that of their fellow citizens."[56] Another observer tells us, "Without trust, there is little basis for social cooperation and voluntary compliance with the laws that could potentially benefit everyone."[57] I don't see a great deal of trust or a sense of common destiny—especially in matters involving Congress—as major players in our current national psyche. As John Fox notes, "If we do not trust Congress's behavior in general, we cannot be expected to embrace the tax system by which it conducts its affairs."[58] And as trust breaks down, the law's legitimacy is called into question as well.

A self-assessed tax contrasts with a government-assessed tax. The most serious problem with a self-assessed tax is that it puts taxpayers in a permanent moral dilemma. This dilemma requires that taxpayers continually assess their self-interest—whether in keeping hold of their money or in paying part of it over to the government—knowing that there must be a balance obtaining between the two but less confident that the current system of income tax has been that perfectly structured to achieve that balance. Fox reports, "The more incentives Congress creates that pit our self-interest against the national interest, the more dysfunctional tax laws become."[59]

Self-Interest

The exclusive promotion of one's own interest and a disregard of the interests of others is often associated with either ethical egoism (prescriptive) or psychological egoism (descriptive), and the line between the two is often blurred.[60] But many ethical egoists understand self-interest to be entwined with the interests of others. In this broader sense, according to Ayn Rand, the belief "that any action, regardless of its nature, is good if it is intended for one's own benefit" is not a proper expression of self-interest.[61] Thus, seeking one's own interest in the context of a self-assessed tax does not necessarily mean trying to free ride on the tax payments of others. But exactly what it does encompass is not always clear.

Assessing one's interest is complicated in part by the difficulty of disengaging self-interest from the interest of the community. For example, Adam Smith's "invisible hand" metaphor indicates that an individual "by pursuing his own interest . . . frequently promotes that of the society more effectively than when he really intends to promote it."[62]

But in the context of taxation, and especially the self-assessment of taxes, Smith's insight may be less helpful than it first appears. In attempting to determine the amount of tax to pay to promote our self-interest most effectively, we are left with the quandary noted earlier. Unlike commerce or trade—where Smith believed that in seeking our interest we will be led to promote the good of the community—leaving to each individual the decision about the amount of taxes to pay means that our personal judgments supplant the wisdom and guidance of the invisible hand but with no assurance that either our self-interest or the interest of the community is being maximized. The complexity of our tax system so obscures our judgment of what is in our own interest that we are rendered incapable of a making a sound determination.

A Moral Problem

John Dewey defined a moral problem not as a struggle between good and bad or right and wrong but as a struggle "between values each of which is an undoubted good in its place but which now get in each other's way."[63] As Dewey also explained, moral problems may arise because of conflicting duties or loyalties,[64] or incompatible ideals or goals,[65] or because a nearby goal is seen as conflicting with a far-off goal.[66] In the case of tax cheating the moral struggle is between the immediate good for the taxpayer and the more remote good for the society the taxpayer is a member and so an indirect beneficiary of.

In *Cheating the Government,* Frank Cowell tells us, "There will normally be a fundamental conflict between private gain and public duty," making tax cheating "appear an attractive option to many citizens."[67] On the one hand taxpayers would like to keep as much of their money as possible and have the freedom to spend it as they choose. On the other hand our ability to keep this money and spend it as we choose depends on the effective operation of government (1) to establish and enforce the laws of the land, (2) to tend to these laws' fair administration by providing an impartial system of law enforcement and courts, (3) to ensure defense against external forces seeking to destroy our way of life, and (4) to oversee and protect our rights (constitutional, property, privacy, and so on). All this costs money.[68]

The Dilemma of Assessing a Taxpayer's Self-Interest

Freedom to spend   ← **Self-interest** →   **Protections of government**

The tension wrought by a self-assessed tax may be seen as a conflict of interest for taxpayers, though the difficulty lies in determining where each taxpayer's interest resides. This was the gist of Adam Smith's comment (quoted in chapter 1) that it is only through the force and authority of conscience "that we can ever make any proper comparison between our own interests and those of other people."[69] That we cannot effectively make this comparison in the arena of the current Tax Code shows how poorly the tax régime appeals to our conscience.

Intertemporal Choice

For some economists and psychologists the decision about tax cheating is characterized as a problem of intertemporal choice. *Intertemporal choice* is a term used in decision theory to describe choices made between costs and benefits occurring at different points in time. "Someone may smoke heavily," according to researchers, "but carefully study the return on various retirement packages. Another may squirrel money away while at the same time giving little thought to electrical efficiency when purchasing an air conditioner. Someone else may devote two decades of his life to establishing a career, and then jeopardize this long-term investment for some highly transient pleasure."[70] According to other writers in the area, "So broad is the domain of intertemporal choice that it is difficult to think of a consequential decision that is *not* an intertemporal choice."[71]

Some commentators argue that the attempt by economists, led by Samuelson, to explain intertemporal choice in terms of perceived discount rates applied to the utility of events in the near future as opposed to events in the more distant future has been a failure. Accordingly, they write, "we believe that economists' understanding of intertemporal choices will progress most rapidly by continuing to import insights from psychology, by relinquishing the assumption that the key to understanding intertemporal choices is finding the right discount rate . . . and by readopting the view that intertemporal choices reflect many distinct considerations and often involve the interplay of several competing motives."[72] In this regard, social scientists have produced a vast literature in decision theory. There is now extensive evidence showing (not surprisingly) that many decisions are made for reasons not strictly logical or rational. How questions or problems are framed, recent events, subjective calculations of probability, and an array of other factors affect decisions, making suspect any generalization or simplification of the process.[73]

In morally evaluating our choice between tax compliance and tax cheating, the uncertainty of what benefits we are supposed to receive from the federal government may skew our decision toward keeping as much of our money as possible. It is one thing to pay taxes, part of which go to fund the Federal Emergency Management Agency (FEMA), for example, with expectations of receiving help in time of need. It is another matter when, as in the aftermath of Hurricane Katrina, the help is misguided, mismanaged, inadequate, and late. The uncertainty of what we can expect to be the benefit of what we pay for is thus a major contributor to the difficulty of the moral dilemma faced by taxpayers in a system of self-assessment.

The Contextual Substructure

Compounding the navigation of this dilemma is the contextual substructure of the income tax system, comprised of three major elements. The first is the political process by which the specific provisions of the Internal Revenue Code have come into existence. Without a central theme or master plan, the diverse Code sections have been clumsily spliced together under the watchful eye of special interests and opposing political and economic ideologies. It is telling that experts predict, "Even if the tax code in its entirety were not supported by a single individual, the odds are against radical change."[74] This is a reflection of the Code's genesis in negotiation, compromise, and trading favors, resulting in a product no one is proud of but no one wants to reopen for debate for fear of losing their pet benefits. The clichéd metaphor of sausage making is frequently employed to describe the process leading to this result.

The second contextual element in the tax substructure is the federal budget and how the tax money is spent. The budget process represents many of the same forces at work that created the Code. Among national defense, health care, education, foreign aid, disaster relief, bailouts of failed institutions of capitalism, interest on the national debt, and space research, the best we can hope for is a compromise no one is particularly happy with. This is the natural result of the Constitution's wording in justifying taxation "to pay the Debts and provide for the common Defense and general Welfare."[75] On this point, Justice Learned Hand observed, "There is indeed no great difficulty in deciding whether a tax is 'to pay the Debts' of the United States; but at times it is hard to say whether a statute is a tax to 'provide for the . . . general Welfare.'"[76] Apologists for the current system may claim that the outcome of a democratic process always reflects the general welfare; but this claim, for reasons addressed in chapter 4, is no more than a hollow tautology.

These first two contextual elements (the sources and uses of tax revenue) are grounded in ethical values and social and political priorities. Wedged between them is the third element. It is the system by which the tax laws are imposed on the nation's income. It involves the process of executing and administering the Tax Code. Starting with the products of the self-assessment process—tax returns—the Internal Revenue Service and the courts are brought to bear. As Slemrod explains, "It is impossible to understand the true impact of a country's tax system by looking only at the tax base and the tax rates applied to that base. A critical inter-mediating factor is how the tax law is administered and enforced."[77] In stark contrast to the elements on either side, which depend for their very existence on moral, social, and political values, the income tax system's administration is designed to operate independently of what is fair or just, or helps this group or hurts another. The execution of the tax system is based on a stern neutrality and disregard for the values that determined where the tax dollars should come from and where they should go. Its administration occurs in an extramoral or amoral framework.[78] We should never know, for example, whether the IRS auditor or Tax Court judge assigned to our case is a Democrat or Republican, socialist or communist, anarchist or fascist, Jew or Muslim, gay or straight, rich or poor. In addi-tion, cheating on the Earned Income Tax Credit (EITC), for example, is not viewed more leniently by the IRS or courts because the cheater is poor and the credit was meant to benefit taxpayers in the lower economic strata.

Sources of tax revenue	Execution and administration	The federal budget
What is taxable income and what is deductible	Impartial, disinterested determination and exaction	Spending priorities and allocations
Infused with moral, political, and social values and ideals	Morally and politically neutral	Infused with moral, political, and social values and ideals

When it comes to administering the tax law, the IRS is constrained by the limits Congress has put on its powers and authority. In general, IRS authority in enforcing and collecting taxes does not include considerations of equity or concerns about a taxpayer's economic status or condition, educational background, medical history or existing physical conditions, mental health, moral standing in the community, stress factors, family circumstances, or employment or unemployment.[79] This issue is addressed again, from the point of view of the courts, in chapter 7.

Tax cheating may be motivated by disagreement with either of the two politically charged elements of the system: the sources of tax revenue or how the money is spent. But tax cheating itself takes place in the middle ground between: execution and administration. Cheating is beating the system's ability to monitor each taxpayer's every economic transaction and how it is reported, characterized, or ignored on a tax return. When viewed in the light of (1) the adversarial nature of the relationship between the taxpayer and the IRS, (2) the dilemma of self-assessment, requiring taxpayers to seek the locus of their self-interest as described earlier, and (3) taxpayers' impotency in judging what is their fair share of the national tax burden—caused by the complexity of the tax system—the current tax régime's inability to engender a moral obligation emerges full-blown.

Nonvoluntary Taxation

Why do we cling to the notions that we must employ a voluntary tax system and that it can be effective? Is it because we don't want to live in a society where the government forces us to do something? If so, aren't we falling for an old politicians' word trick? Calling the tax system voluntary doesn't make it voluntary. Rather than a voluntary or self-assessed system, what is needed—if minimizing tax cheating is the goal—is a system sharing certain features of a real estate tax. We don't self-assess the value of our home or other property, we receive a bill based on a government assessment. We can appeal the assessed value of the property, but this is done in the empirical context of a marketplace, appraisals, construction costs, and the sale of comparable properties. If we choose not to pay the bill, a lien will be put on the property; and if nothing is done, the property will eventually be seized by the government or other lienholder and sold.

A Real Estate Tax

An income tax system abandoning voluntarism would constitute a paradigm shift of the magnitude needed to deal with the tax gap and the unreported income from the underground or shadow economy and from many illegal activities. A nonvoluntary system could take many forms, limited only by our imaginations. The advantage of a real estate tax, as nineteenth-century political economist Henry George pointed out, is that "land cannot be hidden or carried off; its value can be readily ascertained, and the assessment once made, nothing but a receiver is required for collection."[80] Consider the difficulty of hiding a parcel of land from the eyes of the government, or of smuggling it out of the United States to a tax haven. George maintained that "some part of the public revenues is collected from taxes on land, and the machinery for that purpose already exists and could as well be made to collect all as a part."[81] Perhaps policymakers could entertain a national real estate tax, piggybacking on the existing administrative capabilities of local government and using the value of taxpayers' real estate holdings as a proxy for the taxpayers' income—or in Adam Smith's terms—as an index for "the revenue which they respectively enjoy under the protection of the state."[82]

Just as banks are again using budget-based ratios to determine the appropriate size of a mortgage payment relative to the borrower's income, a person's income could be statutorily defined on the basis of the mortgage payment or of its statutory equivalent, the value of the house or other property. This may introduce certain complexities as well, but nothing of the magnitude of the current Code. On the negative side, a Gallup poll reports that the real estate tax is one of the least popular forms of taxation,[83] perhaps because it is so difficult to circumvent.

Another reason why some people oppose a real estate tax is its use to pay for local services, such as airports, libraries, or public schools, from which they perceive there is no direct benefit. Robert McGee suggests that taxpayers who believe that they are not directly benefiting from these services resent having to pay for them. "There are a number of injustices associated with the property tax," according to McGee. "For example, all homeowners have to pay the tax, even if they do not have any children. In effect, they are being forced to pay for the education of other people's children."[84] I would suggest that there is a benefit to living among more-educated rather than less-educated people, even if we have to contribute to this outcome involuntarily. If nothing else, I assume that an enlightened tax policy is more likely to emerge from an educated electorate than from one embalmed in ignorance.

A Presumptive Income Tax

Economist Edward Wolff informs us, "The distributional effects of shifting from the federal personal income tax to one based on real property values or land values depends on the ratio of property (or land) values to income." The more real estate you control, the more income you generally command; thus, employing the value of real estate as an index for income may be defensible.[85] The use of an indirect metric to determine income as a base for an income tax results in what is called a *presumptive income tax,* and has been previously proposed as a tax reform.[86] Though there are probably many options for presuming taxpayers' income, the key would be choosing one that does not rely on the taxpayer's self-assessment.

The IRS already uses indirect methods to determine the income of audited taxpayers who fail to keep adequate records. By assessing increases in a taxpayer's net worth (including real estate), for example, the IRS is able to determine how much income would be needed to support a particular way of life. These methods are frequently employed IRS audit techniques that have been accepted by the courts.[87]

The economic adjustments such a change would require on the part of businesses and homeowners would be fascinating to predict, but that must be left to economists.[88] Such a system would put an end to the intrusiveness of the present régime. Skeptics will point out that ownership of real estate can be hidden through land trusts and similar measures, to which the response is, yes, ownership, but not the real estate itself; take a look at Google Earth (earth.google.com) if you are skeptical. Someone will still receive a tax bill and failure to pay will have consequences. Corruption in the tax system will not be prevented but the relative transparency of real estate valuation, in contrast to income measurement, will make it more challenging for public officials to disguise their misdeeds.[89]

Apart from pundits' predictably negative visceral responses, the most serious challenges to this proposal are likely to be constitutional: Is a presumptive income tax based on real estate holdings really a tax on income as envisioned by the Sixteenth Amendment? In a historic case for the income tax, the Supreme Court in *Pollock v. Farmer's Loan and Trust Company*[90] ruled that the 1894 income tax was unconstitutional because taxing rent from real estate was a direct tax subject to Article I, Section 2, of the Constitution. As such the tax must be apportioned among the states on the basis of their respective populations, though this was not the case with the 1894 tax. But as one critic tells us, "The logic of the Supreme Court's decision in *Pollock,* as well as the Court's effort to draw a constitutional distinction between direct and indirect taxes, can be mystifying and largely unconvincing."[91] This particular issue was settled for rent by the Sixteenth Amendment. But will a tax on the value of real estate—statutorily defined as a proxy for income—be ruled an income tax, whether direct or indirect?[92]

Henry George

Critics familiar with the history of economics will point out that Henry George, in his 1879 book *Progress and Poverty*, presented an impassioned argument for a single tax on land rents, but one that many believe has long since been debunked and left for dead. George's central theme, though not entirely original, was revolutionary and based on his moral beliefs.[93] It represented a fundamental shift in how the problem of taxation was perceived, though it was never seen by mainstream economists as more successful than its competitors "in solving a few problems that the group of practitioners has come to recognize as acute."[94] According to George, the total source of taxation could be shifted to a tax on land and, as one commentator explains, "land is socially a costless asset; we would still have its services if all rent were appropriated by government."[95]

At the core of George's teaching was the distinction between income from rents and active income from labor, and what he saw as inequities arising from this difference. In this he followed John Stuart Mill who made the following observation:

> Suppose there is a kind of income that constantly tends to increase, without any exertion or sacrifice on the part of the owners: those owners constituting a class in the community, whom the natural course of things progressively enriches, consistently with complete passivity on their own part. In such a case it would be no violation of the principles on which private property is founded if the state should appropriate this increase in wealth, or part of it, as it arises. This would not properly be taking anything from anybody; it would merely be applying an accession of wealth, created by circumstances, to the benefit of society, instead of allowing it to become an unearned appendage to the riches of a particular class.[96]

Readers familiar only with Mill's *On Liberty* may be surprised by such language. Is this the same Mill who wrote of government, "But the strongest of all the arguments against the interference of the public with purely personal conduct is that, when it does interfere, the odds are that it interferes wrongly, and in the wrong place"?[97] It is, but in *On Liberty* Mill also said, "Everyone who receives the protection of society owes a return for the benefit."[98] And although Mill opposed a graduated income tax because such a tax imposes "a penalty on people for having worked harder and saved more than their neighbors," he also wrote, "It is not the fortunes which are earned, but those which are unearned, that it is for the public good to place under limitation."[99] In the latter category are gifts and inheritances, including land passed down through generations, which Mill favors taxing "as the most eligible mode of restraining the accumulation of large fortunes in the hands of those who have not earned them by exertion."[100]

George was an evangelist for what he saw as a more just system of taxation, a single tax on land rent. George's book remains the best-selling text on economics in history, and second in sales only to the Bible during the late nineteenth century.[101] Knowledgeable critics, including Todd Buchholz, author of *New Ideas from Dead Economists,* have scoffed at George's ideas.[102] But Nobel economist Milton Friedman once said that of all the ways to tax, "in my opinion the least bad tax is the property tax on the unimproved value of land, the Henry George argument of many years ago."[103] And Harold Groves writes, "George's contribution contained elements of truth that are of enduring importance. They are currently relevant even if only in support of property taxes as against sales taxes [and] capital gains' inclusion in the income tax as against their exclusion."[104]

The difference of opinion on his teachings may come down to which aspect of George's proposal is the focus. According to Groves, George's views are subject to many valid criticisms and yet his doctrine "contains much that . . . has stood the test of time."[105] In *The Worldly Philosophers,* Heilbroner explains that for George, "the injustice of rents not only robbed the capitalist of his honest profit but weighed on the shoulders of the working man as well." Furthermore, rent "represented an unfair distribution of produce to landlords at the expense of workers and industrialists."[106] For George, according to Heilbroner, "the single tax was a religion."[107] But if we strip away the moral fervor and underlying assumptions that drove George's teachings, the question becomes: Is it possible to evaluate the option of a single tax on real estate as a practical solution to the problem of tax cheating?

There are doubtless many economic reasons why such a tax would not work well, including various distortions to the markets. Rents will necessarily increase to allow landlords to cover their additional costs. At the same time, we will be told, real estate prices will be depressed and the market will decline, causing the value of the tax base to shrink, necessitating an increase in the tax rates, leading to further declines in property valuation and decreasing rents. Fortunately, the strictly deductive armchair approach to economics—which produces such dismal certainty in the minds of some—is eventually confronted with the actual behavior of markets, and the outcome is not always so dire as predicted.

Market adjustments to such a dramatic change are inevitable. The cost of owning a home may increase, but without an income tax our net pay will be closer to our gross, leaving more to work with. To reduce taxes, many people may choose to live in smaller homes; fewer corporate headquarters may be built of marble and mahogany. But as one of my real estate–developer clients once told me, "They're not making any new dirt." So finding substitutes for real estate will have limits. I have little doubt that market forces will sort through the issues and find a solution allowing the least dislocation; in this regard we should be reminded that "all things being equal" is not one of these market forces.

Such a proposal would require rethinking the entire federal tax system. Anyone currently benefiting from that system or from tax cheating enabled by it would oppose the change. One economist observes that such change is "politically poisonous" as "the case for any radical reform of tax systems is hard to make."[108] But the benefits of the simplicity and transparency of such a system and of the government's ability to predict tax revenues should not be dismissed lightly. Likewise, respect for the law would be enhanced as taxpayers recognize their common plight. Resulting distortions, such as raising the rent for those least able to afford it, for example, could be dealt with through the kinds of rent subsidy or voucher programs already employed by the Department of Housing and Urban Development (Section Eight Housing, for example). But for those taxpayers who currently pay what income tax the law requires, the change should mean tax relief and a morale boost, knowing they are only paying their share and not also part of someone else's.

Property taxes, according to the nonprofit educational Tax Foundation, are the principal source of revenue for cities, counties, and school districts; so something about them is working.[109] This is part of what is described as the "division of labor in which cities used the property tax, states adopted sales taxes, and the federal government the income tax," a system unique to the United States.[110] But its uniqueness should not be interpreted as a sign of its advantage over another system.

To provide a national real estate tax—or an income tax employing real estate values as a proxy for income—with a fair hearing, it may be beneficial here to briefly distinguish two proposals: (1) the one employed by local governments taxing real estate including land and buildings, and (2) Henry George's dealing only with land rents. The arguments regarding land rents, George's proposal, do not automatically apply to a tax on the value of buildings and land and its improvements. The difference in the two approaches is significant and they must be regarded independently. According to George, the tax on land values is "the most just and equal of all taxes. It falls only upon those who receive from society a peculiar and valuable benefit, and upon them in proportion to the benefit they receive."[111] Under George's vision, "Labor and capital—so often burdened by the patchwork of taxes on labor, savings and entrepreneurs—would be unleashed because none of these would be taxed."[112] This cannot be said of a system also taxing homes and buildings, nor of our income tax. "In common speech," George writes, "we apply the word rent to payments for the use of buildings, machinery, fixtures, etc., as well as to payments for the use of land or other natural capabilities.... But in the economic meaning of rent, payments for the use of any of the products of human exertion are excluded.... [O]nly that part is rent which constitutes the consideration for the use of the land."[113]

Following Adam Smith's lead,[114] George posits four characteristics of an ideal tax: (1) "that it bear as lightly as possible upon production"; (2) "that it be easily and cheaply collected, and fall as directly as may be upon the ultimate payer"; (3) "that it be certain—as to give the least opportunity for tyranny or corruption on the part of officials and the least temptation to law-breaking and evasion on the part of taxpayers"; (4) "that it bear equally—so as to give no citizen an advantage or put any at a disadvantage, as compared with others."[115] According to Richard Fisher, president of the Federal Reserve Bank of Dallas, "The single tax remains one of the most examined, supported and criticized of all the theoretical ideas ever put forth in economics."[116]

Compliance Costs

While I don't want to get off track with a discussion of a federal real estate tax—or an income tax based on real estate values—and it is not my intention to defend Henry George's position, I would like to note that I have broached the idea here as an antidote to the growing problems of tax cheating and the expanding tax gap. The size of the latter problems may determine how hard we want to look at alternatives to the self-assessment model of the Internal Revenue Code. While the underlying tax system is not the focus of this work, any system designed to be fair will fulfill its mission more fully insofar as it can thwart tax cheating. The reason for this, as Schwartz and Orleans point out, is that a "reduction in evasion . . . distribute[s] the tax burden more equitably and add[s] to the sense of legitimacy on which the legal order presumably rests."[117] Even a theoretically ideal tax, from the point of view of encouraging entrepreneurs and saving, investing, and wealth and job creation, may be but an academic pipe dream if the tax's collection is easily jeopardized by wanton cheating.

Compliance costs are an important dimension in a comparison between alternate tax models. The Tax Foundation reports that for 2004 tax compliance costs for the income tax were $244 billion, or 24 percent of federal revenue collected. Ten years earlier compliance costs as a percentage of revenue were 15.6 percent.[118] In addition to dollars spent on accountants, attorneys, and other tax preparers and the IRS, there is the tremendous time allotment, for which the IRS by law provides an estimate for each tax form completed. It has been suggested that the 140 million taxpayers who do file tax returns spend an average of twenty-seven hours annually of "fundamentally unproductive activity," including record keeping, reading instructions, and hunting for deductions.[119] In *Faster,* James Glieck cites a University of Chicago study reporting that presently "four minutes a day goes, on average, to filling out paperwork for the United States Government" (twenty-four hours a year) and that this is approximately the same amount of time devoted to sex.[120]

The costs of compliance, collection, and tax evasion resulting from the present income tax system are "massive," according to Netzer, at about 30 percent for federal income taxes. On the basis of comparative data, the same economist reports, "Taxpayer compliance costs are negligible in the aggregate for the existing property tax in the U.S.," estimated at "less than 2 percent for land value taxation."[121] It is not clear why this much time and money should be expended on a "voluntary" income tax to wind up with a $345 billion annual tax gap, falling tax morale, and a growing disrespect for the law if alternatives are available.

When George proposed a single tax on land, it was in the context of a discussion of taxing land rents, and part of a contentious and historic debate. His ideal tax did not include taxing the improvements made to the land (houses, buildings, factories). Many things have changed since that lively debate. The country has transformed itself from a primarily agricultural economy in the mid-nineteenth century to a postindustrial one in the twenty-first. Changing conditions often require revisiting abandoned ideas if the reasons for their abandonment are tied to circumstances no longer present. In *New Ideas from Dead Economists,* Buchholz advises, "As human relationships and social institutions change, so does the subject of our inquiry."[122] And Keynes pointed out, "Economics is a science of thinking in terms of models joined to the art of choosing models which are relevant to the contemporary world....The object of a model is to segregate the semi-permanent or relatively constant factors from those which are transitory or fluctuating so as to develop a logical way of thinking about the latter, and of understanding the sequences to which they give rise in particular cases."[123]

A constant factor threatening the voluntary income tax system is the ability of some taxpayers to slip through its net. This is why mere tinkering with the Internal Revenue Code or even dramatically altering some of its key provisions, as was done during the Reagan administration, will not provide the needed solution to the problem of tax cheating.[124] "The current income tax system is fundamentally broken," according to the nonprofit Tax Foundation, "and should be replaced with a code adhering to the principles [of]...neutrality, simplicity, stability, transparency, and growth promotion."[125] But others warn of the ambivalence many taxpayers feel regarding a better tax system; a more effective system will also be more burdensome to those successfully cheating the current system.[126]

Complexity and Morals

In searching for a new paradigm it should be observed that it is not complexity itself that is responsible for the loss of the law's moral force. In one study the researchers found that "[t]here is no necessary theoretical link between the complexity of the tax system and its perceived unfairness."[127] Recent psychological research on why people obey the law indicates that the fairness of a legal system is not judged by its final outcome so much as by the formula employed to reach that outcome. "Within the general framework of fairness," these researchers report, "procedural concerns consistently take precedence over distributive concerns."[128] In the case of an income tax this implies that the absolute amount of tax owed is not as significant in judging the fairness of the tax régime as the system used to compute the amount owed, and that the same system is uniformly applied to all taxpayers. "Whether our taxes are fair or not," one commentator reminds us, "is an ethical, not an economic question."[129]

Complexity in the case of the Tax Code is a symptom of other factors. They include: (1) a lack of planning and coordination based on a central goal (raising revenue is now only one of many—and often competing—congressional agenda items), (2) counteracting measures aimed at making the tax fairer to specific constituent groups (as noted earlier, new tax provisions are wedged in among the old in incremental policy making, with little thought to compatibility), and (3) the political market forces that create the law, including horse trading and buying votes with promises.[130] According to Louis Kaplow, the Tax Code "involves the use of a substantial and complex set of rules imposing significant compliance costs on taxpayers and administrators for the purpose of assessing each taxpayer's circumstances more accurately in terms of some notion of their equitable tax burden."[131] But as Friedrich Hayek warned, "There is all the difference in the world between treating people equally and attempting to make them equal."[132]

To illustrate that complexity itself is not the problem, consider complexities occurring in nature. Does the human body's complexity, for example, result in its loss of ethical stature? Not at all, and quite to the contrary. The very complexity of the human body is a source of awe for many; it has led individuals—from Michelangelo to Albert Schweitzer—to revere its complex design. But the Tax Code's complexity is of a different origin. Rube Goldberg's complex machines for performing simple tasks are a metaphor for kind of complexity exhibited by the Tax Code. Consider Goldberg's pencil sharpener and imagine what it might look like if a congressional committee had helped him with the design.

Pencil Sharpener

The Professor gets his think-tank working and evolves the simplified pencil sharpener.

Open window (A) and fly kite (B). String (C) lifts small door (D), allowing moths (E) to escape and eat red flannel shirt (F). As weight of shirt becomes less, shoe (G) steps on switch (H) which heats electric iron (I) and burns hole in pants (J). Smoke (K) enters hole in tree (L), smoking out opossum (M) which jumps into basket (N), pulling rope (O) and lifting cage (P), allowing woodpecker (Q) to chew wood from pencil (R), exposing lead. Emergency knife (S) is always handy in case opossum or the woodpecker gets sick and can't work.

In the case of the human body—and it does not matter whether one ascribes the body's complexity to millions of years of evolution or to divine planning—adherents of either camp can appreciate that within the body's complexity are elements of coordination, support, self-defense, reproduction, consciousness, and internal integrity, rendering it a proper subject for respect and ethical value. The underlying problem with the Tax Code in this regard is not its complexity per se but its unharnessed complexity; there is no central theme, no underlying moral intuition, no wholeness of thought or overall design.

The perception of the law and respect for its integrity are important aspects of the law's moral standing. "Laws perceived to be poorly conceived or downright foolish," we are told "can lead to lowered respect for law generally and greater willingness to flout it."[133] Others argue that "the credibility of the legal code depends on it being perceived as a trustworthy guide to assigning liabilities according to the community's perception of which actions are moral, which are immoral, and how severely the immoral actions should be punished."[134] In one experiment, Nadler explains, "participants exposed to unjust laws indicated a greater likelihood of engaging in...criminal behavior compared to those exposed to just laws."[135] However, these results were least pronounced in the case of tax laws, which is perhaps a function of the difficulty, because of our tax laws' complexity, of judging their relative injustice.

Tax complexity is a problem and its resolution requires understanding what kind of a problem it is. In a seminal paper on complexity in the sciences, Warren Weaver identified two types of complexity—organized and disorganized.[136] By organized complexity Weaver understood problems that involve "dealing simultaneously with a sizable number of factors which are interrelated into an organic whole." As examples he offered, "On what does the price of wheat depend?" and "What is a gene, and how does the original genetic constitution of a living organism express itself in the developed characteristics of the adult?" In contrast, a problem of disorganized complexity is one in which "the number of variables is very large, and one in which each of the many variables has a behavior which is individually erratic, or perhaps totally unknown." "In spite of this helter-skelter, or unknown, behavior of all the individual variables," he explains, "the system as a whole possesses certain orderly and analyzable average properties." The techniques of probability theory and of statistics are used to solve problems of disorganized complexity. As examples he offers the motion of atoms and the operations of a life insurance company that does not know which of its many policyholders will die next, but does know, on average, the frequency of death within the population of which its policyholders are members.

Tax complexity, in the sense in which people speak of it as a problem, is an example of neither organized nor disorganized complexity, though it would be tempting to co-opt the term disorganized complexity—if only we could make predictions about the Tax Code based on statistics or probability. The complexity of the Tax Code is what I call *accretive complexity* caused by the patchwork approach used by legislators. As if filling potholes after the winter's onslaught, the congressional approach to tax legislation frequently involves no more than adding a subsection here or extending or modifying another one over there.

But to say the tax law is complex is not to say the Internal Revenue Code is devoid of any order or logic. It is not as bad, for example, as Jeremy Bentham's characterization, when he invited us to "open what code you will, pitch upon what law you will, the parts of it lie scattered up and down at random, some under one head, some under another, with little or no notice taken of their mutual relations and dependencies."[137] In *The Logic of Tax,* Joseph Dodge says his purpose is to show there is a "rhyme and a reason for a great deal of the tax law of the federal income tax—that more is involved than mere political ox-goring."[138] He then admits there is really more than one system of logic operating simultaneously, one dealing with the definition of income, another with fairness, another with accounting and financial concepts, and another with economic considerations. These diverse logics mean "there is conflict, or at least awkward 'coexistence;'" and thus, the author confesses, "there is no single 'principle' or approach which solves all issues of tax doctrine, theory, or policy."[139]

Though tax complexity is a frequent topic of debate, the difficulty of defining or measuring what is meant by complexity is a stumbling block to tax simplification. If we ask whether the extent of the Code's complexity can be measured—whether the problem is quantifiable, for example—the answer appears to be no. Unlike problems of disorganized complexity, the complexity of the Tax Code does not reveal predictable patterns. Starting with a collection of individual code sections, it would not be possible to derive a formula, for example, that would allow us to predict the nature of the next code section to be enacted, modified, or deleted. The Tax Code thus lacks sufficient order to constitute even disorganized complexity.

Saying the current tax régime lacks a unifying design or organization is not saying that some of its parts are not well thought out to produce a particular end or solve a specific problem. There are elements of elegance in certain aspects of the Code's design that perhaps only the trained eye of an accountant can appreciate. My personal favorite is Subchapter K of the Code, from section 701 to section 761, relating to partnerships. Developed there is a wonderfully complex and aesthetically pleasing format for dealing with partnership transactions, dividing up the income and expenses, keeping track of tax basis, and integrating each partners' share of liabilities.

Belaboring the human body analogy a little longer, however, consider the relative importance of its various parts. The appendix, we supposed until recently, plays no essential role in the body's operation; we could probably operate just as well without toenails or hair on our legs. But if we go much beyond these examples, we find it harder and harder to discover what else in the human body is not somehow helpful or essential to its effective operation. Contrast this with the Internal Revenue Code. Are there sections of the Code that, like the human appendix, could be removed without harming the rest or threatening the integrity of the tax system? No doubt there are many. A more telling question is whether there are parts of the Code that are essential, without which the Code would suffer and cease to function even as well as it does.

Section 61, for example, the heart and vascular system of the Code, defines income—though imprecisely—even using the term being defined within the definition.[140] Since it is an income tax code, this section is central. But if we proceeded through the rest of the Code looking for what parts are critical or defining, we might be surprised at how little of the complexity is essential or part of an overall plan. The Internal Revenue Code is largely a hodgepodge compilation of provisions, some dating back to the nineteenth century. Like a potluck supper, the various sections of the Code have been put on the groaning board together, not based on a central blueprint but out of an unseemly admixture of political compromises. Naturally, it works about as well as other forms of alchemy.

While there are small clusters of code sections that are logically interdependent, a critical reading of the Code will lead to a sense of its characteristic arbitrariness. Here are three examples:

- Why are drug dealers allowed to deduct their cost of goods sold, but not other ordinary and necessary business expenses, while other illegal businesses are not disadvantaged in the same manner?[141] A hired assassin, for example, has a tax advantage over a drug dealer in that the assassin can deduct his business travel costs while the drug dealer may not.[142]

- If health care and health insurance are important national policy issues, why is the deduction for health insurance only available to one-third of the taxpayers (approximately two-thirds use the standard deduction) and subject to a threshold limitation that began at 5 percent in 1942, was increased to 7½ in 1986, and for 2013 has been increased again to 10 percent of Adjusted Gross Income?[143]
- Why are children subject to the Alternative Minimum Tax (AMT) when there is already a special Kiddie tax—requiring children to pay tax at their parents' highest tax rate—if they have "too much" investment income?[144]

Of course there are "reasons" for each of these items individually, but connecting the dots between the individual reasons, to comprehend the underlying public policy philosophy being implemented, is beyond the skills of even the slickest politician.

In the human body, even our unglamorous parts, such as the pancreas or the thyroid gland, have important and well-understood functions. In the case of the Tax Code's complexity it is hard to find a parallel. If this or that section were eviscerated—the deduction of certain personal expenses or the preferential taxation of capital gains, for example—the overall operation of the system would be largely unaffected, though any political constituent who had formerly benefited from that section would certainly protest.

Is There Ever a Time for Draconian Measures?

From its inception in 1913, the Code has grown in response to particular problems facing particular constituencies—in fits and starts—not along a well-thought-out path to an agreed-upon destination. Consider the growth of a cancerous tumor in the human body threatening the body's natural operations—the cancer following a path of destruction—though presaging its own demise through the eventual death of its host. The body's immune system is often insufficient to prevent the growth of cancer cells whose progress depends not on logical steps toward a goal but on rampaging, uncontrolled growth, resulting in the cancer's spread. To compare the historical development of the Internal Revenue Code with the ravaging growth of cancer cells may seem overly dramatic. But in studying how the Code came about and in trying to predict where it is headed, the analogy appears eerily appropriate.

Researchers have determined "that taxpayers may not necessarily consider a complex tax system to be an unfair tax system," because complexity may be necessary to accurately measure income.[145] Though the complexity of the Internal Revenue Code is often cited by the IRS, the public, and the press as a problem, very few individuals have read it.[146] Members of Congress vote on changes or additions to the Code often without reading them. "Senator Moynihan was fond of pointing out that no member of Congress ever read one of these bills before voting on it, and no one person really understood what was in it."[147] Even tax professionals (excluding certain academics), when they do read the Code, limit their reading to a particular Code section or the interplay of a few related sections. The Code's lack of unity makes these practices possible. Though complexity may be cited as a cause of some tax cheating, it is complexity without an articulable unifying principle that causes the Code's lack of moral integrity.

In 2005 then IRS Commissioner Everson stated, "We're moving aggressively to reduce the tax gap. With proper funding, over a number of years we will be able to close a significant portion of the gap. But no one should think we can totally eliminate the gap. That would take Draconian measures and make the government too intrusive. We have to strike the right balance."[148] Consider, however, the aggressive treatment of a cancer—through surgery, chemotherapy, and radiation treatments—each generally quite intrusive. Perhaps there are times for Draconian measures.

Draco was given the job of writing a uniform set of laws for Athens (circa 621 BCE). "[H]e was concerned not with the working of the constitution but with the administration of justice."[149] His revolutionary breakthrough was promulgating a set of written laws applicable to all citizens, replacing a system of oral laws individualized to separate classes in society. The laws were made public and were intended to be understandable to all. Aristotle reports that it was the severity of the punishments imposed by Draco's laws that led to their infamy.[150]

The parallel figure in Spartan tradition was Lycurgus (ca. 800–730 BCE), whose legal system was founded on the principle that the law should not be written but instead internalized by the citizens. According to Plutarch, Lycurgus "would never reduce his laws into writing...for he thought that the most material points, and such as most directly tended to the public welfare, being imprinted on the hearts of their youth by a good discipline, would be sure to remain, and would find a stronger security, than any compulsion would be, in the principles of action formed in them by their best lawgiver, education."[151] Perhaps a goal of current lawgivers should be to simplify the tax law to the extent that ordinary citizens could be educated in its meaning. On this point, one commentator reminds us, "The challenge is not only to educate people about the content of existing legal rules, but in addition, to facilitate a public understanding of the rationale for the existing rules."[152] Here we find the lack of congressional transparency and a failure to achieve a consensus on the meaning of *general welfare,* blocking the road to progress.

According to one historian, Draco's "legal code was remarkable to later minds for its severity. The law of debt, for instance, entitled a creditor in certain cases to enslave, or to sell into slavery, an insolvent debtor and his dependents."[153] When the creditor is the IRS, our law sends criminal tax evaders to prison, which, as we saw in the tax protestor case *Drefke* in chapter 2, is not considered enslavement, yet most do not think it too severe either.

There are occasions when continued tinkering with a serious problem is an indication not that the problem can eventually be solved by just the right combination of adjustments, but rather that the problem as currently conceived is irresolvable. Congress should consider the possibility that the current problem of tax complexity is such a case, requiring not more tinkering but a Draconian paradigm shift.

FOUR

THE MORAL DUTY TO OBEY THE LAW

> A person who, though no doubt highly blamable for violating the laws of his country, is frequently incapable of violating those of natural justice, and would have been, in every respect, an excellent citizen, had not the laws of his country made that a crime which nature never meant to be so.
>
> —Adam Smith, *Wealth of Nations*

Morality and Legality

"For most people," attorney and moral philosopher M. B. E. Smith contends, "violation of the law becomes a matter of moral concern only when it involves an act which is believed to be wrong on grounds apart from its illegality."[1] In the case of tax laws this does not settle the matter, as there is a spectrum of opinion on the moral justification for paying taxes. For example, John Locke believed, "Everyone who enjoys his share of the protection [of the state], should pay out of his estate his proportion for the maintenance of it."[2] While Leo Martinez claims, "If a taxpayer commits a moral wrong by violating the tax code, it is not because she pays less than the morally proper amount but rather because she disobeys the government."[3]

Indeed, whether we have a moral duty to comply with the tax law may depend on whether or not we have a moral duty to comply with the law in general. On the one hand, if we have no such general duty to obey the law, it is hard to see how we could owe a special moral duty to comply with a subset of the law, the Tax Code. On the other hand, there is a widely held notion that we do have a moral duty to obey the law. In *Why People Obey the Law*, psychologist Tom Tyler reports, "Citizens seem to view breaking laws as a violation of their personal morality."[4] This expresses itself in the belief that we should obey the law, or at least much of the law, not simply out of the fear of getting caught, but because the law embodies basic principles we agree with, or in some cases because it enforces basic moral beliefs we subscribe to. Cicero asked, "How will a man behave in the dark if his only fear is a witness and a judge?"[5] I assume, for example, that most citizens refrain from engaging in armed robbery not simply because it's against the law, but because they believe there is something wrong with taking someone's money at gunpoint. This chapter explores the debate about a moral duty to obey the law as a possible basis for a moral duty to obey the Tax Code.

The moral duty to obey the law has been debated at least since Socrates and Plato in ancient Greece. Socrates could have fled Athens to avoid his death sentence but believed it was his moral duty to obey the law. One root of the debate, as Plato pointed out in the *Laws,* is a tension between the need to legislate some moral principles and the dangers of going too far. According to Plato, there are many minor wrongs that are not made illegal because of their frequency and triviality. However, he asserts, such wrongs pose "a real danger to such law as we do impose since the habit of transgression is learned from repetition of these petty misdeeds. Hence, though we are at a loss to legislate on such points, silence about them is also impossible."[6]

The question of the moral quality of the law is central to legal philosophy. The continuum of thought on this question includes, at one end, the position of legal positivists that laws and ethical matters inhabit two distinct realms; and, at the other end, the position of legal naturalists that law is inherently grounded in moral concepts.[7] Legal positivism is represented by jurists including John Austin, H. L. A. Hart, and Hans Kelsen. According to Kelsen, "A legal norm is not valid because it has a certain content."[8] Hart holds that the law's validity is determined independently from its ethical content. Richard Posner says Hart "does not want people to think they have a moral duty to obey any law whose legal validity is unassailable."[9] Another commentator explains, "Legal positivists treat the validity of law and the morality of law as completely separate and advocate, as Socrates did, obedience to even unjust laws."[10]

More recently other writers too have denied that we have a moral duty to obey the law, among the most prolific being Joseph Raz.[11] Raz argues that common reasons provided as to why we have a moral duty to obey the law—prudential reasons, reasons based on setting a good example for others, reasons based on estopple (accepting benefits based on acts or promises made to the detriment of another) or implicit promises or promoting respect for the law, for example—do not prove what they are intended to prove. They show we have many reasons for obeying the law, but not that we have a moral duty to do so.[12]

Legal naturalism—comprised of both a secular version, represented by Lon Fuller and Ronald Dworkin, and a religious version whose best-known advocate is Thomas Aquinas—contends that the law is inextricably bound up with moral principles.[13] From the view of legal naturalism, we are told, "rules of political powers are not really laws, are defective legally, if they fail the test of Natural-Law."[14] This echoes the teachings of Cicero, who wrote that, if laws "were validated by the orders of peoples, the enactments of politicians, and the verdicts of judges, then it would be just to rob, just to commit adultery, just to introduce forged wills, provided those things were approved by the votes or decrees of the populace."[15] A. P. d'Entrèves maintains, "The coercive character of human or positive law is in its essence contradictory to that moral element which the law is supposed to embody."[16] While the secular form of natural law employs logic to make its case, the religious version traces the legitimacy of human law back to its foundation in divine law.

Ethical Relativism and Absolutism

Lurking behind the debate about the relation of morality to the law is a dichotomy of belief about the single-mindedness of morality itself. Does it speak with one voice, as Plato and Kant have argued, or are the claims posed by Machiavelli or Nietzsche correct—that what is right or wrong (not merely what people believe is right or wrong) is relative and changes from time to time and place to place?[17] On the side of relativism are proponents, including Socrates's adversary Thrasymachus, who hold that might makes right.[18]

Complicating an explanation of ethical relativism is the fact that there are various forms depending on what standard ethical values are assumed to be relative to. At one extreme—which some might refer to as subjectivism—ethical values might be relative only to the individual. In that case it is hard to know why they would be called ethical values. In such a situation, any individual could say, for example, "This particular action (murder, fraud, rape, child abuse) is morally permissible only when I do it because I am I, but not when you or someone else does it."[19] This view, however, violates one of the fundamental principles of ethical understanding, which requires that the reason or justification provided for an action's being right or wrong, good or bad, be one anyone might adopt under relevantly similar circumstances. This is the principle of universalizability, which will be discussed in connection with the generalization argument in chapter 5.

In order for my moral justification of an action to hold up, I must be willing to let others employ the same justification in analogous situations. For this reason John Mackie asserts, "What is wrong for you cannot be right for me merely because I am I and you are you."[20] This fundamental notion has been expressed in various ways. Thomas Hobbes, for example, says, "Do not that to another, which thou thinkest unreasonable to be done by another to thyself" is a natural law "approved by all the world."[21] Even children seem to have an intuitive understanding of this principle when they ask their parents, "Why is it okay when you do X, but not when I do it?" Without this perspective, it is difficult to give any meaning to moral terms of approbation or condemnation unless, as some have argued, their use does no more than express subjective feelings of approval or disapproval.[22]

The focus of ethical relativism, however, may be wider than the individual, encompassing a group—familial, religious, professional, political, national—thereby providing apparent plausibility. But when pushed to justify why the same action is right when done by members of one group and wrong when done by members of another group, the ethical relativist must strain to maintain the plausibility of the theory.[23]

If individual relativism is one extreme, at the other we might find (hypothetically) only two competing sources of ethical values, with the proponents of one source accepting the legitimacy of the other source "for the other group," although the two groups' specific beliefs are diametrically opposed. The advice "when in Rome" may be of this origin, as may be the concept of religious tolerance. A proponent of this view might believe that while the moral beliefs of another group are at odds with her own, she must respect that group's right to the opposing view.

But it is not clear that respecting the right to an opposing view is the same as believing it is "right for them." It is hard to imagine, for example, anti-abortion advocates agreeing to a kind of truce with their pro-abortion foes. Can we imagine an anti-abortion mother explaining to her daughter, "Abortion is wrong, but people who accept abortion as a legitimate medical procedure are doing nothing wrong when they have an abortion." Believing it can be "right for them" makes the universilizabiltiy principle relative—or at least posits an alternative moral universe—leaving one to wonder whether or not the adherents of such a view aren't conflating a prescriptive enterprise (ethics) with a descriptive one (sociology, anthropology). Ethical relativism bothers many people because they wonder how competing views of what is right and wrong can both be right. The alternative—one correct ethical position—is ethical absolutism, also troubling to many because of competing claims about which version is correct.[24]

The traditional logic of moral reasoning is based on a widely recognized belief. David Hume wrote: "The notion of morals implies some sentiment common to all mankind, which recommends the same object to general approbation, and makes every man, or most men, agree in the same opinion or decision concerning it."[25] In contemporary ethical theory there are otherwise dissimilar ethical practitioners arguing that ultimately there can be but one correct ethical position. From the twentieth-century British tradition, R. M. Hare asserts that "if we assumed a perfect command of logic and of the facts, they would constrain so severely the moral evaluations that we can make, that in practice we would be bound all to agree to the same ones."[26] Similarly, Michael Smith asserts that "if we are open-minded and thinking clearly then such an argument [about moral opinions] should result in a convergence in moral opinion, a convergence upon the truth."[27] "Apart from all linguistic matters," according to Stephen Toulmin, "it is possible, that, given all relevant facts, people's moral judgements might always agree."[28] Concurring in the result—of a final true or absolute ethical position—but for very different reasons are philosophers from the religious tradition of natural law. Preceding and following Thomas Aquinas are theorists who begin from the assumption that the universe is subject to divine law, which extends to our conduct in the form of the moral law, accessible by reason and the same for all. Thus, ethical absolutism may have a religious or a logical grounding.[29]

The Role of Morality in the Law

If we keep in mind that the debate about the relation of law to morality is taking place not on a solid foundation but on the shifting plates of another ongoing debate—that between ethical absolutism and ethical relativism—we gain added appreciation of the difficulty of the challenge. When we inquire about the relation of law to morality, accordingly, we are assuming a prior answer to the question of absolutism or relativism, one morality or many (sometimes "one true God or many"). Therefore, it may turn out that part of the disagreement between those who believe law is inextricably bound up with morals and those who believe the law is a separate enterprise, not dependent on morality, is based on a more fundamental difference in belief about the nature of ethical values.

In *Law as Moral Judgment,* Beyleveld and Brownsword discuss the complex set of relationships obtaining between legal positivism versus natural law theory on the one hand and ethical relativism versus ethical absolutism on the other.[30]

Legal Naturalism	Legal Positivism
Ethical Absolutism	Ethical Relativism

They argue that while there are general propensities, there is no simple correspondence or one-to-one relationship between, for example, ethical relativism and legal positivism or between ethical absolutism and natural law theory. They also contend that while their own natural law theory depends on an absolutist ethical perspective, this is not a logically necessary relationship.[31] Fortunately, for my purpose, it is not critical to settle this matter; my point here has been to indicate the underlying complexities of the situation, whose ripple effects ultimately impact a discussion of the morality of tax cheating.

And though the matter is not settled, I assume the arguments that have been expended by those who cannot accept a sharp division between law and morality have been sufficient to render a final victory by legal positivism unlikely. By this I mean that legal positivists will never ultimately succeed in winning a consensus that we are dealing with two parallel but unrelated universes—law and morality. As d'Entrèves notes, "Surely not even at the present day does the 'good' citizen think of law merely in the shape of the policeman or the law-court. Nor, on the other hand, does he long hesitate to break laws which he deems morally indefensible, at least when he is sure that he can do so with a fair chance of impunity."[32]

In arguing that we do not have a moral duty to pay our taxes under the current Tax Code, the possibility must still exist that we do have a moral duty to obey the law—under certain circumstances at least—and that being governed under those conditions imposes a moral duty to pay taxes. The nature of the government certainly makes a difference to this duty, as does the form of taxation; but at least within some idealized situation it must be possible that the undertaking of being governed implies a moral duty to pay taxes.

Establishing that we have a moral duty to pay taxes and not just a contractual, institutional, or prudential duty, even under the most ideal form of government (including an ideal form of taxation) may be difficult, but it also seems necessary. Being governed under an ideal system means we value and are willing to pay for the rights, protections, and freedoms such a system provides. This should form the basis for our moral duty to pay taxes. Without the possibility that such a moral duty could arise under ideal conditions, it becomes difficult to know what can be meant by a moral duty to pay taxes. To illustrate this point, consider the following utopian situation. We are governed by a constitutional democracy with fair and open elections. The government is run efficiently and the tax system is unobtrusive. The taxpayers have direct input into the amount of taxes they pay because their elected representatives adhere to the taxpayers' wishes. In addition, the tax revenue is spent in ways generally approved of by the taxpayers. Though this situation can exist only in words, we must be prepared to say that if it did arise, the taxpayers under such a system would have a moral duty to pay their taxes. Absent this possibility, my argument here is superfluous.

Further, it is the belief held by some unspecified portion of the population—that we have a moral obligation to pay income taxes under the current Tax Code—against which I am arguing, and that forms the basis for this inquiry. But if it turns out that there is no direct or necessary link between law and morality, as legal positivists contend—that is, that there is no reason to suppose that we have a moral duty to obey the law—then, again, the purpose of this book is defeated, as I am arguing for a special instance of a more general but opposing principle.

Whether or not and to what extent we have a moral obligation to obey the law is a contentious issue.[33] In general the problem with a "fully general moral obligation to obey the law whatever its content and without regard to the consequences of obeying it," we are told, is that it "represents a moral blank check that government is free to fill in at will or at least within very broad limits."[34] The issue is most acute when we are called upon to obey a law we disagree with. Tyler's research found that "82 percent [of respondents] agreed that 'a person should obey the law even if it goes against what they think is right.'"[35] As one might expect, opinions on this issue are diverse and polarized. On the one hand we are told, "People are often called upon to recognize their moral obligation to obey the law in those cases where they morally disagree with the law."[36] While on the other hand Dworkin says, "It does not follow that a man is morally to blame every time he does what the law prohibits."[37] And Rawls observes "that sometimes we have an obligation to obey what we think, and think correctly, is an unjust law."[38] By contrast Thoreau wrote: "It is not desirable to cultivate a respect for the law, so much as for the right."[39] According to Sidney Hook, "The obligation to obey an unjust law in a democracy is political and not directly moral."[40] Another writer observes, "The question of whether a law is just, is distinct from the question whether it ought to be broken; though the two are related, an answer to the one is not an automatic answer to the other."[41] And George Christie says, "[T]o say that one has a moral obligation to obey the law does not mean that one must necessarily obey the law. Other more important countervailing moral obligations may require that one not obey the law."[42]

When the divine right of kings was accepted as justification for the law, laws by definition were moral, for they were enacted by kings who traced their moral authority back to God.[43] Though some countries still recognize a direct connection between a supreme lawgiver and the law of the state, the United States is not among them. According to Richard Posner, "[T]he enterprise, now several thousand years old, of establishing the existence and content of a natural law that underwrites positive law is hopeless under the conditions of modern American society."[44] From a practical perspective, Posner explains, people obey the law for a multiplicity of reasons, including habit, concern with reputation, considerations of reciprocity, net expected gain, and weighing opportunity costs; so whether or not there is an independent moral obligation to obey the law may be an important consideration for some people but not for others.[45] Still, I believe that in the case of some laws, especially tax laws—where the lion's share of violations are neither detected nor a matter of public record—the importance of a connection between what the law requires and our moral obligations is magnified, since our illegal actions are likely to go undetected.

While there is a long tradition in ethical theory holding that we have a moral duty to obey the law, there is also a more recent but still historic argument about our moral duty to pay taxes. Over five hundred years of this dispute, described in detail in *The Moral Obligation of Paying Just Taxes*, involves the segregation of what are called *penal laws*—which proscribe certain acts and provide penalties for infractions but do not morally obligate us—from other laws for which a moral as well as a legal obligation arises.[46] Thus, questioning the moral status of the Internal Revenue Code is but a contemporary example of a problem drawing debate since the middle ages.

Thomas Aquinas, one of the disputants, taught that law is "an ordination of reason for the common good, made by him who has charge of the community."[47] And more recently Benjamin Cardozo wrote, "The final cause of the law is the welfare of society."[48]According to this view laws are developed for the common good, and that gives them moral authority; the general welfare is the reason the U.S. Constitution authorizes taxes. But different lawmakers obviously have different notions about what constitutes the common good or general welfare. To refine his point, Aquinas incorporates a number of qualifications. Of first importance for Aquinas is the notion that there is a divine or eternal law that human reason is capable of ascertaining, if only imperfectly, and there from obtaining guidance. According to Aquinas, reason informs us that "whatever is a means of preserving human life and of warding off its obstacles belongs to the natural law." In particular, one of these means, he says, is to live in society, and "whatever pertains to this inclination belongs to the natural law."[49] "But," he qualifies, "human laws cover only those aspects of human behaviour which imply a co-ordination with other men. Thus, properly speaking, the laws of men do not primarily aim at promoting virtue, but only at securing a peaceful living together: they do not forbid all that is evil, but only that which imperils society; they do not command all that is good, but only that which pertains to the general welfare."[50] The last presumably includes taxation.

Aquinas further divides man-made laws into just and unjust laws. "If they are just they have the power of binding in conscience, from the eternal law from which they are derived."[51] Unjust laws are man-made and, because they are not binding on conscience, we are not morally obligated to obey them. Thus Aquinas's answer, regarding a moral obligation to pay taxes, is that it extends to just taxes—those aimed at achieving the general welfare—but not to unjust taxes.

So, for Aquinas, tax laws that are man-made and just are examples of laws enacted for the public good and binding on conscience. Aquinas also acknowledges situations where the law inflicts injustice on an individual, and holds that in such cases there is no moral obligation to obey the law. This would presumably extend to unjust tax laws. According to Martin Crowe, because Aquinas does not recognize penal laws—and thus rejects the notion that all tax laws are penal laws—there is nothing in what Aquinas says that precludes tax laws in particular from commanding a moral obligation.[52] However, the problem with our Tax Code, for reasons I have given and others I will later provide, is that it precludes a responsible assessment of the extent to which it embodies justice or fairness or whether its specific provisions were enacted for the public good. If this is not as apparent as I would hope, it may be because—as one critic explains—our leaders have tried "to socialize the population or mold the conception of fairness or justice to fit their policies."[53] The government's use of the expression "voluntary tax system," described in chapter 3, is an obvious example of this process.

Moral Obedience to the Law

Cicero advises that "many harmful and pernicious measures are passed in human communities—measures which come no closer to the name of laws than if a gang of criminals agreed to make some rules."[54] Both legal positivism and legal naturalism agree in this and with Oxford jurist Paul Vinogradoff that "it is impossible to give a definition of law based exclusively on coercion by the State."[55] The law must aim, he argues, "at right and justice, however imperfectly it may achieve this aim in particular cases."[56] "If we omitted this attribute from our definition," he concludes, "we should find it very difficult to draw the line between a law and any kind of arbitrary order as to conduct, e.g. the levying of regular blackmail by a criminal association."[57] This comports with Rawls's assertion that "it is not possible to have an obligation to autocratic and arbitrary forms of government."[58]

What is significant for my primary argument is that proponents of both points of view—legal positivism and natural law—have stated similar requirements for the production of justice in the administration of the law. That is, aside from their differing views about the moral substance of laws, both legal positivists and legal naturalists accept the need for a fundamental structure through which any system of law must operate if it is to be properly called a *legal system*. It was for this reason that Herbert Spencer wrote, "Even Austin [a staunch legal positivist], anxious as he is to establish the unquestionable authority of positive law . . . is obliged, in the last resort, to admit a moral limit to its action over the community."[59] Because of this broader context, "What the legislator hands down" one commentator writes, "follows a dialogue already in progress and enters into a dialogue that continues. The dialogue as a whole is about the welfare of the body politic, a good which is logically antecedent to law and which gives law its point."[60]

Although Hart is a legal positivist—holding that the law's validity is logically independent of morality—he argues that certain moral conditions must be met before the law's application can be considered just: It must involve general standards of conduct communicated to citizens who are "expected to understand and conform to the rules without further official direction," and it must be "intelligible and within the capacity of most to obey."[61] As Hart admits, "If this is what the necessary connexion of law and morality means, we may accept it."[62] The minimum standards that Hart proposes are echoed and amplified by Lon Fuller, a legal naturalist.[63]

Fuller describes a legal utopia "in which all rules are perfectly clear, consistent with one another, known to every citizen, and never retroactive. In this utopia the rules remain constant through time, demand only what is possible, and are scrupulously observed by courts, police, and everyone else charged with their administration."[64] He goes on to point out that while such an utopian view may not be of any practical use "it does suggest eight distinct standards by which excellence in legality may be tested."

The eight conditions for law Fuller describes may be paraphrased as follows:[65] (1) The legal system must have rules, and issues must not be decided on an ad hoc basis. (2) The rules must be publicized. (3) The legal system must utilize no retroactive laws. (4) The rules must be understandable. (5) The legal system must contain no contradictory rules. (6) The rules of the legal system must require no conduct that is beyond the powers of those affected by the rules. (Ought implies can.) (7) The rules of the legal system must not be changed frequently. (8) There must be congruence between the rules as they are announced or promulgated and as they are administered (or enforced).[66]

For Fuller these eight criteria are necessary conditions of a legal system though collectively they may not be sufficient. Since Fuller's criteria apply to a legal system as a whole, it may be questioned whether or not these minimum conditions apply to subsystems of a legal system as well, such as the Tax Code. I assume they do, as ultimately the analysis of their application comes down to individual laws.

The existence of a legal system, and that system's potential for dispensing justice, is one basis for the widely accepted view that we have a moral duty to obey the law. This proposition, in turn, is a premise of the argument that tax cheating is morally wrong. However, the Internal Revenue Code—or at least Congress as its author—regularly violates a number of Fuller's principles. The Code's rules are changed frequently—by one count, 14,000 times since 1986—and often changed retroactively.[67] The tax system allows at least the appearance of some ad hoc decisions (discussed in chapter 5), and its understandability is frequently questioned, which undermines the importance of the fact that it is well publicized; publicizing what is unclear violates the spirit of Fuller's condition. If average citizens must pay someone else to keep them from violating the law—as most taxpayers do when they pay to have their taxes prepared[68]—what does this say about the law's understandability?

Further, (1) whether the tax law contains contradictory rules, or (2) requires conduct beyond the powers of those affected by the rules, or (3) whether the law is administered in the same way it is announced is likely to depend on our ability to comprehend the law's meaning, and is a key component of the tax complexity problem. "Certainly there can be no rational ground," Fuller states, "for asserting that a man can have a moral obligation to obey a legal rule that does not exist, or is kept secret from him, or that came into existence only after he had acted, or was unintelligible, or was contradicted by another rule of the same system, or commanded the impossible, or changed every minute."[69]

One question that affects the issue of tax cheating is whether respect for a legal system can be maintained though that system contains a subsystem—in this case the Tax Code—whose purpose is to supply revenue to the treasury, not to dispense justice (except insofar as justice is coextensive with the Code's many ancillary goals, including redistributing wealth, providing incentives for business and education, and exercising fiscal policy). As Greenawalt explains, "The existence of pockets of injustice within generally just political orders presents a kind of conceptual barrier to understanding the duty to support just institutions as including a general duty to obey the law."[70] Consider an analogy with human life. Can we respect human life (or revere it), as a living system, although it serves as a host for a cancerous tumor? It certainly seems possible. If so, this lends support for the proposition that a legal system may be respected even if it contains a subsystem operating on a principle different from and perhaps antagonistic to the one causing us to respect the law generally. This analogy has limits, however. The cancer's ultimate "success" is inimical to human, life, destroying its host; while collecting tax revenue—at least to a point—is necessary to finance the cost of administering justice. However, taxes are also necessary to pay for any system of law, regardless of how well or poorly it dispenses justice.

Moreover, even if we do owe or feel a general moral obligation to obey the law, that does not mean we cannot violently disapprove of a specific law—to the point of intentionally disobeying it, as in the case of civil disobedience (discussed in chapter 8)—where it is a contrary moral belief that prompts us to violate a law. And if such is true of a particular law, it is certainly possible that an entire category of the law, such as the current Internal Revenue Code, may warrant moral objection.

That we have no moral obligation to obey the Internal Revenue Code is a specific instance of Rawls's general principle that "obligatory ties presuppose just institutions."[71] It is not a coincidence that research shows that a tax system that is perceived as unfair is more prone to tax evasion.[72] As will be explained in chapter 5, there are many reasons for believing the Tax Code is unfair. My focus is on the administrative reasons rather than the substantive reasons that reflect the economic status or often the diametrically opposed political and ideological beliefs of the disputants. Also, as noted in chapter 1, the fairness question is really two separate questions. The fairness of the underlying system of law—promoting this or that social, political, or economic philosophy, and some form of distributive justice—is one front. It is the result of decisions about who should be taxed and at what rates, and produces what Justice Learned Hand described as "statutes that, although they levy taxes that will bring in a net revenue, have an added and incidental purpose."[73] The other front relates to compliance and how the law is administered. This second was the source of concern, cited by Pfohl earlier, that "there must be some guarantee that a high percentage of offenders either really will be punished or at least believe they will be punished."[74] As we have seen,

however, this requirement is not now being met by the tax law, and the situation appears to be getting worse. Though tax cheating and its relation to the administration of the law is the primary subject of this work, either or both concerns regarding fairness may cause us to question our duty to a system devoid of coherent moral grounding.

The Ethics of Tax Evasion

Nineteenth-century political economist Henry George, in speaking of what he called "the ridiculous untruthfulness of income tax returns," observed that "taxes which lack the element of certainty tell most fearfully upon morals."[75] The literature on ethics contains few discussions specifically addressing the morality of tax cheating (especially using or defining the term *cheating*). When the term *tax cheating* is used it is either left undefined or employed to mean tax evasion. Two writers, Robert McGee and Leo Martinez, for example—in separate writings—argue that *tax evasion* is not immoral.[76] McGee offers a thoroughgoing defense of the idea.[77] He first catalogs a number of opposing arguments that conclude that tax evasion is or should be considered immoral. After defusing each argument to his own satisfaction, he takes a markedly libertarian approach to arguing that taxation at its very core is theft by the government. "Where the tax is extracted by force or by the threat of force, as in the case of the income tax, there seems to be no moral duty to give anything whatsoever, because the recipient is a thief." He continues: "Morality involves choice. Where there is no choice, there is no morality." While I am sympathetic to many libertarian perspectives—especially regarding the importance of individual liberty—and agree with McGee's ultimate conclusion that tax cheating under the current Internal Revenue Code is not immoral, his argument comes at a high price as the same conclusion may be established with less drastic assumptions.

Taxation as Theft

One problem with the argument that taxes are theft by the government is that theft has its most practical meaning in the context of the rule of law, because the law defines ownership.[78] As Cass Sunstein and Stephen Holmes point out in *The Cost of Rights: Why Liberty Depends on Taxes,* an owner of property "is an owner only on the precise terms laid down at particular times by specific legislatures and courts."[79] *Black's Law Dictionary* defines property as "an aggregate of rights which are guaranteed and protected by the government."[80] In describing property rights it is common in the law to employ the expression "bundle of rights." The bundle includes the right to use, to possess, to dispose of, and to exclude others from using.[81]

Milton Friedman asserted that "the notion of property, as it has developed over centuries and as it is embodied in our legal codes," involves "complex social creations rather than self-evident propositions."[82] This has become all the more obvious with the explosion of intellectual property rights. Law establishes the meaning of ownership and of property rights, and without government and a legal structure to enforce the law, can there be theft? In a utopian communal society, for example, where by law there is no personal property, there would also be no theft. "If everyone owns everything then, in a sense, no one owns anything."[83]

McGee's perspective on property rights is, however, an extension of a long tradition. Herbert Spencer denied "the alleged creation of rights by government." "Contrariwise," he claimed, "rights having been established more or less clearly before government arises, become obscured as government develops."[84] Dworkin concurs with this notion. "Individuals can have rights against the state" he claims "that are prior to the rights created by explicit legislation."[85] But believing that property rights (and by extension theft) can occur if there is no government, is to overlook either (or both) of two important distinctions—that between (1) mere appropriation or possession of property and legal ownership or (2) moral or natural rights and legal rights. Paul Vinogradoff explains the notions of appropriation and possession in contrast to ownership: "When men have sunk labour and capital in a plot they expect naturally to keep it for themselves and for their nearest."[86] But, he observes, "a dog that has got hold of a bone [also] feels as an 'owner' and resents interference with his right of appropriation."[87] Yet few believe the dog's feelings establish its legal ownership of the bone.

According to Ayn Rand, "no human rights can exist without property rights."[88] Furthermore, she claims, the protection of rights, and in particular property rights, is the only moral purpose of a government.[89] The line between legal rights and natural (or moral) rights was famously illustrated by Thomas Hobbes in his description of the chaotic condition when "men live without a common power to keep them all in awe," when they are "in that condition which is called war; and such a war, as is of every man, against every man. . . . In such condition, there is no place for industry; because the fruit thereof is uncertain."[90] In such a condition, some would add, it is guns rather than good fences that make good neighbors.

John Locke believed that property rights could arise outside of a legal system, but that such rights were strictly limited to what an individual could personally use. *"God has given us all things richly . . . to enjoy. As much as anyone can make use of to any advantage of life before it spoils, so much he may by his labour fix a property in: whatever is beyond this, is more than his share, and belongs to others."*[91] Nevertheless, according to Locke, "The great and *chief end* of men's uniting into common-wealths, and putting themselves under government, is the *preservation of their property."*[92] Jean-Jacques Rousseau agreed that establishing and maintaining property rights is the central role of government. "It is to the law alone that men owe justice and liberty."[93] "The right to property is the most sacred of all the citizens' rights," according to Rousseau, "and more important in certain respects than liberty itself."[94]

Natural or moral rights may be distinguished, but both lack the specific characteristic of enforceability. Jeremy Bentham assessed the value of natural rights with the following pragmatic test. "A man is never the better for having such a natural right; admit that he has it, his condition is not in any respect different from what it would be if he had not had it."[95] The same can be said for moral rights. Holmes and Sunstein tell us, "When they are not backed by legal force moral rights are toothless by definition. Unenforced moral rights are aspirations binding on conscience, not powers binding on officials."[96]

Consent to Taxation

A second problem with McGee's characterization of taxation as theft is that it stacks the deck from the outset by defining theft as "taking of property without the owner's consent" rather than as "illegal taking of property." Even theorists who are wary of much about taxation, such as Austrian economist Ludwig von Mises, believe a certain amount of taxation is necessary and legitimate.[97] McGee makes it tautological that any government taxation (except voluntary contributions) is without the owner's consent "because all governments are illegitimate to the extent that they do not do just what every citizen wants and nothing else"[98]—a practical, if not a logical impossibility. But this raises the question: If taxation has to be voluntary to be legitimate, is there any sense in calling it taxation? Immanuel Kant held that tax "contributions should not be voluntary . . . they must be in fact compulsory political impositions."[99] Wellman and Simmons add: "It takes little imagination to see that governments would have considerable difficulties securing peace and protecting basic moral rights if they could count on the financial support and legal obedience of only those constituents who freely chose to support the government presiding over them."[100]

Locke believed that taxation should be voluntary in the extended sense that it be imposed with the consent of the governed, "giving it either by themselves, or their representatives chosen by them."[101] Rousseau addressed this issue from a democratic, social contract perspective as well:

> It should be remembered here that the foundation of the social pact is property, and its first condition is that each person should be maintained in the peaceful possession of what belongs to him. It is true that by the same treaty each person, at least tacitly, obligates himself to be assessed for a contribution to the public needs, but since this commitment cannot harm the fundamental law, and presupposes that the taxpayers acknowledge the evidence of need, it is clear that in order to be legitimate, this assessment should be voluntary; it should not arise from a particular will, as if it were necessary to have the consent of each citizen, who should pay only what he pleases, which would be directly contrary to the spirit of the confederation, but from a general will by majority votes on the basis of a proportional scale that leaves nothing arbitrary in the rate of taxation.[102]

Thus for Rousseau *voluntary* means arising from a vote. Since we vote for Congress every two years, and Congress is the source of the Internal Revenue Code (the Constitution says tax legislation is supposed to originate in the House),[103] we resubmit the question for a vote on a regular basis, and in this sense our system of taxation is voluntary as intended by Locke and Rousseau. It is also voluntary in the tortured sense explained in chapter 2, relating to self-assessment.[104]

John Locke also claimed that "every man, that hath any possessions, or enjoyment, of any part of the dominions of any government, doth thereby give his *tacit* consent, and is as far forth obligated to observance to the laws of that government, during such enjoyment."[105] But as one theorist observes, "The moral obligation to obey the law turns on basic justice and free acceptance of benefits, but free acceptance is so often problematic and basic injustice so often in controversy that persons frequently regard themselves as not bound by law or by the state's view of law."[106] The question of consent and its relation to obligation, and also the form the consent must take in order to obligate someone to the laws of the land, are contentious issues that, fortunately, I may skirt in this discussion.[107]

With regard to taxes specifically, Locke believed that "governments cannot be supported without great charge, and it is fit everyone who enjoys his share of the protection, should pay out of his estate his proportion for the maintenance of it."[108] McGee disagrees: "Just because some democratically elected government imposes a tax, it does not automatically follow that there is a duty to pay."[109] In contrast to Locke, McGee's view of government requires that consent to taxation be explicit rather than tacit. After a review and rejection of variations of the social contract argument, McGee states: "Taxation is coercive whenever it forces people to part with their property without their explicit consent." One rebuttal to this is the claim that "a state that could not, under specified conditions, 'take' private assets could not protect them effectively, either."[110] Another is that consent may be only a threshold requirement for moral obligation to the laws and not a guarantee, so that even explicit consent may not obligate someone to the government in some cases.[111]

McGee's requirement of explicit consent runs counter to the notion that unless one resides in a country that does not allow its citizens to leave the country, consent (whether explicit or implicit) is given each day a citizen chooses to remain.[112] The choice of a country functions as a marketplace, and everyday citizens of one country—whether legally permitted or not—make the choice to stay or go.[113] Deciding to stay is, in some sense, a vote for that country's legal institutions, including its system of taxation.[114] Whether staying also imposes a moral obligation to the law is a thorny issue among philosophers, legal scholars, and political scientists.[115] John Rawls, for example, claims that the principle of fairness requires a person to "do his part as defined by the rules of an institution when . . . one has voluntarily accepted the benefits of the arrangement or taken advantage of the opportunities it offers to further one's interests."[116]

Martinez finds fault with the implicit consent argument because "if citizens consent by freely choosing to remain, why is there no acknowledgment of the seriousness of this choice, no rituals or formal pledges?" One answer is that it is not a one-time choice, but a daily choice. A second answer is that immigrants do acknowledge the seriousness of their choice by undertaking tremendous risks to life and property in leaving their country of birth for a new home. Likewise, wealthy U.S. citizens who renounce their U.S. citizenship and remove themselves to Belize or the Bahamas or elsewhere for tax-avoidance purposes presumably do so in all seriousness, with knowledge of the sacrifice involved, though perhaps forgetting that the creation of their wealth was enabled by the very system they now renounce.[117] Paraphrasing Rawls quoted above, while they have voluntarily accepted the benefits of the economic and political arrangement and taken advantage of the opportunities it offered to further their interests, they have now turned their backs on their country—yet without the moral outcry awaiting a soldier who deserts his unit or a spy selling secrets to the enemy.

Martinez further claims that "only if citizens could choose to live outside any government's authority would their choice to live within a state amount to consent." This form of argument misconstrues the process of choice in situations of valuation. Requiring another alternative to living in this country or in that country—living outside any governmental authority—as a vantage point for choosing between two governmental alternatives is a flawed approach. There is no final neutral position from which to make valuations.[118] In this context Tony Honoré notes, "A citizen can never emancipate himself from dependence on the state. He can sometimes transfer his allegiance to another state, but such conduct is not a choice between dependence and freedom. It is a choice between depending on the citizens of State A and on those of State B."[119]

Further, it is not possible to value an end without valuing the means leading to that end. Feigning to value the protections of government—our rights as laid out in the Constitution—without consenting to the means necessary to achieving this end, which includes taxation—is simplistically one-dimensional reasoning. Rousseau believed that protecting property rights is the most significant job of government. But he says, "It is no less certain that the maintenance of the state and the government incurs costs and expenses, and, as anyone who grants the end cannot deny the means, it follows that the members of society should contribute some of their assets to its upkeep."[120]

Justifying a Moral Duty

This chapter began with a discussion of the moral duty to obey the law. My argument that we do not have a moral duty to obey the current tax laws has force only to the extent that we do have a moral duty to obey the law generally. So the question remains, do we have a moral duty to obey the law? One answer comes from traditional natural law theories that "assume that government is valuable and that obedience contributes to its effectiveness." These theories, as Greenawalt explains, emphasize benefits conferred on citizens.[121] "The duty to obey the law is related to the benefits the existence of law confers. . . . In being a law-abiding citizen, someone is contributing toward the effectiveness of an institution that is necessary for his own welfare."[122] Accordingly, another observer notes, "acknowledgement of the value of law arises out of rational appraisal of one's own self-interest in the maintenance of coercive social order."[123] One potential problem with tracing our moral obligation to obey the law back to our self-interest is the question of intertemporal choice described in chapter 3. Weighing our self-interest at different times—the present, tomorrow, next year, or in ten years—is not an easy matter. So while our overall or long-range self-interest may best be guaranteed by obeying the law, even when we don't agree with the law, our more limited self-interest may provide reasons for a different choice.

In an article on legal compliance, Robinson and Darley (a lawyer and a psychologist) contend, "The real power to gain compliance with society's rules of prescribed conduct lies not in the threat or reality of official criminal sanction, but in the power of the intertwined forces of social and individual moral control."[124] Their argument is that the law may possess or lack "moral credibility." Though addressing specifically criminal law, the authors believe that "law influences the powerful social forces of normative behavior control through its central role in the creation of shared norms."[125] "If the law has moral authority, it can be a reliable guide in shaping conduct for those cases in which the moral justifica-tions for its prohibitions are not immediately obvious."[126] One key to this process is the public's belief that "the law instantiates their moral beliefs" and "that the law came into being via fair procedures conducted by the appropriate authorities."[127] The fair procedures requirement (or rather its violation)—discussed in chapter 5—helps explain the current Tax Code's lack of moral authority.

Another answer to the question of a moral duty to obey the law may depend finally on whether we act on the assumption that we do. A. P. d'Entrèves proposed to define law "as any rule of human conduct which is recognized as being obligatory."[128] This pragmatic perspective may not satisfy many people. But if you ask yourself whether you would rather live in a society where people believe there is a moral duty to obey the law or one where people feel no such obligation, I believe most would choose the former. In *Is There a Duty to Obey the Law?* Wellman and Simmons support this notion: "What each of us gains from everyone else's compliance with the state's laws is much more valuable than what we lose by having to obey these laws ourselves."[129]

Tony Honoré argues:

> If people believe that there is a prima facie obligation to obey the law of their state, but that this can be overridden by contrary considerations such as the injustice of the law, they will generally obey. If, on the other hand, the existence of a law requiring certain conduct is treated as morally neutral, the tendency will be, apart from fear of sanctions, to choose disobedience in any case in which the burden of obedience seems heavier than the likely advantage to others.[130]

Thus, if the present Tax Code is viewed as morally neutral, as I have argued here that it should be—and the burden of obedience seems heavier to taxpayers than the likely advantage—the practical consequences to the treasury will depend only on our fear of sanctions. This outcome should be viewed with alarm by lawmakers, though there is little evidence that it has even registered on their radar.

One text on deviant behavior begins with the following statement. "If any single factor makes human social life possible and bearable, it is the ability of individuals to predict the behavior of others."[131] The law is concerned with regulating conduct, making behavior more predictable. Individuals calibrate expectations with respect to the conduct of others, allowing planning and anticipating probable responses. In a book on predicting the future, Nicholas Rescher asserts, "All major structures of human socialization—law, custom, habit, routine, tradition—seek to guide our actions into channels that will make the business of life more conveniently manageable through predictability."[132] While tax laws could be on this list, Congress has done little to ensure their inclusion. In a paper on conscience and obedience to the law, David Richards observes, "The scope and force of our moral obligation to obey law in a democracy are more fragile than might be supposed."[133] Most of us, I assume, would prefer that this force be less fragile, if only because our ability to predict other people's behavior is essential to directing our own.

As these comments suggest, when encouraging obedience to the law, an important consideration for lawmakers should be the ability of specific laws or systems of law to appeal to us on a moral level. A society where there is law—but no common moral purpose—results in obedience to the law only from an external perspective to avoid punishment. No government can operate effectively on that basis. Predicting others' behavior in such a society would be crude at best.

Obedience to the tax law is no different, but in this case U.S. lawmakers have failed to see the road they have taken us down. It is no longer sufficient to expect tax compliance based on loyalty, gratitude, or patriotism. I presume most tax cheaters compartmentalize taxes and patriotism and see no conflict between tax cheating and love of country. It is likewise unrealistic to expect someone to pay taxes because the taxes are his or her fair share if, as I have argued, the Tax Code's complexity makes it impossible to know what one's fair share is. In spite of this, a recent poll indicates that 95 percent of taxpayers believe they have a civic duty to pay their fair share of taxes.[134] The juxtaposition of the belief—held by 95 percent of taxpayers—that they have a civic duty to pay their fair share, with the widespread practice of tax cheating as described in chapter 2, indicates how dysfunctional our tax system has become.

But what, if anything, can be done to restore a moral duty to pay taxes? As a start, realigning the sources and uses of tax revenue with a vision of national purpose (the Constitution's "general welfare")[135]—either maximizing liberty for all, or maximizing security for all, or Jefferson's "equal and exact justice to all,"[136] or optimizing life's chances for all, for example—would put tax policy on a recognizable moral foundation. Determining that national purpose—the general welfare—is, of course, another matter. What is clear is that the current Code makes no effort in that direction. This topic is addressed more fully in the next chapter.

FIVE

CHEATING, COMPETITION, AND FAIRNESS

> But the most pernicious of all taxes are the arbitrary. They are commonly converted, by their management, into punishments on industry; and also, by their unavoidable inequality, are more grievous, than by the real burden which they impose.
> —David Hume (1711–1776), "Of Taxes"

Cheating and Competition

Much, but not all, cheating is associated with competition. In this context, cheating is characterized as seeking to gain an advantage by skirting the rules. Baseball fans have endured countless scandals involving steroid use, corked bats, spitballs, greaseballs, and players wagering on games, all in an effort by some players to gain an advantage over the competition. In "Baseball, Cheating, and Tradition," the author frames the question of cheating in terms of an unfair advantage.[1] For reasons stated earlier, I prefer to leave the term *unfair* out of the definition because the fairness or unfairness of cheating can best be assessed in relation to the moral status of the rules violated and only after formulating a morally neutral definition of cheating. "Gaining an advantage by violating the rules" provides this neutral starting point. This refocuses our attention on the moral status of the rules themselves, instead of on the activities of cheating. If the rules require what is immoral, for example, then doing what is right may require cheating.

As evidence that not all cheating occurs in the realm of competition, we can ask: Is cheating on a spouse, cheating on a diet, cheating death, or tax cheating done to garner an advantage over a competitor? In these cases if an advantage is gained it is personal, as there is no opponent. So if cheaters put themselves in what they consider a better position—not necessarily in relation to an opponent or competitor but in relation to a personal ideal or value—competition is only an associated and not an essential element of cheating. This is why we sometimes speak of someone cheating herself.

Though competition is not essential to cheating, it is probably its most common setting, and hence warrants a brief discussion. Competition itself is viewed in different ways. In what can be called the classical view of competition, the goal is to win while strictly adhering to rules of the contest and to best the most formidable opponent. Roman philosopher Seneca tells us, "A gladiator counts it a disgrace to be matched with an inferior; he knows that a victory devoid of danger is a victory devoid of glory."[2] The World Series, the Super Bowl, the Kentucky Derby, Wimbledon, and the World Cup are celebrations of this ideal.

Another view, quite at odds with this outlook, is the win-at-all-costs position exemplified by Rosie Ruiz, the ostensible winner of the 1980 Boston Marathon. Ruiz crossed the finish line first, but it was later determined that she had not run the 26.2 miles but had joined in the race near the end. There are numerous exemplars of this perspective, including Mark McGwire, who hit seventy home runs in 1998; Olympic sprinter Ben Johnson; the East German women's Olympic team of the 1970s; and ice skater Tonya Harding's ex-husband, accused of engineering the 1994 attack on skating rival Nancy Kerrigan's knee. The roster of business cheaters includes a growing number of individuals who did much more than crash their own careers. Recent examples include Angelo Mozilo, former Countrywide Financial Corp. CEO; Bernard Madoff, the $50 billion swindler; and Bernard Ebbers, founder of WorldCom.

These differing views of competition lead to differing views of cheating, and form the basis for a long-standing debate: Is cheating wrong, or only wrong if you get caught? A legend featuring Alexander the Great alleges that his travels brought him to a town that was home to an impenetrable knot binding a yoke to a pole—and subject of an oracle—tied by Gordias, founder of the Phrygian monarchy. The prophecy was that whoever could undo the knot would rule Asia. Many before Alexander had tried and failed. In 333 BCE, according to the legend, Alexander raised his sword and cut the knot in half, and subsequently conquered Asia. Some would say he cheated because he circumvented the rules to achieve his end; he did not undo the knot by untying it. Others might praise his cleverness, arguing that he found an ingenious solution, thinking outside the knot. These represent differing views of competition and consequently of cheating.

An important aspect of competition is knowing your opponent. Understanding tendencies and weaknesses is one key to doing battle. When the government establishes a tax policy, one commentator tells us,

> they are establishing the rules of the game. However, over time taxpayers may begin to feel their taxes are too high relative to what is received in return. Compliance becomes increasingly problematic among those who feel that they are not getting as good a deal as they bargained for. No compliance procedures will work forever. Knowledge of gains and losses, acquired over time, can alter choices.[3]

Thus it is with taxpayers who come to know where the tax law is soft or where the IRS is unlikely to tread.

Legal philosopher H. L. A. Hart states that justice in the application of the law "consists in no more than taking seriously the notion that what is to be applied to a multiplicity of different persons is the same general rule, undeflected by prejudice, interest, or caprice." Such a system "consists primarily of general standards of conduct communicated to classes of persons, who are then expected to understand and conform to the rules without further official direction." In addition, "the rules must satisfy certain conditions: they must be intelligible and within the capacity of most to obey."[4] This also expresses the framework necessary for cheating. There must be a valuable goal and an accepted standard or set of rules for its accomplishment. One implication of this view is that cheating requires rules that are understandable and at least potentially known by those expected to comply with them. How far the rules of the Internal Revenue Code fail either of these tests is part of the reason for a discussion of unintentional cheating in the next chapter.

The commonly voiced complaint that the income tax is unfair because it allows wealthy individuals and large corporations to use "loopholes" within the tax system to avoid or minimize their tax bills is evidence that the present system does not meet Hart's minimum criteria—not because it may be true, but because it is widely believed that there are two standards. Of large corporations, Congressman Lloyd Doggett (D-TX) admitted: "They have the ability to hire the brightest and most creative people in their tax departments. I will tell you they also have demonstrated the ability to hire the best and brightest lobbyists and they have the most flush political action committees in terms of influencing what we do here."[5] Whether well founded or not, the widespread belief or perception that the law—applied to a multiplicity of different persons—is not the same should be a source of concern for Congress. Whether there is empirical evidence for these popular beliefs is beside the point; that they are commonly assumed demonstrates a central reason why the moral status of tax cheating is in question.

John Stuart Mill analyzed the question of tax fairness as partly a problem of compliance. Even if we were to design an otherwise ideal tax system, the inability to enforce its provisions would doom its recognition as fair. "It is to be feared," Mill observes, "that fairness which belongs to the principle of an income-tax cannot be made to attach to it in practice."[6] The underlying design or intention of the tax law may thus be less important for understanding tax cheating in the present context than the effectiveness of its implementation. The fact that taxpayers are left to their own devices to comply—and apparently with no one watching—means the current system is flawed in more than one dimension. Like crimes of opportunity, encouraged by the perceived absence of a deterrent, the current system, even if it were somehow judged fair or just in its underlying principles, leaves taxpayers largely unattended and able to help themselves to what legally belongs to the public treasury.

Criminologists describe techniques of crime control—measures available to limit an individual's chances for or interest in committing a crime. These techniques of situational crime prevention have been classified by Frank Schmalleger under four headings: "(1) increase the effort involved in crime, (2) increase the risks associated with crime commission, (3) reduce the rewards of crime, and (4) reduce the rationalizations that facilitate criminal activity."[7] It should be apparent to anyone familiar with our income tax system that it does a relatively poor job with at least three of these techniques. (1) Tax cheating can be done with minimal effort; all we are doing is reporting numbers from the privacy of our home or office. (2) The risks involved in tax cheating are low; the audit rate has declined precipitously in recent decades, though some taxpayers face a higher risk than others. (3) Reducing the rewards of tax cheating is a more difficult problem, except in connection with increasing the risk. (4) Rationalizations for breaking the tax law are abundant:

- The tax law is complex.
- Our tax system is unfair.
- I need the money just to survive.
- Other people don't pay—why should I?
- The government will just waste the money anyway, and so on.

Collectively, the four crime control techniques provide a menu of options for Congress to choose among, if it decides to tackle the problem.

Hand-to-Hand Combat

The adversarial nature of the present tax system encourages taxpayers to overreach and aggressively seek to minimize their taxes. Since taxpayers are charged with self-assessing their taxable income and preparing their own tax returns, it is no wonder there are problems. One tax historian tells us:

> There is a naked confrontation between the citizen and the state in the income tax system that does not exist with indirect taxes. . . . The demand for taxes on income is backed by an inquisition into the taxpayer's affairs—one's personal life, how one runs one's business, and how one spends one's money. This is the power associated with despots, and every taxpayer knows the tax system is a pocket of totalitarianism in an otherwise free society. This makes taxpayers mad and rebellious. . . . As a general rule, widespread tax evasion is a sure sign a government's tax system is bad.[8]

This criticism is not new. French economist Jean-Baptiste Say (1767–1832), in discussing the consequences of despotic and arbitrary governmental taxation on the contraction of the tax base, observed, "The general distrust and uncertainty of the future induce people of every rank, from the peasant to the pacha, to withdraw a part of their property from the greedy eyes of power."[9] This ability of taxpayers to readily remove income from the view of the IRS—from the greedy eyes of power—accounts for most of what is labeled tax cheating.

To combat this taxpayer disposition, the IRS is empowered to counterattack and interpret the tax law in a manner that will maximize treasury revenue. According to one economist, the government's role in the tax system "combines the roles of rulemaker, victim, and umpire."[10] This adversarial system promotes mistrust and animosity between taxpayers and their government. It incentivizes dishonesty—through the audit selection lottery—where rewards for breaking the law can be great and the odds of getting caught are small. For 2002 the IRS reported auditing fewer than one-half of 1 percent (.48 percent) of all returns filed.[11] In the case of individuals almost two million taxpayers were audited in 1996, while only 735,000 people on average were audited each year during President George

W. Bush's first term—a 63 percent reduction.[12] Though the audit rate has been creeping up and is now at nine-tenths of 1 percent,[13] over against the 1963 rate of 5.8 percent,[14] the odds still favor the tax cheater. This system effectively punishes compliance among honest taxpayers—those who choose not to play the audit lottery; after all, you have to play to win.

Fueling the animosity and mistrust between taxpayers and the IRS is taxpayers' concern for privacy. Interestingly, privacy is both claimed as a right and employed as a smokescreen to cover tax cheating. As one commentator notes, "The social institution of privacy creates a major 'structural hindrance to the flow of information' about deviance to officials in charge of imposing legal sanctions. . . . When law violations occur in private places, as they often do, they are in an immediate sense invisible to law enforcement officials."[15] Yet attempts to increase visibility in the tax system are invariably met with cries of invasion of privacy.

Privacy has another dimension as well. While the privacy of tax returns filed is carefully guarded by the law,[16] the activities producing a taxpayer's income are not. In the spirit of George Orwell's *1984* the tax law allows one taxpayer (though probably not children, as in the novel) to accuse another taxpayer of tax cheating by reporting specific details to the IRS. In a survey of taxpayer attitudes, 58 percent of those questioned agreed that "it is everyone's personal responsibility to report anyone who cheats on their taxes."[17] The IRS Whistleblower Office pays rewards to people who turn in taxpayers who fail to report income and pay the tax they owe. If the IRS uses information provided, it can award the whistleblower up to 30 percent of the amounts it collects. Vindictive ex-spouses and ex-employees are common contributors to this program. This concept is not new. In Venice during the Renaissance it was possible for Italians to charge fellow citizens with tax fraud, but the accusation had to be signed—and if the case was not proven, the accuser would suffer the punishment otherwise awaiting the tax cheater. The IRS system is much less risky for the informant. The IRS pays for information leading to a determination of additional taxes due; if no recovery, no reward is paid to the informant.[18] According to the IRS, even after paying fees to the informant the targeted program is more cost effective than the traditional audit route. This parallels the statistics on financial audits, where auditors uncover very little fraud compared to the amounts reported by whistleblowers or discovered by chance.[19]

Sociologist Robert Merton advised, "Widespread incentives to evade coupled with the widely shared belief that 'everybody does it' along with the tendency to imitate successful evaders leads to the patterned evasion of norms in the face of their continuing claim to legitimacy. Tax evasions, cheating on exams, avoidance of customs duties and currency controls, adultery, and petty theft in business firms provide familiar examples."[20] Like many compliance problems—especially in areas where morality is an insufficient safeguard—tax cheating thus results either from insufficient regulation or regulation that is unenforced or perhaps unenforceable, providing an incentive to pay less tax than the rules require. In recapping the problems caused by lax or inefficient enforcement, legal scholar Lon Fuller echoes Aristotle's warning quoted in the first chapter—about the spirit of obedience to law:

> Government says to the citizen in effect, "These are the rules we expect you to follow. If you follow them, you have our assurance they are the rules that will be applied to your conduct." When this bond of reciprocity is finally and completely ruptured by government, nothing is left on which to ground the citizen's duty to observe the rules. The citizen's predicament becomes more difficult when, though there is no total failure in any direction, there is a general and drastic deterioration in legality.[21]

In terms of tax compliance, the increasing tax gap and growing special interest control of the Tax Code are early warning signs of this breakdown; further, it seems unlikely that disrespect for the law in one area can remain contained.

If we view tax cheating as a form of lying, as some suggest,[22] Mark Twain's comments are applicable to the present discussion. "When whole races and peoples conspire to propagate gigantic mute lies in the interest of tyrannies and shams, why should we care anything about the trifling lies told by individuals? . . . Why should we without shame help the nation lie, and then be ashamed to do a little lying on our own account?"[23] Twain's question—extrapolated to tax cheating—is why should we expect taxpayers to feel moral responsibility for paying their individual taxes when those who design the tax system and control the spending of our taxes appear so unconcerned with the system's moral integrity.

These observations raise uncomfortable questions about our national tax strategy. As a result of the adversarial forum—pitting the taxpayer against the IRS—and the widespread acceptance of tax cheating, the moral sting that should be borne by the term *cheating* is largely lost. So the stigma that attaches itself to lawbreakers in other areas—con artists, pedophiles, sexual predators, child abusers, and rapists—is lost in the case of tax cheaters. Some tax scofflaws, like Willie Nelson and Wesley Snipes, may even rank as folk heroes.[24] The design and implementation of this particular legal subsystem thus renders it a battleground rather than a source of respect and moral obligation.

As noted in chapter 1, this outcome also removes an important disincentive from the government's arsenal. Insofar as people believe that tax cheating is immoral, conscience is enlisted, and the force of morality is added on top of other deterrence factors provided by the law, including the fear of penalties and prison terms. In a discussion of research on tax compliance and the conscience, the authors report that "shame is the threat which has the greatest direct effect" on deterring tax cheating.[25] Since there is at least some evidence that even indirect appeals to the conscience of taxpayers—asking taxpayers about their willingness to "do something for the country as a whole"—have some effect on income reporting,[26] choosing to bypass or ignore taxpayers' moral capacity (as Congress appears willing to do) strikes me as legislative negligence. That the present tax system is structurally incapable of informing the conscience should not be underrated and is taken up in greater detail in chapter 8.

Fairness and Equality

Reducing tax evasion may "serve to distribute the tax burden more equitably and add to the sense of legitimacy on which the legal order presumably rests."[27] This is important, Janice Nadler observes, because empirical research shows that "[w]hen a person evaluates particular legal rules, decisions or practices as unjust, the diminished respect for the legal system that follows can destabilize otherwise law-abiding behavior."[28] The income tax is commonly viewed as unjust or unfair from diverse and often opposing perspectives. Unfairness is interpreted by some to mean the Code's tendency to favor wealthy individuals and large corporations. At a 1990 Congressional hearing on the tax gap, the head of the American Institute of CPAs testified: "The perception that Congress is intentionally allowing wealthy taxpayers and big business to escape taxes legally can be a strong motivation for others to create their own [illegal] tax savings."[29] The Code's underlying design is seen by others as unfair because its goal is the redistribution of wealth. Advocates of this view may agree with George Bernard Shaw, who wrote that "the daily ceremony of dividing the wealth of the country among its inhabitants [should] be conducted that no crumb shall, save as a criminal's ration, go to any able-body adults who are not producing by their personal exertions not only a full equivalent for what they take, but a surplus sufficient to provide for their superannuation and pay back the debt due for their nurture."[30]

John Rawls, in describing his version of a social contract, posits a fictional setting—(what he calls "the original position")—where people don't know the circumstances of their own lives as they are shrouded by a "veil of ignorance." From this fictional setting, rules are formulated—reflecting each person's ignorance of her or his circumstances—leading to a system of justice, as participants hedge their bets. Without the veil of ignorance, according to Rawls, "If a man knew that he was wealthy," for example, "he might find it rational to advance the principle that various taxes for welfare measures be counted as unjust; if he knew that he was poor, he would most likely propose the contrary principle."[31] In fact, however, in the original position we would not know our particular situation and therefore we would be forced to determine what rules would be good under any circumstances. Using such a procedure "no one should be advantaged or disadvantaged by natural fortune or social circumstances in the choice of principles."[32] Congress employs no such tool for seeking objectivity and fairness, leading one observer to write: "Tax policy debates have produced no general consensus on a 'fair' allocation of the tax burden," leading to ambivalence about the Tax Code and ultimately "to ambivalence toward noncompliance as well."[33]

The ancient Stoics taught that we should not behave as if our lot in life defined who we are, since tomorrow may bring a reversal of fortune. To dramatize this belief they appealed to the goddess Fortuna and her Wheel of Fortune as the great equalizer. "Know then," says Seneca, "that your lot in life is changeable, and that whatever befalls any man can befall you also."[34] The $50 billion Madoff Ponzi scheme provided ample evidence for this, as many victims of the fraud went to bed one night millionaires and woke up the next day broke. The sting of misfortune was eased by the IRS when it announced that the victims could write off their losses in full, rather than at the normal pace of $3,000 per year applicable to capital losses arising from "true" investments.[35]

The relative fairness of a tax system depends in part on its justification. Thomas Hobbes believed the primary justification for taxes is defense:

> To equal justice, apperteineth also the equal imposition of taxes; the equality whereof dependeth not on equality of riches, but on the equality of the debt that every man oweth to the commonwealth for his defense. . . . Seeing then the benefit that everyone receiveth thereby, is the enjoyment of life, which is equally dear to poor and rich; the debt

which a poor man oweth them that defend his life, is the same which
a rich man oweth for the defense of his; saving that the rich who have
the service of the poor, may be debtors not only in their own persons
but for many more.[36]

As his final comment indicates, the rich, he believed, should pay more
taxes than the poor—not simply because they are rich—but because
they have more to defend. To capture this fact, Hobbes proposed a form
of consumption tax as the most equitable. "The equality of imposition"
of taxes, according to Hobbes, "consisteth rather in the equality of that
which is consumed, than of the riches of the persons that consume the
same." He concludes: "When the impositions, are laid upon those things
which men consume, every man payeth equally for what he useth; nor is
the commonwealth defrauded by the luxurious waste of private men."[37]
David Hume concurred: "The best taxes are such as are levied upon
consumptions . . . because such taxes are least felt by the people. They
seem, in some measure, voluntary; since a man may chuse how far he will
use the commodity which is taxed."[38]

Presaging the serial importance of "liberty, equality, and fraternity,"
Montesquieu offers a general rule "that taxes may be heavier in proportion
to the liberty of the subject, and that there is a necessity for reducing
them in proportion to the increase of slavery."[39] Except in the case of the
tax protestors discussed in chapter 2—who believe they are slaves of the
state by virtue of the income tax—our celebrated enjoyment of liberty,
according to Montesquieu, means we should expect to be taxed hand-
somely for all the freedoms we enjoy, and glad in the bargain.

But liberty may be sought by some at the expense of equality and
especially of fraternity. Rawls comments: "In comparison with liberty and
equality the idea of fraternity has a lesser place in democratic theory."
By deemphasizing fraternity, especially in deference to liberty, what is
downplayed is, according to Rawls, "a sense of civic friendship and social
solidarity" as well as "a certain equality of social esteem."[40] Thus while we
value freedom and recognize it has a price, we may still prefer that our
neighbor pay more tax so that we can pay less for our common defense
and general welfare. Equality and fraternity are thereby sacrificed to
reduce the cost of freedom.

"The subjects of every state," Adam Smith said, "ought to contribute
towards the support of the government, as nearly as possible, in proportion to their respective abilities; that is, in proportion to the revenue
which they respectively enjoy under the protection of the state."[41] Ability

is measured by results—the revenue enjoyed—not by potential. For Smith the more one has (and thus the more one has to lose) the more one should pay. Some will say this system misaligns incentives, especially for financially successful taxpayers. But viewed from another point of view, wealthy taxpayers also purchase more casualty insurance than others because they have more to protect; and no one finds this unfair.

Even economist Milton Friedman, in describing the benefits of a single-rate (flat) income tax, claimed that the "higher absolute payments" of tax this system would require of persons with higher income—to pay for the additional governmental services they receive (discussed in the next section)—"is not clearly inappropriate on grounds of benefits conferred."[42]

Getting What You Pay For

"A steady reduction in tax compliance," we are told, "need not only be interpreted as a violation of the law, but also as taxpayers' discontent with what they receive for their taxes."[43] However, according to Martinez, because of the law's complexity "it is impossible to levy taxes in proportion to the benefits received by each citizen."[44] In discussing the issue of getting what you pay for, Robert McGee, in an article on paying our "fair share" of taxes, makes it axiomatic that we cannot get what we pay for from the government because "just about any service provided by the government can be provided better and cheaper by the private sector."[45] In another article on the ethics of tax evasion, McGee finds it unlikely that wealthy individuals—and he cites Leona Helmsley and Ross Perot—could possibly have received services from the government of equal value to their income taxes paid. Of Helmsley in particular he writes, "It is difficult to believe that she received more than $100 million in services from the federal government over the years."[46] Accordingly, she would be seen as typical of "wealthy taxpayers who perceive a growing gap in exchange equity between their rising tax burdens and public sector benefits" they receive.[47] But if we include services such as national defense, protection of property rights, regulating stock and bond markets—providing an economic climate where Helmsley was able to build her empire—then it is very possible that her lifetime tax burden was, as Adam Smith put it, in proportion to the revenue she enjoyed under the protection of the state. If $100 million in lifetime income taxes is a reliable number, it would represent 10 percent of her final estate's reported $1 billion value.

In a book describing the breadth and depth of what benefits depend on taxes, Cass Sunstein and Stephen Holmes point out—apropos of Helmsley's real estate fortune—"Markets presuppose a reliable system of recordation, protecting title from never-ending challenge. . . . My rights to enter, use, exclude from, sell, bequeath, mortgage, and abate nuisances threatening 'my' property palpably presuppose a well-organized and well-funded court system."[48] "Where real estate is involved," the same authors contend, "ownership becomes quickly enmeshed with sovereignty. . . . Defense spending is surely the most dramatic example of the dependency of private rights on public resources."[49] Furthermore, "property rights depend on a state that is willing to tax and spend. Property rights are costly to enforce. . . . Protection of property rights can be a valuable investment that increases aggregate wealth over time."[50]

Based on this, it is possible that the graduated income tax may accurately reflect the graduated demands of the wealthy for the protections of government. Sunstein and Holmes argue: "Government must not only repress force and fraud, invest in infrastructure and skills, enforce stockholders' rights, and provide securities exchange oversight and patent and trademark protection. It must legally clarify the status of collateral. And it must regulate the banking sector and credit markets to prevent pyramid schemes and ensure a steady flow of credit to businesses rather than cronies."[51] Investors who placed their life's savings with Bernard Madoff may now wish they had paid a little more in taxes, if so doing would have helped the understaffed SEC protect their "investments." Those who resent paying taxes for anything that does not directly benefit their current situation are underestimating the value of the safety net provided by a justice system, a system of national defense, regulated markets and—as Justice Holmes reminded us—a civilized society.[52]

Thomas Hobbes also chided reluctant taxpayers: "Those levies therefore which are made upon men's estates, by the sovereign authority, are no more but the price of that peace and defence which the sovereignty maintaineth for them."[53] But John Stuart Mill observed, "It is not admissible that the protection of persons and that of property are the sole purposes of government."[54] Thus, the numerous intangible benefits paid for by taxation, which facilitate the process of earning and keeping income and making the undertaking more predictable and less risky—by regulating potentially disruptive factors in the market—cannot be ignored.

It may surprise some that two of the most influential Austrian economists freely acknowledge the importance of taxes. Friedrich Hayek recognized the necessity of taxes for a number of purposes. "Far from advocating . . . a 'minimal state,'" he claims, "we find it unquestionable that in an advanced society government ought to use its power for raising funds by taxation to provide a number of services which for various reasons cannot be provided, or cannot be provided adequately, by the market."[55] Ludwig von Mises tells us, "The maintenance of a government apparatus of courts, police officers, prisons, and of armed forces requires considerable expenditure. To levy taxes for these purposes is fully compatible with the freedom the individual enjoys in a free market economy."[56]

In this regard the authors of *The Cost of Rights* inform us: "Because rights impose costs on private parties as well as on the public budget, they are necessarily worth more to some people than to others. The right to choose one's own defense lawyer"—as Leona Helmsley might have attested to at her tax fraud trial[57]—"is certainly worth more to a wealthy individual than to a poor one."[58] In light of Helmsley's reported claim that only little people pay taxes, Nietzsche's characterization of a criminal as a "debtor who not only refuses to repay the advantages and advances he has received but who even dares to lay hands on his creditor"[59] seems fitting. Unhappily for Helmsey, her creditors included the little people who helped pay for her prosecution.

In one empirical study, researchers found that tax compliance is not affected by a "sense that the tax system is inequitable or unfair." People do not need, the authors contend, "an ideological justification for tax evasion."[60] The authors of that study interpret fairness in terms of taxes being "too high," government waste, general inefficiency of government, and the cost of government outweighing the benefits.[61] They conclude: "Those who support the system admit they cheat about as much as those who say the system is unfair."[62] Other studies, however, report that "an unfair tax system positively influences tax evasion,"[63] with one finding that 42.6 percent of people agree that taxpayers "cheat on their taxes because they feel the tax laws are not fair to them," while 48.8 percent disagreed.[64] Here, as with other empirical research on tax cheating, there is a problem of determining taxpayers' moral attitudes and their sense of duty to pay taxes under the current Internal Revenue Code as opposed to what these attitudes would be under a different or ideal system of taxation. Most research I have reviewed is not specific on this question or deals with people's moral feelings relating to a generalized or unspecified tax régime. This may explain why—as a general proposition—95 percent of U.S. taxpayers believe they have a civic duty to pay their fair share of income taxes;[65] but that in the specific case of the Internal Revenue Code this belief gives way to an unsettling realization that "fair share" has been hijacked by unseen forces inside the Beltway.

In an article examining the ethical implications of a taxpayer's "fair share," McGee offers examples of situations where taxpayers do not receive exactly what they pay for, and he concludes that "fair share generally equals zero, especially in cases where taxes are collected by force [e.g., the current income tax]."[66] I don't claim to know what fairness means in the context of taxation, only that the present Code introduces so many variables that it makes such a determination impossible. But I do think that attempting to measure taxpayers' perceptions of fairness or their belief that taxes are too high, or that government wastes money or is inefficient, or that we do not always receive exactly what we pay for, is not getting at the heart of the problem addressed here. I assume that some people would complain about these problems even under an ideal tax code.

"The perceived fairness of the tax system," according to Danshera Cords, "is influenced by the interaction of the government with taxpayers."[67] But many taxpayers feel that their interaction with the government is illusory. However, there are options. Imagine a federal tax return with a pie chart allocating percentages or providing boxes to check above the signature line—allowing a sense of participation in governance—instructing taxpayers to allocate their taxes among (1) education, (2) national defense, (3) health care, (4) infrastructure, (5) interest on national debt, (6) conservation, (7) alternative energy, (8) space exploration, (9) supporting the arts, (10) combating global warming, (11) law enforcement, (12) foreign aid, (13) congressional junkets, and so on. This would not end tax cheating, of course, but its impact on how people feel about paying what taxes they do pay would certainly be measurable. Those most concerned about national defense, for example, could feel assured that their taxes are contributing to the government service they value most and not some other program whose purpose they disagree with. And though such a system would not sit well with entrenched constituencies—those who prefer the status quo money-driven representative democracy over a California-style limited direct democracy—it would bring us closer to former IRS Commissioner Gibbs's goal that "each of us must understand the vested interest all of us have in fostering voluntary compliance."[68]

The problem Americans express in wanting to "get what you pay for" may be symptomatic of a more general issue raised by a fictional character in the income tax–driven novel, *The Pale King*. Much of the narrative is based on the author's thirteen-month experience as an IRS examiner at the Midwest Regional Examination Center in Peoria, Illinois, during 1985–86. At one point, one of David Foster Wallace's characters says of Americans, "We don't think of ourselves as citizens—parts of something larger to which we have profound responsibilities. We think of ourselves as citizens when it comes to our rights and privileges, but not our responsibilities."[69] To the extent we ignore the intangible benefits of what we pay for and focus only on the direct effects—educating my child versus living among educated citizens—the question becomes one of focus. Seeing the trees but not the forest is also not seeing the saplings, the climatic effects, the soil containment, the potential for forest fires, the animals who call it home, the conversion of carbon dioxide into oxygen, the mutual benefits of an ecosystem, and the multisensual aesthetics of a walk in the woods.

What If Everyone Cheated?

If we move from an economic fairness argument about getting what you pay for to a more fundamental moral argument, we arrive at a formidable objection to the proposition that tax cheating is illegal but not immoral—the question: "What if everyone cheated?" Psychologists who study the influences of social trends on individual behavior recognize that cheating begets more cheating. Former IRS Commissioner Charles Rossotti explains that "as the number of people cutting corners on taxes increases, so does the number of their friends and business competitors who start to think, 'Everybody else is doing it and getting away with it, so why not me?'"[70] Presenting the results of empirical research on trust theory, Dan Kahan tells us that if taxpayers "believe that others are morally motivated to comply, they reciprocate by complying in turn, whether or not they believe they could profitably evade" their tax obligations.[71] On the other hand, the same writer reports that when taxpayers believe others are cheating, they "behave like amoral calculators posited by the conventional theory." As a result, "if taxpayers believe there is even a significant minority of tax cheaters, they may be inclined to cheat as well because the act would have acquired some social validation."[72] The rhetorical question and ethical admonishment "What if everyone cheated?" then begins to lose its force as more people engage in cheating. Though we may be at a tipping point in this regard, it is still worth examining this venerable and often powerful ethical question.

The insight of the universalization principle of moral reasoning, discussed in chapter 4, has been formulated in many ways, from the

Golden Rule to the Categorical Imperative. The generalization argument is grounded in this insight but formulated as a question for testing the plausibility of certain moral claims. In *Generalization in Ethics*, Marcus Singer explains that "the generalization argument has the form: 'If everyone were to do x, the consequences would be disastrous (or undesirable); therefore no one ought to do x'."[73] Accordingly, someone believing that tax cheating is immoral could argue: "No one should cheat because if everyone cheated the consequences would be disastrous." This would provide the basis for a moral duty to pay taxes and undercut the primary argument set forth in this book.

In explaining how the generalization argument applies to paying taxes, Singer quotes the following example from Ewing.

> Suppose a man to urge that he will miss the sum he has to pay [for taxes] much more than it would be missed by society. The absence of the few pounds which he has to pay will not, he may urge, make any perceptible difference whatever to the public funds, but it will make a very perceptible difference to himself, therefore to force him to pay it will do more harm than good; and it will be difficult to answer him if we consider the particular act by itself. But the real answer surely is that he still ought to pay it, because this argument, if admitted at all, would apply to practically everybody, and it would therefore be unfair to him to benefit by other people's taxes while not paying his own share.[74]

According to Singer, this is a valid application of the generalization argument, and "it is presented in a way that is most effective for making clear not only the rational force of the argument but also the conditions that must be met to justify the claim that a certain case is a legitimate exception."[75]

The generalization argument, as Singer explains, is valid unless one of two conditions applies. The first condition he calls *invertability* and the second *reiterability*. These conditions take the form of counterexamples intended to show when the generalized argument does not work. Invertability refers to a feature of the generalization argument when it is initially applied to everyone and subsequently to no one. Consider the following example. "You should not become a doctor, because if everyone became a doctor, the results would be disastrous." If everyone became a doctor there would be no farmers, no school teachers, no truck drivers, and so on. Here, Singer explains, "In a case in which the consequences of everyone's acting in a certain way would be undesirable, while the consequences of no one acting in that way would also be undesirable . . . the argument can be inverted."[76] Both the original argument and its inversion have the same result, which means it is not a valid application of the generalization argument. Neither everyone's becoming a doctor, nor no one's becoming a doctor, is a desirable outcome.

According to Singer, "In order for the generalization argument to have a valid application with respect to some action it is necessary that it not be invertible with respect to that action."[77] In the case of tax cheating, the argument is inverted if we ask, "What would happen if no one cheated on her or his income taxes?" Here the results are the opposite or reverse of the original undesirable outcome. If no one cheated, things would be fine. The generalization of a proposition about income tax cheating is not invertable and is therefore a valid application. While "Everyone should cheat on her or his taxes" would lead to potentially undesirable results, "No one should cheat on her or his taxes" would lead to positive consequences. This is the desired outcome of the generalization argument.

The other form of invalidating counterexample for the generalization argument is found when the argument is reiterable. An argument is reiterable according to Singer "whenever it is applied to some action arbitrarily specified, as part of its description, as taking place at some particular time, or at some particular place, or by some particular person, or in relation to some particular person or thing."[78] Singer illustrates the problem with the following example:

> If everyone were to eat in this restaurant it would get so crowded that no one would be able to do so; therefore no one ought to eat in this restaurant. . . . The reference to *this* restaurant is not essential here; the same argument would apply to *that* restaurant, and to any other one. The argument can obviously be reiterated for every restaurant, and its consequence would be not just that no one ought to eat at this or that restaurant but that no one ought to eat at any restaurant.[79]

Therefore, Singer explains, "Any instance of the generalization argument that is reiterable is invalid."[80] The generalization argument as applied to tax cheating would be reiterable only if it made reference to this or that particular taxpayer or a certain time or place.

Though the generalization argument applied to tax cheating is valid, on the basis of Singer's analysis, its weakness comes from the continuing need to define tax cheating. Validity is a formal requirement of logic, but the soundness and usefulness of a valid argument are limited by any vagueness or ambiguity in the terms used to express the premises. If tax cheating involved everyone's paying less than required by law, the government would have less to spend, and some would argue that this is a good thing. In the current discussion we need to ask just what, in the context of tax cheating, would lead to an undesirable outcome if everyone did it? Martinez asserts, "It requires no great effort to document the 'harm' caused by wholesale tax evasion."[81] But *evasion,* as I have explained, is a legal term with a settled definition. In contrast, proclaiming that "no one should cheat, because if everyone cheated the consequences would be disastrous" provides no real information unless we know what constitutes tax cheating (and perhaps disaster). It is not equivalent to generalizing the claim that everyone should pay taxes because if no one did the result would be disastrous. Cheating for a few may mean paying no taxes, but in its common usage it refers simply to paying less than the amount required by law; as noted earlier most cheating involves reducing but not eliminating taxes.[82] It may be the result of an exaggerated charitable deduction, an unreported cash receipt, or a misreported capital gain. The variations and possibilities are endless, but for most tax cheaters the goal is to adjust the tax to what is felt to be fair or to what is affordable, not to stop paying taxes. "When people think taxes are unfair," one observer explains, "they spend less time reporting carefully and may be motivated to produce what they perceived to be a fair outcome even when this does not conform to the law."[83] The connection between tax cheating and an impending disaster is thus too tenuous to make a convincing argument.

The Uneven Playing Field

John Locke wrote that laws should "not to be varied in particular cases, but to have one rule for rich and poor, for the favorite at court, and the country man at plough."[84] The income tax system can be characterized as a series of general rules and principles qualified by myriad exceptions, many tailored to specific classes of taxpayers. In addition, the administration of the tax system involves a lack of generality in a number of dimensions, violating the fair procedures requirement described in chapter 4. Three examples are discussed here: (1) individualized tax laws affecting one or only a few taxpayers, (2) courts in different parts of the country intentionally interpreting federal tax laws in different ways, and (3) IRS Private Letter Rulings.

Individualized Tax Laws

A minimum criterion for a moral rule is that it applies to everyone equally in pertinently similar circumstances. On the moral force of the law, Justice Oliver Wendell Holmes Jr. wrote that "any legal standard must, in theory, be one which would apply to all men, not specially excepted, under the same circumstances. It is not intended that the public force should fall upon an individual accidentally, or at the whim of any body of men."[85] Friedrich Hayek warned, "Often the content of the rule is indeed of minor importance, provided the same rule is universally enforced."[86] For a law to impart moral force, it must be universally applicable. Like cases must be treated alike, or as Hart stated, "What is to be applied to a multiplicity of different persons is the same general rule, undeflected by prejudice, interest, or caprice."[87] The moral principle of universalizability was most forcefully asserted by Kant in his Categorical Imperative.[88] He held that actions may be justified morally when the actor is able to will that the principle or maxim on which he or she is acting become a universal law—that is, that others acting on the same principle or maxim, under relevantly similar conditions, would also be morally justified. Kant provides an example of a man short of money and seeking a loan. The only way he can borrow the money is by promising to pay it back. But he knows he cannot pay it back. Kant generalizes this circumstance into the following maxim. "Whenever I believe myself short of money, I will borrow money and promise to pay it back, though I know that this will never be done."[89] He then asks, "How would things stand if my maxim became a universal law?"[90] Accordingly, what the individual is proposing is wrong since the principle behind the act cannot be universalized.

While the Tax Code meets the condition of generality when viewed as a whole—the Code applies to everyone—individual sections (or subsections) of the Code frequently reveal the hollowness of this condition. In such cases, it turns out that although anyone coming under the qualifications of the code section will be treated similarly, in fact very few taxpayers—and occasionally only one taxpayer—so qualify. In such cases the general form of the law masks its true substance, a violation of the spirit of the principle that the rule apply to everyone equally. It is for this reason, according to McGee, "that any special interest legislation—a law that benefits some special interest at the expense of the general public—need not be obeyed."[91] Unfortunately, for those of us left behind by special interest legislation we often have no opportunity to obey or disobey; we simply forfeit the benefits that go to others, and perhaps pay more tax to subsidize the fortunate beneficiaries.[92]

"The problems of achieving compliance," one writer explains, "are exacerbated by the slow but steady transformation of the terms of exchange that accompanies the return of politics as usual." One such transformation occurs as "special interest groups negotiate alterations in the contract favorable to themselves."[93] Whether this is another dimension of tax cheating or just a part of the democratic process (or the political game) is an important question, but one with an irreconcilable spectrum of answers. Some of what are popularly called earmarks are tax laws affecting a few taxpayers or only one.[94] Though special interest tax legislation is nothing new, the crypt where the bodies are hidden was opened for a brief period in the late 1990s. The *Taxpayer Relief Act of 1997* contained seventy-nine items that applied to one hundred or fewer taxpayers.[95] The reason we know this is the result of a short-lived law aimed at bringing some transparency to the tax legislation process. The *Line Item Veto Act*,[96] subsequently ruled unconstitutional by the Supreme Court in *Clinton v. City of New York*,[97] required the Congressional Joint Committee on Taxation to prepare a statement identifying each "limited tax benefit"—earmark directed at one hundred or fewer taxpayers—"contained in a bill or resolution."[98] One of these measures, and a target of the president's veto, affected only one taxpayer. Its cost was estimated at "$84 million over five years, allowing for deferral of taxes on the sale of a sugar beet processing facility owned by Dallas businessman Harold Simmons to a farmer-owned cooperative."[99] For those who believe federal legislation should have some bearing on the nation and its general welfare, this was a stretch.

The inclusion of this narrow rule and others like it—what one observer calls "'special interest' provisions buried within the arcane language of the income tax code"[100]—is symptomatic of the lack of authentic generality. A law designed to apply to anyone in a particular class—but where that class has been so narrowly defined as to circumscribe a very few taxpayers—abuses the spirit of the moral principle of universality. The potency of the principle that like cases be treated alike depends on the moral relevancy of the criteria used to determine likeness. Congress has frequently violated this requirement; without it, however, the moral grounding of the Code is eroded. If the sugar beet plant sale mentioned earlier were an isolated incident, it might be forgiven. But the fact that we had a law requiring disclosure of tax items affecting one hundred or fewer taxpayers—even briefly—indicates a general problem with the Tax Code and its moral standing.

The workings of special interest legislation can be instructive for its brazenness. Buried in the massive *Tax Reform Act of 1986* was a provision benefiting one newspaper, the Houston *Chronicle*. Rather than naming the paper, however, Congress elected to describe it in general terms, thereby thumbing its nose at the public in a veiled gesture. Specifically the law change exempted from an effective tax increase (caused by the removal of a tax credit), "any daily newspaper . . . which was first published on December 17, 1855, and which began publication under its current name in 1954, and which is published in a constitutional home rule city . . . which has a population of less than 2,500,000."[101] In spite of its use of the word *any*, Congress intended to benefit only one taxpayer and—like Cinderella's glass slipper—this description fit only one daily newspaper.

With a wondering eye out for the nation's general welfare, Congress has also come to the aid of a small group of high-profile taxpayers—

"Now that we've agreed on the loopholes,
what should the tax laws be?"

professional golfers. The *American Jobs Creation Act of 2004,* which, according to the *Wall Street Journal,* was "larded by Congress with all sorts of goodies for all sorts of industries,"[102] contained a provision designed to limit the benefits of deferred compensation plans for certain wealthy taxpayers. However, the law provided an exception to help out golfers such as Tiger Woods and Vijay Singh. Rather than directly naming the golfers or their professional organization in the law, Congress conferred its benefits only on deferred compensation plans "established or maintained by an organization incorporated on July 2, 1974," the very day the PGA Tour, Inc. was incorporated.[103]

Describing the organization in this way also saved Congress the potential embarrassment of having to explain how the PGA, as well as other sports organizations such as the National Football League (NFL) and National Hockey League (NHL), qualify as nonprofit organizations with tax-exempt status.[104] There may be nothing wrong with providing tax breaks for members of already tax-exempt organizations except that it clearly exposes the lack of direction or political agnosticism of the overall tax strategy. Rather than seeking a settled body of law by aiming the Tax Code in the direction of its constitutional mandate to "provide for the common defense and general welfare,"[105] congressional tax policy often appears to be driven by no more than several hundred fingers testing the current direction of the wind.

An important exception to this lack of direction involves tax breaks for limited classes of taxpayers involving issues of religion. At one time Internal Revenue Code section 512 allowed an exemption from unrelated business income tax [106] for a single radio station operated by a nonprofit religious organization, Loyola University of New Orleans. The wording of The Code subsection disguised its specific intent, however, by stating its exemption in general terms. As Hopkins explains, the criteria were phrased in such a way that the first letter of each of the three tests for exemption identified a call letter of the beneficiary radio station (WWL).[107]

Though most employees and employers are forced to pay into the Social Security system, Code section 3127 allows employees and employers of a particular religious faith to opt out. One might expect the news media to be all over this and the religious group to be growing in popularity. To be eligible for this religious exemption, it must be established that the employees are members of "a recognized religious sect or division thereof which . . . is conscientiously opposed to acceptance of the benefits of any private or public insurance which makes payments in the event of death, disability, old-age, or retirement or makes payments toward the cost of, or provides services for, medical care (including the benefits of any insurance system established by the Social Security Act)." This sounds general and morally relevant. Unfortunately for those who would like to say Thanks-but-no-thanks to Social Security, the law also requires that to qualify for this exemption the religious sect must have established tenets or teachings embodying this opposition to Social Security and the sect must have been in existence at all times since December 31, 1950.[108] This law took effect in 1989 and targets its benefits at the Amish.[109]

The Code contains other special exemptions and benefits for religious organizations, their leaders and donors, apparently on the assumption that the separation of church and state allows or requires this treatment. Ministers, for example, are allowed to receive a tax-free housing allowance from their congregation.[110] Though benefiting from this special rule, ministers are still able to deduct the mortgage interest and taxes on their homes.[111] While doing good some ministers have therefore done quite well.

Churches are not required to file tax returns (Form 990) with the IRS—regardless of the size of their revenue—although this is mandatory for other categories of 501(c)(3) tax-exempt organizations.[112] As a result, while we know little about the financial dealings of churches, we have public access to extensive information on other nonprofits, including sources of revenue, how their funds are spent, and their boards of directors' names and salaries. There is even a special rule limiting the IRS's ability to audit a church, requiring prior approval by a higher authority.[113]

Regarding the double standard favoring the church in the tax law, Thoreau quipped, "I did not see why the schoolmaster should be taxed to support the priest, and not the priest the schoolmaster."[114] In attempting to administer the separation of church and state, the dim light of congressional imprecision fails to disclose a slippery slope—not interfering with the practice of a religion is not the same as helping to subsidize a religion with tax dollars. For this reason Ronald Dworkin asks, "Does a right to religious liberty include the right not to have one's taxes used for any purpose that helps a religion to survive? Or simply not to have one's taxes used to benefit one religion at the expense of another."[115] The Supreme Court's interpretation of the First Amendment's Establishment Clause, prohibiting the establishment of an official religion or other preference for one religion over another (or for religion over nonreligion)—as it relates to taxation—is addressed in chapter 8.

In 1934 the Supreme Court used the phrase "legislative grace" in reference to the deductibility of certain items in *New Colonial Ice. Co.*

v. Helvering.[116] The phrase caught on in the courts and the proposition, "deductions are a matter of legislative grace" has now been cited in more than 2,500 tax cases. The use of the term *grace,* of which John Calvin made so much, is a remnant of the deference common law has traditionally shown for God's law. Calvin—trained as an attorney before he became a preacher—said "God's grace is illustrated by the fact that he does not give away salvation indiscriminately, but gives to some what he denies to others."[117] To the extent the tax laws show deference to the elect—whether for religious or other reasons—legislators have conferred upon themselves the role of bestowing grace with the tax law. "The Gospel is not preached to everyone,"[118] Calvin reminds us, but a well-directed campaign contribution also couldn't hurt our odds of achieving tax salvation.

In addition to religious organizations, certain other charitable groups or their donors have been singled out for tax blessings as well. The *American Jobs Creation Act of 2004* authorized a new charitable deduction available only to certain whaling captains recognized by the Alaska Eskimo Whaling Commission.[119] That the law applies equally to all such whaling captains is of little consolation to the rest of us. The *Pension Protection Act of 2006* added a special charitable deduction for taxidermy property and defined such property as a "work of art which is the reproduction or preservation of an animal, in whole or in part" and which must, the law stipulates, contain part of the body of the dead animal.[120] The dead-animals-as-art movement is apparently alive and well, and politically connected; and the rest of us therefore are subsidizing a few big-game hunters—for if these were not valuable deductions they would not have made their way into the Code. The inclusion of special provisions—whether benefiting big business or big-game hunters—is a sinister sport played by lawmakers and it results in a lack of respect for the law, perhaps aiding and abetting tax cheating. This is not a new problem; Adam Smith warned, "Where there is at least a general suspicion of much unnecessary expense, and great misapplication of the public revenue, the laws which guard it are little respected."[121]

Even in a sea of arbitrary-sounding tax rules, it is often possible to spot an unusually arbitrary new rule that prompts suspicions of personalized tax deals for the well connected. In the 2009 *American Recovery and Reinvestment Act,* for example, a special temporary adjustment was made to an already arbitrary rule reducing from ten years to seven years the waiting period to avoid taxation upon the sale of certain assets, but only for 2009 and 2010 (or to five years in 2011) and only for S Corporations.[122] Unlike many other changes made at the time, it is difficult to tie this change to stimulating the economy. My limited grapevine, a recently retired IRS agent I talked to, indicated that the rule change was prompted by the family needs of a large Modesto, California, wine maker.[123]

That such "private tax laws" apply to so few taxpayers exposes their origins in blatant political favoritism. The additional fact that these special interest laws are often worded in general terms, employing "any" and "all" as if they were universal, only intensifies the perceived injustice of the situation and provokes renewed cynicism at Congress's arrogance in attempting to conceal its political misdeeds. As one ethicist observes, "If an Italian patriot propounds the maxim that the interests of all boot-shaped countries should be specially favored, we shall not accept this as universalized if it is a mere dodge for not using the proper name 'Italy.'"[124]

Aggravating the problem of exclusive categories of taxpayers favored by specific legislation is its unknowable extent. As Sheldon Pollack explains, "The fundamental problem of contemporary American tax policymaking is that it seldom has any overall direction and is simply too accessible to too many private interests at once."[125] In their book *Showdown at Gucci Gulch,* the authors vividly describe the massive special interest lobbying process that took place in the two years before the passage of the *Tax Reform Act of 1986.* As they report, "So much money was floating around Washington that even lawmakers themselves began to look askance."[126]

Unfortunately for the moral integrity of the Tax Code, the individual-izing of tax provisions is not new. In *The Rape of the Taxpayer,* Phillip Stern chronicles a batch of special code sections "secretly" incorporated into a piece of tax legislation in 1969. Among these provisions were section 49(b)(10), designed to save Uniroyal Corporation $3 million in taxes. Another special rule saved Lockheed Corporation $14 million and McDonald Douglas Corporation $6.5 million. Litton Industries, Mobil Oil Corporation, individuals Gwendolyn Cafritz and Louis B. Mayer, and the estate of Charles E. Merrill (of Merrill Lynch) each procured a personalized tax benefit.[127] While Stern contends that some of these provisions can be identified by their retroactive effective dates, "one of the main difficulties in identifying the special provision is the conspiracy of silence entered into by those who know who is getting what from which provision."[128]

The Uneven Bench

The court system plays a role in ensuring that federal tax laws are not interpreted uniformly, thereby exposing taxpayers to geographical differences in what constitutes their fair share. One understandable reason for this outcome is that federal courts in different judicial districts, from time to time, interpret the same complex tax law in different ways. In some cases, the disparity is eventually brought to the attention of the Supreme Court, whose ruling on the matter brings harmony to the districts.

Supreme Court Justice William O. Douglas, in a dissenting opinion, argued that "if it is the law, we should require observance of it—not merely by taxpayers but by the government as well."[129] The federal courts are also the government and taxpayers have a right to expect consistency across state lines in their interpretation of federal tax laws. Aggravating the geographical problem, however, is the fact that the IRS may choose not to follow the decision of a federal court, except the U.S. Supreme Court. If the IRS loses a case, it may, undeterred, continue to attack other taxpayers as if it had never lost. Thus, taxpayers willing to pursue their disagreement with the IRS through the court system are effectively bound by different rules from taxpayers who, for financial or other reasons, don't or can't do so. For its part at least the IRS is forthright in this practice in that it often announces publicly the rulings against it that it intends to follow and those in which it believes the court was wrong. This process is carried out through the IRS's reporting of its acquiescence or nonacquiescence with a specific court's decision.[130]

Adding to taxpayers' woes in understanding regional differences in the meaning of the Internal Revenue Code is a policy followed by the U.S. Tax Court. This policy derives from the Court's decision in *Golsen v. Commissioner of the Internal Revenue Service*.[131] In applying this rule, the Tax Court—a federal court administering a federal law—will rule differently in different parts of the country on exactly the same issue. Thus, the federal law as administered in California (ninth circuit) may differ from the same federal law as administered in Maine (first circuit).

Under the Golsen Rule, the Tax Court overrides its own considered judgment when the court to which the case is appealable disagrees with the Tax Court on a particular issue. The court's integrity is thereby traded off for "efficient and harmonious judicial administration,"[132] calling for the Tax Court to follow a decision in an earlier case by the court to which the present case is appealable. This is an expedient approach that can be seen either as efficient—since if the Tax Court follows its own reasoning, it is likely to be overturned on appeal—or it can be seen as a face-saving device for the Tax Court since it reduces the number of its decisions that will be overturned—and as Judge Posner of the Seventh Circuit informs us, "Most judges are highly sensitive to being reversed."[133] In addition, however, it has a numbing effect on the public's perceptions of the legal system. More than one court, in considering a prior decision and reasonings on a particular issue, has reversed itself, citing a flaw or error in its prior interpretation of the law. "Judges must be allowed to change their minds," Posner claims, "even though the consequence will be an 'arbitrary' distinction between litigants in period one and those in period two."[134] This is a critical piece of the judicial process. But in prejudging the outcome of an anticipated appeal—a kind of self-censoring of its conscience—the Tax Court with its Golsen Rule ensures that the appeals court it disagrees with will never have the chance to reconsider, perhaps never finding that, after all, the Tax Court was right.[135]

The Code permits "small" Tax Court cases (under $50,000 in dispute) to be handled differently than larger cases.[136] This represents approximately one-half of the cases heard by the Tax Court. Specifically, the Code stipulates that decisions of the Small Case Division "shall not be reviewed in any other court and shall not be treated as a precedent for any other case." Even here, however, the Tax Court applies the Golsen rule, prompting the question why the court should not apply its best reasoning in these cases, at least, rather than deferring to the appeals court to which the case can never be appealed.[137]

Personalized Tax Rulings

In the administration of the tax law, there is a third example in which the law fails to achieve a satisfactory level of generality, potentially failing to treat like cases alike. It is practiced by the Internal Revenue Service in issuing Private Letter Rulings. These rulings are issued to a specific taxpayer for a fee in response to an inquiry on how the Internal Revenue Service will treat a specific proposed transaction. The amount of the fee—ranging from $625 to $14,000—gives some indication of who is or is not obtaining such rulings.[138] A Private Letter Ruling applies only to the taxpayer who requested it and "may not be used or cited as precedent by another taxpayer."[139] The IRS issues such rulings in response to a taxpayer's written inquiry "filed prior to the filing of returns or reports that are required by the tax laws, about its status for tax purposes or the tax effects of its acts or transactions."[140] Private Letter Rulings represent an administrative work-around in response to a problem of Congress's own creation: the Code's complexity.

To those of us outside the Beltway's powerful force field, there is something bizarre about a system in which an agency of the executive branch raises money by selling information to taxpayers on how it intends to interpret the federal tax laws in the special case of the taxpayer writing the check. Though tax practitioners may defend the system as a form of insurance for themselves against malpractice—although paid for by their clients—from a theoretical standpoint, such a procedure projects the perception of the ad hoc administration of the Tax Code. The historical parallel with the church's selling indulgences during the Middle Ages—ensuring that the departed soul enjoyed an advantageous eternal experience—will be left to another time.

The purpose of exploring these three aspects of our tax system was to expose their lack of authentic generality. In describing the attributes of a tax régime capable of appealing to taxpayers on a moral level, to enforceability we must add transparency and generality. Like cases must be treated in a like manner—verifiably and in the light of day—and "like" must be broadly construed as not to include only a handful of taxpayers or sometimes only one.[141]

The administration of the tax system, described in chapter 3, is by design an amoral enterprise. But the tax law itself is directed by the Constitution to the general welfare—necessarily a moral ideal. In an article on the importance of a moral "buy-in" to the criminal law, the authors write, "Enhancing the criminal law's moral credibility requires more than anything, that the criminal law make clear to the public that its overriding concern is doing justice."[142] While focusing on the criminal law, the authors' central point applies to tax law as well. Getting people to obey the law requires that they generally see a connection between what has been outlawed or required and their moral intuitions.

Since fear of legal sanctions is only one component of ensuring voluntary tax compliance, the more legitimate the law is perceived to be the more lawmakers can count on voluntary compliance. Infusing legitimacy into the tax law would require Congress to focus on overarching national issues and priorities, which should be addressed by a federal law. Without that focus, Robinson and Darley warn, "those who perceive the political authority that governs them to be less legitimate are more likely to engage in acts of social or political protest," such as tax cheating, tax protesting, or even tax defiance.[143]

SIX

UNINTENTIONAL CHEATING

> Every man, to be sure, is desirous of pushing off from himself
> the burden of any tax, which is imposed, and of laying it upon
> others: But as every man has the same inclination, and is upon
> the defensive, no set of men can be supposed to prevail altogether
> in this contest.
>
> —David Hume (1711–1776), "Of Taxes"

A Fork in the Road

I have no doubt that most tax cheating is intentional. One field study found that 17 percent of taxpayers intend to cheat on their tax returns.[1] Strong indirect evidence is provided by the fact that individual taxpayers will engage in more risky tax behavior if they owe money than if they are due a refund. In my accounting practice I encountered this phenomenon on an anecdotal basis. Taxpayers who were accustomed to receiving refunds would commonly dig deeper for more deductions once they were told they were going to have to pay the IRS. While digging for more deductions is not itself cheating, risk-prone behavior may induce taxpayers to invoke questionable deductions when trying to get out of a tax-due position.

Psychological research supports this finding. Cognitive psychologists Tversky and Kahneman found that individuals are "generally risk averse when it comes to gains and risk seeking when it comes to losses."[2] Known as prospect theory, this account of human action has been tested in a number of settings, including predicting the behavior of gamblers and taxpayers.

In a tax setting, individuals may view the amount of income tax withheld and paid to the IRS as a sort of gain. If they have to pay additional taxes they view this as a loss. "The theory predicts that taxpayers would be risk averse in a refund situation and risk seeking in a taxes due position."[3] Taxpayers are thus more willing to take exaggerated or questionable deductions if this will keep them from having to write a check to the U.S. Treasury. If taxpayers are due a refund, they will not go to the same effort to increase the refund, even if the absolute amount of tax reduction is the same in both cases. This behavior must obviously be intentional.

In attempting to comprehend the nature of cheating, a number of elements have come to light. These elements, as fleshed out to this point, include (1) standards or rules violated, (2) a judgment or feeling that something is not fair (though it may be the rules that are seen as unfair), (3) the use of fraud or deceit, (4) an act undertaken to gain an advantage, (5) competition, and (6) intention. As mentioned earlier, some traits may be essential or defining and some only associated or secondary. In chapter 5, for example, competition was determined to be associated with cheating but not an essential characteristic. Because *cheating* is applied in such diverse contexts as education, marital infidelity, dieting, sports, and taxation, insisting there must be a core of essential or defining characteristics may be unreasonable. Philosophers from Socrates in ancient Greece to Ludwig Wittgenstein in twentieth-century Europe have addressed this issue armed with their own special theories.

Wittgenstein warned that we must be on the alert for mere family resemblance when looking for elements common to a set of items called by the same name.[4] His point was that within a family, resemblances may be only piecemeal. Taken as a group, there may be no one feature that all members of the family share, yet there is an overall resemblance within the group. Wittgenstein's observation—"we see a patchwork of similarities overlapping and crisscrossing: sometimes overall similarities, sometimes similarities of detail."[5] This could be the case with cheating, dooming our search for a unifying set of characteristics.

A starting point in this regard—and a key to understanding tax cheating—is determining whether intention is required for cheating or whether cheating may be unintentional. This will call the necessity of deceit and fraud into question, together with an action's being undertaken to gain an advantage, as these are all products of intention.

At the extreme one could argue that all income tax cheating is unintentional; for how can you cheat on rules that you cannot fully understand? The chess game featured in Lewis Carroll's *Through the Looking Glass* is a metaphor for this problem. Alice finds herself in the midst of a life-sized chess game taking place all around her. The chess pieces move of their own accord and for reasons that are not obviously related to the rules of the game. Yet, to say that anyone is cheating would be dubious, because the game takes place in a dream. In explaining one of the game's rules to Alice, the Red Queen proclaims, "Now, *here*, you see, it takes all the running *you* can do, to keep in the same place. If you want to get somewhere else, you must run at least twice as fast as that."[6] As more than one court has observed, when the tax law is unclear, a taxpayer lacks the requisite intent to violate it willfully.[7] While it first appears logical that cheating requires an understanding of the rules, I would still like to address this question, in case such logic is a stumbling block to understanding tax cheating.

The key to defining tax cheating may come down to a paradox resulting from a juxtaposition of its various elements. Consider the following syllogism, which employs two of these elements.

- All cheating is done to gain an advantage.
- Some cheating is unintentional.
- Therefore: Some unintentional acts are done to gain an advantage.

Since the argument is formally valid—but the conclusion is contradictory—the truth of one or both of the premises is called into question.[8] Of these, whether cheating can be unintentional appears more doubtful than whether cheating is done to gain an advantage. But even the latter proposition can be questioned, since gaining an advantage generally implies competition, but not all cheating, as we saw in chapter 5, occurs in a competitive arena. It may be that only the end result of gaining an advantage is essential to cheating and not the intention to cheat. Whether some cheating is unintentional will be the focus of the remainder of this chapter. The answer will provide a fuller understanding of tax cheating and how it manifests itself under the current Tax Code.

Cheating and Justice

Injustice, according to John Rawls, involves applying arbitrary distinctions in assigning people basic rights and duties.[9] A question worth considering at this point is whether cheating isn't simply a subcategory of injustice. But if we examine cases, we find that not all cheating involves injustice and not all injustice involves cheating. Cheating applies to specific actions; and while injustice may also concern actions, its scope is wider than cheating as it also describes institutions and political arrangements such as apartheid or slavery that apply arbitrary distinctions in assigning rights and duties. Such conditions, as Rawls points out, fail to provide a "proper balance between competing claims to the advantages of social life."[10]

Another difference distinguishing some instances of cheating from injustice is the moral dimension. Injustice is inextricably a moral notion. Cheating, as I am arguing, can be associated with moral concerns or not. So while there is overlap in that some instances of cheating may also be described as unjust, injustice is not a defining characteristic of cheating.

Justice is employed in evaluating and interpreting rules, as well as in establishing rules, and always in a context of right or wrong, good or bad. Once rules are in place, and whether they are believed to be just or not, cheating may result when rules are violated. But whether the result is also an injustice cannot be determined simply from the fact that there is cheating. We must look to the underlying ethical status of the rules.

Supreme Court Justice Robert H. Jackson once referred to the tax law as a "field beset with invisible boomerangs."[11] One problem with our current income tax system is that the diversity and complexity of its rules makes it impossible to say whether it is just or fair. While some tax rules were no doubt drafted with an eye to fairness, opposing views of fairness have left the whole structure beyond the realm of judgment. The graduated income tax, for example, is felt by some to address an injustice by taxing at a higher rate those who earn greater income.[12] Others obviously disagree, some holding that a flat rate of tax for everyone or perhaps a tax on everyone but themselves would be just. This is why justice and morality are bound together but cheating and morality are not. Interestingly, taxpayers with opposing views about taxation, tax rates, and justice are equally capable of cheating on their taxes.

In the Old Testament notion of justice as an eye for an eye[13] there is an additional factor distinguishing cheating from injustice. In this framework, acts of cheating may be avenged by further acts of cheating to even the score, so that justice would presumably be achieved because someone cheated in retaliation. An example of marital infidelity might be viewed in this way. One spouse cheats, engaging in an extramarital affair. The other spouse gets even by doing the same.

Affirmative action may also provide an example of this phenomenon. If we believe the system (laws, social norms, institutions) was, in the past, set up to favor a certain class of individuals—by applying arbitrary distinctions in assigning people basic rights and duties[14]—and now it is time to correct this injustice by allowing the disadvantaged individuals (or their descendents) an advantage in competitive situations, some will say this is institutionalized cheating. One person gets into medical school and another gets a promotion, not by following the rules of the competition but as a remedy for a previous injustice. In this case the person who followed the rules and otherwise met the qualifications may feel cheated because he or she is rejected though qualified.

It is for these reasons that an adequate definition of cheating must be morally neutral, since it is the moral status of the rules being flouted that determines the moral status of the cheating. While it may be hard to dislodge the moral tone from the meaning of cheating, and so view cheating in an objective or clinical light, what may help us is recognizing that cheating an unjust system—such as slavery, apartheid, or a corrupt government or ruthless dictator bent on violating human rights or practicing genocide—may be good.[15]

Fair Share Argument

In the case of tax cheating it is not necessarily other taxpayers who are being cheated but the system of tax law or its integrity. If a budget is based on projected income tax revenues, and if these projections naïvely fail to assume a certain amount of tax cheating, then the resources available to fulfill the demands of the budget will be short. Governments are used to deficits and have means for dealing with them. Some insist, however, that tax cheating is cheating other taxpayers, causing them to pay more than their fair share.

A Zero-Sum Process

The fair share argument claims that if one taxpayer cheats on his or her income taxes, more of the tax burden is pushed onto the rest of the taxpayers—a pecuniary externality. Expressing this truism, John Stuart Mill observed, "If any one bears less than his fair share of the burden, some other person must suffer more than his share."[16] Here, taxation is viewed as a zero-sum process. The amount others are being asked to pay (which, incidentally, may or may not be their fair share in any event) is being increased by the actions of someone else who is cheating and thereby paying less than the rules require.[17] In a public poll, 62 percent of taxpayers reported believing that if others cheat it increases their taxes.[18]

Cheating that rises to the level of ethically significant does so because harm is inflicted on some individual (or group of individuals) by the unilateral actions or decisions of another. Jeremy Bentham refers to actions such as tax cheating as offenses against the public or the state—on account of the "distant mischief [they threaten to bring] upon an unassignable indefinite multitude . . . although no particular individual should appear more likely to be a sufferer . . . than another."[19] Cheated individuals are harmed because, while they adhered to the rules, they were disadvantaged by others who skirted those rules. The student who cheats on the entrance exam and scores well is admitted to medical school, leaving the student who followed the rules but earns a lower but passing score to seek a different career. The affected individual is shoved off course by the unconsented-to action of another. In the realm of actions characterized as unethical, consider how many fit this model, from child abuse to discrimination in the workplace, from Bernard Madoff's Ponzi scheme to global warming, the ethical issue arises because the actions of some people (or organizations) alter the life path of others, though without—and generally against—their consent.

But is it true that if one individual pays less tax than the rules require (cheats) this shortfall will have to be made up by someone else?[20] One insight is provided by John Scholz who explains, "If we compare a system in which everyone cheated by the same percentage with a system in which no one cheated, the system with evaders could raise the same revenue as the system with honest taxpayers by adjusting the tax rate rather than by increasing enforcement."[21] But this does not address the issue of people cheating by different percentages or of some people cheating and others not. "Other things being equal," economists Slemrod and Bakija inform us, tax cheating "means higher tax rates and a heavier burden for the many people who are honest and who have little opportunity to cheat."[22] In her testimony before Congress in 2007, Nina Olson, the National Taxpayer Advocate, reported on this "extraordinary burden to ask our nation's compliant taxpayers to bear every year," and which she estimated at "an average 'surtax' [per household] of about $2,680 to subsidize noncompliance."[23] But if dividing the amount of the tax gap by the number of compliant taxpayers is good theater, it is unhelpful economics. The situation is more complex than this; all things are not held constant, as the model requires. As with any dynamic system, deductive reasoning will not explain everything.

It is for this reason that one observer asserts, "One common bit of nonsense published by the tax bureau is that the evader forces the honest taxpayer to pay more. But tax burdens that are evaded or avoided are not assumed by others. If my neighbor operates off the books and pays no tax, my tax rates do not increase. . . . The less tax paid, the less the government has to spend."[24] This helps to explain how in the United States, during the late 1990s, the treasury reported a surplus although the tax gap was still in the range of $250 billion.

Rules without Reasons

To understand the relationship between tax cheating and paying our fair share, it is important to recognize two aspects of our tax system. The first is that each taxpayer's required annual tax is computed independently and in isolation, not as a percentage of a predetermined amount. Thus, if one person or corporation pays less than the rules require, this simply means the Treasury Department receives less than it would have if that taxpayer had paid the amount the rules require. It does not mean that someone else, or even everyone else, will receive an additional bill from the IRS requesting them to pick up the difference—the amount left unpaid by cheaters—or that tax rates will automatically escalate. Tax cheating from this perspective fits Adam Smith's description of crimes "that do not immediately or directly hurt any particular person; but their remote consequences, it is supposed, do produce, or might produce, either a considerable inconveniency, or a great disorder in the society."[25]

The second relevant aspect of our tax system was discussed in chapter 3 and relates to our inability to know, even if no one ever cheated, whether we are paying our fair share. The complexity of the Tax Code—resulting from multiple constituencies each clamoring for fairness in some particular aspect of the law—has produced a heterogeneous coagulate of opposing claims to fairness rather than an integrated whole starting with an agreed-on notion of what fairness would look like. Because of this, believing that a tax cheater is causing us to pay more than our fair share is an illusion, since we have no reliable benchmark to know what constitutes our fair share. This kind of uncertainty is antithetical to a moral obligation to pay taxes, if the moral obligation argument rests on each individual's paying his or her fair share.

"The certainty of what each individual ought to pay is, in taxation," according to Adam Smith, "a matter of so great importance, that a very considerable degree of inequality . . . is not near so great an evil as a very small degree of uncertainty."[26] Accordingly, knowing how our share of the tax burden was arrived at—even if the amount is determined unfair—is therefore preferable to the uncertainty of our current system in which any two (or ten) taxpayers with the same spendable income are likely to pay different amounts of tax but for no logically defensible reason.

A Moving Target

Much economic reasoning—and hence public policy—relies on a static view of the forces at work; what is often required, however, is dynamic and evolutionary thinking. Grahm and Dodd, in their classic work on valuing stocks, wrote, "There can be no such thing as a scientific prediction of economic events under human control. The very 'dependability' of such a prediction will cause human actions which will invalidate it."[27] According to Steven Hawking, "At sufficiently high levels of technological development we may have a turbulent economy, with irregular variations and sensitive dependence on initial condition. One may argue that we now live in such an economy."[28] For this reason some economists embrace a more fluid form of analysis based on principles of physics—viewing economic changes as potentially chaotic, leading to the evolution of unique states. In this respect we may be at a tipping point. In a book on chaos, David Ruelle tells us,

> Textbooks of economics are largely concerned with equilibrium situations between economic agents with perfect foresight. The textbooks may give you the impression that the role of the legislators and government officials is to find and implement an equilibrium that is particularly favorable for the community. The examples of chaos in physics teach us, however, that certain dynamical situations do not produce equilibrium but rather a chaotic, unpredictable time evolution. Legislators and government officials are thus faced with the possibility that their decisions, intended to produce a better equilibrium, will in fact lead to wild and unpredictable fluctuations, with possibly quite disastrous effects. The complexity of today's economics encourages such chaotic behavior, and our theoretical understanding in this domain remains very limited.[29]

The unexpected global economic events of September 2008 are a powerful reminder of this assessment.

According to E. O. Wilson, author of *Consilience*, "In economics and the remainder of the social sciences as well, the translation from individual to aggregate behavior is the key analytic problem. Yet in these disciplines the exact nature and sources of individual behavior are rarely considered. Instead, the knowledge used by the modelers is that of folk psychology, based mostly on the common perception of unaided intuition."[30] The combination of using folk psychology to understand taxpayer behavior and a closed-end deductive economic model to predict the consequences of governmental actions—including changes to the tax code—means that legislators are operating with outmoded tools. It is no wonder that the tax gap is growing.

Is there a sound reason to believe that the tax gap problem is not a dynamic and evolving situation that will produce more tax cheating as knowledge of its magnitude and mismanagement resonates with previously compliant taxpayers, eroding confidence in the government's ability to effect a solution? In a book on tax reform, economists Slemrod and Bakija write, "Human nature being what it is, it won't work to just announce how to calculate the tax base and what tax rates to apply, and rely on taxpayers' sense of duty. . . . Some dutiful people will undoubtedly pay what they owe, but many others would not. Over time the ranks of the dutiful will shrink, as they see how they are being taken advantage of by the others."[31]

Returning to the argument that one person's failure to pay taxes means another taxpayer pays more, someone opposed to tax cheating on moral grounds could say: "Yes in the short run and on a limited basis one taxpayer's tax cheating need not be made up by others. But in the long run and especially if a majority of taxpayers embarked on a plan to cheat on their income taxes, the total amount received by the Treasury Department would shrink so much that government services would have to be cut or curtailed or tax rates on honest taxpayers raised to unconscionable levels." At that point for sure, some might insist, tax cheating is morally wrong because it results in the diminution of government services for those who have paid what taxes the rules require (though for some that amount is none). Compliant taxpayers are now getting less than they are paying for— less education, bumpier roads, reduced national defense and the like—and are in fact subsidizing the cheaters.

But if taxpayers are being hurt by tax cheaters—in that everyone now receives less government service—this applies to the cheaters as well; they also are receiving less government service. Are they now being cheated by their own cheating? And what about those otherwise compliant taxpayers whose income is below the threshold requiring them to pay, or who receive the Earned Income Tax Credit? Upon reflection, this debate is no longer about tax cheating but has strayed to a debate about tax policy, distributive justice, and social philosophy and how much government is too much or too little, and even about representative democracy, as the majority, in this illustration, would effectively have voted with their wallets to reduce tax revenues, and thereby curtail government services. The argument that one person's tax cheating is another person's tax increase, while intuitively appealing for its simplicity, masks the complexity of the underlying dynamic economic system.

Thinking of tax cheating as a simple problem of addition and subtraction—a zero-sum process—underestimates the seriousness of the problem by leading us to believe the solution is a simple matter of adjusting factors of an equation. To a point, collecting more taxes from honest taxpayers—or at least those unfortunate enough to have little

opportunity to cheat—will solve the equation. But adding in variables of human behavior— rarely quantifiable to the required degree—allows for change in the way honest taxpayers feel about tax cheating. One such change may be their recognition that cheating the present tax system is illegal but not immoral.

Unintended Cheating

Most studies of tax cheating focus on intentional acts. One report summarizes common scenarios:

- Tax preparers who craft phony returns for others and don't bother to file themselves.
- Self-employed persons who write off their personal expenses or deduct their hobby losses from their income.
- Concealed capital gains from the sale of stocks, or real estate, or art work, or antiques.
- Immigrant workers who live tax free.
- Independent businesspeople whose living expenses are paid for by offshore corporations.[32]

In 2010 The Treasury Inspector General for Tax Administration released a report on the growing problem of prisoners receiving refunds after filing fraudulent tax returns. [33] Others have cataloged additional examples.[34]

Intentional cheating has been the subject of experiments applying, for example, the reasoned-action model of psychologists Fishbein and Ajzen.[35] Such experiments involve attempting to predict the behavior of taxpayers on the basis of antecedent conditions, including background factors, behavioral beliefs, normative beliefs, control beliefs, attitude toward a particular behavior, acknowledgment of a perceived norm, perceived behavioral control, and intention.[36] About this model, one commentator notes: "When considering behavioral intentions in the context of tax evasion it is not a simple matter to see how all these criteria could be met."[37]

"We assume," say Fishbein and Ajzen, "that human social behavior follows reasonably and often spontaneously from the information or beliefs people possess about the behavior under consideration."[38] In addition, "The theory suggests that intention is the best single predictor of behavior but that it is also important to take skills and abilities as well as environmental factors (i.e., behavioral control) into account."[39]

Insofar as some tax cheating is unintentional, then, we could surmise either that this behavior is unpredictable or, paradoxically, that it is not really behavior in the required sense, as it lacks the key component of intention.

The portion of the tax gap pie composed of unintentional tax cheating—referred to by one commentator as "unknowing noncompliance"[40]—is undetermined. As explained in chapter 3, the IRS admits, "The data do not reveal how much of the gap is attributable to willful non-compliance or carelessness and how much is the result of a lack of understanding [of the taxpayer's] . . . full tax obligation."[41] But Justice Holmes reminds us, regarding the importance of intention in law, "It is no doubt true that there are many cases in which the criminal could not have known that he was breaking the law, but to admit the excuse at all would be to encourage ignorance where the law-maker has determined to make men know and obey, and justice to the individual is rightly outweighed by the larger interests on the other side of the scales."[42]

Even determining whether some cheating is intentional or unintentional poses a problem. One writer explains: "Tax rules are constantly defined and redefined through political decision making, agency rule making, court decisions, and the interpretation of rules by tax officials. Taxpaying behavior occurs in the context of this continuously renegotiated set of rules. A behavior that is compliant one year may be noncompliant the next."[43]

In dealing with ethical questions, defining a key term or at least limiting a term's meaning or coining a new term often proves helpful. In *Our Criminal Society*, for example, the author, in speaking of tax cheating, uses the phrase "nonprofessional fraud," which, conceptually, has much to recommend it.[44] The fraud is nonprofessional because it is not what the taxpayer does for a living. Deciding whether cheating can be unintentional is difficult because the determination is not based on empirical evidence, it is controlled by definition. Consider a mistake made in applying the tax law resulting from the intention not to study the tax law diligently. While reckless disregard of the law is recognized as one extreme, degrees of diligence make knowing our true level of responsibility for studying the law uncertain. Pinning down the meaning of unintentional requires careful consideration of its diverse applications. Is a drunk driver's accident rendered intentional because he intended to buy the whiskey that made him drunk? Is this situation altered if the individual is an alcoholic? In some cases waiting for more empirical evidence or further study is fruitless. A similar situation arises in other ethical contexts. Waiting for medical science finally to proclaim the point in a pregnancy when a small cluster of cells constitutes a human life with a soul and attendant rights—bringing an end to the religious controversy surrounding abortion—is equally a confusion about the respective roles of definition and empirical science.

A fork in the road appears when we ask: Are we better able to deal practically with the problem of tax cheating if we hold out for a definition of cheating that requires all cheating to be intentional, or if we settle on a definition that allows both intentional and unintentional cheating? I believe the latter choice proves more fruitful to understanding and dealing with the problems of tax cheating, in part because it decouples tax cheating from ethics. Ethics by definition deals with intentional choices. Earlier illustrations indicate that the IRS accepts this broader definition as well, recognizing that in its administrative role there should be no moral stigma attached to tax cheating. Recall also that it was Congress that coined the euphemism "erroneous item"[45] to describe inaccuracies that I would call tax cheating, further obfuscating the fuzzy boundary between intentional and unintentional.

Thus, in the discussion that follows, I will assume that tax cheating may be either intentional or unintentional and does not require the associated characteristics noted at the outset of this chapter, those of (1) fraud or deceit, (2) competition, (3) intention, or (4) acting with the intention of gaining an advantage. The remaining essential characteristics of tax cheating are therefore (1) rules, stated or implied, (2) the violation of which puts someone at an advantage, and (3) the judgment or feeling that the advantage gained by some is unfair (though this may be the result of seeing the rules themselves as unfair). Note that the advantage gained by the cheater is a result of violating rules, perhaps out of confusion or ignorance, and that gaining an advantage was not necessarily the reason the rules were violated. Also, because the current tax system does not transparently determine each taxpayer's fair share of the tax burden, the judgment or feeling that some have gained an unfair advantage cannot be established in the way cheating in other contexts can be. In defining cheating in this way, I bifurcate tax cheating into intentional and unintentional, making explicit its lack of a necessary ethical dimension. This parallels the taxation of income which does not concern itself with the moral status of either the taxpayer or the source of the income; all income is taxable from whatever source derived.

Unintentional as well as intentional tax cheating is often character-ized by the IRS as negligent. Negligence implies a failure to meet the expected standard of care in filing a tax return. The term *negligence* is broadly defined to include a failure to make a reasonable attempt to comply with the provisions of the Code.[46] A reasonable attempt may include taking the time and effort to become familiar with the intricacies of the tax law or hiring someone who is. This may be accomplished by employing a professional tax adviser, but even then the taxpayer is held responsible for evaluating the professional's knowledge of the tax law, thereby acting "reasonably and in good faith." The IRS regulations place the onus on the taxpayer to distinguish between a professional tax adviser and others who provide tax advice. As described in more detail in chapter 7, if a taxpayer seeks tax advice from "someone that he knew, or should have known, lacked knowledge in the relevant aspects of Federal tax law" even though the taxpayer sought (and paid for) tax advice, he or she would have "failed to act reasonably or in good faith."[47] The explanations a taxpayer offers for his actions are unimportant for assessing negligence, only the facts that a rule was violated, that the taxpayer should have known better, and that additional tax is owed. The taxpayer's excuses fall on deaf ears.

Viewing tax cheating from this angle has other analogies in the law, where some violations require only wrongdoing while others require requisite intention. Unintentional tax cheating is comparable, for example, to the legal concept of strict liability. Strict liability is "liability without fault."[48] If a liquor store sells beer to an underage customer, local statutes may shut the store down, even though the customer looked old enough and, upon request, produced an authentic-looking (but fake) driver's license, showing the proper age. It is strict liability because there are no excuses and no defense.

In the case of a manufacturer, strict liability in tort law (civil wrong) is based on the assumption that the finished product, on the basis of its nature and intended use, is safe and ready for use (or consumption) for its ordinary and foreseeable purpose or function. If the product is defective or unreasonably dangerous, the manufacturer is liable for damages. A hammer, for example, is presumed safe for pounding nails even though occasionally you may pound your thumb. But if under normal use the head of the hammer flies off injuring someone, the manufacturer cannot defend itself by asserting that it intended to build a safe product: that is assumed. A product is unreasonably dangerous if it poses a danger beyond what would be contemplated by the ordinary consumer.

As with strict liability, tax negligence does not remove the agent's responsibility. What a taxpayer meant to do or tried to do (with limited exceptions for tax fraud) is of no consequence to the system. The results of a taxpayer's actions are presumed to encompass the taxpayer's intention to understand and comply with the law. Thus, asserting confusion or lack of understanding of the law does not diminish the taxpayer's liability. If you did not understand the rule—the law assumes—you should have taken steps to remedy this shortcoming.[49] To illustrate this perspective and the meaning of unintentional cheating, consider professional football.

The Meaning of Cheating in Football

Reporting on the results of an IRS focus group relating to tax cheating, a former IRS Commissioner said that people justify tax cheating by seeing it as "a game" and believing "you can get away with whatever you can."[50] No doubt many games are popularly viewed in this light, including many professional sports. Professional football provides a useful framework for analyzing the meaning of cheating and the significance of intention.

In football, as in other sports, rule violations are a normal part of each game and are dealt with through penalties, whether assessed in yards on the field, disqualification of a player, or fines. Because of differing views of competition noted in chapter 5, some may consider rule violations cheating, others as fair competition and just part of the game. When a rule violation can be accomplished without getting caught, it is often beneficial to one team and detrimental to the other. As a matter of strategy, an intentional rule violation, although detected by the officials, may still be worth the accompanying penalty, as when a player engages in defensive pass interference to prevent a touchdown.

Football penalties include roughing the passer (15 yards),[51] intentional grounding (10 yards and loss of down),[52] holding an opponent (10 yards),[53] more than eleven players on the field while the ball is in play (5 yards),[54] unnecessary roughness (15 yards and disqualification if flagrant),[55] and "twisting, turning, or pulling the face mask" (15 yards).[56] Each is a sanctioned violation and may also constitute cheating.

It is important to observe from the outset, however, that with a few exceptions, the imposition of these penalties does not depend on the intention of the player(s) involved. The same penalty is meted out whether the violation of the rule is intentional or accidental. Twisting, turning, or pulling a face mask may be done to hurt an opposing player or inadvertently in the frenzy of an attempted tackle.

Like many questions in football, whether or not rule infractions constitute cheating is likely to result in a lively debate among football fans. Part of the controversy depends on the fact that the word *cheating* is used both in moral contexts and in other contexts where it has no moral import, often without recognition of this difference. When cheating in school is rebuked, including plagiarizing, stealing exams, and so on, there is clearly a moral judgment intended. But if a tennis player "cheats" to the left in anticipation of the ball coming to her backhand, there is certainly no moral implication in the description. To the extent that many (or most) rules in sports are arbitrary, it can be argued that they carry no moral import and hence cheating these rules cannot be wrong in a moral sense. This is supported by the fact that actions that would be considered morally wrong in daily life such as tackling in professional football—which would be considered assault—are only penalized if the tackle is determined to involve unnecessary roughness.[57]

In football violations resulting in penalties, it is apparent that the infractions are called and penalties assessed on the basis of physical evidence, largely without addressing the motives of the players. A player attempting to block a kick may be trying as hard as possible not to brush against the kicker and yet he does so. A flag is thrown by the official and the penalty is assessed. The player violated a rule. The player tried not to run into the kicker, but he failed. Fortunately, there is no need to determine whether he tried hard enough, for as philosopher of law Lon Fuller reminds us, "Nothing can be more baffling than to attempt to measure how vigorously a man intended to do that which he has failed to do."[58] If the player's act is cheating, it is unintentional cheating.

When the same penalty is applied to an action whether or not the player intended to violate the rule, it is clear that the penalty is not imposed for cheating in the moral sense. Even if the original purpose of a rule was to address an ethical concern, such as avoiding permanent injury to a player, the rule's administration is based on objective standards of what observably happened. Justice Holmes explained this phenomenon as it occurs in the law. "The standards of the law are external standards, and however much it may take moral considerations into account, it does so only for the purpose of drawing a line between such bodily motions and rests as it permits, and such as it does not. What the law really forbids, and the only thing it forbids, is the act on the wrong side of the line, be that act blameworthy or otherwise."[59]

Contrasting this with income tax compliance, if a claimed deduction cannot be established with credible evidence and aligned with a specific statutory provision, it is disallowed by the IRS. The same penalty is imposed whether a taxpayer's failure to maintain adequate records is the result of ignorance or an honest mistake. The irrelevance of taxpayers' subjective intent was dramatically affirmed by one court that claimed "nineteen bishops swearing as to taxpayers' subjective intent would not carry this argument because it contends an irrelevant fact."[60]

Moral Turpitude

Just as intention is not relevant to most football penalties, moral degeneracy is not essential for tax cheating. Cheating may be committed by taxpayers whose rap sheet is otherwise spotless, or should be. In the case of a Roman Catholic priest, *Timothy Thomas Noah*, the IRS imposed a negligence penalty for Noah's failure to report all his income and for claiming erroneous deductions. The court summarized the case: "There are far too many errors on his return to be excused. There were substantial amounts of underreported income, duplicated deductions, [and] deductions of personal items as business expenses."[61] Negligence is the label for actions on the wrong side of the line, whether intentional or not.

The Supreme Court declared that "moral turpitude is not a touchstone of taxability."[62] Moral turpitude refers to actions generally considered to be violations of accepted moral norms. Fraud, perjury, assault, and rape, for example, all reflect a lack of regard for others and for the moral or social norms of the community. Applied to the income tax system, the court's pronouncement means that the law's operations are blind to the moral standing of the source of income or its recipient; all income is taxable from whatever source derived. Illegal income is taxable just like legal income. In general, the same deductions are allowed to an illegal business as to a legal one.[63] The Tax Court in *Pittsburgh Milk Co.* employed the proposition in connection with the allowance of a discount given by the milk company to its customers; the discount was illegal under state law.[64] The court stated that although "we voice no approval of the business ethics of such concealment . . . moral turpitude is not a touchstone of taxability."

The moral turpitude claim was made in the context of embezzled funds in *Wilcox*—where the court asked "whether the taxpayer in fact received a statutory gain, profit or benefit"—that is, income. The Supreme Court in that case said no, based on the embezzler's offsetting liability to return the embezzled funds.[65] In *James*, a later case also involving embezzled funds, the Supreme Court reconsidered and reversed its view, holding that embezzled funds are income.[66] This remains the law and supports the proposition that accessions to wealth are income regardless of the ethicality of their origins, and regardless of the embezzler's intentions or whether he "meant to pay the money back."

When we reflect on the fact that income is taxable whether legally or illegally derived, we gain an added perspective on tax cheating. Tax cheating, whatever it is finally determined to mean, can take place in the context of a legal business or an illegal business. A drug dealer may accurately report his income or he might cheat by overstating his cost of goods sold and understating his ending inventory. As former IRS Commissioner Gibbs observed, some people have the ability to "compartmentalize morality—to be more ethical in some parts of their lives than in others . . . effectively separating tax cheating from other immoral actions and in the process, sparing himself or herself any guilt."[67] Honor among thieves is just a special case.

Note that Commissioner Gibbs's framing of the situation in terms of ethical compartmentalization, however, assumes that tax cheating is unethical. Like many others, he ignores the more drastic possibility proposed in this book, that the income tax system has been so manipulated (or some might say mangled) in its construction and reconstruction—trying to be all things to all people, at least in some aspect—as to render its operations beyond the moral realm. Viewed in this light, the ability to compartmentalize our thinking about income taxes seems less surprising.

Moral Credentials

An alternative explanation to moral compartmentalizing is provided by recent research on *moral credentials*. This theory, which has its basis in social psychology, "holds that people feel licensed to act on questionable motives when they have previously established their credentials as a person of pure motives."[68] As individuals establish a track record of moral credentials, they are buttressed in taking actions that would otherwise put them in a morally suspect light.[69] Further, "people's thoughts and behavior are often guided by a 'working' level of moral self-regard that fluctuates from moment to moment according to situational influences."[70] Thus, people who otherwise scrupulously adhere to the letter and spirit of the law may feel they have banked enough moral capital to expend some on bending the tax laws. In this regard, "bolstering people's moral self-regard can license them to act in more morally problematic ways in the future."[71] This helps explain the widespread practice of tax cheating among otherwise law-abiding citizens.[72] They have established their moral credentials in other aspects of their lives, allowing them to stray in their tax dealings.

Negligence Penalty

When a taxpayer acts negligently in preparing a tax return, the IRS imposes a penalty.[73] Negligence is this context is devoid of moral import. The term *negligence* is defined to include any failure to make a reasonable attempt to comply with the pertinent provisions of the Code. The same penalty is imposed for disregard of the tax laws, where the term *disregard* includes any careless, reckless, or intentional aspects of a tax return's preparation.[74] Negligence, like penalties in football, is assessed in spite of and without regard to the taxpayer's intent. As we have seen, the moral import of the word *cheating* requires some degree of intention and purpose. In this sense, tax penalties are assessed—the IRS throws the flag—on the basis of observable events, without consideration of intentions or excuses, except insofar as intentions are relevant—as in the case of fraud—and can objectively be inferred from observable actions.

If *cheating* is to retain its moral sting, then unintentional, objective, or technical violations of a rule must be differentiated from intentional violations. But if the word *cheating* is used to describe any infraction—regardless of intention—then cheating takes on a more benign meaning and necessarily loses its moral significance. When the IRS imposes penalties, disallows deductions, includes additional reportable income, or makes other adjustments to a taxpayer's account, it is not doing so in response to tax cheating in any moral sense but because the law was violated. "Many rules," sociologist Howard Becker informs us, "are quite technical and may really be said to have their base, not in some general value, but rather in an effort to make peace between other and earlier rules."[75] This is clearly the case with many tax rules. The tax law embodies "tasks of economic allocation," according to Fuller, and "cannot be effectively performed within the limits set by the internal morality of law. The attempt to accomplish such tasks through adjudicative forms is certain to result in inefficiency, hypocrisy, moral confusion, and frustration."[76] Administration of our current tax law is not a moral enterprise, nor is it an immoral one. It is extra-moral and thus incapable of commanding or requiring a moral response from us.

Blaming the Messenger

Only when we get to the level of tax fraud do intentions become relevant for the IRS, and even then intentions are determined from observable actions, not from reading states of mind. In the case of criminal tax fraud, a formidable burden of proof switches to the IRS and the evidence presented must show a pattern of conduct normally associated with someone who knows the rules and takes deliberate steps to undercut and defeat the law's purpose. Tax fraud generally involves specific kinds of conduct including deceptive measures undertaken to cover the taxpayer's tracks (shredding documents, hiding assets, falsifying records).

As the Tax Court informs us, "Fraud is never to be presumed. It must be proved by clear and convincing evidence. Moreover, the burden of proving fraud rests on the Government."[77] After describing the inadequacies of a taxpayer's records, which contributed to the findings of an IRS audit, the court in *Marinzulich* reported that the taxpayers were guilty of poor judgment but held that "poor judgment and ignorance are not tantamount to fraud. There is lacking one essential element, the very heart of the fraud issue, namely, the intent to defraud the Government by calculating tax evasion."[78]

The penalty for willful failure to file a return, supply information, or pay tax,[79] for example, requires intention but, as explained in chapter 7, willfulness must be inferred from a taxpayer's overt actions. At a certain point in football, the imposition of penalties takes into account intentions as well. The NFL's rules contain a prohibition against "extraordinarily unfair acts."[80] In 2010 the NFL fined the New York Jets $100,000 for violating league rules when assistant coach Sal Alosi tripped Miami Dolphins cornerback Nolan Carroll on the sideline during a punt return.[81] New England Patriots head coach Bill Belichick was fined by the NFL in 2007 for videotaping signals by New York Jets coaches during the first game of the season, hardly something undertaken by mistake.[82]

Even in a sport such as football that features violence and physical injury as integral parts, the existence, survival, and welfare of the game requires boundaries to players' violent actions. An argument can be made that actions designed to permanently injure an opposing player and end his career are not only violations of the rules of the game but also immoral. But the boundaries enclosing a sport are not necessarily moral limits, though they may take the spectators' moral values into account. The rules are calculated to provide maximum enjoyment to the spectators and maximum revenue for the businesses—the result of managerial and marketing decisions—or to protect team owners' investments in the players—the result of economic or investment concerns.

There is no doubt a point where attempts to increase fans' enjoyment of a competition may cross an ethical line for the majority of fans. But when this is the case, the decision on the rules is not made *for* moral reasons but *in recognition* of the spectators' moral objections, and these are two very different matters. To illustrate, imagine an overzealous football league announcing a new halftime entertainment—a small dog wearing a football helmet is to be catapulted through the goal posts into a net. Assume, further, that a substantial majority of fans are disgusted by this prospect. When the league meets to reconsider its decision, it is not doing so for moral reasons—it has already shown its hand—but in reaction to the moral outcry of its customers. Much of the tax law appears to be fashioned by this same strategy; bills are drafted based on revenue needs and then modified in reaction to lobbyists' demands or the public's indignation and protests.

While moral outrage may also be expressed at specific aspects of the Tax Code or its implementation, such expressions of outrage are isolated and local and not generally directed at the Code itself. During 1996 and 1997, the Senate held hearings on reported IRS abuse of taxpayers, resulting in a moral outcry by the news media and then the public. Senator William Roth Jr. (R-DE) of the Senate Finance Committee chaired the hearings. In *The Power to Destroy,* a book he wrote after the hearings, he expressed dismay that no earlier Senate Finance Committee had ever held hearings on the IRS.[83] The issues involved an agency of government apparently abusing its authority in the treatment of its citizens, as documented by testimony of taxpayers at the hearings. Similar outrage has been expressed in the past at the Department of Veterans Affairs, FEMA, the Food and Drug Administration, and other agencies of government, indicating that it is not the specific issue of taxes that caused the moral groundswell, but the government's apparently callous treatment of citizens.

The congressional hearings on the IRS, one critic points out, "were televised, widely discussed in the media, and conducted in a 'circus-like atmosphere.' Much of the testimony was later determined to be erroneous."[84] As a result of the hearings, however, Congress passed the *IRS Restructuring and Reform Act of 1998.* This bill sets restrictions on IRS discretion and provides numerous safeguards for taxpayers.[85] That

Congress took this step, however, is scapegoating. Rather than recognizing that the IRS has been asked to perform a task comparable to that of Sisyphus—rolling the boulder uphill only to watch it roll down again—Congress effectively washed its hands of the problem—and of its central role in designing, creating, and enabling it—and instead attacked the messenger. In the earlier football example, this would be the equivalent to the league's blaming the officials on the field for allowing the hapless dog to be traumatized at halftime. For Congress the ploy apparently worked, as the media and the public took their eye off the ball—the lawmakers—and focused outrage at the IRS. But as Justice Holmes reminds us, "even a dog distinguishes between being stumbled over and being kicked."[86] The IRS was kicked.

The significance of recognizing unintentional cheating, whether in football or in taxes, is to allow the discussion to move past the need to determine a person's motives—motives that may not be known even to the person acting. Additionally, acknowledging unintentional cheating makes it clear that cheating in this context is not a moral indictment. The administration of the income tax system takes place in a moral vacuum; it is not aimed at dispensing justice or fairness, except insofar as the law's short leash allows. Thus, our limited allegiance to the tax régime is based on paying for the services and protections we demand from government. This is not equivalent to acknowledging a moral responsibility to obey the Tax Code. According to McGee, "Just because you may benefit from a certain expenditure, it does not automatically follow that there is a moral duty to pay."[87] Tax cheating thus takes place outside the moral realm. In football each team has an opponent and the officials control the quality of competition (and sometimes the outcome of the game). Unfortunately, with the present income tax system the taxpayers' opponent is often seen as the officials—the IRS—rather than the team on the other side of the field, Congress.

In the next chapter we look at the courts' role, which includes mediating between the IRS, the Tax Code, and taxpayers.

SEVEN

THE COURTS, EQUITY, AND TAXES DUE

For, since one man is part of the community, each man, in all that he is and has, belongs to the community; just as a part, in all that it is, belongs to the whole. Thus also nature inflicts a loss on the part in order to save the whole, so that on this account such laws as these, which impose proportionate burdens, are just and binding in conscience, and are legal laws."

—Thomas Aquinas (1225–1274), *Summa Theologica*

Taxes and Equity

Aristotle taught: "The magistrate or magistrates should regulate those matters only on which the laws are unable to speak with precision owing to the difficulty of any general principle embracing all particulars."[1] According to one legal scholar, Aristotle is calling attention to the fact that

> legal rules are necessarily general, while the circumstances of every case are particular, and . . . it is beyond the power of human insight and science to lay down in advance rules which will fit all future variations and complications of practice. Therefore law must be supplemented by equity; there must be a power of adaptation and flexible treatment, sometimes suggesting decisions which will be at variance with formally recognized law, and yet will turn out to be intrinsically just.[2]

Further, as Aristotle notes, equity is "a rectification of legal justice." Thus, he reports, "when the law states a general rule, and a case arises under this that is exceptional, then it is right, where the legislator owing to the generality of his language has erred in not covering that case, to correct the omission by a ruling such as the legislator himself would have given if he had been present there and as he would have enacted if he had been aware of the circumstances."[3] A contemporary observer writes, therefore: "Though equity is supplemental to positive law, it is not merely an optional supplement."[4]

Insofar as the courts are the final arbiter of the law, their authority to give weight to considerations of equity is an element of their jurisdiction. In tax law, however, there is little room for considerations of equity, and the courts generally respect this fact. Unlike the criminal law, the tax law does not allow for excuses or defenses relating to our personal circumstances: how we were treated as children, our physical or mental condition, what we have ingested, or our "diminished capacity," are of no relevance in determining the amount of tax we owe.[5]

This fact is illustrated in *Roberts,* heard by the U.S. Tax Court.[6] The case involves a man who, in July 1997, requested a distribution from his former employer's 401(k) plan. Before receiving the distribution, Roberts was sentenced by a court to confinement in an alcohol rehabilitation center. In August of the same year, while he was still confined to the center, a distribution check from the 401(k) plan was received at his residence.

In November 1997, Roberts was released from the rehabilitation center and concurrently re-confined in the Los Angeles county jail to serve the remainder of his sentence. He was released in February 1998, and during May of that year he cashed the distribution check. He did not report the distribution as income on his 1997 federal income tax return, as the IRS believed appropriate. The IRS therefore determined the gross distribution of $24,867.37 was unreported income for 1997.

The disagreement between Roberts and the IRS centered on Roberts's ability to cash the check or deposit it in his bank account. The Code provides a general rule that income for an individual, such as the 401(k) distribution, be included in the tax year during which it is actually or constructively received by the taxpayer.[7] The phrase "constructively received" is the subject of much litigation and refers to situations where, although the cash or check may not literally have been in the taxpayer's hand, it was within reach. The IRS argued that Roberts constructively or effectively received the check in 1997, when it arrived at his residence, and therefore his failure to report the distribution was improper. Roberts argued that, despite receipt of the check at his residence during August 1997, he could not cash it until May 1998, after his release from jail. So he argued that the 401(k) distribution should not be included in his income for 1997.

Had Roberts been living at home during 1997 when the check arrived, there would have been no dispute and he should have included the payment in his income for 1997. But a taxpayer can argue that there was a substantial limitation or restriction on his actually receiving the payment which allows him to report the income in a later year. This is an exception to the rule that holds a taxpayer accountable for income that, while not literally received in cash, is available to him, perhaps with a little effort. The court in *Roberts* took a hard line on what constitutes a "substantial limitation or restriction," ruling that merely being confined to an alcohol rehabilitation center or jail is not enough. The taxpayer's incarceration "was not a sufficient impediment to his control over the check that was received at his residence during 1997. He had access to a telephone," the court insisted, "and there were individuals who could have assisted petitioner in cashing the check." Therefore, ruled the court, "we hold that the distribution [of] income was available to petitioner and, except for his own inaction while in alcohol rehabilitation [and jail], was subject to his will and control in 1997."

Telling someone you were unable to do X because you were confined to an alcohol rehabilitation facility by court order and subsequently transferred directly to jail will excuse you from numerous obligations, because it is a substantial limitation or restriction on your freedom. But paying taxes on time is not one of them. This no-nonsense approach is typical in tax cases because of how the law was drafted, rarely referring to principles of equity. The phrase "extenuating circumstances," for example, does not appear at all in the Code; "reasonable cause" and "inequitable" do appear on rare occasions, but then only in relation to specific actions connected with specific code sections, including relief for an innocent spouse and waiving the negligence penalty, both topics to be discussed later in the chapter.

Rules and Principles

Ronald Dworkin describes the rules that laws state in terms of their reliance or lack of reliance on principles employed in their application. Some rules, for example, contain a qualifying term such as *reasonable, unjust,* or *significant* that "makes the application of the rule which contains it depend to some extent upon the principles or policies lying beyond the rule."[8]

According to Dworkin, a principle is a "standard that is to be observed, not because it will advance or secure an economic, political, or social situation deemed desirable, but because it is a requirement of justice or fairness or some other dimension of morality."[9] Furthermore, he explains, "the difference between legal principles and legal rules is a logical distinction. Both sets of standards point to particular decisions about legal obligation in particular circumstances, but they differ in the character of the direction they give. Rules are applicable in an all-or-nothing fashion."[10] While there are tax principles that were employed in the Internal Revenue Code's drafting, for the most part it consists of all-or-nothing rules. Many of these rules contain exceptions; but, again, the application of an exception is most often also an all-or-nothing affair, unless the exception contains qualifiers such as *unreasonable* or *inequitable*.

The following examples illustrate the courts' application of a principle to overturn the results of a tax rule. In *Blackman v. Commissioner*,[11] the taxpayer's house was destroyed in a fire. On his tax return Blackman claimed a casualty loss as allowed by the rule of Code section 165. The court noted the rule: "Section 165(a) allows a deduction for 'any loss sustained during the taxable year and not compensated for by insurance or otherwise.'" Section 165(c)(3) provides that the deduction allowed is to be limited to losses arising from "fire, storm, shipwreck, or other casualty, or from theft." Further, according to the court, "the Commissioner [IRS] concedes that the petitioner sustained a loss through fire." Thus, the court set out the specific rules governing the case. However, the IRS also argued that the taxpayer intentionally set the fire that destroyed his home, and that allowing the deduction would frustrate public policy, "and that, therefore, under the doctrine of *Commissioner v. Heininger*[12] and subsequent cases, the petitioner is not entitled to a deduction for the damage caused by his fire."[13] Here a legal principle involving public policy was invoked to prevent the application of the rule allowing a deduction for the loss resulting from a fire. According to the Supreme Court in *Heininger*, "Courts have traditionally disallowed business expense and casualty loss deductions under section 162 or 165 where national or State public policies would be frustrated by the consequences of allowing the deduction."[14]

In *Highway Farms, Inc. v. U.S.*,[15] the district court found that a taxpayer's application of a tax rule, while adhering to the letter of the law, violated its spirit by ignoring a basic principle. The rule permits in-kind payments to agricultural workers to escape Social Security tax. Though still subject to income tax, avoiding Social Security tax saves the employer and the employee 7.65 percent each of the payment (total of 15.3 percent of the amount of the in-kind wage). In this case the in-kind payment took the form of a hog given to each of two employees who were officers of the corporation. In reviewing the details of the transaction, the IRS (and subsequently the court) believed the hogs in this case were not really in-kind payments. According to the court, "the transferred hogs and the Highway Farms hogs were loaded onto the same truck and sold to the same hog buyer on the same terms." The hogs were never physically delivered to the employees nor did the employees attempt to sell the hogs. Shortly after the hogs' sale by the corporation, a cash payment was made to the employees.

The spirit of the law seeks to reduce the tax and corresponding administrative burdens associated with assessing Social Security on in-kind payments for the performance of agricultural labor. It is one of many pro-farm and pro-agriculture provisions in the Code. The court believed that in this case, however, the rule was being abused in a tax-avoidance scheme. The court found that because the in-kind-payment hogs were never segregated from the other hogs nor delivered to the employees, nor subject to their control, the hogs became a cash substitute (cash equivalent) and therefore there would have been no difference in the transaction if the corporation had simply sold the hogs and turned over the cash to the employees. "Because the hogs were market-ready at the time of transfer," the court reasoned, "there was little risk that they could not almost immediately be converted into cash."

In this case, the principle applied to overcome the application of the rule—that in-kind payments are treated differently than cash payments in an agricultural labor setting—is that receiving an in-kind payment must be significantly different than receiving cash by shifting risk of ownership to the recipient. But when the results of the in-kind payment transaction are indiscernible from the results of a cash payment, the fact that the payment was in-kind (in form) should be ignored and the transaction treated as a cash payment reflecting its substance.

A key difference between principles and rules, as Dworkin points out, is that more than one principle may affect the application of a rule and these principles may carry different weight and pull the argument in different directions. By contrast, "if two rules conflict, one of them cannot be a valid rule."[16] In *Blackman* (casualty-loss house fire), had the principle of fairness been introduced by the taxpayer to urge that the casualty loss deduction be allowed since he had a powerful personal reason for starting the original fire—but had no idea the fire would spread and burn down the house—there would have been a clash between the principle of fairness and the principle requiring that tax deductions not frustrate public policy.[17] Such conflicts between principles are rare in the administration of the tax law because most tax rules are administered without reference to any principle of equity, justice, or fairness.

The Innocent Spouse Rules

I have emphasized throughout this book that the administration of the Internal Revenue Code is, by design, carried out in a moral void. Collecting taxes is too serious a business to allow for questions of fairness or equity. Such questions, it is presumed, have previously been addressed in the design of the law in reference to its moral underpinnings. But as most provisions in the Tax Code are subject to one or more exceptions, so too is this generalization. So I would like to describe one particular provision

Tax justice tips the scales
to accommodate the law.

of the Code that includes both the terms *equitable relief* and *inequitable* and was put in the Code to redress what many perceived as a particularly unfair outcome of the tax collection process. Potentially, this provision affects half of the married couples in the United States as a result of filing a joint tax return (given the divorce rate is about 50 percent).

A long-standing rule in the Code imposes joint liability for the tax due on a joint tax return. This means the IRS is empowered to collect 100 percent of the tax due from either spouse. Normally this is not a problem for married couples, but in certain situations it can become a big one.[18] The most common situation involves divorce, where taxes are still owed on a joint tax return filed before the divorce. This is especially acute when one spouse was unaware that the other had unreported income or had taken unwarranted deductions on the joint return. The Tax Code and IRS regulations refer to these examples of tax cheating euphemistically as *erroneous items*.[19] "An erroneous item is any item resulting in an understatement or deficiency in tax to the extent that such item is omitted from, or improperly reported (including improperly characterized) on an individual income tax return."[20] Examples of erroneous items include ordinary income reported as a capital gain so as to be taxed at a lower tax rate, the deduction of an expense that is personal and hence nondeductible, and unreported income from an investment or other source. Each is also an instance of tax cheating (either intentional or unintentional), as I have defined the term.

To illustrate the problem addressed by the innocent spouse rules, consider the following. A couple files a joint tax return each year during their seven-year marriage. Both spouses work outside the home. The husband is an accountant for a national marketing organization. As a result of his position, and as a means of financing his gambling hobby, the husband embezzles funds from his employer. The embezzled money is income but it is never deposited to the couple's checking account nor reported on their tax return, and the wife has no knowledge of the situation. When the husband's embezzling is discovered by his employer, he is fired and arrested. He is tried and sentenced. During these events, the couple gets a divorce.

When the IRS learns of the unreported income, it audits the former couple's joint returns. Assume for the example that the husband has embezzled $100,000 a year for two years before being discovered. Assume further that the tax assessed by the IRS on the missing income, including penalties and interest, is a total of $100,000 for the two years. Since the husband is in jail, the IRS pursues the former wife for 100 percent of the tax and penalty, as she is jointly responsible for the liability. For situations such as this the Code provides an escape hatch for an innocent spouse, in this case the wife. The relief offered by section 6015 of the Code consists of a series of conditions to be met—one dealing specifically with concerns of equity—which, if satisfied, will allow the innocent spouse to elude the joint tax liability. In this example the former wife applies to the IRS to have her joint liability severed, that she not be held liable for the tax on her former husband's erroneous item of embezzled and unreported income.[21]

While couples filing joint returns are generally held jointly liable for the tax due, if an erroneous item is attributable to one spouse and the other spouse "establishes that in signing the return he or she did not know, and had no reason to know"[22] that there was an understatement of tax resulting from the erroneous item, the innocent spouse can be relieved of the liability for the tax attributable to the guilty spouse's actions. The burden of proving that the innocent spouse had no direct or indirect knowledge of the tax cheating falls on the spouse seeking relief.

It should be noted that questions about whether a taxpayer knew or did not know something are rare in the Code.[23] Generally taxpayers are presumed to know the facts and conditions of their own tax returns as well as the requirements of law. In making its determination whether the spouse is innocent or not the IRS is charged with taking into account all the facts and circumstances and if as a result it determines that it is "inequitable" to hold the spouse making the claim for relief responsible for the tax, the joint liability may be divided and apportioned between the former spouses with the appealing taxpayer thereby awarded innocent-spouse relief.

One key to avoiding joint liability, as mentioned, involves the innocent spouse's proving that he or she neither knew of nor had reason to know of the understated tax. Whether the innocent spouse "had reason to know" is interpreted strictly. The IRS and the courts look at four factors: (1) the education and relative financial sophistication of the innocent spouse, (2) the innocent spouse's involvement in the family financial affairs, (3) the presence of expenditures that appear lavish, and (4) the guilty spouse's evasiveness and deceit concerning the couple's finances, especially in respect to the erroneous item.[24]

In assessing the education of a spouse the courts look specifically at a college degree and business experience as marks of a sophisticated taxpayer and a reason to question the appealing spouse's innocence. If the spouses discussed their finances and the innocent spouse was involved in paying the bills or making other financial decisions, the courts interpret this as involvement in the family financial affairs and as a mark against spouse's innocence. If the couple's spending habits changed from one year to the next—bigger house, fancier car, more lavish vacations—it is expected that both spouses would take note and have an explanation for these changes. And, on the other hand, if the spouse responsible for the erroneous item was secretive and withheld information from the innocent spouse, this may indicate that the innocent spouse did not have reason to know of the erroneous item in the joint tax return. This latter requirement has involved the courts at least once in an armchair psychological analysis of the marital dynamic.

In *Butler v. Commissioner*, the court explained that the taxpayers "were married at the time they filed their petition, are currently married, and have always had a 'smooth' marital relationship."[25] In addition, it was recited that the husband "has always applied all of his income toward the benefit of his family." The issue giving rise to the claim for innocent-spouse relief by the wife involved a legal settlement awarded to the husband that was taxable to the couple but was not reported on their joint tax return. The settlement was the outcome of a business venture in a nursery that the husband had undertaken against the wife's advice. "Petitioner testified that she never approved of his involvement in the nursery business." According to the court, the wife further testified that "their discussions on the subject [of the nursery] were almost always argumentative." Summarizing its findings the court stated that the wife never favored her "husband's involvement with the nursery, and their discussions on the subject were usually contentious." In spite of this the court proclaimed, "We fail to believe that petitioner's husband would negotiate a settlement that would allow him to walk away from the financial misery of the nursery with money left over without telling his wife at least minimal facts about its nature and scope." The court's analysis overlooks the possibility that the husband did not choose to share the proceeds of the settlement with his wife since she never approved of the venture in the first place.

In concluding their rejection of the wife's claim for innocent-spouse relief, the court asserted, "At a minimum, given her experience in the family's financial affairs, [and] her knowledge of the settlement," the wife should have inquired into whether the income from the settlement "was properly accounted for on the tax return." It is apparent from this example that for the IRS and the courts, the bar is set rather high in measuring whether a taxpayer knew or had reason to know of an erroneous item. It is presumed that each spouse analyzes the tax return, reflects on the events of the past year, and asks questions of the preparer of the return and of each other. Based on my thirty years of preparing tax returns this is a naïve expectation and certainly not the norm. If a would-be innocent spouse simply signs the return, delegating responsibility for the correctness of the return to the other spouse—as I have observed commonly occurs—he or she is opening the door to the IRS's asserting "you could have known, if you had but asked the right questions." This is certainly an extra ace up the government's sleeve, and shows that even when the law makes reference to equitable principles, the taxpayer may be held to moral standards of marital commitment well beyond the institution's legal bonds, especially for taxpayers in rocky marriages or on the brink of divorce.

The Courts and Equity

The Supreme Court has stated a general proposition that is applicable throughout the court system with respect to the tax law—"Arguments of equity have little force in construing the boundaries of exclusions and deductions from income many of which, to be administrable, must be arbitrary."[26] In applying the Code's arbitrary rules the court's equity straight jacket was dramatically demonstrated in the *Estate of Kalahasthi v.U.S.*. The administrators for the taxpayer's estate sought tax relief available to victims of the September 11, 2001, terrorist attacks.[27] The taxpayer's husband, Pendyala Vamsikrishna, was a passenger on American Airlines Flight 11 when it was hijacked and crashed into the north tower of the World Trade Center in New York. The court ruled that the decedent-wife Prasanna Kalahasthi, who committed suicide by hanging herself a month after her husband's death, wasn't eligible for the Code's reduced tax rate[28] as a "victim" of the attacks, since her death was not a direct result of the tragedy within meaning of the Code.[29] In her two suicide notes Kalahasthi stated that she was killing herself because she did not choose to face life without her husband. District Court Judge Margaret M. Morrow interpreted the Code narrowly to require that the "specified terrorist victim"[30] must have suffered physical injury as a direct result of the September 11 attacks. In addition, according to the court, "Kalahasthi's suicide must be viewed as an intervening cause that precludes a finding she died 'as a result of' the terrorist attacks." While "victim status" wasn't necessarily confined to only those present at the scene of the attacks, the court ruled that the statute was limited to those whose death was the result of wounds or injuries resulting from the attacks, which did not encompass the wife's suicide. In summarizing its approach to this case, the court explained that "because the reduced tax rate in [Internal Revenue Code] § 2201 is equivalent to a tax deduction (and hence a matter of legislative grace),[31] strict construction is applicable. This means that any ambiguity in the statutory definition of 'specified terrorist victim' must be resolved against Kalahasthi and in favor of the government."

In a treatise on Tax Court litigation, legal scholar Nina Crimm states, "The Tax Court is a court of limited jurisdiction that lacks general equitable powers to expand its statutorily prescribed jurisdiction."[32] The Tax Court's statutorily prescribed jurisdiction involves the determination of the tax due in a dispute between a taxpayer and the Internal Revenue Service.[33] The court's jurisdiction is limited to interpreting and applying the rules of the Internal Revenue Code. The latter body of law—in its application, though not necessarily in is design—as I have shown, is generally devoid of moral, equitable, or other considerations related to fairness.[34] "Because of the historical development and the Article I status of the Tax Court," Crimm reports, "some questions have arisen as to whether the court is empowered to use principles of equity in dealing with cases."[35] The answer, she says is yes, but only in a very limited set of circumstances. On rare occasions the court has applied "such equity-based principles as equitable estoppel, abuse of discretion, waiver, duty of consistency, the tax benefit rule, laches, substantial compliance, equitable reformation, and equitable recoupment."[36] But these issues are raised primarily in the context of dealings between the IRS and a taxpayer, not generally in the taxpayer's dealing with the Code.

To illustrate the Tax Court's limited employment of these principles of equity, consider the treatment of the first listed. Equitable estoppel is a judicial doctrine that "precludes a party from denying his acts or representations which induced another to act to his detriment."[37] After listing five specific conditions for estoppel, the Tax Court in *Norfolk Southern v. Commissioner* concluded that "estoppel requires a finding that a claimant [taxpayer] relied on the Government's [IRS's] representations and suffered a detriment because of that reliance."[38] But, according to another court, the doctrine of estoppel may be applied against the IRS only "with utmost caution and restraint."[39] Further, according to the Tax Court, the IRS's "discretion generally will be upheld unless there is evidence of unconscionable injury or undue hardship suffered by the taxpayer through reliance on the erroneous position [of the IRS] . . . or the circumstances reveal an unfair disparity in the Commissioner's treatment of similarly situated taxpayers."[40] In *Schuster v. Commissioner*, another court observed: "Such situations must necessarily be rare, for the policy in favor of an efficient collection of the public revenue outweighs the policy of the estoppel doctrine in its usual and customary context."[41] In *Manocchio v. Commissioner*, after praising the taxpayer for presenting a strong argument for applying the doctrine of estoppel against the IRS—for retroactively correcting and then applying an IRS Revenue Ruling the taxpayer had relied on in its original form—the court nonetheless denied the applicability of estoppel.[42] According to the court, "absent highly unusual circumstances, respondent [IRS] has very broad discretion to correct a mistake of law in a ruling and to do so with retroactive effect."[43] This is the case even if the taxpayer previously relied on erroneous IRS pronouncements to his or her detriment.

In another case, summarizing its general lack of concern for mitigating taxpayer circumstances involved in various tax choices or elections, the Tax Court announced, "Oversight, poor judgment, ignorance of the law, misunderstanding of the law, unawareness of the tax consequences of making an election, miscalculation, and unexpected subsequent events have all been held insufficient to mitigating the binding effect of elections made under a variety of provisions of the Code."[44]

Equity, Subjectivity, and Negligence

In a few circumstances, however, the courts have proved more lenient than the IRS. In its court-generated Cohan Rule for estimating expenses in the absence of proper records, and when dealing with taxpayer negligence, the courts have occasionally come to the aid of the taxpayer.

The Cohan Rule

In a case well known to tax practitioners, *Cohan v. Commissioner*,[45] the court established a principle beneficial to taxpayers who fail to comply with strict recordkeeping requirements. In the Cohan case, musical composer and playwright George M. Cohan had appealed the findings of an IRS audit to the Board of Tax Appeals and subsequently to the U.S. Court of Appeals. In particular, his travel and entertainment expenses had been questioned and disallowed because he had failed to keep the necessary records. The appeals court knew that the celebrity traveled extensively and consequently allowed Cohan's travel costs on the joint conditions that the taxpayer could prove that he did travel and that there was a reasonable basis for determining the travel costs. In upholding Cohan's deductions, Justice Learned Hand explained his reasoning.

In the production of his plays Cohan was obliged to be free-handed in entertaining actors, employees, and, as he naïvely adds, dramatic critics. He had also to travel much, at times with his attorney. These expenses amounted to substantial sums, but he kept no account and probably could not have done so. . . . Absolute certainty in such matters is usually impossible and is not necessary; the Board should make as close an approximation as it can, bearing heavily if it chooses upon the taxpayer whose inexactitude is of his own making. But to allow nothing at all appears to us inconsistent with saying that something was spent. True, we do not know how many trips Cohan made, nor how large his entertainments were; yet there was obviously some basis for computation, if necessary by drawing upon the Board's personal estimates of the minimum of such expenses. . . . It is not fatal that the result will inevitably be speculative; many important decisions must be such.

In a more recent case, the Tax Court employed the Cohan Rule to estimate both the moving expenses and a casualty loss for an unfortunate Florida taxpayer who had been in his new home for only a short time when it was hit by Hurricane Wilma in 2005. According to the taxpayer, he "lived in water for four days" and subsequently "all his property was destroyed by the water . . . and everything was taken out to the street in dumpsters." Although his records were also destroyed in the same disaster, the court allowed that he had actually moved and that whatever he had moved was now gone and permitted an estimated amount for the deductions disallowed by the IRS. In so doing the court credited the taxpayer's credible testimony.

The Cohan Rule is often cited by taxpayers who fail to keep adequate records; but in most cases the courts generally do bear more heavily "upon the taxpayer whose inexactitude is of his own making." Gambling is an activity where taxpayers frequently fail to maintain adequate records, for example, and thus seek the courts' help in applying the Cohan Rule. Rarely do the courts comply. The taxpayer in *Zielonka* was not allowed to deduct $140,830 of gambling losses for 1992 to offset his gambling winnings of a like amount.[46] The court noted that the amount of gambling losses sustained by the taxpayer is a matter of facts and circumstances and must be decided on the evidence presented.

Taxpayer Negligence

When the IRS determines that a taxpayer underreported income, the taxpayer may be liable for an "accuracy-related penalty" for any portion of an underpayment attributable to, among other things, a substantial understatement of income tax.[47] A substantial understatement is one that exceeds whichever is greater (1) 10 percent of the tax required to be shown on the return, or (2) $5,000 ($10,000 for corporations).[48] The penalty applies to several taxpayer abuses, among the most frequently cited being negligence or disregard of rules or regulations.[49] The term *negligence* is defined to include any failure to make a reasonable attempt to comply with the provisions of the Code, and the term *disregard* includes any careless, reckless, or intentional disregard.[50] As explained in chapter 6, both the courts and the IRS presume that taxpayers are familiar with the law and understand its application and their responsibilities with respect to paying taxes.

A taxpayer may contest the imposition of a negligence penalty by showing he or she acted reasonably and in good faith.[51] Congress appointed the IRS to specify criteria for determining reasonableness and good faith.[52] One way of establishing reasonableness and good faith, for example, is by showing reliance on a professional tax adviser. If a taxpayer faced with a negligence penalty can demonstrate that the cause of the negligence was advice from a professional tax adviser, the relief provided by the Code's "reasonable cause exception for underpayments" may be forthcoming.[53] But for the IRS, demonstrating good-faith reliance on a professional tax adviser involves assessing both the level of professionalism of the tax adviser and the level of sophistication of the taxpayer.[54] Thus, a taxpayer already snared in the Tax Code's complexity is now asked to judge the qualifications of his or her adviser.

The IRS regulations impose a distinction between a professional tax adviser and others who provide tax advice, though without providing specific guidance on how this distinction is determined. The onus of determining the difference is thus put on the taxpayer.[55] Taxpayers are charged with understanding the Tax Code well enough to determine whether an adviser's knowledge of the law is adequate. Since roughly 60 percent of taxpayers use the services of a paid tax preparer, knowing whether reliance on that preparer's advice will protect them from a negligence penalty is significant.[56] According to the regulations (and noted in chapter 6), if a taxpayer seeks tax advice from "someone that he knew, or should have known, lacked knowledge in the relevant aspects of Federal tax law," he or she will have "failed to act reasonably or in good faith."

A taxpayer assessed with a negligence penalty may appeal the IRS's action to the courts. In *Boyle,* the Supreme Court held: "Whether the elements that constitute 'reasonable cause' are present in a given situation is a question of fact, but what elements must be present to constitute 'reasonable cause' is a question of law."[57] The test applied by the Tax Court in *Neonatology Associates,* for example, relieving a taxpayer of an IRS-imposed negligence penalty, generally follows the regulations requiring that a taxpayer reasonably relied on a professional tax adviser and that the adviser was a competent professional with sufficient expertise to justify the taxpayer's reliance.[58] In addition it must be found that the taxpayer provided necessary and accurate information to the adviser, and that the taxpayer relied in good faith on the adviser's judgment.

"Reliance on professional advice," as clarified by the court in *Van Scoten,* can in certain circumstances "provide a defense to a negligence penalty. But reliance on such advice must be reasonable."[59] The court indicated that part of the test for reasonableness hinges on the tax adviser's independence from the taxpayer. As one observer points out, "a court will scrutinize the relationship between the adviser and the taxpayer to decide whether a true 'advisory' relationship existed." [60] The promoter selling tax shelters may give tax advice to a customer, for example, but the court will presume the advice is not independent and hence the taxpayer's reliance is not reasonable. Reliance on a tax adviser "may be unreasonable when it is placed on insiders, promoters, or their offering materials, or when the person relied upon has an inherent conflict of interest that the taxpayer knew or should have known about."[61]

Thus, whether the taxpayer acted with reasonable cause and in good faith depends upon "all the pertinent facts and circumstances, including the taxpayer's reasonable reliance on a professional tax adviser, the taxpayer's efforts to assess his or her proper tax liability, and the knowledge and experience of the taxpayer."[62] Adding to the challenge, reasonable cause also "requires that the taxpayer have exercised ordinary business care and prudence."[63] Finally, when the law is unclear, it is unreasonable for the IRS to impose a negligence penalty in the first place.[64]

In a 2008 decision, *Stadnyk,* the Tax Court considered the propriety of a negligence penalty imposed on a taxpayer who claimed to have received professional tax advice.[65] The advice concerned whether or not a personal injury award of $49,000 was taxable.[66] Under the law, if the award is directly related to a *physical* personal injury, the proceeds of the settlement (except for punitive damages) are excludable from income. In *Stadnyk*, the wife had received the settlement award but, according to the court, "the mediation agreement did not state the basis for the award or allocate the award in any way."

The basis for the physical injury claim the taxpayer asserted against the bank was her alleged false imprisonment. Her arrest by the police and subsequent detention arose from a dispute with the bank about a dishonored check. According to the court, the wife "admitted that she did not suffer physical harm during the course of her arrest and detention. She was not grabbed, jerked around, or bruised. Rather, petitioners argue[d] that physical restraint and detention constitute physical injury."[67] The court disagreed with the wife and held that the settlement from the bank was unrelated to any physical injury, and hence was taxable income.

But the court also held that the IRS's negligence penalty was out of place. The court observed, "Petitioners relied on statements made by their attorney, [the bank's] attorney, and the mediator during the course of the mediation conference that the settlement award would not be subject to Federal income tax." However, according to the court, "none of those individuals had specialized knowledge in the tax law." In spite of this fact and the fact that the taxpayers did not seek additional professional tax advice after receiving a Form 1099 for $49,000—relying instead on the opinions of personal injury attorneys rather than tax attorneys—the court held that they had "acted reasonably and in good faith when following their advice."

This outcome is at odds with the strict requirements for reasonable cause and good faith set forth above by both the IRS in its regulations and the court in *Neonatology Associates*, and raises the question of what responsibility a taxpayer bears for seeking professional tax advice and in what way the quality of the tax advice is to be judged. In particular, is acting reasonably and in good faith "when following" tax advice (the court's words) equivalent to acting reasonably and in good faith in *seeking* professional tax advice (the emphasis of the regulations). The second implies a higher standard of responsibility for taxpayers than simply following faithfully whatever advice is provided. The IRS standard, which is more rigorous, states that "reliance on ... the advice of a professional tax adviser ... does not necessarily demonstrate reasonable cause and good faith," unless "under all the circumstances, such reliance was reasonable and the taxpayer acted in good faith."[68] The court in *Stadnyk* applied a lower standard by making reliance on advice of professionals (non-tax attorneys) equivalent to reasonable reliance on professional tax advisers.

Also relevant to the appropriateness of a negligence penalty, according to IRS regulations, is the relative sophistication of the taxpayer.[69] This judgment is sometimes made on the basis of formal education. "The higher the level of the taxpayer's education, the less likely the courts are willing to accept a claim that he acted in good faith in following his adviser's questionable advice."[70] However, it is not obvious whether a lack of sophistication especially requires a taxpayer to seek a professional tax adviser or, on the contrary, a lack of sophistication excuses the taxpayer from knowing that the tax issue is sufficiently complex that a professional tax adviser should be consulted.[71]

In some cases the court has found that although a taxpayer may have acted in good faith, there was no reasonable cause.[72] In *Tamberella*, the taxpayer claimed that his mental illness constituted "reasonable cause" for his not reporting $89,840 of settlement income.[73] But the court explained that "while the settlement agreement specifically put Tamberella on notice that some or all of the $89,840 might be taxable, he did not seek the advice of a tax professional." Further, the taxpayer's claim of mental illness was undermined by the fact that "throughout the relevant period, Tamberella was able to manage his personal affairs and even represented himself in a lawsuit he brought against his former employer for denied unemployment benefits."

There are numerous cases dealing with the assessment of a negligence penalty by the IRS. Their varying results expose the subjectivity of determining "good faith" and "reasonable cause," as well as the uneven scrutiny the courts give the credentials of the taxpayer's tax adviser or the sophistication of the taxpayer. In addition, and more important, this problem further compounds the ethical dilemma discussed in chapter 3 requiring taxpayers to determine where their interests lie in a tax system relying on self-assessment. The law's reliance on a standard of reasonableness and good faith may appear to open the door to the application of equity by the courts. But equity appearing in this guise is a false promise, born of subjectivity; its unpredictability cannot reliably guide the decisions and actions of taxpayers.

The Bankrupt Taxpayer

The U.S. Bankruptcy Court is empowered to discharge or forgive income taxes after a certain lapse of time, unless there is evidence that the taxpayer had previously tried to "evade or defeat" these taxes.[74] Some have argued that in forgiving taxes in such instances, the court is giving weight to a moral judgment. For example, in an article on the ethics of tax evasion, Martinez argues that it is the perceived immorality of tax evasion that prompts the Bankruptcy Court to balk at discharging previously evaded taxes.[75] The cases he cites mention the immorality of tax evasion, but their decisions are not based on morals but on the law. Martinez reports, for example that "one court tells us unequivocally, 'there is always a moral obligation to pay taxes,'" The case he cites, *Snyder v. Routzahn,* states: "There is always a moral obligation to pay taxes, which is sufficient to support the consideration for their voluntary discharge after the tolling of the statute."[76] This means the right to have one's taxes discharged or forgiven in bankruptcy, after the legally prescribed period, is based on the taxpayer's prior moral obligation to pay those taxes. This context frames the court's more limited meaning: don't ask the law for relief from an obligation unless you previously acknowledged that obligation. This requirement is formalized in the law for taxpayers who owe taxes but fail to file a tax return, or who file a fraudulent return.[77] In both these cases the bankruptcy law forbids forgiving taxes of a taxpayer who previously cheated the system. The court in *Snyder v. Routzahn* also states: "It is in the nature of mortals to avoid the payment of taxes, if there is any escape." Splicing the threads of the court's view of taxes and morality together, we are left with the tax cheating version of biblical original sin—it's wrong, but we can't help it.

In *Simone,* also a Bankruptcy Court decision, the question addressed was whether income taxes are dischargeable in bankruptcy when there is evidence that the taxpayer could have paid them but chose instead to spend the money on insignia of lifestyle (thirty-foot boat and Jaguar XJ6 and so on).[78] The Bankruptcy Code provides that taxes may not be discharged if the debtor made a willful attempt "in any manner to evade or defeat such tax."[79] In this case, willfulness was determined not as a state of mind but based on the taxpayer's admission that he "did a lot of things knowing [he] owed the IRS money."

Acknowledging there was a tax liability combined with sufficient means to pay the tax and the choice to use the money for discretionary spending was enough to evidence willfulness. Therefore the taxpayer's tax debts were not forgiven. In reaching its conclusion the court relied on *Fegeley,* another bankruptcy case, which had adopted a "civil willfulness standard where a debtor satisfies the *mens rea* criteria [the "mental state requirement" of bad intentions] of the evasion of a tax obligation if the evasion was voluntary, conscious, and intentional."[80] The court concluded, "Commissions of civil activities constituting moral turpitude are not required. Omission of payment with the ability to pay is adequate."[81] Moral turpitude, as discussed in chapter 6, refers to actions generally considered to be violations of accepted moral norms (fraud, perjury, assault, rape). The taxpayer-debtor's only required wrong is therefore mismanaging the priorities of his finances. In addition, as explained in chapter 1, when the law is "vague or highly debatable," a defendant lacks the requisite intent to violate it and his actions, therefore, cannot be willful.[82]

In *Fegeley*, the Bankruptcy Court had originally allowed the discharge of the taxpayer's income tax debts because—although he had failed to file returns for a number of years, had asked his employer to pay him as an independent contractor rather than have taxes withheld from his paycheck, and possessed sufficient funds to pay the taxes had he chosen to—the taxpayer had not displayed traditional "badges of fraud" (falsifying records, concealing assets, hiding income, destroying documents) required to find he attempted to "evade or defeat" the tax.[83] The district court reversed this finding and the appeals court upheld the district court. "We observe," the appeals opinion states, "the majority of courts have found that affirmative conduct by a debtor designed to evade or defeat a tax is not required. Rather, section 523(a)(1)(C) [Bankruptcy Code] circumscribes acts of culpable omission as well as acts of commission." Tax cheating therefore encompasses what we fail to do if the consequences of the failure are foreseeable and it leads to the same result as an overt action.

Interpreting the Law—Transparency

Cicero wrote that "injustices often occur through a species of trickery which takes the form of an extremely clever but willful interpretation of the law."[84] Jeremy Bentham argues that "interpretation," when applied to the law, is a "euphemism for *alteration*."[85] Italian criminologist Cesare Beccaria (1738–1794), was one of the earliest to theorize about the causes of criminality and cheating. In *On Crimes and Punishments*, he laid out a general principle that is certainly applicable to the complexity of the current income Tax Code. "If the interpretation of laws is an evil, another evil, evidently, is the obscurity that makes interpretation necessary."[86] In the present context, this means don't blame the taxpayer for fashioning the rules to fit his or her intent if Congress drafted the law allowing such flexibility. In addition, Beccaria adds, "And this evil would be very great indeed where the laws are written in a language that is foreign to a people, forcing it to rely on a handful of men because it is unable to judge for itself."[87] While his reference may have been to a different (or foreign) language, his criticism is fitting for the present Internal Revenue Code—a law written in a language foreign to many people. The fact that the majority of taxpayers must pay others to have their taxes calculated is certainly forcing them to rely on a handful of people because they are unable to judge for themselves.[88]

Economist and philosopher Adam Smith (1723–1790) is generally credited with first enumerating criteria that make one form of taxation preferable to another. "The tax which each individual is bound to pay" according to Smith "ought to be certain, and not arbitrary. The time of payment, the manner of payment, the quantity to be paid, ought all to be clear and plain to the contributor, and to every other person."[89] The most telling point among Smith's criteria is that the payer of the tax should have as much knowledge and understanding of the tax as the collector. Though we may facetiously believe this is the case with the current Internal Revenue Code—with the IRS and the taxpayer equally befuddled—Smith's point is that there should be no mystery, no element of doubt, regarding what is to be taxed and how much it is to be taxed and when. Each individual should have an understanding of how his neighbor's tax is computed and that it is in the same manner as his own.[90] Although we are far from Smith's goal, the courts, true to their role, have refused to step in the middle. As one court bluntly stated, "We dismiss this 'confusion in the law' argument outright. The complexities of our tax code notwithstanding, a taxpayer cloaked in ignorance will find no safe haven from liability imposed by law."[91] However, the courts frequently must do their own interpreting, as they are the final arbiter of the law's meaning. In one case, where the court was called upon to determine if the sale of land produced capital gain or ordinary income, the court described its uneasy role: "Finding ourselves engulfed in a fog of decisions with gossamer-like distinctions, and a quagmire of unworkable, unreliable, and often irrelevant tests, we take the route of ad hoc exploration."[92]

Thus, the administration of the law is generally adversarial, as chronicled in chapter 5—with the IRS interpreting the law in a way most favorable to raising revenue—but taxpayers interpreting it most favorably to themselves. This tension between the taxpayer, the IRS, and the Tax Code, as argued in chapter 3, is a central reason we have no moral duty to comply with the tax law. As adversarial parties in a legal dispute, our duties are restricted to the law and its requirements and do not include an additional layer of moral duty, especially a duty to cut the IRS any slack. The IRS has its job to do and we have ours. Our overarching moral duty to obey the law is trumped in this case by the fact that the tax law's administration is, by law, carried out without considerations of equity and therefore in a moral void.

While the design of the U.S. income tax system has obvious roots in ethics and political and social philosophy, the administration of the tax law, as described in chapter 3, is carried out largely without reference to justice or fairness. The administration of the law by the IRS and the courts is thus by design amoral or extra-moral. By law, the administration of the Internal Revenue Code requires the IRS and the courts to ignore otherwise morally relevant excuses (age, mental capacity, education, sanity, personal circumstances, medical conditions, and so on). Likewise, the courts, as illustrated above, are not empowered to consider issues of equity or fairness in their adjudication of disputes. Terms occurring in the tax law, including examples in this chapter—reasonable cause, inequitable, and good faith—while appearing to relax the unbending rules of revenue collection, should not be relied upon as a safe harbor or safety net. The administration of the tax régime—within the framework of the current Internal Revenue Code—is, by design, devoid of moral grounding. In the next chapter we will look at some possible remedies for this condition.

EIGHT

COMPLIANCE, COMPLEXITY, CONSCIENCE, AND FAIRNESS

The whole practice of public finance has been developed in an endeavor to outwit the taxpayer and to induce him to pay more than he is aware of, and to make him agree to expenditure in the belief that somebody else will be made to pay for it.
—Friedrich Hayek (1899–1992), *Law, Legislation, and Liberty*

The Moral Dimension of Tax Compliance

From a public policy perspective, if compliance with the income tax laws is a growing problem, it is important to consider all the tools available for promoting obedience to the law. A number of such measures have been suggested and debated. They include (1) increasing the perceived fairness of the tax system,[1] (2) increasing the audit rate,[2] (3) decreasing the perception that the government is wasting tax dollars,[3] (4) reducing privacy restrictions and thereby exposing more taxpayers to the stigma of tax cheater,[4] (5) simplifying the law and increasing taxpayers' understanding of their legal obligations,[5] (6) improving the deterrence effects of tax penalties,[6] (7) reducing the perception that most people cheat,[7] (8) reducing negative perceptions of the IRS,[8] (9) increasing trust in the government,[9] (10) reducing the tax rates,[10] (11) increasing the tax rates,[11] (12) increasing efficiency of tax compliance by reducing expenditure of time and money,[12] (13) reducing opportunity for cheating by increasing third-party reporting,[13] (14) rewarding taxpayers for compliance,[14] (15) increasing individuals' feelings of guilt about tax cheating through promoting moral commitment to the law,[15] and (16) positively affecting moral beliefs about tax cheating by, for example, appealing to conscience.[16] Few, if any, of these suggestions have gone uncriticized. And they come from accountants, criminologists, economists, and legal scholars approaching the problem from the perspective of their respective disciplines, not necessarily giving weight to factors outside their own purview.

The insight that moral or ethical beliefs can affect tax compliance has spawned a growing body of empirical studies.[17] Summarizing the outcome of their experiments on the influence of ethical considerations on tax compliance, researchers report, "There was moderate agreement among participants that income taxes were necessary to a smoothly functioning society and that, in principle, tax evasion was morally wrong."[18] In an article on taxes and morals, Leo Martinez asserts, "The interplay of morals and taxes is crucial to tax collection. . . . If there is no moral obligation to pay taxes, the state can expect its citizens to weigh only the law or purely legal consequences in deciding whether compliance with tax laws makes sense as a matter of personal choice."[19] This may be the basis for the current willingness of so many taxpayers to play the tax audit lottery.

Seeing this consequence, others weighed in on how best to improve taxpayers' moral response to paying taxes. One study employing a sampling of public opinion on tax evasion reports that although "not all taxpayers will view tax evasion with the same sense of morality, and there are people who do not respond to morals," yet, "individual moral beliefs are highly significant in tax compliance decisions."[20]

A pivotal question is whether the ever-growing tax gap, and its implications for tax compliance, should be viewed as a consequence of the moral failings of taxpayers and therefore a solution requires enhancing their moral capacities,[21] or whether that approach is misguided and the solution to the problem should be sought in examining the Tax Code's failure—due to its complexity and its reliance on self-assessment and other features examined earlier to afford effective moral incentives.

If the problem appears to be the waning force of moral obligation on tax compliance, as some contend, we should be prepared to recognize this erosion of moral feeling as a symptom of another problem rather than the ultimate cause of increasing noncompliance. Thus, the tax law's weakening moral tug should be seen as a warning sign to Congress that it has strayed too far from what taxpayers feel is a morally defensible system of taxation. Nina Olson, the IRS National Taxpayer Advocate, testified before the Senate that "when honest taxpayers feel like chumps, some of them start fudging too. And when that happens, voluntary payments drop even more, necessitating more examination and collection actions. This sense that the system is unfair can result in a vicious cycle of increased noncompliance and increased enforcement."[22] The relation between the law and morality is a dynamic one. As the law veers from the path of what the public feels is right or fair, the law's ability to guide conduct—except by fear of formal sanctions—is by the same degree diluted and its moral force weakened.

One discovery leading to our understanding of the importance of ethics in encouraging tax compliance arose from the inadequacy of neoclassical economic theory, which overestimated the extent of tax cheating. As explained in chapter 3, economists manipulating marginal tax savings produced by cheating and the risks of an audit determined that, if taxpayers were acting rationally we should expect a good deal more tax cheating than now occurs.[23] These results led others to infer that noneconomic factors were guiding some decisions on tax compliance and that these factors included ethical values or moral sentiments.

Alternatively, it has been suggested, people may not cheat as much as expected, not as an expression of ethical values but because they would like to maintain their good reputations. The claim is founded on a Machiavellian-style game theory analysis allowing that a reputation is a personal asset to be honed and polished to achieve its maximum benefit. An important aspect of social life, we are told, is that people value their reputations, and "will take steps to protect them." The same researcher tells us that people avoid tax cheating to avoid being stigmatized as tax cheats so that others will trust them.[24] In either case, whether the moral feelings are real or only feigned for the sake of appearances, the belief that tax cheating is morally wrong is assumed to be one factor promoting tax compliance. Thus, Congress, by "designing" the Internal Revenue Code in its present form, has bypassed the opportunity to add the weight of conscience to the list of incentives for complying with the tax laws.

A study in the late 1960s—employing a control group and based on questions posed to U.S. taxpayers shortly before the tax filing deadline—found differences in the effectiveness of appeals to conscience that cut across socioeconomic, religious, and educational lines. In particular, the study found that appeals to conscience change attitudes toward tax compliance most among "the best and least well-educated, those employed by others, and Protestants and Jews." Appeals to conscience had little effect on those in the highest economic class. Generally, appeals to conscience were found more effective than threats of sanctions. For some taxpayers threats of sanctions were even counterproductive.[25]

Interestingly, harking back to the discussion of small business and its contribution to the tax gap in chapter 2, this same study found a significant difference in susceptibility to appeals to conscience between the self-employed and those who work for others. Moral appeals "only moderately moved" the self-employed to report more income. For employees such appeals had more than three times the effect.[26]

The Matthew Effect

Since 2002, the IRS Oversight Board has conducted random taxpayer attitude surveys. One of the survey questions asks, "Is it every American's civic duty to pay their fair share of taxes?" Since the survey began, a little over 70 percent of taxpayers "completely agree" that they have this duty, and another 25 percent "mostly agree."[27] One conclusion I would like to develop from the arguments in the earlier chapters—especially chapters 3 and 6—is that even if someone accepts a civic (or moral) duty to pay her or his fair share of the tax burden, under the current system there is simply no way to know whether this has occurred: in the present tax climate, fair share has lost its meaning. Thus, while the IRS Oversight Board may take heart that 95 percent of Americans agree that they have a civic duty to pay their fair share, the Board should recognize that such a high rate of agreement is a hollow victory if there is no consensus on what constitutes a fair share.

While I argued earlier that complexity alone is not the reason for our lack of a moral duty to pay our taxes, one aspect of our system's complexity is its confounding of the fair share calculation. If we don't believe the current system is determining our fair share, by default we believe the system is unfair. Much of the Tax Code's complexity and our inability to locate our fair share can be traced to the congressional decision to bifurcate income into what is taxed and what is not, rather than taxing all income "from whatever source derived" as permitted by the Sixteenth Amendment. According to John Fox's calculations, "The tax laws currently allow massive amounts of income to be [legally] siphoned away from taxable income."[28] The same writer explains, "Congress undermines the effectiveness of progressive tax rates by allowing so much income of middle- and upper-income taxpayers . . . to escape status as taxable income."[29] More than 45 percent of income potentially available for taxation is legally excluded, although this untaxed income is not spread proportionately to taxpayers' incomes, the primary benefits going to those in the highest tax brackets.[30] This is an extension of what sociologist

Robert Merton called the Matthew Effect.[31] "For whosoever hath, to him shall be given, and he shall have more abundance."[32]

While it stands to reason that tax incentives, including deductions, exemptions, reduced capital gains rates, and other breaks are of the greatest potential benefit to taxpayers in the highest tax brackets, crafting tax breaks specifically for those in the highest brackets, as Fox points out, undercuts the original purpose of a progressive tax rate system. In addition, when the purported justification for certain tax benefits is the advantages they offer to middle or lower-income taxpayers, while in fact they do those taxpayers very little good but have their greatest impact on the wealthiest among us—the congressional shell game is exposed. Two examples of this phenomenon are described here, the itemized deduction for home mortgage interest and the business deduction for employer-provided health insurance. In both cases the greatest benefit goes to those whomsoever already hath, although each is popularly conceived as an incentive or benefit aimed at helping the struggling average taxpayer.

Home Mortgage Interest Deduction

The term *tax expenditure* is used by economists and politicians who deal in tax policy to differentiate what avoids taxation (or reduces what is taxed)—and is thereby subsidized—from what is taxed. Income earned but used to pay deductible mortgage interest is an example. Fox tells us, "Congress subsidizes all sorts of programs . . . by creating special provisions in the tax laws that reduce government receipts."[33] *Tax expenditure* is an unfortunate term, for it further obfuscates the ordinary taxpayer's understanding of the tax régime. In everyday English a tax expenditure sounds like spending money generated from taxes; that is not its meaning on Capitol Hill. One economist tells us, "The term 'tax expenditure' refers to departures from the normal tax structure designed to favor a particular industry, activity, or class of persons."[34]

The U.S. Government Accountability Office (GAO) lists as examples of tax expenditures "tax exemptions, exclusions, deductions, credits, and deferrals"[35] and has criticized their widespread use in the Code. Effectively, tax expenditures represent the cost—in lost tax revenue—caused by items afforded special tax status and benefiting special groups of taxpayers. As a consequence of, "having placed so much income beyond the government's reach," according to Fox, "Congress adopts much higher tax rates than would otherwise be necessary to raise a given amount of tax revenue."[36] Ronald Pasquariello explains that "[t]he effect of tax expenditure is to subsidize a particular activity. The home mortgage interest deduction subsidizes home buying. In this sense, it is no different from a budget outlay."[37] Further, Leonard Burman tells us, "The mortgage interest deduction is the largest housing subsidy by far and dwarfs the size of not only other tax expenditures but also other direct expenditures for housing in the federal budget."[38]

At first glance, this deduction appears to be an incentive: the government's way of encouraging home ownership. By helping someone who might not otherwise buy a house to afford the monthly payments, the deduction can be seen as encouraging taxpayers to take the step from renting to buying. In theory the additional cost of the mortgage payment is subsidized by a deduction for the mortgage interest paid. But this deduction is only available to people who itemize deductions—roughly 35 percent of taxpayers—leaving no benefit to those at the lower end of the home-buying spectrum, those who use the standard deduction and are frequently less affluent.

To provide any tax relief, the mortgage interest paid plus other itemized deductions must exceed the standard deduction. For 2010, for example, for a married couple, the standard deduction was $11,400. Added to other itemized deductions, the benefit derived from the mortgage interest deduction is only the amount greater than the standard deduction. Thus, except for those with hefty mortgages where the interest component greatly exceeds the amount of the standard deduction ($11,400), the purported tax savings benefit is greatly diluted or largely illusory. To illustrate, assume my marginal tax rate is 25 percent and my itemized deductions as a result of my home mortgage interest are $12,400; in this case my benefit from the mortgage interest deduction is only $250 ($12,400 − 11,400 = 1,000 x .25 = $250) or 2 percent of the interest paid.[39] Such a meager savings would hardly encourage me to purchase a house with all the attendant risk and looming costs.

At the other end of the economic spectrum, the greatest tax benefits from the mortgage interest deduction (tax expenditure) go to those paying taxes at the highest marginal tax rates. These are also taxpayers who would likely buy a house even without a government subsidy. If my mortgage interest is $48,000[40] and if my marginal tax rate is 35 percent, my benefit is $12,810 ($48,000 − 11,400 = 36,600 x .35 = $12,810) or 27 percent of the interest paid, a significant subsidy. In addition, the mortgage interest deduction is available to those with a second home, meaning the government's subsidy for the mortgage interest on the second home is effectively greater (in the above example 35 percent) than the mortgage interest subsidy for the first home since the standard deduction has already been subtracted from the benefit of the interest on the first mortgage. As Burman explains, "The subsidy has been criticized as an upside down subsidy that provides the greatest benefit to upper middle class and upper class homeowners, while the greatest needs are among lower-income families struggling to pay rent or afford a home."[41] The GAO explains that "tax expenditures may not be an effective way to achieve federal goals if targeting them to entities or activities meant to receive the benefits is difficult, if they subsidize activities that would have been undertaken without their stimulus, or if they serve to exacerbate other key private sector and public policy challenges."[42] The federal government's encouraging home ownership for higher-income taxpayers—the primary beneficiaries of the mortgage interest deduction—is an example of a subsidy for an action that would have been undertaken without this stimulus.

Those who oppose a consumption tax on the basis that it is regressive—that its burden weighs heaviest on taxpayers at the lower end of the economic spectrum because they spend all their earnings—may need to reconsider this opposition in light of the actual as opposed to the nominal results of the current progressive income tax system. If, as Fox claims, the current progressive system has been so emasculated—through the numerous deductions, exemptions, and credits that provide their greatest benefit to those at the high end of the economic spectrum[43]—that it is actually regressive, the comparison of formal definitions of *regressive* and *progressive* may be less useful than a comparison of the results of these systems once they have been retrofitted to the needs of those inside the Beltway.

Employer-Provided Health Insurance

The same kinds of problems have been documented for the tax benefits of employer-provided health insurance. "The tax expenditure [for health insurance] is regressive," says Joseph Antos, "providing a greater subsidy to those with good jobs and high incomes and much less to the unemployed and disadvantaged."[44] "The tax code gives far less benefit to people who purchase their health care directly rather than through insurance. . . . Tax filers who itemize may deduct out-of-pocket health spending that exceeds 7.5 percent of their adjusted gross income."[45] Further, according to Antos,

The tax exclusion [for health insurance] favors those with higher taxable incomes and discriminates among individuals based on their employment status. After income and payroll taxes, a high earner could save as much as 50 cents for every dollar spent on health insurance premiums, at the margin. In contrast, a low earner might save as little as three cents on the dollar for employer-sponsored insurance. People without access to employer-sponsored insurance are not helped by the exclusion, regardless of their income or health status.[46]

As with homeownership, Burman and Gruber explain that "the tax exclusion [for health insurance] is not only upside down from an equity perspective, it is also poorly designed to change behavior. The high-income people who benefit most from the tax exclusion would also be most likely to purchase insurance without a subsidy."[47]

While specific expenditure items may be criticized, there is a more fundamental problem with this fiscal technique—"We do not know if [tax expenditures] have achieved their objectives, how they have done so, who is using them, how they compare to other means of achieving the same goals."[48] Compounding this problem, reports Pasquariello, "they have not been periodically reviewed as are direct expenditures."[49] The GAO points out that "[a]mong the many causes of tax code complexity is the growing number of preferential provisions in the code, defined in statute as tax expenditures. . . . The number of these tax expenditures has more than doubled from 67 in 1974 to 161 in 2006."[50] Former IRS Commissioner Rossotti observed that "the reason the tax code has so many pages . . . is that almost every page is a compromise over whose constituents are going to get, or not get, a tax break, and how much that tax break is going to 'cost' in lost tax revenue."[51]

Our Vision of a Fair Share

Currently, as these examples show, the tax expenditure approach to taxation, employing the exclusions, credits, deferrals, and deductions peppered throughout the Code—in an attempt to encourage certain actions and discourage others—serves to further blur our vision of a fair share. Two taxpayers (or ten) with the same amount of spendable income will rarely pay the same amount of tax.[52] There is little reason, therefore, to believe that the end result of the Code's machinations is our fair share. Fortunately, Pasquariello writes, "Many of the tax expenditures now on the books can be easily converted into direct expenditures. . . . This kind of restructuring would unmask the irrationality and fundamental unfairness of many of our tax expenditure programs. . . . A clear advantage in simple justice to restructuring tax loopholes as direct expenditures is that it would simplify the complexity of the tax system while providing a way to monitor the benefits."[53]

"A broad-base low-rate system," Fox explains, "would give taxpayers greater confidence that others bear their fair share of the tax load. More favorable perceptions about the tax system would increase taxpayer compliance with the tax laws."[54] Only if we possessed a uniform and all-inclusive definition of income and knew that everyone was paying a certain percentage of his or her income into the treasury, could we even know what share we are paying, and possibly whether it is also our fair share.

"Our only hope is gridlock
among the special interest groups."

One impediment to achieving the end of a clear and precise Code is the fact that Congress has not set as a goal establishing a settled body of law. The Code's rules are changed frequently and often changed retroactively. Increasingly, the goals expressed in the Code have become narrower and more short-sighted. "There are now 141 temporary provisions that expire nearly every year" according to Senator Max Baucus (D-MT).[55] This procedure provides flexibility for Congress, but not without a price. Frequent changes in the Code fuel new problems with compliance and new disagreements over the meaning of the law.

The complexity of the current Internal Revenue Code and our knowledge of the growing tax gap currently renders this judgment impossible. Aggravating the situation, Slemrod warns, if the tax law is selectively enforced then "what is apparently a tax base finely tuned to reflect individual differences in ability to pay may, in fact, produce a capricious distribution of tax liabilities."[56] The selective enforcement of the Tax Code is evidenced by the IRS's focus on matching documents for those taxpayers in "the system," while its enforcement efforts against those scofflaws operating outside the system, in the cash and criminal economies or tax havens, by necessity are situational and ad hoc.

When the Alternative Minimum Tax was established—then just the Minimum Tax—by the Tax Reform Act of 1969, it was in response to reports of that "155 people in the United States with income over $200,000 paid no income tax in 1966."[57] Though these taxpayers had reduced their taxable incomes through judicious—but legal—tax planning, this was seen by many as unfair. The 1969 Minimum Tax was intended to ensure that wealthy taxpayers (including corporations) would pay at least some tax in spite of their use of tax shelters and other means enabled by Congress and referred to as tax preference items.

The general explanation accompanying the Tax Reform Act of 1976, prepared by the Joint Committee on Taxation, addressed the ineffectiveness of the 1969 legislation in meeting its objective. Some high-income taxpayers, it was claimed, were still "not paying their fair share of taxes."[58] In 1974, the minimum tax on individuals had raised "only $130 million, a small fraction of tax-preferred income."[59] This led, in the 1976 tax legislation, to an increased tax rate for the minimum tax and a reduced exemption amount. Forty years after its inception—as the result of a lack of congressional foresight regarding inflation—the AMT applies to millions of taxpayers, including children—not all wealthy—and is now claimed to be unfair to them.[60] For 2007, the AMT impacted 4.1 million returns, increasing the treasury's take by $24.1 billion.[61] Among these, the AMT snagged 3,836 taxpayers with adjusted gross incomes between $10,000 and $15,000.[62]

The piecemeal strategy employed by Congress for generating tax fairness is like handing out candy on Halloween; the cloak of darkness and the masks worn by the lobbyists means we don't know who came back for seconds or who never made it to our door. The slice of the pie that represents each taxpayer's share of the tax burden has thus been cut with a hand trembling under the weight of so many guiding principles as to render its relation to the total indeterminable. In the end the Code is a black box: we send our tax data through the system and our tax liability is the result. While the math involved is generally not complex, the reasons for many of the calculations are inexplicable.

In his 2005 book *Many Unhappy Returns,* former IRS Commissioner Charles Rossotti says, "Ultimately, the American people will have a tax system only as good as they demand from the president and Congress. But in the last decade, the presidents and Congress have not been giving Americans what they deserve. Instead, the elected leaders have consistently made politically expedient decisions that are leading to a steady deterioration of the system, to the enormous detriment of all honest taxpayers."[63]

Adam Smith expressed a moral intuition (noted in chapter 5) regarding the fairness of a tax system: "The subjects of every state ought to contribute towards the support of the government, as nearly as possible, in proportion to their respective abilities; that is, in proportion to the revenue which they respectively enjoy under the protection of the state."[64] In general terms, a tax on income could accomplish this, though varying congressional interpretations of Smith's words "in proportion to their respective abilities" may open the door to a Code like the current one featuring countless exclusions, deductions, credits, and other refinements intended to ensure everyone's abilities have been properly accounted for, especially those of favored constituencies. If self-assessment is the method used to determine the "revenue enjoyed under the protection of the state," however, we will end up with the same complexity and compliance problems we are now seeking to solve. This shows that even using a simple moral principle as a starting point will not help if the legislative process required to enact the tax laws is focused on spinning the moral principle to someone's political advantage rather than on promoting the general welfare.

It could be argued that in a democracy, tax laws passed by duly elected representatives are fair by definition and therefore each taxpayer's computed tax must be his or her fair share. According to one expert, the tax process is "an accurate reflection of public opinion."[65] John Mackie responds that a reciprocal obligation to obey the law arises "only if the compromise that the body of laws as a whole represents is itself reasonable and fair. Democracy in itself is far from sufficient to ensure this."[66] The notion that democracy ensures fair tax policy is also countered by the practical outcome of special interest lobbying, which greatly affects our tax laws; while lawmakers represent those who vote for them, they also represent those who support their campaigns financially. John Scholz reports that "members of tax-writing committees, and particularly the chairmen, receive considerably greater contributions than the average congressman."[67] There is ancient wisdom, however, holding that no person can serve two masters.[68] In answer to this complaint it can be argued that each of us is a constituent of one or more special interests and thus our voice is heard along with everyone else's. But though everyone's voice may be heard, each voice is not recorded equally in the construction of the Code, leaving no reason to believe that an "invisible hand" has somehow distributed the tax burden fairly among taxpayers. How can each of us pull our weight when the scales determining our weight has not been calibrated to a standard?

If it is impossible to know whether each of us is paying our fair share, any moral (or civic) duty to comply with the income tax laws based on the fair-share principle is doomed. This exacerbates the moral problem described in chapter 3—the problem resulting from self-assessment. If we believe we are being asked to pay more than our fair share—though we can never be sure what that is—and the means for adjusting our share is left within reach, what should we expect the upshot to be but tax cheating?

The Moral Quality of Actions

It is generally accepted that some actions have moral significance and others do not. John Dewey asked, "May acts be voluntary, that is, be expressions of desire, intent, choice, and habitual disposition, and yet be morally neutral, indifferent? To all appearances the answer must be in the affirmative."[69] On the other hand, he points out, "Many acts are done not only without thought of their moral quality but with practically no thought of any kind. Yet these acts are preconditions of other acts having significant value."[70] A logical consequence of this view, according to Dewey is that "every act has *potential* moral significance, because it is, through its consequences, part of a larger whole of behavior."[71] To this he adds, however, "It would be rather morbid if a moral issue were raised in connection with each act; we should probably suspect some mental disorder if it were, at least some weakness in power of decision."[72] These comments raise the specter that the moral quality of actions—not whether they are right or wrong, but whether they are proper objects of moral valuation at all—is not absolute, but found along a continuum.

Where does this put tax cheating? Unlike slavery, child abuse, or rape—where the action's immorality is generally acknowledged and thus not dependant on the law—tax cheating is not an identifiable action in itself but the characterization of a particular action or series of actions. Not reporting an item of income can result from a mistake, a choice, or confusion over the law's meaning. Rape cannot be committed by mistake, except perhaps as to the victim. Tax cheating is an especially challenging problem for IRS officials because it involves "inherently low-visibility acts"—reporting income and deductions—that "are not wrongful themselves."[73] Not reporting taxable income is against the law, but its moral import is a separate question. As noted earlier the moral quality of cheating depends on the moral status of the underlying rules being violated.

In an article on tax cheating Hans Sherrer argues that even tax evasion—the most blatant example of tax cheating—is not an objective label. "The thoughts, motivations, and purpose of any action that can be superficially construed as tax evasion cannot be ascertained from the mere observance and recording of one's actions—because engaging in an activity is not in and of itself tax evasion."[74] Psychologists Fishbein and Ajzen concur: "It can often be difficult to assess with direct observation whether a particular behavior was performed. If we observe people at the opera or a lecture we can say they were present, but we cannot be sure that they were actually listening."[75] The omission of an item of income results in an incorrect tax return and perhaps in tax cheating, but the reason for the omission is a separate matter, and its moral import yet another.

Enlisting Conscience in Reducing Tax Cheating

Conscience, whatever that term is determined to mean, is recognized as insufficient by itself to foster compliance with the tax law. It is for this reason that the law contains penalties and other legal sanctions and that the IRS conducts audits. But in recognizing that conscience by itself is not enough, Congress has taken the further but unwarranted step of discarding its potential benefits and focusing only on legal remedies. Thus, the fact that the conscience itself is insufficient "does not explain . . . why conscience is not combined with the threat of sanction."[76] The solutions for many problems are found in the combination of different influences. Diplomacy is described as employing both a carrot and a stick; weight loss unfortunately requires both diet and exercise; and excelling at sports requires both talent and discipline. Likewise, another observer tells us, "the interplay of morals and taxes is crucial to tax collection."[77]

Adam Smith asked, "What can be added to the happiness of the man who is in health, who is out of debt, and has a clear conscience?"[78] At present, penalties, fear of the IRS, and the threat of prison time are used to encourage compliance with the Internal Revenue Code. The conscience could be added to these deterrents. But I have argued throughout this book that the tax system is so structured as to preclude its status as a moral compass. So the question becomes how, if at all, can the U.S. income tax régime be reformed so that it appeals to the conscience—that is, appeals to the moral values shared by large sections of the population, thereby increasing compliance?

Though it will shock no one, a starting point for Congress—if it would employ the force of morality on the side of tax compliance—is to rethink the necessity of the Code's rambling complexity. Some have claimed that the Code's complexity has been caused by continual refinements necessary to accurately effect tax fairness.[79] Paradoxically, even if this is historically accurate, the end result puts any judgment on the success of the project beyond reach: the Code's complexity makes it impossible to determine anyone's fair share. A simpler set of rules should provide a more effective guide to what is expected of taxpayers and why. It could allow us to see that two people (or ten) enjoying the same spendable revenue under the protection of the state must pay the same tax. If Congress wants to provide special incentives or assistance to particular groups it could continue to do so outside the Tax Code in directed programs such as low-income housing, welfare, or grants for education or research.

Utilizing the potential of the conscience has practical benefits. Wilbert Moore, a sociologist, informs us: "Internalization of norms has the great social advantage of reducing the necessity of surveillance and discipline."[80] E. A. Posner concurs: "If people can be made to act properly because of social norms, rather than because of fear of legal sanction, then the desired behavior can be obtained at less cost."[81] If the tax system can be reengineered to facilitate such internalization, perhaps much of what the Internal Revenue Code attempts to do by threat of sanction could be accomplished more effectively through the individual conscience.

Social psychologist Albert Bandura emphasizes the importance of modeling in learning, because life is not long enough to learn everything by trial and error.[82] Regarding the modeling of moral reasoning he points out that "modeling influences do not invariably produce changes in moral reasoning [because] . . . people cannot be much influenced by modeled opinions if they do not understand them."[83] It is hard to know what ethical values the current Code projects, though if Congress chooses it could remedy this problem.

What is Conscience?

If there is something answering to the name *conscience,* it is an influence promising to limit our range of conduct. One of my students described it as a "speed bump" in the process of making a choice with ethical implications. Your conscience won't prevent you from choosing a certain alternative, but it may prompt you to regret that choice later and anticipation of this regret may influence your choice. But if conscience is a speed bump, familiarity with its effects means we may become inured to its influence. Plato taught that "the habit of transgression is learned from repetition."[84] Joseph Wells, founder of the Association for Certified Fraud Examiners, points out that "the first time we do something contrary to our morals, it bothers us. As we repeat the act, it becomes easier."[85] This process of *adaptation,* is described by one psychologist as a "ubiquitous feature of human psychology . . . [whereby] we get used to things, and then we start to take them for granted."[86] Tax compliance is subject to these same influences; failing to file or failing to report income or relying on trumped-up deductions may give pause at first, but once undertaken can become the new norm. Before engaging in tax cheating taxpayers may fear an audit or believe they will be found out by the IRS. But with continued noncompliance resulting in no negative consequences, taxpayers adapt to this environment and old feelings of anxiety are swept away.

Conscience is not a term commonly used in contemporary U.S. psychology, nor is it well defined. And conscience has been only a "secondary or peripheral topic in writings on moral philosophy."[87] According to Philip Cary, "Conscience originally meant someone is in on a secret with you."[88] Latin *con* (with) *scientia* (knowledge)—he or she "knew with you some secret."[89] In its religious context conscience became "the inner witness inside you who knows what you have done and will bear witness against you."[90] It is "your awareness of where you stand before God. Something in your own memory that will testify against you."[91]

In a book on the religious characterization of conscience, the author tells us, "Conscience is generally understood as the judgment about the morality of an act to be done or omitted or already done or omitted by the person."[92] Justin Aronfreed, a psychologist, reports that "conscience is the term that has been used traditionally to refer to the cognitive and affective processes which constitute an internalized moral governor over an individual's conduct."[93] The same writer tells us, "One aspect of conscience that helps us to identify its presence, and to distinguish it from other evaluative systems . . . is our own experience of its affective intensity and our observation of the same intensity when it is apparent in the behavior of others."[94] Another observer writes, "Conscience is not a purely intellectual concern. . . . A person with a conscience is also capable of experiencing specifically moral

www.mchumor.com

"We consult those with whom we agree, which is why I rarely consult my conscience."

emotions and of being moved to perform those actions which he believes to be moral."[95]

Theories of how the conscience is formed and on the veracity of its pronouncements abound. The Bible speaks of "the work of the law written in their hearts, their conscience also bearing witness to their thoughts."[96] Hamlet famously confessed, "Conscience doth make cowards of us all."[97] Nineteenth-century English author Leslie Stephen proclaimed: "The conscience is the utterance of the public spirit of the race, ordering us to obey the primary conditions of its welfare, and it acts not the less forcibly though we may not understand the source of its authority or the end at which it is aiming."[98] According to Freud, "The super-ego is an agency which has been inferred by us, and conscience is a function which we ascribe, among other functions, to that agency."[99] And theologian and anti-Nazi martyr Dietrich Bonhoeffer wrote, "Conscience is concerned not with man's relation to God and to other men but with man's relation to himself."[100]

Research in evolutionary psychology has plumbed the origins of conscience. In *The Moral Animal*, Robert Wright describes the evolutionary purpose of conscience in terms of the adaptability it provides.[101] In the case of those with whom we share genes (our kin), conscience provides guidance on our choice of actions. "The transmission of moral instruction from old to young parallels the transmission of genetic instruction and is sometimes indistinguishable in its effects."[102] Wright goes on, "The aim of conscience, in dealings with nonkin, is to cultivate a reputation for generosity and decency, whatever the reality."[103]

Conscience and Ethics

Psychologists who study socialization explain how we come to have the ethical norms we do, but that explanation cannot justify the norms themselves as the contents of our conscience. Describing ethical phenomena in psychological terms is a slippery business because it presupposes an ethical bias. In his psychological research on moral influences on behavior, Lawrence Kohlberg offered a descriptive evaluation of the sources of conscience.[104] His work resulted in the development of a view of moral conduct in which individuals are seen as operating at one of six distinct stages.

In Kohlberg's hierarchy of stages of moral development, any given person may never develop his or her moral reasoning beyond one of the lower stages; and very few people reach the sixth stage. The six stages are as follows:

1. Punishment. A punishment and obedience orientation in which the goal is to avoid punishment and to display deference for superior power.
2. Reward. An orientation involving conduct engaged in to obtain rewards to satisfy the self's egoistic needs.

In these first two stages, values informing the conscience are found in external occurrences, in bad consequences, or in positive rewards rather than in persons or standards.

3. Approval. In the "good/bad person" orientation, the motivation is to gain approval and please others and avoid disapproval.
4. Duty. This orientation maintains the social order and involves a motivation to fulfill one's duty and show respect for authority.

In the third and fourth stages, moral values arise in performing approved roles, in maintaining the conventional order and in fulfilling the expectations of others.

5. Contractual. In the social-contract orientation an individual's goal is to follow society-maintaining principles involving respect of others.
6. Ethical autonomy. The final stage—"principles of choice involving appeal to logical universality and consistency"—requires "orientation to conscience as a directing agent to mutual respect and trust."[105]

In the last two stages, moral value resides in the self's conformity to shared or internally generated standards and internally acknowledged rights or duties.

Psychologist B. F. Skinner, in *Beyond Freedom and Dignity,* claimed: "Man has not evolved as an ethical or moral animal. He has evolved to the point at which he has constructed an ethical or moral culture."[106] The meaning of *ethical* or *moral* used to describe behavior in the social sciences is descriptive rather than prescriptive. Ethical conduct is thus a certain kind of behavior that has been molded by a social environment. It is behavior that shows outward signs of "taking account" of the behavior and responses of others. "The more the individual is responsible for the decision of the group, and for his own actions in their consequences for the group," according to Kohlberg, "the more must he take the roles of others in it."[107] Ethical behavior in this sense can be contrasted with the "selfish" behavior of an infant, who has not yet learned to adjust her actions to the needs or rights of others. In the tradition of ethical thought extending back to Socrates, it is only the last three stages of Kohlberg's scheme (4, 5, 6) that would be recognized by moral philosophers as falling within the realm of ethical reasoning, and for some only number 6 would be.

Some taxpayers view the rules "only from the external point of view as a sign of possible punishment,"[108] fearing the IRS, and fines and imprisonment—Kohlberg's first stage—and this forms the basis for their level of tax compliance. Other taxpayers may operate on one of the other five levels. The progression from the first stage to the sixth stage is a gradual change in focus from what is external to the individual (and to which the individual reacts), to standards and principles internal to and generated by the individual (over which the individual has control). Writing on our ethical maturation, Kohlberg maintains that, "the development of moral capacities . . . involves an orientation to internal norms."[109] If he is correct about these stages, it is also the case that some taxpayers will be "stuck" at each level and never progress to a higher stage of ethical response. Each level represents a different way that the conscience operates and is therefore capable of being appealed to by different means. Though different taxpayers may relate to paying taxes from any one of the six stages, the Code itself encourages compliance only on the first level—punishment—the lowest stage.

The Code and Conscience

Even if we agreed that the Congress should do more to align the Code with moral incentives, the issue of influencing the conscience is a different matter. Simply moralizing or preaching or appealing to our patriotism or loyalty or sense of duty can have little lasting effect. As Torgler informs us, "Moral suasion has hardly any effect on taxpayer's compliance behavior. Those in the [experiment's] treatment group did not significantly change their payment timeliness more than did those in the control group."[110]

Speed bumps don't slow every driver, but this does not mean they serve no purpose. Aronfreed, in *Conduct and Conscience,* notes: "Just as internal control of conduct does not presuppose conscience, it is conversely true that conscience does not insure internalized control of conduct."[111] To bypass the chance to influence tax compliance positively, however, by framing the Code's rules in a form more likely to bring conscience into play, is certainly to forego an opportunity for increasing compliance and for reducing resentment of the tax system and thereby reduce tax cheating. B. F. Skinner argued, "We cannot use good sense in human affairs unless someone engages in the design and construction of environmental conditions which affect the behavior of men."[112] This includes ethical behavior generally and tax compliance in particular. Skinner continues, "We are all controlled by the world in which we live, and part of that world has been and will be constructed by men. The question is this: Are we to be controlled by accident, by tyrants, or by ourselves in effective cultural designs?"[113] Redesigning the Tax Code with this in mind would be a positive step, thereby infusing tax cheating with a moral valence and shrouding tax cheaters with a moral stigma.

Although reworking the Code, making it more "conscience-friendly," is not proposed as the final solution to tax cheating's current lack of moral import, the suggested revision—creating transparency in the Code, thereby allowing us to judge its relative fairness in allocating our portion—may edge us closer to acknowledging tax cheating as a moral wrong. As John Carroll writes, "It is not desirable for a tax system to make criminals out of so many people that it has to continually monitor, frighten, and punish them. It would be better if people saw the value of paying their taxes, and that taxpaying behavior was simple and clear."[114]

"Conscience," one writer tells us, "relies on the moral quality of the groups to which we belong. We gain our moral bearings from the communities we're born into and deliberately choose, beginning with family and extending to peers, other adults, religious and professional communities. We carry their voices, for better and for worse."[115] Reducing tax cheating requires designing a Tax Code that provides an additional voice; this means a Code's guidance must be capable of instilling a certain emotional charge in beliefs about neglecting the rules—that is, of triggering moral feelings in people when they are faced with certain choices.

Ends and Means

Taxation is necessary to allow government to protect our lives, rights, and property. Taxes are *not* a necessary evil; they are simply the means to a valued end. Though we commonly speak of ends and means in isolation, John Dewey warned that "ends are appraised in the same evaluations in which things as means are weighed.... For what is deliberation except weighing various alternative desires (and hence end-values) in terms of the conditions that are the means of their execution, and which, as means, determine the consequences actually arrived at?"[116] As a result, Dewey argues, the

> arbitrary selection of some one part of the attained consequences as *the* end and hence as the warrant of means used (no matter how objectionable are their *other* consequences) is the result of holding that *it*, as *the* end, is an end-in-itself. . . . [This procedure] discloses in a striking manner the fallacy involved in the position that ends have value independent of appraisal of means involved and independent of their own further causal efficacy.[117]

This insight brings out a central problem with current tax policy. We view and evaluate the ends for which taxation is used as cut off from the means by which taxes are raised. We do not ask, for example, how money should be raised for the military as opposed to how it should be raised for education. With some exceptions such as Social Security the budget is based on the assumption that raising revenue is a separate issue from how the money is spent. The notion that taxation is an evil is thus fueled by its isolation as *only* a means to undetermined ends with which we often disagree. A system integrating the means of taxation with the ends for which tax revenues are employed would offer the basis for a moral duty to pay taxes. One such option was described briefly in chapter 5: allowing taxpayers the opportunity on their tax returns to designate the uses of at least part of their personal tax burden. Ayn Rand suggested that where feasible taxes be raised voluntarily like user fees. Under such a system, for example, a tax would be charged on the value of contracts—including those for sales, financing transactions, leases, and insurance—that would pay for the court system that adjudicates any resulting disputes.[118] Allowing taxpayer participation is the key; and this key works best in a transparent system where each of us can see how our share was determined and know that other taxpayers are subject to the same rules. In the words of H. L. A. Hart, quoted in chapter 5, this "consists in no more than taking seriously the notion that what is to be applied to a multiplicity of different persons is the same general rule, undeflected by prejudice, interest, or caprice."[119]

Conscientious Objectors

George Bernard Shaw proclaimed: "All men are anarchists with regard to laws which are against their consciences."[120] For some taxpayers our tax system requires a violation of conscience. At a hearing before the House Ways and Means Committee in 1993, a number of conscientious objectors were allowed to testify. One tax objector stated, "As a member of the Mennonite Church, which has emphasized a peace witness for more than 450 years, I am a conscientious objector to war. . . . This not only forbids participation in war, it also raises ethical questions about my payment through taxes for weapons of war. . . . I am glad to pay taxes for services which help needy people and which establish a more just society. However, my conscience is deeply violated when I am required to pay taxes for the support of a military machine and military actions which are contrary to my faith in Jesus Christ."[121]

The courts have struggled with what authority to accord to individual conscience. In *U.S. v. Macintosh* a Canadian was denied U.S. citizenship by the Supreme Court because he stated he could bear arms only in a war he believed morally justified.[122] The court reversed its opinion in 1946 in *Girouard v. U.S.*, awarding another Canadian, a Seventh Day Adventist, U.S. citizenship although he declared he was prohibited by his religion from bearing arms but was willing to work for the war effort in a noncombatant role.[123] The court backed its reversal of the earlier decision citing Justice Holmes's 1929 dissenting opinion in *Schwimmer*.[124] The court wrote, "The victory for freedom of thought recorded in our Bill of Rights recognizes that in the domain of conscience there is a moral power higher than the State."[125]

"When the conscientious objector violates the law," Hugo Bedau explains, "he or she does so primarily in order to avoid conduct condemned by personal conscience even though required by public law."[126] This perspective allows us to distinguish conscientious objection from civil disobedience, though the first is a precondition for the second. The aim of conscientious objection is individual or personal while civil disobedience is public, often seeking support from others to bring about a law change.

The actions of conscientious objection may be minor or token or may reach a level leading to civil disobedience. Conscientious objection related to taxes generally involves opposition to war and taxes used to finance war. In *Muste v. Commissioner*, A. J. Muste, a Presbyterian minister who was also a member of the Society of Friends (Quakers) protested the expenditure of 60 percent of his tax dollars on war.[127] Muste was a pacifist and for thirty years a member of the Fellowship of Reconciliation, an organization opposed to war. Until filing with the U.S. Tax Court, his conscientious objection to taxes had been a personal matter. His situation came to the attention of the IRS when he stopped filing tax returns and instead sent the IRS letters of explanation. In one of these letters he wrote, "I have come as the result of long reflection and prayer to the conviction that I at least am in conscience bound, in the present period . . . to challenge the right of the government to tax me for waging war." Unlike many of the tax protestor cases discussed in chapter 2, where the court was less than sympathetic and often dismissive of the protestor's claim, the Tax Court in *Muste* offered a patient and thorough discussion of the facts and law. In its opinion the court stated, "The power to tax is the one great power upon which the whole national fabric is based. It is necessary to the existence and prosperity of a nation as is the air he breathes to the natural man. It is not only the power to destroy, but it is also the power to keep alive." In specific response to Muste's appeal to his constitutional rights, the court asserted, "The Constitution does not relieve a pacifist or a conscientious objector of the duty to pay taxes, even though they may be used for war or preparation for defense."

A monograph published by the War Resistors League describes methods of conscientious objection and protest against the portion of the income tax applicable to war and related defense activities.[128] But taxpayers believing that their tax dollars are being allocated in specific ways raises the question of the fungibility of money. The assumption of those who object to their taxes being used for war is that if X percent of the national budget goes to financing war, for example, this means X percent of *their* tax dollars do so as well.[129] The War Resistors League accepts this assumption and argues, "The taxes you pay to the government cannot be earmarked for the constructive functions of the government,"[130] though I have suggested earlier that they could be so earmarked by the taxpayer, if so permitted, on his or her tax return.

George Bernard Shaw addressed the question of monetary fungibility in his play *Major Barbara,* but from the another direction. In Shaw's play the question raised is whether a charity, the Salvation Army, may refuse donations from sources opposed to the charity's mission, in particular donations from a whisky distiller and a munitions manufacturer.[131] As Shaw argues, "refusing to accept money from anybody except sweet old ladies with independent incomes and gentle and lovely ways of life" will not do—because this income also may be traced ultimately to what he calls its "industrial source," including "poisonous canned meat and all the rest of it."[132] "The notion," Shaw concludes, "that you can earmark certain coins as tainted is an unpractical individualist superstition."[133]

If this is true for the sources of charitable donations, the same principle should apply to tax revenue. Believing a given taxpayer's money may be traced to a particular use, such as war, is equally superstitious as believing it can be traced it to its original source—as Republican money or Democratic or anti-abortion or pro-union or otherwise designating its moral or political origin. A politician refusing to allocate tax revenues he claimed had come from anti-abortion taxpayers, for example, to fund a family planning agency (advocating abortion as a legitimate planning option) illustrates Shaw's point. My actual tax dollars may as readily go to pay a groundskeeper who mows the White House lawn as to pay a nurse employed in a veterans hospital in Albuquerque.

In a manual on *War Tax Resistance,* the authors present a series of possible actions aimed at frustrating tax collection.[134] All are illegal, but some are relatively minor, such as an employee's claiming enough exemptions to ensure that less than the required amount of tax is withheld. When the tax filing deadline arrives, the tax objector may file a return still withholding the portion of the tax he believes is allocated to making war. Though penalties and interest will accrue, the taxpayer can drag out the collection process as long as practicable. As the manual points out, the statute of limitations on collecting income taxes is ten years,[135] so protracting the collection process for that long will constitute a victory for the war tax resistor. Even if the amount due must eventually be paid to the IRS, the resistor's conscience is clear and he or she can then say, "At least I didn't give up without a good fight."

Many of the strategies described in the manual involve appeals to constitutional arguments and are indistinguishable—except for their motivation—from tax protestor arguments described in chapter 2. The First Amendment argument relying on religious freedom, however, is unique to conscientious objectors. As described in chapter 2, constitutional tax protestor arguments often attempt to show that the income tax system itself is unconstitutional. On the other hand, some pacifists argue not that the income tax is unconstitutional but that the First Amendment protects their right not to pay taxes for war, since the First Amendment prohibits the government from denying the free exercise of religion. The courts have uniformly rejected this claim. In a 1990 case the Supreme Court declared, "The free exercise of religion means, first and foremost, the right to believe and profess whatever religious doctrine one desires. Thus, the First Amendment obviously excludes 'all governmental regulation of religious beliefs as such.'"[136] According to the court, "The tax system could not function if denominations were allowed to challenge the tax system because tax payments were spent in a manner that violates their religious belief."[137] Rejecting the taxpayer's argument, the court concluded, "If prohibiting the exercise of religion is not the object of the tax but merely the incidental effect of a generally applicable and otherwise valid provision, the First Amendment has not been offended."

Justice William O. Douglas, in a concurring opinion in the Supreme Court's *Sherbert v. Verner*, explained, "The fact that government cannot exact from me a surrender of one iota of my religious scruples does not, of course, mean that I can demand of government a sum of money, the better to exercise them. For the Free Exercise Clause is written in terms of what the government cannot do to the individual, not in terms of what the individual can exact from the government."[138] Thus, the payment of taxes and their ultimate use are issues beyond the grasp of the First Amendment's protection of religious freedom.

Civil Disobedience

Because garden-variety tax cheating is done covertly, it is not civil disobedience. In a text on business ethics written almost a century ago, the author asserts, "The courage to oppose unjust laws is obviously not legal; it is of course illegal but it also transcends legality. When the individual takes this position, he is exercising the highest right he has as a moral personality. His sincerity is tested by the amount of punishment or sacrifice he is willing to face in pursuing what he regards as right."[139] In the case of tax protestors or conscientious objectors the punishment ranges from a $5,000 frivolous-tax-return penalty to time in prison.[140]

A discussion of civil disobedience may bring to mind such figures as Socrates, Thoreau, Gandhi, Martin Luther King Jr., and Jack Kevorkian. Defining civil disobedience is itself a moral endeavor since, like many moral questions, the framing of the definition presupposes a particular moral stance. Civil disobedience, at a minimum, involves disobeying a given law voluntarily because the law is believed unjust, in full acceptance of the sanctions to follow.[141] Furthermore, disobeying a law because it does not personally benefit us is not civil disobedience, nor is disobeying the law to take advantage of those who do obey it (free-riding). Civil disobedience is not merely defiance, rebelliousness, or obstinacy. "By looking exclusively at the act of disobedience," Konvitz asserts, "one sees only half of the event. The punishment is the other half, which is just as essential to the person as the act of disobedience; for even as he breaks the law, he means at the same time to restore its wholeness."[142]

According to Bedau, the purpose of civil disobedience "is to frustrate and then change the law itself, by making an appeal to conscience, the conscience of the authorities, especially the conscience of the majority of the public—the conscience, in short, of whoever it is that issues, enforces, and supports the law as an exercise in public moral education, as a tactic to achieve law reform."[143] The initiator of such change is what sociologist Howard Becker calls a moral entrepreneur.[144] Moral entrepreneurs are crusaders for a formerly unacknowledged moral cause who attempt to redefine a social condition by drawing attention to an unrecognized problem. According to Becker, "Even though a practice may be harmful in an objective sense to the group in which it occurs, the harm needs to be discovered and pointed out. People must be made to feel that something ought to be done about it."[145] Sociologist Stephen Pfohl points out that this is how child abuse became a recognized problem. "Despite documentary evidence of child beating throughout the ages, the 'discovery' of child abuse as deviance and its subsequent criminalization are recent phenomena. In a four-year period beginning in 1962, the legislatures of all fifty states passed statutes against the caretaker's abuse of children."[146]

Like entrepreneurs in business, who, according to economist Joseph Schumpeter, reform or revolutionize the pattern of production by "exploiting . . . an untried technological possibility for producing a new commodity or producing an old one in a new way,"[147] a moral entrepreneur probes and expands the moral frontier in recognizing an overlooked moral problem. As Becker notes, the change in moral beliefs and consequently the consciences of individuals, is the result of a "moral enterprise."[148] Tax cheating is objectively harmful "to the group in which it occurs"—to the United States, to honest taxpayers, to respect for the law, and to the financing of government programs—but this problem is awaiting someone to make people feel that "something ought to be done about it."

John Rawls offers a definition of civil disobedience that is specifically aimed at a democracy and in particular "a nearly just society, one that is well-ordered for the most part but in which some serious violations of justice nevertheless do occur."[149] Rawls's definition comprehends civil disobedience as "a public, nonviolent, conscientious yet political act contrary to law usually done with the aim of bringing about a change in the law or policies of the government. By acting in this way one addresses the sense of justice of the majority of the community and declares that in one's considered opinion the principles of social cooperation among free and equal men are not being respected."[150]

Tax cheating itself is rarely a public activity, though it could be undertaken in a way that includes the characteristics listed by Rawls. Thus, tax cheating could be performed as an act of civil disobedience, with a public display of signing and filing a tax return containing an illegal deduction or omitting taxable income and awaiting the sanctions. Some tax protestors may fall into this category, though public sympathy has yet to attach to these acts.

Part of the reason for this public response may be a condition imposed by Gandhi, an icon of civil disobedience, requiring the critic of a law to have established a track record of legal compliance before seeking change. In Gandhi's view, the laws of society should always be obeyed by a person "intelligently and of his own free will, because he considers it to be his sacred duty to do so. It is only when a person has thus obeyed the laws of society scrupulously that he is in a position to judge as to which particular rules are good and just and which unjust and iniquitous. Only then does the right accrue to him of the civil disobedience of certain laws in well-defined circumstances."[151] A scofflaw who adds tax cheating to his roster of misdeeds is thus not engaged in civil disobedience.[152]

Thoreau emphasized a different aspect of civil disobedience: "Those who, while they disapprove of the character and measures of a government, yield to it their allegiance and support are undoubtedly its most conscientious supporters, and so frequently the most serious obstacles to reform."[153] From this point of view, tax cheating, if done to bring pressure on the government to reform a broken system, becomes not only permissible but morally obligatory. While many contemporary opponents of our tax system may agree with Thoreau in principle, and attend polite media-sponsored protest rallies, it is unlikely that many of these same "activists" could summons the courage to face Thoreau's challenge—"When I meet a government which says to me, 'Your money or your life,' why should I be in haste to give it my money?"[154]

For many tax objectors, the difference between immorality and inconvenience has been obscured, and simply hiding the money—whether in the underground economy or in tax haven bank accounts—seems an easier solution. While some tax cheating may also be civil disobedience, most is not, as its goal is not a public display of defiance and acceptance of the legal consequences, but a secretive attempt to slip something past the IRS for personal gain.

Though I have no crystal ball, it is possible that discontent with the present Tax Code will eventually lead to widespread tax protesting and civil disobedience. Although more limited in scope, the Prohibition era in American history may be instructive. In an article on flouting the law, Nadler writes, "Toward the end of the prohibition era, prominent leaders worried that such widespread lawlessness had weakened respect for the law generally, leading to widespread diminished compliance with laws unrelated to prohibition."[155] If tax cheating spreads through any kind of organized movement, the direct loss of revenue may seem but a shadow compared to the indirect effects caused by a loss of respect for the law generally and for our political leaders in particular.

In this book I have tried to show what tax cheating entails, why it is a problem, who is affected by the problem, and where the sources of the problem lie. While it was not my aim to name a specific solution, I have posed ingredients of such a solution along the way. Eliminating (or minimizing) self-assessment is one approach, though much income is difficult to assess in any other way. Reducing complexity by reducing reliance on tax expenditures (shadow subsidies) and refocusing the tax on its original mission of raising revenue—while making some attempt to associate the sources and uses of revenue—would be a start. Enforceability and transparency are critical conditions for any tax system asking taxpayers to pay their fair share. In *Why People Obey the Law*, Tyler reports that "[l]egal authorities must restrict the activities of those over whom they exercise power, but at the same time their effectiveness depends ultimately on their ability to secure voluntary public compliance with their directives."[156] In a work on the psychology of tax, Lewis tells us: "Changes in attitudes towards taxation may be reflections of a more gradual and important change in moral values. If this is so, attempts to understand attitudes without recourse to underlying values or ideological belief systems may be doomed."[157] While exploring the problem of tax cheating I have attempted to clear some of the rubble standing in the way of honest dialog on tax reform. By disabusing taxpayers of any moral obligation to pay taxes under the current system, I hope to have helped the cause of a rational debate in the marketplace of ideas and perhaps sparked the interest of a moral entrepreneur.

AFTERWORD

In January 2012, the IRS released an updated estimate of the tax gap as of 2006 showing a 30 percent increase from its previous report. The tax gap is the amount of taxes the IRS estimates go missing each year because of underreported income, nonfiling, or underpayment of taxes. The previous estimate—referred to in this book—was $345 billion annually and was for 2001. For 2006, the IRS increased its annual estimate to $450 billion. In its explanation of the new figures, the IRS reports: "The growth in the tax gap over the five years was concentrated in the under-reporting and underpayment forms of noncompliance, which jointly account for more than nine out of ten tax gap dollars. The nonfiling portion of the gap hardly changed. The underreporting gap grew by 32%; the underpayment gap grew by 38%; and the nonfiling gap grew by 4%. The overall gap grew by 30%, slightly more than the growth in overall tax liabilities."

The tax gap is an index of the amount of tax cheating by those in the system, and its calculation ignores illegal income and other undocu-mented income sources. If the tax gap continues to grow by 30 percent every five years, for 2011 it would stand at $585 billion. In 2011, Congress set a goal of saving $1 trillion over ten years, through budget cuts and possibly tax increases (though effected through reductions in deductions or other tax expenditures). As their efforts continue, over half this amount is slipping through their fingers each year as a result of cheating a flawed tax system.

In this book I have tried to show what tax cheating entails, why it is a problem, who is affected by the problem, and where the sources of the problem lie. I have laid out the causes of the tax gap and the reasons to believe it will continue to grow. Primary among these reasons are the voluntary (self-assessment) model of taxation and decreasing respect for the Tax Code and its authors—resulting from its complexity and the factors producing this complexity. The system's lack of transparency makes it impossible for taxpayers to know whether they are paying their fair share, or their share and part of someone else's. What was supposed to be a system voluntary in name only is apparently being transformed into a system voluntary in practice, at least for some with income sources not subject to reporting and tax withholding and for those fortunate enough to benefit from special provisions enacted with their welfare in mind. In a 2011 article in the *New York Times*, billionaire Warren Buffet said of these tax breaks, "These and other blessings are showered upon us by legislators in Washington who feel compelled to protect us, much as if we were spotted owls or some other endangered species." The factors causing the tax gap, tax complexity, lack of transparency, self-assessment, tax cheating, and a loss of respect for the law and its moral standing are all under congressional control; because of this concentration of control, slowing the pace of tax cheating will entail not only tax reform, but campaign-finance reform and term limit restrictions, as these issues are all interrelated.

NOTES

Chapter One. Tax Cheating—The Problem

1. Oliver Wendell Holmes Jr., *The Common Law* (Mineola, NY: Dover, 1991), 50. Richard Posner calls Holmes "the leading figure in American jurisprudence." Richard A. Posner, *Problems of Jurisprudence* (Cambridge: Harvard University Press, 1990), 19.

2. Posner, *Problems of Jurisprudence,* 334. For background on this issue see the author's, "Establishing Basis for Gambling Losses," *The Tax Advisor* (June 2007).

3. U.S. Department of Justice Press Release, Erik C. Peterson United States Attorney Western District of Wisconsin, May 22, 2009. "Jerome M. Koosman, 66, of Osceola, Wis., pleaded guilty today in U.S. District Court in Madison to a charge that he failed to file his 2002 federal tax return.... Koosman faces a maximum penalty of one year in prison and a $25,000 fine.... Koosman was required to file federal tax returns for 2002, 2003, and 2004, and he willfully failed to file those returns. Koosman, [is] a retired major league baseball player who played in the major leagues from 1967 through 1985 for the New York Mets, Minnesota Twins, Chicago White Sox, and Philadelphia Phillies."

4. U.S. Department of Justice press release, September 22, 2009. "Orlando, Florida—United States Attorney A. Brian Albritton announces that Jimmie L. Thorpe, a/k/a Jim Thorpe (age 60, of Heathrow, Florida) today pleaded guilty to two counts of failing to pay income taxes. Thorpe faces a maximum penalty of two years in federal prison and a $4,125,152.54 fine.... According to the plea agreement, Thorpe was a professional golfer on the Professional Golf Association (PGA) Champions Tour.... In 2002, 2003, and 2004, Thorpe received gross income of approximately $1,610,460.01, $1,916,209.13, and $1,838,485.31, respectively, on which he owed, but did not pay, income taxes in the amount of $659,286.74, $717,384.18, and $685,905.35, respectively."

5. In 1990 Willie Nelson reportedly owed the IRS $23 million. At least part of this amount was the result of disallowed losses arising from tax shelters Nelson claimed his former accountants at Price Waterhouse had recommended. In negotiations with the Internal Revenue Service on how Nelson's tax bill would be paid it was decided that Nelson would release a new CD, *The IRS Tapes: Who'll Buy My Memories.* According to the agreement, part of the proceeds

from the CD's sales would be allocated to paying Nelson's past due taxes. *New York Times,* Sept. 2, 1991.

6. U.S. Department of Justice press releases, May 7, 2009, and May 30, 2007.

7. U.S. House of Rep., Committee on Ways and Means, Statement of the Internal Revenue Service on *Tax Proposals Related to Legislation to Legalize Internet Gambling,* May 19, 2010, Appendix.

8. U.S. Department of Justice press release, April 13, 2009, "Justice Department Highlights FY 2008 Tax Enforcement Results" WWW.USDOJ.GOV. Petition filed in U.S. District Court, Southern District of Florida.

9. Ibid.

10. IRS Information Release 2011-14. "The Internal Revenue Service announced today a special voluntary disclosure initiative designed to bring offshore money back into the U.S. tax system and help people with undisclosed income from hidden offshore accounts get current with their taxes. The new voluntary disclosure initiative will be available through Aug. 31, 2011." The program assesses a 25 percent penalty and requires filing of eight years of tax returns.

11. Frank A. Cowell, *Cheating the Government: The Economics of Evasion* (Cambridge: The MIT Press, 1990), 195.

12. Aristotle, *Politics,* trans. Benjamin Jowitt, 5:8.

13. IRS, "Reducing the Federal Tax Gap: A Report on Improving Voluntary Compliance," August 2, 2007.

14. IRS News Release 84-123 (Nov. 30, 1984).

15. Harvey S. Rosen, *Public Finance,* 7th ed. (Boston: McGraw-Hill Irwin, 2005), 349.

16. Internal Revenue Code § 6015(b)(1)(B) "Relief from joint and several liability on joint return" and Internal Revenue Service Reg. § 1.6015-1(h)(4). According to IRS Regulations, "An erroneous item is any item resulting in an understatement or deficiency in tax to the extent that such item is omitted from, or improperly reported (including improperly characterized) on an individual income tax return."

17. To anticipate one objection from the outset, I am using the terms *moral* and *ethical* as interchangeable. As a result there may be readers who believe I have used *moral* when I should have used *ethical* or vice versa. My reason for not distinguishing between ethical and moral is in part because common usage does not clearly distinguish between them and also because, as Sidgwick noted, "the term 'moral' is commonly used as synonymous with 'ethical' (moralis being the Latin translation of [the Greek term] ethikos)." Henry Sidgwick, *Outlines of the History of Ethics* (Indianapolis: Hackett, 1988), 11.

18. Readers interested international perspectives on the ethics of tax evasion are directed to Robert W. McGee, ed., *The Ethics of Tax Evasion* (South Orange, NJ: The Dumont Institute of Public Policy Research, 1998), and Robert W. McGee, "Three Views on the Ethics of Tax Evasion," *Journal of Business Ethics* 67 (2006): 15–35.

19. There are many discussions of the legitimacy of government and of what obligations citizens owe to their government. For example, see Ruth C. A. Higgins, *The Moral Limits of Law: Obedience, Respect, and Legitimacy* (Oxford: Oxford University Press, 2004).

20. Cowell, *Cheating the Government,* 24.

21. Rosen, *Public Finance,* 349.

22. Comm v. Newman, 159 F2d 848 (2d Cir 1947).

23. See Gunn, who argues that employing a motives test for some tax avoidance and not for others is a problem. In particular he argues that "the question of whether particular conduct was tax-motivated should be irrelevant to the decision whether that conduct should be taxed in a certain way." Alan Gunn, "Tax Avoidance," *Michigan Law Review* 76 (1978): 733.

24. The Supreme Court set out three tests to determine when tax avoidance becomes an issue of tax cheating in *Frank Lyon Co. v. US*, 435 US 561 (1978). The *Patient Protection and Affordable Care Act* of *2010* codified the concept of economic substance in Internal Revenue Code § 7701(o). To have economic substance a transaction must change the taxpayer's economic position in a meaningful way (apart from federal income tax) and the taxpayer must have a substantial purpose (aside from the federal income tax) for entering into the transaction. References to the Code throughout are to the Internal Revenue Code of 1986 as amended (hereinafter abbreviated IRC) unless indicated otherwise. References within the Internal Revenue Code are to section numbers (hereinafter abbreviated §).

25. J. W. von Goethe, *Faust*, trans. Barker Fairley, in *Selected Works* (New York: Random House, 2000), 882.

26. Rosen, *Public Finance*, 349.

27. John Dewey, *The Quest for Certainty* (New York: G. P. Putnam's Sons, [1929] 1960), 7.

28. John Dewey, *Logic: The Theory of Inquiry* (New York: Holt, Rinehart and Winston, 1938), 107.

29. Edward M. Schur, *Our Criminal Society: The Social and Legal Sources of Crime in America* (Englewood Cliffs, NJ: Prentice-Hall, 1969), 164.

30. Benno Torgler, *Tax Compliance and Tax Morale* (Northampton, MA: Edward Elgar, 2007), 104.

31. Denis M. Hanno and George R. Violette, "An Analysis of Moral and Social Influences on Taxpayer Behavior," *Behavioral Research in Accounting*, vol. 8, supp. (1996).

32. Philip M. Reckers, Debra L. Sanders, and Stephen J. Roark, "The Influence of Ethical Attitudes on Taxpayer Compliance," *National Tax Journal* 47, no. 4 (Dec. 1994).

33. Tom R. Tyler, *Why People Obey the Law* (Princeton: Princeton University Press, 2006), 45.

34. John L. Mackie, *Ethics: Inventing Right and Wrong* (New York: Penguin Books, 1977), 210.

35. Richard D. Schwartz and Sonya Orleans, "On Legal Sanctions," *University of Chicago Law Review* (1967): 274.

36. Adam Smith, *The Theory of Moral Sentiments* (Indianapolis: Liberty Fund reprint of Oxford University Press edition [1759] 1976), 134.

37. Tyler, *Why People Obey the Law*, 64–65.

38. Henry David Thoreau, *Civil Disobedience* (New York: Quill Pen, 2008), 8.

39. IRS Fact Sheet 2002-07 (2002).

40. John Stuart Mill, *Principles of Political Economy*, abridged by J. Laurence Laughlin (New York: Appleton and Company, 1884), 539.

41. R. E. Hall and A. Rabushka, *The Flat Tax*, 2d ed. (Stanford, CA: Hoover Institution Press, 1995), 57.

42. For an overview of the meaning of distributive justice, including five common alternatives (equality, need, merit and achievement, contribution or "due return," and effort), see Joel Feinberg, *Social Philosophy* (Englewood Cliffs, NJ: Prentice-Hall, 1973), 107–17. According to Feinberg, distributive justice "is reserved for economic distributions, particularly the justice of differences in economic income between classes, and of various schemes of taxation which discriminate in different ways between classes" (107).

43. Rome I, Ltd. v. Comm, 96 TC 697, 704 (1991).

44. Richard Robinson, *Definition* (Oxford: Oxford University Press, 1954), 19. "By 'lexical definition' I mean reporting the customary or dictionary meaning of a word."

45. *Black's Law Dictionary*, abridged 6th ed. (St. Paul: West, 1991).

46. R. M. Hare, *Moral Thinking: Its Levels, Method, and Point* (Oxford: Clarendon Press, 1981), 4. Aware of Hare's claim, Mackie adds the following restriction. "No substantive moral conclusions or serious constraints on moral views can be derived from either the meanings of moral terms or the logic of moral discourse." Mackie, *Ethics*, 105.

47. Stuart P. Green, *Lying, Cheating, and Stealing: A Moral Theory of White-Collar Crime* (Oxford: Oxford University Press, 2006), 57.

48. Robert A. Kagan, "On the Visibility of Income Tax Law Violations," in *Tax Compliance vol. 2: Social Science Perspectives*, ed. Jeffrey A. Roth and John T. Scholz (Philadelphia: University of Pennsylvania Press, 1989), 103.

49. Towne v. Eisner, 245 US 418, 425 (1918).

50. Robinson, *Definition*, 19.

51. Howard Becker, *Outsiders: Studies in the Sociology of Deviance* (New York: The Free Press, 1963), 204.

52. Ibid., 204–205.

53. Ibid., 205.

54. For a discussion of a number of issues related to this topic see Eric A Posner, "Law and Social Norms: The Case of Tax Compliance" *Virginia Law Review* 86 (2000): 1781. Posner has suggested that lessening the privacy restrictions on tax scofflaws might result in increased tax compliance, as tax cheaters face public scrutiny. Scott and Grasmick found that social stigma can be an important deterrent to tax cheating when motivation to cheat is high. Wilbur J. Scott and Harold G. Grasmick, "Deterrence and Income Tax Cheating: Testing Interaction Hypotheses in Utilitarian Theories," *The Journal of Applied Behavioral Science* (1981): 395–408.

55. The Dru Sjodin National Sex Offender Public Website (NSOPW), coordinated by the U.S. Department of Justice, is a cooperative effort between jurisdictions hosting public sex offender registries and the federal government (http://www.nsopw.gov).

56. IRS News Release 84-55 (April 13, 1984).

57. Bret H. Leiker,"The Ethics of Tax Evasion as Analyzed through the Philosophy of Jean-Jacques Rousseau," *Journal of Accounting, Ethics & Public Policy* 1 no. 1 (1998), reprinted in McGee, *The Ethics of Tax Evasion*, 90.

58. Roper Starch poll, Sept. 8, 1999. Only 8 percent of the respondents believed that some tax cheating "here and there" was all right while 3 percent indicated that "as much [cheating] as possible" was permissible. The same survey indicated that a majority of respondents believe that "if someone cheats on his or her

taxes in a 'minor' way, such as not reporting a small amount of income" that someone should be punished. *Wall Street Journal*, Sept. 22, 1999.

59. See Charles R. Tittle, *Sanctions and Social Deviance: The Question of Deterrence* (New York: Praeger, 1980), 48–49. Based on various demographics the disapproval rates were between 79 and 97 percent.

60. Young v. Comm, 783 F2d 1201, 1204 (5th Cir 1986).

61. Dante Alighieri, *The Divine Comedy*, trans. Mark Musa (New York: Penguin Books, 1984), vol. I, *Inferno*, canto 11.

62. H. L. A. Hart, *The Concept of Law* (London: Oxford University Press, 1961), 88.

63. Tyler, *Why People Obey the Law*, 46. "Just as respondents almost universally feel that breaking the law is immoral, they feel a strong obligation to obey the law: both personal morality and the legitimacy of legal authorities encourage citizens to be law-abiding."

64. Michael R. Gottfredson and Travis Hirschi, *A General Theory of Crime* (Stanford: Stanford University Press, 1990), 16–17. According to the IRS the average age of high-income nonfilers is forty-nine. U.S. House of Representatives, Committee on Ways and Means, Subcommittee on Oversight hearing, *Taxpayers Who Fail to File Federal Income Tax Returns*, Statement of Margaret Milner Richardson, Commissioner of Internal Revenue, 103rd Cong., 1st sess., Oct. 26, 1993. Porcano found that more tax evaders were single than married but that neither age nor sex was not a significant factor. Thomas M. Porcano, "Correlates of Tax Evasion," *Journal of Economic Psychology* 9 (1988): 47–67.

65. Jeremy Bentham, *Of Laws in General* (London: The Athlone Press, 1970), 215.

66. IRC § 6663.

67. IRC § 7201.

68. IRS "Program and Emphasis Areas for IRS Criminal Investigation" http://www.irs.gov/compliance/enforcement/.

69. IRC § 7201.

70. IRC § 7203.

71. IRC § 7206.

72. IRC § 7206.

73. A recent audit by the Treasury Inspector General for Tax Administration indicated that 48,887 prison inmates with no wages had successfully obtained tax refunds from the IRS through March 24, 2010. See "Expanded Access to Wage and Withholding Can Improve Identification of Fraudulent Tax Returns," Sept. 30, 2010, Reference Number: 2010-40-129. Also, IRC § 6103(k)(10). Commenting on tax return fraud by prison inmates, former IRS Commissioner Everson indicated that a new Electronic Fraud Detection System (EFDS) has been designed to screen returns for potential fraudulent refunds. U.S. House of Representatives, Subcommittee on Oversight of the Committee on Ways and Means, *Hearing on Internal Revenue Service Operations and the Tax Gap*, 110th Cong., 1st sess., March 20, 2007.

74. See, for example, the author's, "501(c)(3) Money Laundering Deterrents Off Target," *The International Journal of Not-for-Profit Law* 10, no. 4 (2008).

75. *Pomponio*, 429 U.S. 10 (1976).

76. Fink, for example, reports successful criminal defenses including ignorance of the law, ignorance of the contents of a tax return, reliance on others, confusion in applicable tax law, mental disease or defect and family problems, alcoholism

and ill health. Robert S. Fink, *Tax Fraud—Audits, Investigations, Prosecutions* (New York: Matthew Bender, 1980), § 18.04.

77. *Critzer*, 498 F2d 1160 (4th Cir 1974). Also, *Garber*, 607 F2d (5th Cir 1979).

78. *IRS Databook*, IRS Criminal Investigation, Criminal Investigation Statistical Data "Criminal Investigation Program, by Status or Disposition," FY 2010. About 41 percent of the investigations involve legal income and 59 percent involve illegal income.

79. Han Sherrer, "The Illusion of Tax Evasion," in McGee, *The Ethics of Tax Evasion*, 121; italics in original.

80. Ed Hedemann, *War Tax Resistance: A Guide to Withholding Your Support from the Military*, 5th ed., ed. Ruth Benn and Ed Hedemann (New York: War Resisters League, 2003), 14.

81. While the mean discrepancy was just under $2 million, the median was about $569,000. Nancy B. Nichols and Robert C. Richardson, "Criminal Investigations of Taxpayer Fraud," *Journal of Legal Tax Research* 4 (2006): 34–48.

82. IRS Statistical Data—Nonfiler Investigations—Criminal Investigation (CI).

83. U.S. House of Representatives, Subcommittee on Oversight hearing, *Taxpayers Who Fail to File Federal Income Tax Returns*, Rep. J. J. Pickle (D. Texas) Chair, 103rd Cong., 1st sess., Oct.26, 1993.

84. The IRS definition of non-filers includes people for whom the IRS has received tax returns in the past but not for the current year or has received some form of third-party tax report, such as a Form 1099 for interest income or SSA-1099 for Social Security, but received no tax return. Taxpayers in this category may be in full compliance with the law because their taxable income is below the required reporting threshold.

85. Margaret Levi, *Of Rule and Revenue* (Berkeley: University of California Press, 1988), 54.

86. See, for example, Amos Tversky and Daniel Kahneman, "Availability: A Heuristic for Judging Frequency and Probability," in *Judgment Under Uncertainty: Heuristics and Biases*, ed. Daniel Kahneman, Paul Slovic, and Amos Tversky (Cambridge: Cambridge University Press, 1982).

87. H. Kunreuther, R. Ginsberg, L. Miller, P. Sagi, P. Slovic, B. Borkan, and N. Katz, *Disaster Insurance Protection: Public Policy Lessons* (New York: Wiley, 1978).

88. Tyler, *Why People Obey the Law*, 67.

89. Kunreuther et al., 241.

90. Edward O. Wilson, *Consilience: The Unity of Knowledge* (New York: Vintage Books, 1998), 219–20.

91. Mackie, *Ethics*, 210.

92. Michael I. Saltzman, *IRS Practice and Procedure* (Boston: Warren, Gorham, and Lamont, 1981), ¶7.01.

93. Gottfredson and Hirschi, *A General Theory of Crime*, xv.

94. Spies v. US, 317 US 492, 495 (1943). It should be noted that this case predates the imposition of withholding on wages.

95. Steven Klepper and Daniel Nagin, "The Anatomy of Tax Evasion," *Journal of Law, Economics, & Organization* 5, no. 1 (1989): 1–24.

96. Richard D. Schwartz and Sonya Orleans, "On Legal Sanctions," *University of Chicago Law Review* 34 (1967): 274.

97. Jeffrey A. Dubin, "Criminal Investigation Enforcement Activities and Taxpayer Noncompliance," *Public Finance Review* 35 (July 2007): 500–29.

98. Harold G. Grasmick and Robert J. Bursik Jr., "Conscience, Significant Others, and Rational Choice: Extending the Deterrence Model," *Law & Society Review* 24, no. 3 (1990).

99. Stephen Pfohl, *Images of Deviance and Social Control: A Sociological History*, 2d ed. (New York: McGraw-Hill, 1994), 92.

100. Alan Lewis, *The Psychology of Taxation* (New York: St. Martin's, 1982), 132.

101. Tversky and Kahneman, "Availability: A Heuristic for Judging Frequency and Probability," in *Judgment Under Uncertainty: Heuristics and Biases*, ed. Daniel Kahneman, Paul Slovic, and Amos Tversky (Cambridge: Cambridge University Press, 1982), 178.

102. Barry Schwartz, *The Paradox of Choice* (New York: HarperCollins, 2004), 58–60.

103. Ibid.

104. Tversky and Kahneman, "Availability," 11.

105. Ibid., 164.

106. Dubin, "Criminal Investigation Enforcement Activities and Taxpayer Noncompliance." IRS National Taxpayer Advocate Nina E. Olson reports that, "IRS researchers have estimated that the indirect effect of an average examination on voluntary compliance is between six and 12 time the amount of the proposed adjustment," written statement before the Committee on the Budget, United States Senate, "The Causes of and Solutions to the Federal Tax Gap," Feb. 15, 2006: 1–19.

107. John S. Carroll, "How Taxpayers Think about Their Taxes: Frames and Values," in *Why People Pay Taxes*, ed. J. Slemrod (Ann Arbor: University of Michigan Press, 1992), 47.

108. Danshera Cords, "Tax Protestors and Penalties: Ensuring Perceived Fairness and Mitigating Systemic Costs," *Brigham Young University Law Review* (2005): 1515, 1526.

109. Tittle, *Sanctions and Social Deviance*, 9.

110. Dan M. Kahan, "Trust, Collective Action, and Law," *Boston University Law Review* 81, no. 2 (April 2001): 333.

111. For a dated but still enlightening discussion of civil tax penalties, see Michael Asimow, "Civil Penalties for Inaccurate and Delinquent Tax Returns," *UCLA Law Review* 23, no. 4 (1976): 637.

112. Paul A. Samuelson and William D. Nordhaus, *Economics*, 14th ed. (New York: McGraw-Hill, 1992), 5.

113. Otto H. Chang, Donald R. Nichols, and Joseph J. Schultz, "Taxpayer Attitudes Toward Tax Audit Risk," *Journal of Economic Psychology* 8 (1987): 299–309.

114. Dick J. Hessing, Henk Elffers, Henry S. J. Robben, and Paul Webley, "Does Deterrence Deter? Measuring the Effect of Deterrence on Tax Compliance in Field Studies and Experimental Studies," in *Why People Pay Taxes: Tax Compliance and Enforcement*, ed. Joel Slemrod (Ann Arbor: University of Michigan Press, 1992), 304.

115. Ryan C. Amacher, and Holley H. Ulbrich, *Principles of Economics*, 5th ed. (Cincinnati: SouthWestern, 1992), 15.

116. U.S. Department of the Treasury, Office of Tax Policy, "A Comprehensive Strategy for Reducing the Tax Gap" (Sept. 26, 2006), 9.

117. The GAO has criticized Congress for failing to index most penalties to inflation, thus systematically reducing their sting each year. See "Tax Compliance:

Inflation Has Significantly Decreased the Real Value of Some Penalties,"
GAO-07-1062, Aug. 23, 2007.

118. The requirement to file Form 8854 is imposed by § 877A and the $10,000
penalty is imposed by § 6039G(c).

119. Gottfredson and Hirschi, *A General Theory of Crime* (1990), 75. As an example
of an economist taking this approach, the authors quote Gary Becker: "A useful
theory of criminal behavior can dispense with special theories of anomie,
psychological inadequacies, or inheritance of special traits, and simply extend
the economist's usual analysis of choice," Gottfredson and Hirschi (1990), p. 72.
Quoted from Gary Becker, "Crime and Punishment: An Economic Approach," in
Essays in the Economics of Crime and Punishment, ed. G. Becker and W. Landes
(New York: Columbia University Press, 1974), 1–54.

120. Carroll, "Compliance with the Law: A Decision-Making Approach to
Taxpaying."

121. Cords, *Tax Protestors and Penalties*, 1554.

122. Torgler, *Tax Compliance*, 75.

123. This information on uneven penalty abatement was developed further in an
article by the author, "Tax Penalties and Deterrence," *The CPA Journal* (Sept.
2010).

124. IRS Publication 55B Data Book, 2009, Table 17 "Civil Penalties Assessed and
Abated, by Type of Tax and type of Penalty" FY 2009.

125. One of the lowest abatement rates reported is for civil fraud penalties, ranging
from 0 percent up to 10 percent, depending on the type of tax involved. In
this case, the percentage of the number of penalties abated closely mirrors the
percentage of the amounts abated, indicating no apparent advantage for more
prosperous taxpayers.

126. IRC § 6404.

127. Torgler, *Tax Compliance*, 245.

128. IRS Publication 55B Data Book, 2009, Table 17, "Civil Penalties Assessed and
Abated, by Type of Tax and type of Penalty" FY 2009.

129. If the IRS says it didn't receive a payment or tax return, the burden is on the
taxpayer to prove it was received. The Internal Revenue Code allows non–elec-
tronically filed returns and payments to follow the "timely mailed equals timely
filed" rule of Reg. § 301.7502-1.

130. Green, *Lying, Cheating, and Stealing*, 247.

131. Ibid.

132. Robert W. McGee, "Is Tax Evasion Unethical?" *Kansas Law Review* 42 (1994):
411; Leo P. Martinez, "Taxes, Morals, and Legitimacy," *Brigham Young University
Law Review* (1994): 521.

133. Martinez, "Taxes, Morals, and Legitimacy," 547.

134. Paul Vinogradoff, *Common Sense in Law* (New York: Henry Holt, 1913).

135. K. D. Deane, "Law, Morality and Tax Evasion," *Anglo-American Law Review* 13,
no. 1 (1984): 1.

136. IRC § 6662.

Chapter Two. The Tax Gap, Tax Protestors, and Small Business

1. Ingo Walter, *The Secret Money Market: Inside the Dark World of Tax Evasion,
Financial Fraud, Insider Trading, Money Laundering, and Capital Flight* (New
York: HarperCollins, 1990), 84.

2. When a taxpayer fails to file a return, IRC § 6020 authorizes the service to prepare a substitute for return ("SFR") in order to assess the tax.

3. Flora v. US, 362 US 145, 176 (1960).

4. IRS, "Anti-Tax Law Evasions Schemes—Law and Arguments (Section I)" http://www.irs.gov/businesses/small/.

5. Robert Kidder and Craig McEwen, "Taxpaying Behavior in Social Context: A Tentative Typology of Tax Compliance and Noncompliance," in *Tax Compliance vol. 2: Social Science Perspectives*, ed. Jeffrey A. Roth and John T. Scholz (Philadelphia: University of Pennsylvania Press, 1989), 48.

6. John Stuart Mill, *Principles of Political Economy*, abridged by J. Laurence Laughlin (New York: Appleton and Company, 1884), 585–86.

7. Debra L. Sanders, Phillip M. J. Reckers and Govind S. Iyer, "Influence of Accountability and Penalty Awareness on Tax Compliance," *Journal of the American Taxation Association* 30, no. 2 (Fall 2008).

8. J. Slemrod and J. Bakija, *Taxing Ourselves* (Cambridge: The MIT Press, 1996), 145.

9. In its 2009 Taxpayer Attitude Survey, the Internal Revenue Service's Oversight Board asked taxpayers: "Is it every American's civic duty to pay their fair share of taxes?" Respondents strongly believe it is, with 70 percent claiming they "completely agree" and 25 percent that they "mostly agree." IRS Oversight Board 2009 Taxpayer Attitude Survey, Feb. 2010, table 2.

10. IRS Oversight Board, 2009 Taxpayer Attitude Survey.

11. Peter Eric Hendrickson, *Cracking the Code* (n.p., 2003), 27–28.

12. US v. Connor, 898 F2d 942, 943-44 (3d Cir 1990).

13. U. S. Department of Justice press release, "Justice Department Highlights FY 2008 Tax Enforcement Results," April 13, 2009. WWW.USDOJ.GOV.

14. Michael A Cabirac v. Comm, 120 TC 163 (2003).

15. United States v. Moore, 627 F2d 830 (7th Cir 1980). An exception to this rule is found in *United States v. Long*, 618 F2d 74, 75 (9th Cir 1980) where the court ruled that a return containing only zeros could constitute a return for purposes of IRC § 7203.

16. IRS, http://www.irs.gov/compliance/enforcement/.

17. *Brushaber v. Union Pacific Railroad Co.*, 240 US 1 (1916), relying on the Sixteenth Amendment in holding that the income tax provisions of the *Tariff Act of 1913* were not unconstitutional.

18. Ibid. The taxing power of the Congress is established by Art. I, § 8 of the Constitution: "The Congress shall have power to lay and collect taxes, duties, imposts and excises." There are two limitations on this power. First, as the same section also provides, "all duties, imposts and excises shall be uniform throughout the United States." Second, as provided in Art. I § 9, "No capitation, or other direct, tax shall be laid, unless in proportion to the census or enumeration herein before directed to be taken." See also Art. I, § 2, cl. 3 "direct taxes shall be apportioned among the several states which may be included within this union, according to their respective numbers."

19. IRS Rev. Rul. 2005-19, 2005-1 CB 819, March 14, 2005.

20. Knoblauch v. Comm, 749 F2d 200, 201 (5th Cir 1984).

21. Phillips v. Comm, 283 US 589, 595-99 (1931). "The right of the United States to collect its internal revenue by summary administrative proceedings has long been settled. Where, as here, adequate opportunity is afforded for a later judicial determination of the legal rights, summary proceedings to secure

prompt performance of pecuniary obligations to the government have been consistently sustained."

22. The Court in *Fein* stated, "There is nothing unusual about retroactive tax laws. . . . Most such retroactive enactments have been upheld as against due-process challenges, on the theory that some limited retroactivity is necessary as a practical matter to prevent the revenue loss that would result if taxpayers, aware of a likely impending change in the law, were permitted to order their affairs freely to avoid the effect of the change." Fein v. US, 730 F2d 1211 (1984).

23. United States v. Stillhammer, 706 F2d 1072, 1076-77 (10th Cir 1983).

24. IRS Rev. Rul. 2005-19. In *US v. Glen Murphy*, 269 F3d 1130, the taxpayer argued that he was being forced to choose between his Fifth and Sixth Amendment rights because in order to receive the services of a public defender he had to disclose financial information evidencing his eligibility. The court was unsympathetic.

25. United States v. Sullivan, 274 US 259, 263-64 (1927). Also, in *California v. Byers*, 402 US 424, 427-29 (1971) the court stated "the remote possibility of incrimination is insufficient to defeat strong policies of disclosure called for by" the income tax.

26. IRS Rev. Rul. 2005-19. 2005-1 CB 819, March 14, 2005.

27. Abney v. Campbell, 206 F2d 836, 841 (5th Cir 1953).

28. United States v. Drefke, 707 F2d 978, 983 (8th Cir 1983) "The Thirteenth Amendment, however, is inapplicable where involuntary servitude is imposed as punishment for a crime."

29. Hendrickson, *Cracking the Code,* 6.

30. US v. Ward, 833 F2d 1538 (11th Cir 1987).

31. *Becraft, Jr.,* 64 AFTR 2d 89-5656 (9th Cir 1989). The court in this case sought to bring sanctions against attorney Becraft for continuing to pursue the same arguments which the court had already deemed frivolous. The court gave Becraft an opportunity to explain why he should not pay a $2,500 fine to which Becraft provided a "several hundred page reply." In the end the court imposed the sanction citing Becraft's repeated use of the same constitutional challenges to the Tax Code that had already been ruled inapplicable in earlier cases.

32. U. S. Department of Justice press release, April 13, 2009, "Justice Department Highlights FY 2008 Tax Enforcement Results." WWW.USDOJ.GOV.

33. O'Driscoll v. IRS, 1991 U S Dist LEXIS 9829, at 5-6 (ED Pa 1991).

34. US v. Gerads, 999 F2d 962 (8th Cir 1993).

35. Solomon v. Comm, TC Memo 1993-509, 66. In *US v. Glen Murphy*, 469 F3d 1130, a chiropractor appeared before the Court of Appeals for the Seventh Circuit and said, "Equality under the law is paramount and mandatory by law. I Glen James clan Murphy, a Wisconsin national of the republic of Wisconsin, a titled sovereign, am able to handle and represent me concerning all my affairs. In commerce when being forced to testify all my common law rights are reserved" [*sic*].

36. Rev. Rul. 2004-28, 2004-12 IRB 624, March 1, 2004.

37. U. S. Department of Justice press release, April 13, 2009, "Justice Department Highlights FY 2008 Tax Enforcement Results." WWW.USDOJ.GOV. "Nathan J. Hochman, Assistant Attorney General for the Justice Department's Tax Divi-

sion, announced the launch of the National Tax Defier Initiative or TAXDEF on Tuesday, April 8, 2008."

38. U. S. Department of Justice press release, April 24, 2008. "OCALA, Fla—U.S. District Judge Wm. Terrell Hodges today sentenced Wesley Trent Snipes to three years imprisonment for charges of failing to file income tax returns. 'Snipes' long prison sentence should send a loud and crystal clear message to all tax defiers that if they engage in similar tax defier conduct, they face joining him . . . as inmates in prison,' said Nathan J. Hochman, Assistant Attorney General of the Justice Department's Tax Division."

39. The reference to the marketplace of ideas has been used by the Supreme Court more than one hundred times. See W. Wat Hopkins, "The Supreme Court Defines the Marketplace of Ideas," *Journalism and Mass Communication Quarterly* 73, no. 1 (Spring 1996). See, for example, Justice Holmes's dissenting opinion in *Abrams v. US,* 250 US 616, 630 (1919).

40. Peter Eric Hendrickson's book *Cracking the Code* is featured at http://www.losthorizons.com/Cracking_the_Code.htm. According to this site, "Hendrickson delves deep into the history, statutes and case law behind the Code to reveal its startling and liberating secrets; and unless you live in a cave, you need to know what he's uncovered. Once you've finished 'Cracking the Code', the tax laws will never mean the same thing to you, or your bank account, again!" The book employs an argument similar to the one in *US v. Rhodes,* 921 FSupp 261, 264 (MD Pa 1996), where the taxpayers claimed that they were not "persons" as defined by the Internal Revenue Code, and hence not subject to federal income tax.

41. US v. Sloan, 939 F2d 499, 499-500 (7th Cir 1991).

42. The *Tax Relief Health Care Act of 2006* amended IRC § 6702 to allow imposition of a $5,000 penalty for frivolous tax returns. There are other tax protestor arguments as well. In *Williams v. Comm,* 114 TC 136 (2004) the court rejected the taxpayer's argument that only foreign source income is taxable. In *US v. Rickman,* 638 F2d, 182 (10th Cir 1980) the court rejected the taxpayer's claim that payments received in the form of Federal Reserve Notes are not taxable income since the notes can't be exchanged for gold or silver.

43. "As a grand finale," according to the court, "Murphy did not even file income tax returns from 2001–2003, despite telling his bank that he had done so (and even producing a completed 2001 form) as part of a home refinancing application. In any event, he says he was a victim of AAA, which took him to the cleaners to the tune of $274,000." US v. Murphy, 469 F3d 1130 (2006).

44. Danshera Cords, "Tax Protestors and Penalties: Ensuring Perceived Fairness and Mitigating Systemic Costs," *Brigham Young University Law Review* (2005): 1515.

45. Ibid.

46. IRS Fact Sheet 2005-38, March 29, 2005.

47. Estimates reported by Ann D. Witte and Diane F. Woodbury, "The Effect of Tax Laws and Tax Administration on Tax Compliance: The Case of the U.S. Individual Income Tax," *National Tax Journal,* 38 (March 1985): 1–14. According to Malamud and Parry, the use of the term *tax gap* originated in 1983 and made its way into the mainstream in a 1984 *Newsweek* article. In the *Newsweek* article the tax gap in 1984 was estimated at $100 billion, having more than doubled from ten years earlier. Richard B. Malamud and Richard O. Parry, "It's Time to

do Something About the Tax Gap," *Houston Business and Tax Journal* 9 (2008): 1. Joel Slemrod reported the IRS estimate at $84.9 billion for 1987, "comprising more than 20 percent of tax liability." *Why People Pay Taxes*, ed. J. Slemrod (Ann Arbor: University of Michigan Press, 1992), 1.

48. Internal Revenue Service, Washington, DC, 1996, "Federal Tax Compliance Research: Individual Income Tax Gap Estimates for 1985, 1988, and 1992," Publication 1415 (Rev. 4-96).

49. Dick Netzer, "The Relevance and Feasibility of Land Value Taxation in the Rich Countries," in *Land Value Taxation: Can It and Will It Work Today?*, ed. Dick Netzer (Cambridge, MA: Lincoln Institute of Land Policy, 1998), 124.

50. IRS, "Reducing the Federal Tax Gap." Note that the original estimate of a tax gap ("gross gap") for a particular year is reduced in subsequent years as the IRS collects part of the unreported or unpaid taxes due resulting in the "net gap." By 2006 the IRS reported collecting $55 billion from the 2001 gap, leaving the net gap for that year at $290 billion. IRS News Release IR-2006-28 (Feb. 14, 2006). Since the tax gap has not been calculated for each year, there is no cumulative figure representing the total amount due from taxpayers. Were the figures available, and using the 2006 net tax gap for 2001 figure as an average annual estimate, the total would be $290 billion x 10 (since the statute of limitations on collections is ten years) or $2.9 trillion. But even that figure would be a conservative estimate since for taxpayers who have not filed returns, the ten-year collection period would not have started yet.

51. Donald L. Bartlett and James B. Steele, *The Great American Tax Dodge* (Boston: Little, Brown, 2000), 13.

52. Cords, "Tax Protestors and Penalties."

53. IRS News Release 88-77, April 15, 1988.

54. According to the nonprofit National Association for Shoplifting Prevention (NASP), "More than $13 billion worth of goods are stolen from retailers each year. That's more than $35 million per day," http://www.shopliftingprevention. org/. Like all illegal income, the value of the shoplifted items is included in taxable income.

55. IRS, "Reducing the Federal Tax Gap."

56. Walter, *The Secret Money Market*, 14.

57. Ibid., 85.

58. Dick J. Hessing, Henk Elffers, Henry S. J. Robben, and Paul Webley, "Does Deterrence Deter? Measuring the Effect of Deterrence on Tax Compliance in Field Studies and Experimental Studies," in *Why People Pay Taxes: Tax Compliance and Enforcement*, ed. Joel Slemrod (Ann Arbor: University of Michigan Press, 1992).

59. U.S. House of Representatives, Hearing Before the Subcommittee on Oversight of the Committee on Ways and Means, *Hearing on Internal Revenue Service Operations and the Tax Gap*, 110th Cong., 1st sess. March 20, 2007.

60. Peter Reuter and Edwin M. Truman, *Chasing Dirty Money: The Fight Against Money Laundering* (Washington, DC: Institute for International Economics, 2004), 23.

61. U.S. House of Representatives, *Hearing on Internal Revenue Service Operations and the Tax Gap*, Commissioner Everson testifying, 110th Cong., 1st sess. March 20, 2007.

62. Ronen Palan, Richard Murphy, and Christian Chavagneux, *Tax Havens: How Globalization Really Works* (Ithaca: Cornell University Press, 2010), 62–63.

63. Association of Certified Fraud Examiners, "2010 Report to the Nations on Occupational Fraud and Abuse," Austin, TX.

64. Note that the IRS computes the tax gap as a percentage of a predetermined amount of tax revenue comprised of what is collected plus what should be collected. Using this method the tax gap appears to be 16.3 percent of the total expected tax collections. However, as noted earlier, when the amount of the tax gap is taken as a percentage of the actual taxes collected, it is 20 percent.

65. IRS, "Reducing the Federal Tax Gap," 18.

66. Bloomquist cites growing income inequality as a cause of tax cheating. Kim M. Bloomquist, "Tax Evasion, Income Inequality, and Opportunity Costs of Compliance," *National Tax Association Proceedings, 96th Annual Conference on Taxation,* 2003(a).

67. Internal Revenue Service *2010 Databook,* Table 14, Information Reporting Program, Fiscal Year 2010. The number of information returns (Forms 1099 and W-2) reported is 2,686,941,000. The number of individual returns filed for the same period is 141,167,000. The result is about nineteen information returns per individual tax return filed (assuming most information returns are issued to individuals).

68. Though legislation was passed in 2010 requiring extensive Form 1099 reporting, 2011 legislation repealed the 2010 rules. The imposition of the 2010 reporting rules was a justified by the additional amount of revenue it was expected to generate from taxpayers who would otherwise not report their income. In 2011, small business objections to the additional paperwork apparently overcame the need for the additional tax revenue. The *Comprehensive 1099 Taxpayer Protection and Repayment of Exchange Subsidy Overpayments Act of 2011* repealed both the expanded Form 1099 information reporting requirements mandated by § 9006(c) of the *Patient Protection and Affordable Care Act,* PL 111-148, codified as IRC § 6041, and also the 1099 reporting requirements imposed on taxpayers who receive rental income enacted as part of 2010 *Small Business Jobs Act,* PL 111-240.

69. Kim M. Bloomquist, "Trends as Changes in Variance: The Case of Noncompliance," Working paper, presented at IRS Research Conference (June 2003)(b). Bloomquist reports the matchable percentages decreased from 91.3 percent to 81.6 percent between 1980 and 2000.

70. David Callahan, *The Cheating Culture: Why Americans are Doing Wrong to Get Ahead* (New York: Harcourt, 2004), 171. He adds, "Following the money will naturally lead to a much greater focus on upper-income earners, a shift which is long overdue."

71. General Accounting Office (GAO) 1990. "IRS Can Use Tax Gap Data to Improve Its Programs for Reducing Noncompliance." In 2004 the GAO changed its name to the Government Accountability Office.

72. IRS, "Reducing the Federal Tax Gap," 10–11.

73. Richard D. Schwartz and Sonya Orleans, "On Legal Sanctions," *University of Chicago Law Review* 34 (1967): 274.

74. IRS, "The Tax Gap Facts and Figures," March 2005. http://www.irs.gov.

75. Joel Slemrod, "The Return to Tax Simplification: an Econometric Analysis," *Public Finance Review* 17, no. 3 (1989). Although there is required reporting

for the gross proceeds from sales of real estate as well as stocks and other securities, the amount of gain to report is left up to the taxpayer. For this kind of tax cheating, a gain can easily be converted by the taxpayer into a loss since it is only the sales price and not the cost or basis of the asset that is reported to the IRS.

76. Slemrod and Bakija, *Taxing Ourselves,* 149.

77. For 2007 the IRS estimated that there are were 32.1 million businesses in the United States of which 23.1 million were sole proprietors, 4 million were small business corporations (S Corporations), 1.9 million were C (regular taxpaying) corporations, and 3.1 million were partnerships (of which 1.8 million are limited-liability companies). More than 90 percent of corporations are closely held (not publicly traded). The estimate of 31.9 million small businesses is the total of sole proprietorships, S corporations, 90 percent of C corporations, and partnerships. Source: IRS SOI Tax Stats, Table 1—Number of Businesses, Business Receipts, Net Income, and Deficit, by Form of Business and Industry, Tax Years 1980–2007.

78. Walter, *The Secret Money Market,* 86.

79. Eric M. Rice, "The Corporate Tax Gap: Evidence of Tax Compliance by Small Corporations," in *Why People Pay Taxes: Tax Compliance and Enforcement,* ed. Joel Slemrod (Ann Arbor: University of Michigan Press, 1992), 132.

80. Nancy B. Nichols and Robert C. Richardson, "Criminal Investigations of Taxpayer Fraud," *Journal of Legal Tax Research* 4 (2006). In the study of almost six hundred cases, 23 percent were self-employed persons and 45 percent were owners of small businesses operated in the form of another entity—for example, the owners of corporations.

81. Bloomquist 2003(a), "Tax Evasion, Income Inequality, and Opportunity Costs."

82. Bloomquist 2003(b), "Trends as Changes in Variance."

83. Bloomquist 2003(a), "Tax Evasion, Income Inequality, and Opportunity Costs."

84. Bloomquist 2003(b), "Trends as Changes in Variance."

85. Slemrod, *Why People Pay Taxes,* See Fox for an elaboration of this argument.

86. K. D. Deane, "Law, Morality, and Tax Evasion," *Anglo-American Law Review* 13, no. 1 (1984): 1.

87. IRC § 1361(b)(1)(a) Subchapter S (small business) Corporations.

88. IRC § 1244 stock allowing ordinary loss rather than capital loss.

89. IRC § 1202 reduced taxable income on sale of stock held five years or more.

90. IRC § 172 net operating loss (NOL) three year carryback for small business; IRC § 55(e) exemption for small corporate businesses from Alternative Minimum Tax (AMT) if average revenue is less than $5 million for three prior years.

91. IRC § 47R credit for health insurance for small business.

92. Eric M. Rice, "The Corporate Tax Gap: Evidence of Tax Compliance by Small Corporations," in *Why People Pay Taxes.*

93. Ibid., 134.

94. Ibid., 148. Though this observation was the result of an empirical study, by deduction, of two businesses that are identical in every way, except one cheats on its income tax and the other doesn't, the cheating business must necessarily be more profitable.

95. Ibid., 138.

96. Government Accountability Office, "Tax Gap: IRS Has Modernized Its Business Nonfiler Program but Could Benefit from More Evaluation and Use of Third-Party Data," GAO-10-950, August 31, 2010.

97. Michael Asimow, "Civil Penalties for Inaccurate and Delinquent Tax Returns," *UCLA Law Review* 23, no. 4 (April 1976): 637.

98. Matthew N. Murray, "Would Tax Evasion and Tax Avoidance Undermine a National Retail Sales Tax?" in *Tax Policy in the Real World*, ed. Joel Slemrod (Cambridge: Cambridge University Press, 1999), 69.

99. Robert A. Kagan, "On the Visibility of Income Tax Law Violations."

100. Leo P. Martinez, "Taxes, Morals, and Legitimacy," *Brigham Young University Law Review* (1994): 521, 558.

101. Robert A. Kagan, "On the Visibility of Income Tax Law Violations," in *Tax Compliance vol. 2: Social Science Perspectives*, ed. Jeffrey A. Roth and John T. Scholz (Philadelphia: University of Pennsylvania Press, 1989), 115.

102. The Government Accountability Office (GAO) has produced a great number of reports suggesting how to tackle the tax gap problem. A 2007 GAO report "TAX GAP, A Strategy for Reducing the Gap Should Include Options for Addressing Sole Proprietor Noncompliance," makes a number of useful suggestions. Of course it is up to Congress to take action.

103. Montesquieu, *The Spirit of the Laws*, book VI, chap. 13.

104. U.S. House of Representatives, *Hearing on Internal Revenue Service Operations and the Tax Gap*, 110th Cong., 1st sess. March 20, 2007.

105. Nina E. Olson, National Taxpayer Advocate, "The Causes of and Solutions to the Federal Tax Gap," Written statement before the Committee on the Budget United States Senate, Feb. 15, 2006. "Ninety-nine percent (99%) of income subject to withholding is reported on taxpayers' income tax returns."

106. Income received through credit and debit card transactions is to be reported to the Internal Revenue Service starting in 2011. Banks and other payment settlement services will need to report gross annual receipts for each merchant. Exceptions are made for merchants who receive less than $20,000 for the year or who process fewer than two hundred such transactions during the year. This rule was part of the *2008 Housing Assistance Tax Act*. IRC § 6050W requires retailers to file information returns, Form 1099-K, and report payment card transactions—including debit, credit, gift cards, and co-branded cards—as well as third-party network transactions, on a gross basis. Regulations affect transactions beginning on January 1, 2011.

107. Michael J. Graetz, *The U.S. Income Tax: What It Is, How it Got That Way, and Where We Go from Here* (New York: W. W. Norton, 1999), 97. Violette reports that for taxpayers who receive cash income, communicating sanctions has little effect. George Violette, "Effects of Communicating Sanctions on Taxpayer Compliance," *The Journal of the American Taxation Association* (Fall 1989): 92–104.

108. Jeremy Bentham, *Of Laws in General* (London: The Athlone Press, 1970), 214.

109. IRS Oversight Board, 2009 Taxpayer Attitude Survey, Feb. 2010. Another 24 percent of taxpayers say the fear of an IRS audit "somewhat influences" their behavior and 36 percent report very little or no influence from this fear. The ambiguity of the question leaves open the possibility that some taxpayers don't fear an IRS audit because they are in compliance.

110. Carolyn Webber and Aaron Wildavsky, *A History of Taxation and Expenditure in the Western World* (New York: Simon and Schuster, 1986), 554.

111. The tax law treats a constructive dividend in the same way as an actual (planned) dividend distribution. See Lengsfield v. Comm, 241 F2d 5088 (CA-5 1957). As a result, even a constructive dividend (discovered by the IRS during an audit)—under the law in effect at the time of this writing—is eligible to be classified as a qualified dividend and therefore taxed at a maximum individual tax rate of 15 percent. This is no doubt an unplanned incentive for tax cheating.

112. The IRS and the courts employ the "hardheaded business person test" to determine the quality of a financial transaction. The use of this term is traceable to *Forman Co., Inc. v. Comm*, 453 F2d 1144 (2d Cir 1972).

113. See *Brockhouse v. US*, 749 F2d 1248 (7th Cir 1984) for an illustration of this problem in the opposite direction, a loan from the shareholder to the corporation where interest was unreported.

114. U.S. General Accounting Office (GAO), Washington, D.C., "Taxpayer Compliance: Reducing the Income Tax Gap," 1995, 1, GGD-95-176.

115. Mill, *Principles of Political Economy*, 555.

116. U.S. House of Representatives, Hearing Before the Subcommittee on Oversight of the Committee on Ways and Means, *Hearing on Internal Revenue Service Operations and the Tax Gap*, 110th Cong., 1st sess., March 20, 2007.

117. Richard B. Malamud and Richard O. Parry, "It's Time to Do Something About the Tax Gap," *Houston Business and Tax Journal* 9 (2008): 1.

118. For more specific examples see Mark Siegel, *Tax Cheating: Hide and Seek with the IRS*, Mesa, AZ: Blue Sky Press, 1988. Also, the IRS Web site allows access to audit guides used for training IRS employees. These guides feature a number of categories of small business and the directions provided to IRS examiners in dealing with specific kinds of small business.

119. Nancy B. Nichols and Robert C. Richardson, "Criminal Investigations of Taxpayer Fraud," *Journal of Legal Tax Research* 4 (2006).

120. See note 77.

121. Joel Slemrod, "The Return to Tax Simplification: an Econometric Analysis," *Public Finance Review* 17, no. 3 (1989).

122. IRS Fact Sheet 2005-14, March 2005.

123. R. E. Hall and A. Rabushka, *The Flat Tax*, 2nd ed. (Stanford, CA: Hoover Institution Press, 1995), 58.

124. Slemrod, "The Return to Tax Simplification."

125. According to McGee, "One problem with any individual income tax, whether progressive or flat rate, especially in emerging economies, is that it is difficult to collect." Robert W. McGee, *The Philosophy of Taxation and Public Finance* (Boston: Kluwer Academic Publishers, 2004), 213.

126. *PBS Online Newshour*, "A debate on changing and flattening the U.S. tax system," Margaret Warner reports, January 17, 1995.

127. Robert A. Kagan, "On the Visibility of Income Tax Law Violations," in *Tax Compliance vol. 2: Social Science Perspectives*, ed. Jeffrey A. Roth and John T. Scholz (Philadelphia: University of Pennsylvania Press, 1989), 99.

128. James Q. Wilson and George L. Kelling, "Broken Windows," *Atlantic Monthly* 249, no. 3 (March 1982).

129. George L. Kelling and Catherine M. Coles, *Fixing Broken Windows* (New York: Touchstone, 1996), xv.

130. David C. Rowe, *Biology and Crime* (Los Angeles: Roxbury, 2002), 123.

131. See, for example, Bernard E. Harcourt and Jens Ludwig, "Broken Windows: New Evidence from New York City and a Five-City Social Experiment," *The University of Chicago Law Review* 73, no.1 (Winter 2006): 271.

132. For an analysis of opportunity and opportunism, see the author's *Opportunity: Optimizing Life's Chances* (Amherst, NY: Prometheus Books, 2006), 168–83.

133. See, for example, Joseph T. Wells, *Principles of Fraud Examination* (Hoboken: John Wiley and Sons, 2005), 13.

134. Niccolò Machiavelli, *The Prince,* trans. Peter Bondanella and Mark Musa (New York: Penguin Books, 1979), 115. To this advice Cowell adds, "It becomes impossible to evade a provision of the tax law that is never actually enforced; you know you are never going to be chased, so there is no point taking evasive action." Frank A. Cowell, *Cheating the Government: The Economics of Evasion* (Cambridge: The MIT Press, 1990), 13.

135. John T. Scholz, "Compliance Research and the Political Context of Tax Administration," in *Tax Compliance vol. 2: Social Science Perspectives,* ed. Jeffrey A. Roth and John T. Scholz (Philadelphia: University of Pennsylvania Press, 1989), 12.

136. Richard A. Posner, "Theories of Economic Regulation," *Bell Journal of Economics and Management Science* 5 (1974): 335–58.

137. One of the tools used in the federal government's battle against money laundering is IRC § 6050I's reporting requirement for cash received in a trade or business if the amount exceeds $10,000.

138. Friedrich Nietzsche, *The Genealogy of Morals,* trans. Francis Golffing (New York: Doubleday, 1956), 205.

139. Section 511 of the *Tax Increase Prevention and Reconciliation Act of 2005* (TIPRA). The proposed regulations reflect changes in the law required by IRC § 3402(t).

140. For background see J. D. McKinnon and R. Wells, "Self-employed blamed for 'tax gap': IRS taxpayer advocate proposes withholding from contractor payments," *Wall Street Journal,* Jan. 15, 2004.

141. The Associated General Contractors of America Web site announced, "AGC has made full repeal of the 3 percent withholding law a top priority for the 111th Congress. During the 110th Congress (2007-08), a bill to repeal the law enjoyed the bipartisan support of 260 co-sponsors in the House and 15 co-sponsors in the Senate. The legislation has been reintroduced in the 111th Congress. AGC has also made full repeal of the law a top priority in the economic stimulus package." http://www.agc.org/cs/advocacy/regulatory_action_details?id=140.

142. According to an Associated General Contractors of America, news release, January 27, 2011, "The bill introduced by Senator Brown [S. 164, Senator Scott Brown (R-MA)] would offset the roughly $11 billion cost to repeal the 3 percent withholding law by using unobligated *Recovery Act* funds," http://news.agc.org/2011/01/27/senators-introduce-bills-to-repeal-1099-paperwork-mandate-3-percent-withholding/.

143. Charles O. Rossotti, *Many Unhappy Returns: One Man's Quest to Turn Around the Most Unpopular Organization in the World* (Boston: Harvard Business School Press, 2005), 271.

144. Report of the Treasury Inspector General for Tax Administration (TIGTA), "Existing Practices Allowed IRS Contactors to Receive Payments While Owing

Delinquent Taxes," Report number 2011-30-013 (Feb. 4, 2011). According to the report the IRS paid contractors $356 million in 2009 although the same contractors owed the IRS $3.8 million in back taxes.
145. Margaret Levi, *Of Rule and Revenue* (Berkeley: University of California Press, 1988), 49.

Chapter Three. Tax Complexity

1. Margaret Levi, *Of Rule and Revenue* (Berkeley: University of California Press, 1988), 49.
2. U.S. House of Rep., rep. no. 5, Committee Reports on Act of October 3, 1913, 63rd Cong., 1st sess., April 22, 1913. Reprinted in U.S. Bureau of Internal Revenue Bulletin, Cumulative Bulletin 1939-1, pt. 2 (January-June 1939).
3. U.S. House of Rep., rep. no. 2475 on the Revenue Act of 1936, 74th Cong., 2nd sess., April 12, 1936. Reprinted in U.S. Bureau of Internal Revenue Bulletin, Cumulative Bulletin 1939-1, pt. 2 (January-June 1939).
4. IRS Publication 4832, "History of the U.S. Tax Return Preparation Industry" (Rev. Dec. 2009) Catalog No. 54119P.
5. Ingo Walter, *The Secret Money Market: Inside the Dark World of Tax Evasion, Financial Fraud, Insider Trading, Money Laundering, and Capital Flight* (New York: HarperCollins, 1990), 79.
6. Senate, Committee on the Budget, written statement by Nina E. Olson, National Taxpayer Advocate, The Causes of and Solutions to the Federal Tax Gap, Feb. 15, 2006, 107th Cong., 1st sess.
7. John O. Fox, *If Americans Really Understood the Income Tax: Uncovering Our Most Expensive Ignorance* (Boulder: Westview, 2001), 38.
8. Louis Kaplow, "How Tax Complexity and Enforcement Affect the Equality and Efficiency of the Income Tax," *National Tax Journal* 49, no. 1 (March 1996): 135–50.
9. The statute that defines tax expenditures is *The Congressional Budget and Impoundment Control Act of 1974*, P. L. No. 93-344, § 3, 88 Stat. 299, July 12, 1974 (codified at 2 USC § 622[3]).
10. IRS Publication 4832, "History of the U.S. Tax Return Preparation Industry."
11. IRS Fact Sheet-2006-20, June 9, 2006.
12. Benno Torgler, *Tax Compliance and Tax Morale* (Northampton, MA: Edward Elgar, 2007), 56.
13. Congressman Steny Hoyer, news release July 13, 2004, reporting on a speech at a Tax Policy Center Forum (a joint venture of the Brookings Institution and the Urban Institute).
14. Charles O. Rossotti, *Many Unhappy Returns: One Man's Quest to Turn Around the Most Unpopular Organization in the World* (Boston: Harvard Business School Press, 2005), 272.
15. Ibid.
16. Tax Foundation, www.taxfoundation.org, figures are for 2005.
17. Jeffrey H. Birnbaum, "The Road to Riches Is Called K Street: Lobbying Firms Hire More, Pay More, Charge More to Influence Government," *Washington Post*, Wed., June 22, 2005. One result of special provisions in the Code is that "83 percent of the tax code does not apply at all to the 71 percent of taxpayers who get all of their income from wages and investment income," Rossotti, *Many Unhappy Returns*, 274.

18. Jean-Baptiste Say, *A Treatise on Political Economy,* trans. C. R. Prinsep (New Brunswick: Transaction, [1836] 2001), 121.

19. IRC § 152(c)(4) "Special rule relating to 2 or more who can claim the same qualifying child." Parents are given preference over other blood relatives. If more than one non-parent qualifies and no parent qualifies, then the non-parent with the highest Adjusted Gross Income is awarded the child's dependency exemption.

20. IRS Reg. § 1.152-4 Special rule for a child of divorced or separate parents or parents who live apart. Technically, the regulation's wording is correct, because it is possible that one (or both) of the parents has a fiscal tax year rather than a calendar tax year, though this is very rare.

21. IRC § 152(c)(4).

22. Saul Bellow's character Professor Moses Herzog, in a letter to the president, complains, "Dear Mr. President, Internal Revenue regulations will turn us into a nation of bookkeepers. The life of every citizen is becoming a business. This, it seems to me, is one of the worst interpretations of the meaning of human life history has ever seen. Man's life not a business." Saul Bellow, *Herzog* (New York: Penguin Books, 1961), 14.

23. Richard A. Posner, *Problems of Jurisprudence* (Cambridge: Harvard University Press, 1990), 334.

24. Richard J. Herrnstein and Charles Murray, *The Bell Curve: Intelligence and Class Structure in American Life* (New York: Simon and Schuster, 1994), 541.

25. IRS News Release 84-123, Nov. 30, 1984.

26. J. W. von Goethe, *Faust,* trans. Barker Fairley, in *Selected Works* (New York: Random House, 2000), 765.

27. K. D. Deane, "Law, Morality and Tax Evasion," *Anglo-American Law Review* 13, no. 1 (1984): 1.

28. Jeremy Bentham, *Of Laws in General* (London: The Athlone Press, 1970), 236.

29. Sheldon D. Pollack, *The Failure of U.S. Tax Policy: Revenue and Politics* (University Park: Pennsylvania State University Press, 1996), 14. Congress, at least in 1976, was aware of this problem. "Simplification must be an ongoing process, and the individual provisions of the tax law must be reexamined periodically to see how they contribute to the complexity of the tax law. Unless this reexamination occurs, the tax law will grow gradually more complicated as new provisions are added to achieve new goals of society." General Explanation of the *Tax Reform Act of 1976,* PL 94-455, 94th Cong., Dec. 29, 1976.

30. Pollack, *The Failure of U.S. Tax Policy,* 267–68.

31. Carolyn Webber and Aaron Wildavsky, *A History of Taxation and Expenditure in the Western World* (New York: Simon and Schuster, 1986), 554.

32. Walter, *The Secret Money Market,* 87.

33. The principle that equal amounts of income should pay equal amounts of tax is referred to as horizontal equality.

34. *The Wall Street Journal,* Wed., July 26, 2000.

35. IRS "Reducing the Federal Tax Gap," 50.

36. Thomas S. Kuhn, *The Structure of Scientific Revolutions* (Chicago: University of Chicago Press, 1996), 10.

37. Ibid., 17–18.

38. Ibid., 23.

39. R. E. Hall and A. Rabushka, *The Flat Tax,* 2nd ed. (Stanford, CA: Hoover Institution Press, 1995), 57.

40. Matthew N. Murray, "Would Tax Evasion and Tax Avoidance Undermine a National Retail Sales Tax?" in *Tax Policy in the Real World*, ed. Joel Slemrod (Cambridge: Cambridge University Press, 1999). According to Murray, in changing from the income tax to a national sales tax "incentives and opportunities for both tax avoidance and tax evasion will be sustained, although the specific avenues for reducing one's tax liability may change." 71.

41. Joel Slemrod, "The Return to Tax Simplification: an Econometric Analysis," *Public Finance Review* 17, no. 3 (1989).

42. John Stuart Mill, *Principles of Political Economy*, abridged J. Laurence Laughlin (New York: Appleton and Company, 1884), 556.

43. *Republic*, trans. Paul Shorey, bk. 1, 343d.

44. CBS *60 Minutes* (April 19, 2009).

45. IRS "Reducing the Federal Tax Gap," 17.

46. Ibid.

47. See Senator William V. Roth Jr. and William H. Nixon, *The Power to Destroy* (New York: Atlantic Monthly Press, 1999), 1.

48. Harvey S. Rosen, *Public Finance*, 7th ed. (Boston: McGraw-Hill Irwin, 2005), 350.

49. Torgler, *Tax Compliance and Tax Morale*, 175.

50. Eric A. Posner, "Law and Social Norms: The Case of Tax Compliance," *Virginia Law Review* 86 (2000): 1781.

51. Donna D. Bobek and Richard C. Hatfield, "An Investigation of the Theory of Planned Behavior and the Role of Moral Obligation in Tax Compliance," *Behavioral Research in Accounting*, vol. 15, (2003).

52. B. Erard and J. S. Feinstein, "The Role of Moral Sentiments and Audit Perceptions in Tax Compliance," *Public Finance* 49 (1994), 70–89; quoted in Benno Torgler, *Tax Compliance and Tax Morale* (Northampton, MA: Edward Elgar, 2007), 240.

53. Rosen, *Public Finance*, 351.

54. Gideon Yaniv, "The Tax Compliance Demand Curve: A Diagrammatical Approach to Income Tax Evasion," *Journal of Economic Education* (Spring 2009). See also Michael J. Graetz, *The U.S. Income Tax: What It Is, How it Got That Way, and Where We Go from Here* (New York: W. W. Norton, 1999), 105.

55. Cicero, *On Obligations*, trans. P. G. Walsh (Oxford: Oxford University Press, 2000), 92.

56. David Callahan, *The Cheating Culture: Why Americans are Doing Wrong to Get Ahead* (New York: Harcourt, 2004), 178–79.

57. John T. Scholz, "Trust, Taxes, and Compliance," in *Trust and Governance*, ed. Valerie Braithwaite and Margaret Levi (New York: Russell Sage Foundation, 1998), 137.

58. John O. Fox, *If Americans Really Understood the Income Tax: Uncovering Our Most Expensive Ignorance* (Boulder: Westview, 2001), 4.

59. Ibid., 15.

60. The psychological doctrine holding that we naturally seek our own interests is referred to as psychological egoism. By contrast, ethical egoism is the belief that we *should* seek our own interest as an ethical ideal. For a general discussion of psychological versus ethical egoism see John Hospers, *Human Conduct: An Introduction to the Problems of Ethics* (New York: Harcourt, Brace and World, 1961), 141–55.

61. Ayn Rand, *The Virtue of Selfishness: A New Concept of Egoism* (New York: Signet Books, 1964), ix.

62. Adam Smith, *Wealth of Nations* (New York: Prometheus Books, [1776] 1991), 351–52. On this topic, Rachels observes that not all attempts to justify ethical egoism are egoistic; many are like Smith's call for promoting the public interest by pursuing our personal interest. While advancing our self-interest is equated by some with selfishness—with seeking personal advantage at the expense of those we deal with—others agree with Rand or Smith in linking the pursuit of self-interest with the good of the community (even as an unintended consequence). James Rachels, *The Elements of Moral Philosophy* (New York: McGraw-Hill, 2010), 70–71.

63. John Dewey and James H. Tufts, *Ethics*, Second ed. revised (New York: Henry Holt, 1932), 174.

64. Ibid.

65. Ibid.

66. Ibid., 200.

67. Frank A. Cowell, *Cheating the Government: The Economics of Evasion* (Cambridge: The MIT Press, 1990), 195.

68. For a more complete cataloging of what taxes pay for see Stephen Holmes and Cass R. Sunstein, *The Cost of Rights: Why Liberty Depends on Taxes* (New York: W. W. Norton, 1999).

69. Adam Smith, *The Theory of Moral Sentiments* (Indianapolis: Liberty Fund reprint of Oxford University Press edition, [1759] 1976), 134.

70. Shane Frederick, George Loewenstein and Ted O'Donoghue, "Time Discounting and Time Preference: A Critical Review," in *Time and Decision: Economic and Psychological Perspectives on Intertemporal Choice*, ed. George Loewenstein, Daniel Read, and Roy F. Baumeister (New York: Russell Sage Foundation, 2003), 66.

71. Loewenstein et al., *Time and Decision*, 2.

72. Frederick et al., "Time Discounting and Time Preference," 67.

73. For an overview of the impact of decision theory on tax compliance, see John S. Carroll, "Compliance with the Law: A Decision-Making Approach to Taxpaying," *Law and Human Behavior* 11, no. 4, (1987).

74. Webber and Wildavsky, *A History of Taxation and Expenditure in the Western World*, 534.

75. U.S. Constitution, Art 1, § 8.

76. Learned Hand, *The Bill of Rights* (New York: Atheneum, 1979), 13.

77. Joel Slemrod, ed. *Why People Pay Taxes* (Ann Arbor: The University of Michigan Press, 1992), 1.

78. "An amoral or non-moral practical discourse is one in which values lack at least one of the defining features of moral values—justificatory force, universalisability, and categoricality." Deryck Beyleveld and Roger Brown-sword, *Law as a Moral Judgment* (Sheffield, UK: Sheffield Academic Press, 1994), 153.

79. It should be kept in mind that I am discussing the process of assessing the proper amount of taxes due, where personal circumstances have no bearing. This is in contrast with IRS collection procedures which do allow for installment payments and offers in compromise that do take the taxpayer's ability to pay into consideration.

80. Henry George, *Progress and Poverty* (New York: Robert Schalkenbach Foundation, 1953), 414. The relative ease with which real estate taxes can be collected is reflected in the growing market for the purchase and sale of tax lien certificates. These financial instruments represent the right to receive past due real estate taxes and are purchased from the local government taxing authority. As with the practice of tax farming in ancient Athens and Rome, the private collection of public revenues shifts the risk of collection (at a price) from the government to the investor or speculator. See Webber and Wildavsky, *A History of Taxation*, 113–16. Levi tells us, "The tax farmers purchase contracts to collect revenue in a given area and time period. The government receives the funds in advance of their actual collection." Levi, *Of Rule and Revenue*, 71–72.

81. George, *Progress and Poverty*, 414.

82. Adam Smith, "Of Taxes," in *Wealth of Nations*, 498.

83. Gallup Organization, April 4–7, 2005. Local property taxes were rated the least popular form of tax with 42 percent indicating it is the least fair tax. Other taxes in the poll included the federal income tax, state income tax, state sales tax, and federal Social Security tax.

84. Robert W. McGee, *The Philosophy of Taxation and Public Finance* (Boston: Kluwer Academic Press, 2004), 256.

85. Edward N. Wolff, "Distributional Consequences of a National Land Value Tax on Real Property in the United States," in *Land Value Taxation: Can It and Will It Work Today?*, ed. Dick Netzer (Cambridge, MA: Lincoln Institute of Land Policy, 1998), 78–79. Wolff points out that this "ratio increases uniformly with age until years 70–74, and then declines."

86. Christian R. Jaramillo, "On the Use of Presumptive Income Taxes to Alleviate the Burden of Income Tax Compliance," *National Tax Association Proceedings, 96th Annual Conference on Taxation* (2003).

87. The net worth method for determining income was upheld by the Supreme Court in *Holland v. US*, 348 US121 (1954), which explains the procedure. In *Holland* the taxpayers had records but the IRS reconstruction of their income was based on comparative balance sheets using historical costs at the beginning and end of the tax year. To this increase was added all estimated consumption expenditures for the year. Previously the Supreme Court had only sanctioned this method where the taxpayer had no records. See *Johnson*, 319 US 503.

88. See for example, Wolff, "Distributional Consequences of a National Land Value Tax on Real Property in the United States."

89. But note the example in chapter 2 indicating how cheating the real estate tax can be accomplished by understating the value of the property.

90. 157 US 429 (1895); 158 US 601 (1895) (rehearing).

91. Pollack, *The Failure of U.S. Tax Policy*, 48.

92. For a historical treatment of the controversy surrounding direct versus indirect taxes, including one expert's assessment that "there are almost as many classifications of direct and indirect taxes are there are authors," see *Marrita Murphy and Daniel J. Leveille v. Comm*, 460 F3d 79 (US Ct of App DC Cir, 2006).

93. For a discussion of economic influences on George, including David Ricardo and John Stuart Mill, see Harold M. Groves, *Tax Philosophers: Two Hundred*

Years of Thought in Great Britain and the United States, ed. Donald J. Curran (Madison: University of Wisconsin Press, 1974), 123–26.

94. Kuhn, *The Structure of Scientific Revolutions*, 23.
95. Groves, *Tax Philosophers*, 130.
96. Mill, *Principles of Political Economy*, 546.
97. John Stuart Mill, *On Liberty* (Chicago: Henry Regnery, 1955), 122.
98. Mill, *On Liberty*, .
99. Mill, *Principles of Political Economy*, 541–42. Mill's preference, for which he gives Bentham credit, was for a single rate of income tax (flat tax) that excluded a base amount representing the income required for necessities. According to Mill, this is an application of the "maxim that equal sacrifice ought to be demanded from all," (540), and marks the "difference between a tax which can be saved from luxuries and one which trenches, in ever so small a degree, upon the necessities of life," (541).
100. Mill, *Principles of Political Economy*, 542.
101. Richard Fisher, "Henry George: Antiprotectionist Giant of American Economics," in *Economic Insight*. Federal Reserve Bank of Dallas, vol. 10 no. 2 (2005).
102. Todd G. Buchholz, *New Ideas from Dead Economists* (New York: Penguin Books, 1989), 78.
103. Fisher, "Henry George," quoting Milton Friedman from an interview published in *Human Events*, Nov 19, 1979.
104. Groves, *Tax Philosophers*, 130.
105. Ibid.
106. Robert L. Heilbroner, *The Worldly Philosophers: The Lives, Times and Ideas of the Great Economic Thinkers*, 3rd ed. (New York: Simon and Schuster, 1953), 170.
107. Ibid., 172.
108. Dick Netzer, "The Relevance and Feasibility of Land Value Taxation in the Rich Countries," in *Land Value Taxation*, 109–10.
109. Tax Foundation, www.taxfoundation.org.
110. Webber and Wildavsky, *A History of Taxation and Expenditure in the Western World*, 552.
111. George, *Progress and Poverty*, 421.
112. Fisher, "Henry George."
113. George, *Progress and Poverty*, 165.
114. Smith, *Wealth of Nations*, 499. These are referred to as Smith's four canons of taxation: equality, convenience, certainty, and economy.
115. George, *Progress and Poverty*, 408.
116. Fisher, "Henry George."
117. Richard D. Schwartz and Sonya Orleans, "On Legal Sanctions," *University of Chicago Law Review* 34 (1967): 274, 284.
118. Tax Foundation, www.taxfoundation.org. McGee cites other studies putting the cost of raising revenue at between 24 and 47 percent of revenue raised. See Robert W. McGee, "The Individual Income Tax," in *The Philosophy of Taxation and Public Finance*, 211–13.
119. Slemrod and Bakija, *Taxing Ourselves*, 2.
120. James Gleick, *Faster* (New York: Pantheon Books, 1999), 127–28.
121. Netzer, "The Relevance and Feasibility of Land Value Taxation," 125.

122. Buchholz, *New Ideas from Dead Economists,* 4.
123. John Maynard Keynes, "Economic Model Construction and Econometrics,"1938. Reprinted in *The Philosophy of Economics,* ed. Daniel M. Hausman, 2nd ed. (Cambridge: Cambridge University Press, 1994), 286.
124. In the General Explanation of the *Tax Reform Act of 1986,* H.R. Conf. Rep. No. 841, 99th Cong., 2d sess. 7 (1986) we are told the "primary objective is to ensure that individuals with similar income pay similar amounts of tax."
125. Tax Foundation, www.taxfoundation.org.
126. Joel Slemrod, "On Voluntary Compliance, Voluntary Taxes and Social Capital," *National Tax Journal* 51, no. 3 (1998).
127. Adam Forest and Steven M. Sheffrin, "Complexity and Compliance: An Empirical Investigation," *National Tax Journal* 55, no. 1 (March 2002): 75–88.
128. Tom R. Tyler, *Why People Obey the Law* (Princeton: Princeton University Press, 2006), 97.
129. Ronald Pasquariello, *Tax Justice: Social and Moral Aspects of American Tax Policy* (Lanham: MD, University Press of America, 1985), 41.
130. Forest and Sheffrin, "Complexity and Compliance: An Empirical Investigation," citing Warskett, Winter, and Hettich (1998).
131. Louis Kaplow, "How Tax Complexity and Enforcement Affect the Equality and Efficiency of the Income Tax," *National Tax Journal* 49, no. 1 (March 1996): 135–50.
132. Friedrich A. Hayek, *Individualism and Economic Order* (Chicago: University of Chicago Press 1948), 16.
133. Janice Nadler, "Flouting the Law," *Texas Law Review* 83 (2005): 1399.
134. Paul H. Robinson and John M. Darley, "The Utility of Desert" *Northwestern University Law Review* 91, no. 2 (1997): 453.
135. Nadler, "Flouting the Law."
136. Warren Weaver, "Science and Complexity," *American Scientist* 36 (1948): 536.
137. Bentham, *Of Laws in General,* 159.
138. Joseph M. Dodge, *The Logic of Tax: Federal Income Tax Theory and Policy* (St. Paul: West, 1989), v–vii.
139. Ibid., p. v.
140. "§ 61 Gross income defined. (a) General definition. Except as otherwise provided in this subtitle, gross income means all income from whatever source derived...."
141. IRC § 280E prohibits the deduction from gross income of ordinary and necessary business expenses for those engaged in illegal drug trafficking. However, IRS Reg. § 1.61-(3)(a) defines gross income as sales minus cost of goods sold, thereby permitting even drug dealers a deduction for their cost of goods in arriving at their gross income. For a suggested solution to the problem caused by section 280E, see The National Cannabis Industry Association, "Income Tax Preparation for Cannabis Dispensaries: An Accountant's Worksheet for Minimizing the Impact of IRC Section 280E." http://thecannabisindustry. org/.
142. See US v. Tafoya, 757 F2d 1522 (1985). Tafoya was a professional assassin who failed to report his income and claimed that his gross receipts were only reimbursements for his business expenses, including travel. "According to Tafoya, he 'fronted' the expense of costly international travel and received only partial reimbursement."

143. IRC § 213. For a discussion of this issue by the author and co-author Pingjing Qiao, see "How States Employ the Income Tax to Effect Health Care Measures: Encouraging the Purchase of Health Insurance," *Journal of State Taxation* (Feb. 2011).

144. For an explanation of this problem see the author's "Children and the AMT: Saved by the Kiddie Tax," *The CPA Journal* (Nov. 2011).

145. Forest and Sheffrin, "Complexity and Compliance: An Empirical Investigation."

146. According to Rubenfield and Pandit, "One cannot continually argue that our complicated system of taxation is the sole reason for the extensive tax cheating, and that simplifying our tax system will solve the problem. . . . Ultimately, the question becomes whether, short of a complete overhaul of the system of taxation, [the] types of 'innocent' activities that result in lost tax revenues can ever be stopped." Alan Rubenfield and Ganesh M. Pandit, "Tax 'Cheating' by Ordinary Taxpayers: Does the Underreporting of Income Contribute to the 'Tax Gap'?" *The CPA Journal,* March 25, 2009.

147. Rossotti, *Many Unhappy Returns,* 273.

148. "New IRS Study Provides Preliminary Tax Gap Estimate" IRS IR-2005-38, March 29, 2005.

149. N. G. L. Hammond, *A History of Greece to 322 B.C.* (Oxford: The Clarendon Press, 1959), 156.

150. Aristotle, *Politics,* trans. Benjamin Jowett (New York: Modern Library, 1943), bk. II, chap. 12, 1274b.

151. Plutarch. *Plutarch's Lives,* the Dryden trans. (New York: The Modern Library, 2001), 63.

152. Nadler, "Flouting the Law," 1437.

153. Hammond, *A History of Greece,* 156.

Chapter Four. The Moral Duty to Obey the Law

1. M. B. E. Smith, "Is There a Prima Facie Obligation to Obey the Law?" *Yale Law Journal* 82 (1974): 950. Reprinted in *The Duty to Obey the Law,* ed. William A. Edmundson (New York: Roman and Littlefield,1999).

2. John Locke, *Second Treatise of Government,* ed. C. B. Macpherson (Cambridge: Hackett, [1690] 1980), § 140.

3. Leo P. Martinez, "Taxes, Morals, and Legitimacy," *Brigham Young University Law Review* (1994): 521, 525.

4. Tom R. Tyler, *Why People Obey the Law* (Princeton: Princeton University Press, 2006), 44.

5. Cicero, *The Laws,* in *The Republic and the Laws,* trans. Niall Rudd (Oxford: Oxford University Press, 1998), book 1: 41.

6. Plato, *Laws,* trans. A. E. Taylor, VII, 788 b.

7. I have simplified the range of differences represented by legal positivism and legal naturalism since this is an important but background issue to the present discussion. The relation of morality to legality may be questioned from a number of points of view, which are well expressed in H. L. A. Hart's *Law, Liberty, and Morality* (New York: Vintage Books, 1963).

8. Hans Kelsen, *The Pure Theory of Law,* trans. Max Knight, (Berkeley: University of California Press, 1967), 198.

9. Richard A. Posner, *Problems of Jurisprudence* (Cambridge: Harvard University Press, 1990), 229.

10. Martinez, "Taxes, Morals, and Legitimacy."

11. See, for example, Joseph Raz, "The Obligation to Obey the Law," and "Respect for the Law," in *The Authority of Law* (Oxford: Oxford University Press, 1979).

12. Raz, *The Authority of Law*, 233–49.

13. I would like to avoid putting too much emphasis on labels as they ultimately have no bearing on my arguments. Some readers may object to my use of the term *legal naturalism* in a narrower (or broader) sense than the tradition of natural law, whose most prominent spokesman was Thomas Aquinas. Kent Greenawalt, for example, in the context of his discussion of the natural law, states that Lon Fuller and Ronald Dworkin "accept too little of the traditional position to count as natural law theories" (1987, 194 n. 3). By indicating that there is both a religious version and a secular version it should be apparent that there are both similarities and differences under the umbrella term natural law. Others may object to the term *legal naturalism* because they believe it should be used to describe the philosophy of Karl Marx.

14. Deryck Beyleveld and Roger Brownsword, *Law as a Moral Judgment* (Sheffield, UK: Sheffield Academic Press, 1994), 152.

15. Cicero *The Laws*, book 1:43.

16. A. P. d'Entrèves, *Natural Law*, 2nd ed. (London: Hutchinson, 1951), 84.

17. I mention Machiavelli and Nietzsche not because their versions of ethical relativism are particularly well argued but because they are well-known representatives. Among Machiavelli's views that can be interpreted as relativistic: "A wise ruler, therefore, cannot and should not keep his word when such an observance of faith would be to his disadvantage and when the reasons which made him promise are removed." Niccolò Machiavelli, *The Prince*, trans. Peter Bondanella and Mark Musa (New York: Penguin Books, 1979), 134. Nietzsche claimed, "To speak of right and wrong *per se* makes no sense at all." Friedrich Nietzsche, *The Genealogy of Morals*, trans. Francis Golffing (New York: Doubleday, 1956), 208.

18. Thrasymachus, a character in Plato's dialogue *The Republic,* proclaims that justice is "nothing else than the interest of the stronger" (338c).

19. For a more complete explanation of ethical relativism and its logical consequences, see John Hospers, *Human Conduct: An Introduction to the Problems of Ethics* (New York: Harcourt, Brace and World, 1961), 36–38.

20. John L. Mackie, *Ethics: Inventing Right and Wrong* (New York: Penguin Books, 1977), 83–84.

21. Thomas Hobbes, *Leviathan: Or the Matter, Forme and Power of a Commonwealth Ecclesiasticall and Civil,* ed. Michael Oakeshott (London: Collier-Macmillan, 1962), ch. 26, 203; italics in original.

22. On the emotive view of ethics see Charles L. Stevenson, *Ethics and Language* (New Haven: Yale University Press 1944) and *Facts and Values: Studies in Ethical Analysis* (New Haven: Yale University Press, 1963).

23. However, see Richard A. Posner, *The Problematics of Moral and Legal Theory* (Cambridge: Harvard University Press, 1999). In chapter 1, Posner presents a unique, careful, and pragmatic defense of an enlightened form of ethical relativism.

24. For an exploration of the many subtleties of relativism and subjectivism as opposed to objectivism, see Mackie, *Ethics*.

25. David Hume, *An Enquiry Concerning the Principles of Morals* (La Salle, IL: Open Court, [1777] 1966), 110.

26. R. M. Hare, *Moral Thinking: Its Levels, Method, and Point* (Oxford: Clarendon Press, 1981), 6.

27. Michael Smith, *The Moral Problem* (Oxford: Blackwell, 1995), 5–6.

28. Stephen Toulmin, *Reason in Ethics* (Cambridge: Cambridge University Press, 1968), 20–21.

29. For a contemporary discussion of its religious context see d'Entrèves, *Natural Law*. For a contemporary discussion and defense of its logical context see Beyleved and Brownsword, *Law as a Moral Judgment*.

30. Beyleved and Brownsword, *Law,* especially 150–58. The authors also describe two types of moral relativism: (1) "moral relativism which derives from *amoralism*" and (2) "moral relativism which derives from the view that moral reason does not necessitate any specific moral principles" (153; italics in original).

31. Beyleved and Brownsword, *Law,* 33.

32. d'Entrèves, *Natural Law,* 90.

33. Martinez, for example, says, "Legal and political philosophers of all persuasions have failed to produce a convincing argument for a moral duty to obey the law" (567).

34. Rolf Sartorius, "Political Authority and Political Obligation" *Virginia Law Review* 67, no. 1 (Feb. 1981): 3.

35. *Why People Obey the Law,* 45.

36. Jeffrie G. Murphy and Jules L. Coleman, *Philosophy of Law* (Boulder: Westview, 1990), 17–18.

37. Ronald Dworkin, *Taking Rights Seriously* (Cambridge: Harvard University Press, 1977), 9.

38. John Rawls, "Legal Obligation and the Duty of Fair Play," in *Law and Philosophy: A Symposium,* ed. Sidney Hook. (New York: New York University Press, 1964), 5.

39. Henry David Thoreau, *Civil Disobedience* (New York: Quill Pen, 2008), 2.

40. Sidney Hook, "Law, Justice, and Obedience," in *Law and Philosophy: A Symposium,* ed. Sidney Hook (New York: New York University Press 1964), 57.

41. Marcus George Singer, *Generalization in Ethics* (New York: Atheneum, 1971), 74–75.

42. George C. Christie, "On the Moral Obligation to Obey the Law," *Duke Law Journal* 6 (1990).

43. "It is surely self-evident that where the legal order is a moral order it generates a moral obligation of support and respect." Beyleveld and Brownsword, 329.

44. Posner, *Problems of Jurisprudence,* 235.

45. Ibid., 223–34.

46. Martin I. Crowe, *The Moral Obligation of Paying Just Taxes* (Washington, DC: The Catholic University Press of America, 1944), 28.

47. Thomas Aquinas, *Summa Theologica,* in *The Great Books of the Western World,* vol. 20, translated by Fathers of the English Dominican Province, revised by Daniel J. Sullivan (Chicago: Encyclopedia Britannica, 1952), first part of the second part, ques. 90, art. 4.

48. Benjamin Cardozo, *The Nature of the Judicial Process* (New Haven: Yale University Press, 1921), 66.

49. Aquinas, *Summa Theologica,* first part of the second part, ques. 94, art. 3.

50. d'Entrèves, 84, citing Aquinas, first part of the second part, ques. 72, art. 4, and ques. 96, arts. 2 and 3.

51. Aquinas, *Summa Theologica*, first part of the second part, ques. 96, art. 4.

52. Crowe, *The Moral Obligation of Paying Just Taxes*, 85.

53. Margaret Levi, *Of Rule and Revenue* (Berkeley: University of California Press, 1988), 52.

54. Cicero, *The Laws*, bk. 2:13.

55. Paul Vinogradoff, *Common Sense in Law* (New York: Henry Holt, 1913), 43.

56. Ibid., 42.

57. Ibid.

58. John Rawls, *A Theory of Justice* (Cambridge: Harvard University Press, 1971), 112.

59. Herbert Spencer, *The Man Versus the State* (Indianapolis: The Liberty Fund, [1884]1982), 132.

60. Bernard P. Dauenhauer, "On Strengthening the Law's Obligatory Character" *Georgia Law Review* 18, no. 4 (1984): 821.

61. H. L. A. Hart, *The Concept of Law* (London: Oxford University Press, 1961), 202.

62. Ibid.

63. Affirming this, Beyleveld and Brownsword write, "We take it that it is common ground between legal positivists and natural-law theorists that the concept of legal obligation is tied to the concept of legal validity. It is legally valid rules, and only legally valid rules, which generate legal obligations. For both sides, legal obligations are obligations arising under rules of law." Beyleveld and Brownsword, *Law*, 326.

64. Lon L. Fuller, *The Morality of Law* (New Haven: Yale University Press, 1964), 41.

65. Ibid., 38–39.

66. Ibid., 42.

67. Steve Forbes claimed that the Internal Revenue Code had been changed 14,000 times since 1986 in an interview on CNBC (Nov. 3, 2010). See Gunn, who questions the idea that laws should not be retroactive. On the one hand, he points out, if they are retroactive for everyone then this is not violating the principle of treating like cases alike. On the other hand, he notes that judges often and properly change the law retroactively, especially if doing so is needed to counteract the unanticipated results of a particular law. Alan Gunn, "Tax Avoidance" *Michigan Law Review* 76, no. 5 (1978): 733, n.117.

68. In Calendar Year 2009, the Internal Revenue Service (IRS) processed approximately 83.1 million individual Federal income tax returns prepared by paid preparers. This is 59.4 percent of the 140 million total returns filed. Report of the Treasury Inspector General for Tax Administration, Sept. 30, 2010 (Reference Number: 2010-40-127).

69. Fuller, *The Morality of Law*, 39.

70. Kent Greenawalt, *Conflicts of Law and Morality* (Oxford: Oxford University Press, 1987), 166.

71. Rawls, *A Theory of Justice*, 112.

72. Adam Forest and Steven M. Sheffrin, "Complexity and Compliance: An Empirical Investigation," *National Tax Journal* 55, no. 1 (March 2002): 75–88. Like much empirical research on tax compliance, these findings are contradicted

by other research. See, for example, Thomas M. Porcano, "Correlates of Tax Evasion," *Journal of Economic Psychology* 9 (1988): 47–67, who found that tax evasion is unrelated to the fairness of the tax. Pointing to a possible resolution to this conflict of findings, Tom Tyler differentiates the fairness of the procedures by which the amount of tax is determined from the absolute amount of tax owed, finding that the latter is not as important to taxpayers as the former. In judging fairness, "procedural concerns consistently take precedence over distributive concerns." Tyler, *Why People Obey the Law,* 97.

73. Learned Hand, *The Bill of Rights* (New York: Atheneum, 1979), 47.

74. Stephen Pfohl, *Images of Deviance and Social Control: A Sociological History,* 2nd ed. (New York: McGraw-Hill, 1994), 92.

75. Henry George, *Progress and Poverty* (New York: Robert Schalkenbach Foundation, 1953), 416–17.

76. See Robert W. McGee, "Is Tax Evasion Unethical?" *Kansas Law Review* 42 (1994): 411; Robert W. McGee, ed., *The Ethics of Tax Evasion* (South Orange, NJ: The Dumont Institute of Public Policy Research, 1998); Robert W. McGee, "Three Views on the Ethics of Tax Evasion," *Journal of Business Ethics* 67 (2006): 15–35; Martinez, "Taxes, Morals, and Legitimacy": 521.

77. McGee, "Is Tax Evasion Unethical?."

78. George Christie notes, "What constitutes 'theft,' 'fraud,' or 'stealing' are profoundly influenced by legal analysis—indeed, 'theft' and 'fraud' are legal terms of art." "On the Moral Obligation to Obey the Law," 1311.

79. Stephen Holmes and Cass R. Sunstein, *The Cost of Rights: Why Liberty Depends on Taxes* (New York: W. W. Norton, 1999), 67.

80. "Property." *Black's Law Dictionary,* abridged 6th ed. (St. Paul: West, 1991), 845.

81. Ibid.

82. Milton Friedman, *Capitalism and Freedom* (Chicago: The University of Chicago Press, 2002), 26.

83. Holmes and Sunstein, *The Cost of Rights,* 149.

84. Spencer, *The Man Versus the State,* 153.

85. Dworkin, *Taking Rights Seriously,* xi.

86. Paul Vinogradoff, *Custom and Right* (Union, New Jersey: The Lawbook Exchange, [1925] 2000), 101.

87. Ibid., 69.

88. Ayn Rand, *The Virtue of Selfishness: A New Concept of Egoism* (New York: Signet, 1964), 91.

89. Ibid., 33.

90. Hobbes, *Leviathan,* 100.

91. Locke, *Second Treatise of Government,* § 31; italics in original.

92. Ibid., § 124; italics in original.

93. Jean-Jacques Rousseau, *Discourse on Political Economy,* trans. Julia Conway Bondanella, in *Rousseau's Political Writings* (New York: W. W. Norton, 1988), 64.

94. Ibid., 75.

95. Jeremy Bentham, *The Theory of Fictions* (Patterson, NJ: Littlefield, Adams, 1959), 119.

96. Holmes and Sunstein, *The Cost of Rights,* 17. "Every first-year law student learns that private property is not an 'object' or a 'thing' but a complex bundle of

rights. Property is a legally constructed social relation, a cluster of legislatively and judicially created and judicially enforceable rules of access and exclusion" (59).

97. According to Mises, "Taxes are necessary. But the system of discriminatory taxation universally accepted under the misleading name of progressive taxation of income and inheritance is not a mode of taxation. It is rather a mode of disguised expropriation of the successful capitalists and entrepreneurs . . . [and] is incompatible with the preservation of the market economy." Ludwig von Mises, *Human Action: A Treatise on Economics,* 3rd rev. ed. (San Francisco: Fox and Wilkes, 1949), 807.

98. McGee, "Is Tax Evasion Unethical?"

99. Immanuel Kant, *The Metaphysics of Morals,* in *Political Writings,* trans. H. B. Nisbet (Cambridge: Cambridge University Press, [1797] 1991), 150.

100. Christopher Wellman and John Simmons, *Is There a Duty to Obey the Law?* (Cambridge: Cambridge University Press, 2005), 44.

101. Locke, *Second Treatise of Government,* § 140.

102. Rousseau, *Discourse on Political Economy,* 80–81.

103. United States Constitution, Art I, Sec 7, cl 1.

104. The meaning of voluntary in this context is a contentious issue. McGee, for example, says, "It cannot be said that legislators represent the will of the majority or even of their constituents. . . . It cannot be said that taxation is voluntary just because some people voted to elect some legislators who passed tax laws." Robert W. McGee, "An Ethical Look at Paying Your 'Fair Share' of Taxes," *Journal of Accounting, Ethics & Public Policy.* 2, no. 2 (Spring 1999).

105. Locke, *Second Treatise of Government,* § 119; italics in original.

106. David A. J. Richards, "Conscience, Human Rights, and the Anarchist Challenge to the Obligation to Obey the Law," *Georgia Law Review* 18 (1984) 771.

107. For a general discussion of consent, which addresses the difference between the attitude of consent and the act of consent as well as the debate about the meaning and significance of tacit or implied consent, see A. John Simmons, *Moral Principles and Political Obligations* (Princeton: Princeton University Press, 1979), especially 79–100.

108. Locke, *Second Treatise of Government,* § 140.

109. McGee, "Three Views on the Ethics of Tax Evasion," 15–35.

110. Holmes and Sunstein, *The Cost of Rights,* 61.

111. Simmons, 87–95. "While consent, be it tacit or express, may still be the firmest ground for political obligation (in that people who have consented probably have fewer doubts about their obligations than others), it must be admitted that in most modern states consent will only bind the smallest minority of citizens to obedience." *Moral Principles and Political Obligations,* 93–94.

112. For a defense of the position that accepting the benefits of a legal system, voting and not leaving the country establish a legal duty but not a moral duty to obey the law see Mark Tunick, "The Moral Obligation to Obey the Law," *Journal of Social Philosophy* 33, no. 5 (Fall 2002): 464–82.

113. On this question, Simmons writes: "Could a formal choice situation, like the one described by Socrates, make continued residence a sign of consent? Joseph Tussman has answered this question in the affirmative. As long as the situation makes it clear that one who remains a resident is aware of the significance of so remaining, and as long as there remains a genuine alternative to giving

one's tacit consent, then residence will be a sign of consent." *Moral Principles and Political Obligations*, 98, quoting Joseph Tussman, *Obligation and the Body Politic* (Oxford: Oxford University Press, 1960), 38.

114. Hume believed this is an unrealistic argument because of the inconvenience of leaving one's native country. See "Of the Original Contract," *Essays Moral Political and Literary*, ed. Eugene F. Miller (Indianapolis: Liberty Fund, 1985), 465–87.

115. For one discussion of this question see, Simmons, *Moral Principles and Political Obligations*, 76–100.

116. Rawls, *A Theory of Justice*, 111–12.

117. Individuals with a net worth of $2 million or more and who terminate long-term residency or U.S. citizenship are subject to IRC § 877 and § 877A rules requiring IRS reporting. These rules include a requirement to file IRS Form 8854 disclosing information on their income and assets or facing a $10,000 penalty.

118. John Dewey points out, "The worse or evil is a rejected good. In deliberation and before choice no evil presents itself as evil. Until it is rejected it is a competing good." John Dewey, *Human Nature and Conduct* (New York: Henry Holt, 1922), 278.

119. Tony Honoré, "Must We Obey? Necessity as a Ground of Obligation" *Virginia Law Review* 67 (Feb. 1981): 39.

120. Rousseau, *Discourse on Political Economy*, 75. Holmes and Sunstein observe, "Rights cannot be protected or enforced without public funding and support." *The Cost of Rights*, 15.

121. Greenawalt, *Conflicts of Law and Morality*, 160.

122. Ibid., 162.

123. P. Soper, "Obligation to Obey the Law," in *Issues in Contemporary Legal Philosophy: The Influence of H. L. A. Hart*, ed. R. Gravison (Oxford: Oxford University Press, 1987), quoted in Greenawalt (1987), 171.

124. Paul H. Robinson, and John M. Darley, "The Utility of Desert" *Northwestern University Law Review* 91, no. 2 (1997): 453.

125. Ibid.

126. Ibid.

127. Ibid.

128. d'Entrèves, *Natural Law*, 132.

129. Wellman and Simmons, *Is There a Duty to Obey the Law?* 17.

130. Honoré, "Must We Obey? Necessity as a Ground of Obligation."

131. Charles H. McCaghy, Timothy A. Capron, and J. D. Jamieson, *Deviant Behavior*, 6th ed. (Boston: Pearson Education, 2003), 3.

132. Nicholas Rescher, *Predicting the Future: An Introduction to the Theory of Forecasting* (Albany: State University of New York Press, 1998), 5.

133. Richards, "Conscience, Human Rights, and the Anarchist Challenge to the Obligation to Obey the Law," 771.

134. IRS Oversight Board 2009 Taxpayer Attitude Survey, table 2. As noted in chapter 1, 87 percent believe they have a moral duty, as reported by a *Wall Street Journal* poll.

135. U.S. Constitution, Art 1, sec 8.

136. Thomas Jefferson, *The Political Writings of Thomas Jefferson*, ed. Merrill D. Peterson (Chapel Hill: University of North Carolina Press, 1993), 141.

Chapter Five. Cheating, Competition, and Fairness

1. Randolph Freezel, "Baseball, Cheating, and Tradition: Would Kant Cork His Bat?," in *Baseball and Philosophy: Thinking Outside the Batter's Box*, ed. Eric Bronson (Chicago: Open Court, 2004).

2. Seneca, *Moral Essays*, vol.1, trans. John W. Basore. Loeb Classical Library (Cambridge: Harvard University Press, 1928), 17.

3. Margaret Levi, *Of Rule and Revenue* (Berkeley: University of California Press, 1988), 48.

4. H. L. A. Hart, *The Concept of Law* (London: Oxford University Press, 1961), 202.

5. U.S. House of Representatives, Hearing Before the Subcommittee on Oversight of the Committee on Ways and Means, *Hearing on Internal Revenue Service Operations and the Tax Gap*, 110th Cong., 1st sess., March 20, 2007.

6. John Stuart Mill, *Principles of Political Economy*, abridged by J. Laurence Laughlin (New York: Appleton, 1884), 556.

7. Frank Schmalleger, *Criminology Today*, 3rd ed. (Upper Saddle River, NJ: Prentice-Hall, 2002), 121.

8. Charles Adams, *For Good and Evil: The Impact of Taxes of the Course of Civilization* (London: Madison Books, 1993), 395–96.

9. Jean-Baptiste Say, *A Treatise on Political Economy*, trans. C. R. Prinsep (New Brunswick, NJ: Transaction, [1836] 2001), 118.

10. Frank A. Cowell, *Cheating the Government: The Economics of Evasion* (Cambridge: The MIT Press, 1990), 5.

11. IRS SOI Table 6a. Examination Coverage (Including EITC) All Taxpayers, By Examination Class Fiscal Years 1996–2002.

12. IRS, "The Tax Gap Facts and Figures," March 2005.

13. IRS SOI Table 9a. Examination Coverage: Recommended and Average Recommended Additional Tax After Examination, by Type and Size of Return, Fiscal Year 2009. Note that .9 of one percent is the IRS average for 2009. For individuals with Adjusted Gross Incomes (AGIs) under $100,000 the rate is lower and for taxpayers with AGIs above $200,000 it is higher. For those with AGIs between $1 million and $5 million, for example, the rate is 5.35 percent. Source: IRS Data Book, 2009.

14. George Violette, "Effects of Communicating Sanctions on Taxpayer Compliance," *The Journal of the American Taxation Association* (Fall 1989).

15. Robert A. Kagan, "On the Visibility of Income Tax Law Violations," in *Tax Compliance vol. 2: Social Science Perspectives*, ed. Jeffrey A. Roth and John T. Scholz (Philadelphia: University of Pennsylvania Press, 1989), 78.

16. Internal Revenue Code § 6103 Confidentiality and disclosure of returns and return information. Also § 7217 Prohibition on executive branch influence over taxpayer audits and other investigations.

17. IRS Oversight Board 2009 Taxpayer Attitude Survey. The 58 percent include taxpayers who "completely agree" and "mostly agree."

18. IRC § 7623 Expenses of detection of underpayments and fraud, etc.

19. According to KPMG's 1998 *Fraud Survey of 5,000 U. S. Companies and Organizations*, external auditors discover only 4–5 percent of fraud, while 28–37 percent is discovered by chance. Whistleblowing employees account for 51–58 percent of fraud discovery. Similar results were reported by the Association of Certified

Fraud Examiners in their 2010 *Report to the Nations on Occupational Fraud and Abuse*. They found that 4.6 percent of fraud was discovered by external auditors, 8.3 percent by accident, and 40.2 percent from tips (whistleblowers) (Austin, TX).

20. Robert K. Merton, *On Social Structure and Science*, ed. Piotr Sztompka (Chicago: University of Chicago Press, 1996), 14.

21. Lon L. Fuller, *The Morality of Law* (New Haven: Yale University Press, 1964), 39–40.

22. Robert B. Cialdini, "Social Motivations to Comply: Norms, Values, and Principles," in *Taxpayer Compliance vol. 2: Social Science Perspectives*, ed. Jeffrey A. Roth and John T. Scholz (Philadelphia: University of Pennsylvania Press, 1989), 210.

23. Mark Twain, *Mark Twain on the Damned Human Race*, ed. Janet Smith (New York: Hill and Wang, 1962), 30.

24. See note 5 in ch. 1 on Willie Nelson and note 38 in ch. 2 on Wesley Snipes.

25. Harold G. Grasmick and Robert J. Bursik Jr., "Conscience, Significant Others, and Rational Choice: Extending the Deterrence Model," *Law & Society Review* 24, no. 3 (1990).

26. Richard D. Schwartz and Sonya Orleans, "On Legal Sanctions," *University of Chicago Law Review* 34 (1967): 274.

27. Ibid.

28. Janice Nadler, "Flouting the Law," *Texas Law Review* 83 (2005): 1399, 1401.

29. U.S. Congress, House Committee on Ways and Means, Subcommittee on Oversight, *"Tax Gap" and Taxpayer Noncompliance* (Washington, DC: Government Printing Office, 1990), 214–15. Quoted in David Callahan, *The Cheating Culture: Why Americans are Doing Wrong to Get Ahead* (New York: Harcourt, 2004), 178.

30. George Bernard Shaw, Preface, in *Major Barbara* (New York: Penguin Books, 1957), 47.

31. John Rawls, *A Theory of Justice* (Cambridge: Harvard University Press, 1971), 18–19.

32. Ibid., 18.

33. John T. Scholz, "Compliance Research and the Political Context of Tax Administration," in *Tax Compliance vol. 2: Social Science Perspectives*, ed. Jeffrey A. Roth and John T. Scholz (Philadelphia: University of Pennsylvania Press, 1989), 28.

34. Seneca, "On Tranquility of Mind," in *Moral Essays* vol. 2, trans. John W. Basore. Loeb Classical Library (Cambridge: Harvard University Press, 1932), 259.

35. Rev. Rul. 2009-9, IRB 2009-14, 735, April 6, 2009. The IRS's reasoning that the Madoff scheme was not an investment but a fraud leads to a slippery slope. Investors in AIG or Countrywide Mortgage or Lehman Brothers or other casualties of the financial crisis of 2008 may wonder where the line is drawn between unwarranted risk taking or gross negligence and fraud.

36. Thomas Hobbes, *Leviathan: Or the Matter, Forme and Power of a Commonwealth Ecclesiasticall and Civil*, ed. Michael Oakeshott (London: Collier-Macmillan, 1962), ch. 30, 254–55.

37. Ibid.

38. Hume "Of Taxes," in *Essays Moral Political and Literary*, ed. Eugene F. Miller (Indianapolis: Liberty Fund, 1985), 345. John Stuart Mill agreed as well. "If,

indeed, reliance could be placed on the conscience of the contributors, or sufficient security taken for the correctness of their statements by collateral precautions, the proper mode of assessing an income-tax would be to tax only the part of income devoted to expenditure, exempting that which is saved." Mill, *Principles of Political Economy*, 545.

39. Charles De. Montesquieu, *The Spirit of the Laws*, trans., Thomas Nugent and rev. J. V. Prichard. In *The Great Books of the Western World*, vol. 38 (Chicago: Encyclopedia Britannica, 1952), book XIII, ch. 14, 12.

40. Rawls, *A Theory of Justice*, 105.

41. Adam Smith, "Of Taxes," *Wealth of Nations* (New York: Prometheus Books, [1776]1991), [bk. 5, ch. 2, pt. 2] 198.

42. Milton Friedman, *Capitalism and Freedom* (Chicago: The University of Chicago Press, 2002), 175.

43. Lars P. Feld and Bruno S. Frey "Tax Compliance as the Result of a Psychological Tax Contract: The Role of Incentives and Responsive Regulation," *Law & Policy* 29, no. 1 (Jan. 2007).

44. Leo P. Martinez, "Taxes, Morals, and Legitimacy," *Brigham Young University Law Review* (1994): 521, 543.

45. Robert W. McGee, "An Ethical Look at Paying Your 'Fair Share' of Taxes," *Journal of Ethics, Accounting & Public Policy* 2, no. 2 (Spring 1999).

46. Robert W. McGee, *The Ethics of Tax Evasion*, ed. Robert W. McGee (South Orange, NJ: The Dumont Institute of Public Policy Research, 1998), 32.

47. Kim M. Bloomquist, "Tax Evasion, Income Inequality and Opportunity Costs of Compliance," *National Tax Association Proceedings, 96th Annual Conference on Taxation*, 2003(a).

48. Stephen Holmes and Cass R. Sunstein, *The Cost of Rights: Why Liberty Depends on Taxes* (New York: W. W. Norton, 1999), 60.

49. Ibid., 63.

50. Ibid., 61.

51. Ibid., 75.

52. The quote attributed to Oliver Wendell Holmes Jr., "Taxes are the price we pay for a civilized society" is phrased "Taxes are what we pay for civilized society," in his dissenting opinion in *Compania General De Tabacos De Filipinas v. Collector of Internal Revenue*, 275 US 87, 100, (1927).

53. Thomas Hobbes, *De Corpore Politico* (Oxford: Oxford University Press, 1994), 137.

54. Mill, *Principles of Political Economy*, 540.

55. Friedrich A Hayek, *Law, Legislation and Liberty*, vol. 3 *The Political Order of a Free People* (Chicago: University of Chicago Press, 1979), 41.

56. Ludwig von Mises, *Human Action: A Treatise on Economics*, 3rd revised ed. (San Francisco: Fox and Wilkes, 1949), 282.

57. United States v. Helmsley, 941 F2d 71, (2d Cir 1991), cert. denied, 502 US 1091 (1992).

58. Holmes and Sunstein, *The Cost of Rights*, 21.

59. Friedrich Nietzsche, *The Genealogy of Morals*, trans. Francis Golffing (New York: Doubleday, 1956), 203.

60. Robert Mason and Lyle. D. Calvin, "A Study of Admitted Tax Evasion," *Law and Society Review* 13 (1978): 78.

61. Ibid.

62. Ibid.

63. Adam Forest and Steven M. Sheffrin, "Complexity and Compliance: An Empirical Investigation," *National Tax Journal* 55, no. 1 (March 2002): 75–88.

64. Michael Asimow, "Civil Penalties for Inaccurate and Delinquent Tax Returns," *UCLA Law Review* 23, no. 4 (1976): 637.

65. IRS Oversight Board, 2009 Taxpayer Attitude Survey, asked taxpayers: "Is it every American's civic duty to pay their fair share of taxes?" Respondents strongly believe it is, with 70 percent claiming they "completely agree" and 25 percent that they "mostly agree." Very few issues of public life garner such consensus.

66. McGee, "An Ethical Look at Paying Your 'Fair Share' of Taxes."

67. Danshera Cords, "Tax Protestors and Penalties: Ensuring Perceived Fairness and Mitigating Systemic Costs," *Brigham Young University Law Review* (2005): 1515.

68. IRS News Release 88-77, April 15, 1988.

69. David Foster Wallace, *The Pale King* (New York: Little Brown, 2011), 130.

70. Charles O. Rossotti, *Many Unhappy Returns: One Man's Quest to Turn Around the Most Unpopular Organization in the World* (Boston: Harvard Business School Press, 2005), 271.

71. Dan M. Kahan, "Trust, Collective Action, and Law," *Boston University Law Review* 81, no. 2 (April 2001): 333.

72. Robert B. Cialdini, "Social Motivations to Comply: Norms, Values, and Principles," in *Taxpayer Compliance vol. 2: Social Science Perspectives,* ed. Jeffrey A. Roth and John T. Scholz (Philadelphia: University of Pennsylvania Press, 1989), 215.

73. Marcus George Singer, *Generalization in Ethics* (New York: Atheneum, 1971), 61.

74. Quoted by Singer (86–87), from A. C. Ewing, *The Definition of Good* (New York: Macmillan, 1947).

75. Singer, *Generalization in Ethics,* 86–87.

76. Ibid., 72.

77. Ibid.

78. Ibid., 81.

79. Ibid.

80. Ibid., 81–82.

81. Martinez, "Taxes, Morals, and Legitimacy," 521, 557.

82. Yankelovich, Skelly, and White, Inc. "Taxpayer Attitudes Survey: Final Report," Public Opinion Survey Prepared for the Public Affairs Division, Internal Revenue Service (New York, 1984).

83. John S. Carroll, "Compliance with the Law: A Decision-Making Approach to Taxpaying," *Law and Human Behavior* 11, no. 4 (1987): 47.

84. Locke, *Second Treatise of Government,* § 142.

85. Oliver Wendell Holmes Jr., *The Common Law* (Mineola, NY: Dover, 1991), 110.

86. Friedrich A. Hayek, *The Road to Serfdom* (Chicago: University of Chicago Press, 1944), 80.

87. Hart, *The Concept of Law,* 202.

88. Immanuel Kant, *Groundwork of the Metaphysic of Morals,* trans. H. J. Paton (New York: Harper and Row, 1964), 89.

89. Ibid., 90.

90. Ibid.
91. Robert W. McGee, "Three Views on the Ethics of Tax Evasion," *Journal of Business Ethics* 67 (2006): 15–35.
92. Though we may not be able to obey or disobey special interest legislation because it is aimed at a particular industry or group of taxpayers—from which we are specifically excluded—we may sometimes be able to vote against these provisions with our wallets. If we do not care for the special interest legislation that benefits the dairy industry, for example, we can eat less cheese.
93. Levi, *Of Rule and Revenue*, 49.
94. The term *tax earmark* is also used to refer to a tax that is tied to a specific tax base and is intended to pay for a particular good or service. For a discussion of ethical issues generated by this form of earmarked tax system, see Robert W. McGee, "Earmarking Taxes," in *The Philosophy of Taxation and Public Finance* (Boston: Kluwer, 2004), 163–70.
95. Title XVII sect. 1701 Identification of Limited Tax Benefits Subject to Line Item Veto.
96. P. L. 104-130.
97. Clinton v. City of New York, 524 US 417. In its syllabus of the case the Supreme Court writes, "The President exercised his authority under the [*Line Item Veto Act,* 2 U.S.C. § 691 *et seq.*] by canceling § 4722(c) of the *Balanced Budget Act of 1997,* "which permitted the owners of certain food refiners and processors to defer recognition of capital gains if they sold their stock to eligible farmers' cooperatives."
98. *Taxpayer Relief Act of 1997.*
99. The *Dallas Morning News*, August 8, 1997. Act § 1175. This provision was subject to the president's line-item veto and was in fact vetoed. However, the veto was subject to a constitutional challenge to the *Line Item Veto Act* itself in *Clinton v. City of New York.*
100. Sheldon D. Pollack, *The Failure of U.S. Tax Policy: Revenue and Politics* (University Park: The Pennsylvania State University Press, 1996), 4.
101. § 1171(a) of P.L. 99-514 repealed an ESOP credit in IRC § 38, but exempted the *Houston Chronicle* from such repeal. Code § 41. P.L. 99-514, § 1177(b), [as amended by Sec. 1011B(1) of P.L. 100-647] provides transitional rules for changes made by Subtitle C of Title XI (§§ 1171-1177) of the Act: "(b) Subtitle not to apply to certain newspaper."
102. "Ace in the Hole: Golfers Make the Cut in Retirement Round," *Wall Street Journal,* October 14, 2004. According to the article, "As the bill moved through Congress in June, a crush of influential lawmakers attended the PGA Tour's Booz-Allen Classic at Avenel Country Club in Maryland, where they played with the pros."
103. IRC § 409A as amended by HR 4520, Act § 855(d)(3)(C). "(3) Exception for nonelective deferred compensation . . . (C) which is established or maintained by an organization incorporated on July 2, 1974."
104. The PGA's IRS Form 990 (as well as that of the NFL and NHL) lists its tax-exempt status as 501(c)(6)—"Business leagues, chambers of commerce, real-estate boards, boards of trade, or professional football leagues . . . not organized for profit and no part of the net earnings of which inures to the benefit of any private shareholder or individual." While the PGA is not a charity, it made donations in 2009 to a number of organizations that are 501(c)(3) charities

including $7,943,563 to the World Golf Foundation, $11,756 to the Humane Society of Northeast Florida, and $9,640 to the Child Cancer Fund.

105. US Const, Art 1, § 8.

106. This is a tax imposed by IRC § 512 and § 513 on income earned by otherwise tax-exempt organizations that is generated by activities outside the purview of the tax-exempt purpose for which they were formed.

107. Bruce Hopkins, *A Legal Guide to Starting and Managing a Nonprofit Organization* (New York: John Wiley and Sons, 1993), 34. Philip M. Stern, *The Rape of the Taxpayer* (New York: Vintage Books, 1974), 40, confirms this as well.

108. Internal Revenue Code § 3127 and § 1402(g).

109. See James Glenn Harwood, "Religiously-Based Social Security Exemptions: Who is Eligible, How did they Develop, and are the Exemptions Consistent with the Religion Clauses and the Religious Freedom Restoration Act (RFRA)?" *Akron Tax Journal* 17 (2002): 1. The Supreme Court in *US v. Lee*, 455 US, 258-261 (1990) dealt with this issue, leading to the law change. In Lee, "an Amish employer, on behalf of himself and his employees, sought exemption from collection and payment of Social Security taxes on the ground that the Amish faith prohibited participation in governmental support programs." The Court rejected the claim. *Employment Division of the Oregon Department of Human Resources v. Smith*, 494 US 872. Individuals claim the exemption from Social Security and Self-Employment taxes by filing IRS Form 4029.

110. IRC § 107.

111. IRC § 165(a)(6) and Rev. Rul. 87-32, 1987-1 C.B. 131.

112. IRC § 6033(a)(3).

113. See *Living Word Christian Center*, 103 AFTR 2d 20069-714 and IRC § 7611 Restrictions on church tax inquiries and examinations § 7611(a)(1)(B)(2) "The requirements of this paragraph are met with respect to any church tax inquiry if *an appropriate high-level Treasury official* reasonably believes . . . "; emphasis added.

114. Henry David Thoreau, *Civil Disobedience* (New York: Quill Pen, 2008), 13.

115. Ronald Dworkin, *Taking Rights Seriously* (Cambridge: Harvard University Press, 1977), 107.

116. New Colonial Ice Co. v. Helvering, 292 U.S. 435 (1934).

117. John Calvin, *The Institutes of Christian Religion*, ed. Tony Lane and Hilary Osborne (Grand Rapids: Baker Book House, 1986), 3:12:21.

118. Ibid.

119. IRC § 170(n).

120. IRC § 170(f)(15).

121. Smith, *Wealth of Nations*, 563.

122. *American Recovery and Reinvestment Act*, P.L. 111-5, § 2014. "Temporary Reduction in Recognition Period for Built-in Gains Tax."

123. The particular wine operation was founded in 1933.

124. John L. Mackie, *Ethics: Inventing Right and Wrong* (New York: Penguin Books, 1977), 85.

125. Pollack, *The Failure of U.S. Tax Policy: Revenue and Politics*, 25.

126. Jeffrey H. Birnbaum and Alan S. Murray, *Showdown at Gucci Gulch: Lawmakers, Lobbyists, and the Unlikely Triumph of Tax Reform* (New York: Vintage Books, 1987), 181.

127. Philip M. Stern, *The Rape of the Taxpayer* (New York: Vintage Books, 1974), ch. 3.
128. Ibid., 57.
129. Arrowsmith v. Comm of Internal Revenue, 73 SCt 71 (1952).
130. The IRS generally announces its intentions to acquiesce or not in an Action on Decision (AOD) published in the IRS Internal Revenue Bulletin and later included in the IRS Cumulative Bulletin. The IRS does not register its intention on each case nor is it required to do so.
131. Golsen v. Comm, 54 TC 742, 756-758 (1970), aff'd on another issue, 445 F2d 985 (10th Cir 1971).
132. Ibid.
133. Richard A. Posner, *Problems of Jurisprudence* (Cambridge: Harvard University Press, 1990), 224.
134. Ibid., 333.
135. Contributing to the seriousness of this problem is the fact that the judges in the U.S. Tax Court are specialists in the tax law while their counterparts in the Appeals court are generalists, dealing with the full spectrum of federal issues.
136. IRC § 7463.
137. See Carlton M. Smith, "Does the Tax Court's Use of its Golsen Rule in Unappealable Small Tax Cases Hurt the Poor?" *Journal of Tax Practice and Procedure*, Cardozo Legal Studies Research Paper No. 249 (2009).
138. The user fees are set out in Rev. Proc. 2011-1, Appendix A. Though not accorded precedential authority by the Internal Revenue Code § 6110(j)(3), tax practitioners often find Private Letter Rulings (PLRs) helpful for discerning the general approach the IRS may take on a particular issue. Many tax practitioners also accord weight to Private Letter Rulings because they are listed in Reg. § 1.6661-3(b) and § 1.6662-4(d) as "substantial authority," but this relates only to avoiding the "substantial understatement" penalty of § 6662, not the weight they are accorded in a court of law.
139. In *Rowan Cos, Inc. v. US*, 101 SCt 2288 (1981), for example, the Supreme Court criticized the IRS for issuing rulings that were inconsistent with one another with respect to what constitutes wages for FICA purposes. Private Letter Rulings are made available in redacted form through Freedom of Information requests as a result of the court's ruling in *Tax Analysts v. IRS*, 81 AFTR 2d 98-1784, (DC-Dist Col 1998).
140. IRS Rev. Proc. 2011-1.
141. As noted in chapter 3, note 78, "An amoral or non-moral practical discourse is one in which values lack at least one of the defining features of moral values—justificatory force, universalisability, and categoricality." Deryck Beyleveld and Roger Brownsword, *Law as a Moral Judgment* (Sheffield, UK: Sheffield Academic Press, 1994), 153.
142. Paul H. Robinson, and John M. Darley, "The Utility of Desert," *Northwestern University Law Review* 91, no. 2 (1997): 453.
143. Ibid.

Chapter Six. Unintentional Cheating

1. Harold G. Grasmick and Robert J. Bursik Jr., "Conscience, Significant Others, and Rational Choice: Extending the Deterrence Model," *Law & Society Review* 24, no. 3 (1990): 837–61.

2. Scott Plous, *The Psychology of Judgment and Decision Making* (New York: McGraw-Hill, 1993), 98.

3. Philip M. Reckers, Debra L. Sanders, and Stephen J. Roark, "The Influence of Ethical Attitudes on Taxpayer Compliance," *National Tax Journal* 47, no. 4 (Dec. 1994): 825–36.

4. Ludwig Wittgenstein, *Philosophical Investigations*, 3rd ed., trans. G. E. M. Anscombe (Englewood Cliffs, NJ: Prentice-Hall), 67.

5. Ibid., 66.

6. Lewis Carroll, *Through the Looking Glass*, in *The Annotated Alice*, intro. and notes Martin Gardner (Cleveland: World, 1960), 210; italics in original. In the annotation to this quote, Gardner says, "This has probably been quoted more often (usually in reference to rapidly changing political situations) than any other passage in the *Alice* books."

7. *Critzer*, 498 F2d 1160 (4th Cir 1974). Also, *Garber*, 607 F2d (5th Cir 1979).

8. The syllogism has a formal relation between its middle term, major term, and minor term and fits valid form AII 3rd figure.

9. John Rawls, *A Theory of Justice* (Cambridge: Harvard University Press, 1971), 5.

10. Ibid.

11. Dissenting opinion in *Arrowsmith v. Comm*, 73 SCt 71 (1952).

12. The principle of vertical equity is the foundation of the progressive tax rate structure. But according to Fox other aspects of the tax code, specifically tax expenditures discussed in chapter 8, have undermined the effects of the higher rates for many taxpayers by allowing larger deductions as well. "Having placed so much income beyond the government's reach, Congress adopts much higher tax rates than would otherwise be necessary to raise a given amount of tax revenue," John O. Fox, *If Americans Really Understood the Income Tax: Uncovering Our Most Expensive Ignorance* (Boulder: Westview, 2001), 12.

13. Exod. 21:23–27.

14. John Rawls, *A Theory of Justice*, 5.

15. A different argument than the one proposed in this book can be made that under some circumstances, withholding tax payments is the morally proper thing to do. This argument could be asserted when the government is hopelessly corrupt or is intent on perpetrating evil upon its citizens. In a number of works, Robert W. McGee examines situations from an international perspective where committing tax fraud may be the morally defensible thing to do. See, for example, *The Philosophy of Taxation and Public Finance* (Boston: Kluwer, 2004).

16. John Stuart Mill, *Principles of Political Economy*, abridged by J. Laurence Laughlin (New York: Appleton, 1884), 539.

17. For additional versions of the fair share argument see Robert W. McGee, ed., *The Ethics of Tax Evasion* (South Orange, NJ: The Dumont Institute of Public Policy Research, 1998), 18–19.

18. Jeffrey D. Eicher, Thomas J. Stuhldreher, and Wendy L. Stuhldreher, "Taxes and Ethics: Taxpayer Attitudes Over Time," *Journal of Tax Practice & Procedure*, (June-July, 2007): 29–37.

19. Jeremy Bentham, *The Principles of Morals and Legislation* (Amherst, NY: Prometheus Books, 1988), 207.

20. See note 12 above. According to Fox, "Special income exclusions and deductions, as drafted by Congress, are anti-egalitarian. They operate regressively:

The great bulk of the tax savings from special social and economic programs in the tax laws redound to the benefit of more able taxpayers" (40).

21. John T. Scholz, "Compliance Research and the Political Context of Tax Administration," in *Tax Compliance vol. 2: Social Science Perspectives,* ed. Jeffrey A. Roth and John T. Scholz (Philadelphia: University of Pennsylvania Press, 1989), 27.

22. Joel Slemrod, and J. Bakija, *Taxing Ourselves* (Cambridge: The MIT Press, 1996), 3.

23. U.S. House of Representatives, Committee on the Budget, written Statement of Nina E. Olson, National Taxpayer Advocate, On the IRS and the Tax Gap, February 16, 2007. In her calculation she indicates the net tax gap is $290 billion, less than the original $345 billion gross estimate for 2001 by the amount of taxes that had subsequently been collected by 2007. By statute, the IRS has ten years to collect past-due taxes (IRC § 6502 Collection after assessment).

24. Charles Adams, *For Good and Evil: The Impact of Taxes of the Course of Civilization* (London: Madison Books, 1993), 398.

25. Adam Smith, *The Theory of Moral Sentiments* (Indianapolis: Liberty Fund reprint of Oxford University Press edition [1759] 1976), 90.

26. Adam Smith, *Wealth of Nations* (Amherst, NY: Prometheus Books, [1776] 1991), [bk. 5, chap. 2, pt. 2] 499.

27. Benjamin Grahm and David Dodd, *Security Analysis* (New York: McGraw-Hill, 1934), 609.

28. Stephen Hawking, "The Future of the Universe," in *Predicting the Future,* ed. Leo Howe and Alan Wain (Cambridge: Cambridge University Press, 1993), 83.

29. David Ruelle, *Chance and Chaos* (Princeton: Princeton University Press, 1991), 84–85.

30. Edward O. Wilson, *Consilience: The Unity of Knowledge* (New York: Vintage Books, 1998), 219–20.

31. Slemrod and Bakija, *Taxing Ourselves,* 145.

32. Donald L. Bartlett and James B. Steele, *The Great American Tax Dodge* (Boston: Little, Brown, 2000), 49–50.

33. See report: "Significant Problems Still Exist with Internal Revenue Service Efforts to Identify Prisoner Tax Refund Fraud," December 29, 2010, Reference Number: 2011-40-009.

34. See for example Robert A. Kagan, "On the Visibility of Income Tax Law Violations," in *Tax Compliance vol. 2: Social Science Perspectives,* ed. Jeffrey A. Roth and John T. Scholz (Philadelphia: University of Pennsylvania Press, 1989).

35. See for example Donna D. Bobek and Richard C. Hatfield, "An Investigation of the Theory of Planned Behavior and the Role of Moral Obligation in Tax Compliance," *Behavioral Research in Accounting* 15 (2003): 13–38; Dennis M. Hanno and George R. Violette, "An Analysis of Moral and Social Influences on Taxpayer Behavior," *Behavioral Research in Accounting* 8, supp. (1996): 57–75.

36. Martin Fishbein and Icek Ajzen, *Predicting and Changing Behavior: The Reasoned Action Approach* (New York: Psychology Press, 2010), 22.

37. Alan Lewis, *The Psychology of Taxation* (New York: St. Martin's, 1982), 171.

38. Fishbein and Ajzen, *Predicting and Changing Behavior,* 20.

39. Ibid., 21.

40. Robert Kidder and Craig McEwen, "Taxpaying Behavior in Social Context: A Tentative Typology of Tax Compliance and Noncompliance," in *Tax Compliance vol. 2: Social Science Perspectives,* ed. Jeffrey A. Roth and John T. Scholz (Philadelphia: University of Pennsylvania Press, 1989), 58.

41. IRS Fact Sheet-2006-20, June 2006.

42. Oliver Wendell Holmes Jr., *The Common Law* (Mineola, NY: Dover, 1991), 48.

43. Kidder and McEwen, "Taxpaying Behavior in Social Context," 56.

44. Edward M. Schur, *Our Criminal Society: The Social and Legal Sources of Crime in America* (Englewood Cliffs, NJ: Prentice-Hall, 1969), 163.

45. Internal Revenue Service Reg. § 1.6015-1(h)(4). "An erroneous item is any item resulting in an understatement or deficiency in tax to the extent that such item is omitted from, or improperly reported (including improperly characterized) on an individual income tax return."

46. IRC § 6662(c).

47. IRS Reg. § 1.6664-4(b)(2). For a more detailed discussion of this topic see the author's "Assessing Professional Tax Advice and the Sophistication of the Taxpayer: 6664 Reasonable Cause and Good Faith Exception," *Tax Adviser* (Dec. 2009).

48. *Black's Law Dictionary,* abridged sixth ed. (St. Paul: West, 1991).

49. These high expectations regarding citizens' presumed knowledge of the tax law should be evaluated in light of expectations in other areas. For example, a 2003 Gallup © poll found that 31 percent of the Americans surveyed could not name the current vice president of the United States and 43 percent of the Americans surveyed could not provide the name of the third branch of government when supplied with the legislative and executive. In addition, 53 percent did not know the name of the first ten amendments to the U.S. Constitution. The Gallup poll results are based on telephone interviews with 1,008 national adults, aged eighteen and older, conducted Aug. 28 through Sept. 15, 2003, with a margin of sampling error of ±3 percentage points.

50. IRS New Release 84-55, April 13, 1984.

51. National Football League, *Official Rules of the NFL* (Chicago: Triumph Books, 2008), Rule 12 sec. 2 art. 12.

52. Ibid., Rule 8 sec. 3 art. 1.

53. Ibid., Rule 12 sec.1 art. 4.

54. Ibid., Rule 5 sec. 1 art. 1.

55. Ibid., Rule 12 sec. 2 art. 8.

56. Ibid., Rule 12 sec. 2 art. 5.

57. Ibid., Rule 12 sec. 2 art. 8.

58. Lon Fuller, *The Morality of Law* (New Haven: Yale University Press, 1964), 43.

59. Holmes, *The Common Law,* 110.

60. Young v. Comm, 783 F2d 1201, 1204 (5th Cir 1986). Judge Higginbotham stated further, "The Commissioner did not have access to the taxpayers' workpapers and was not otherwise informed of their state of mind."

61. *Timothy Thomas Noah,* TC Memo 1992-18 (1992).

62. Comm v. Wilcox, 66 SCt 546 (1946).

63. A business that is illegal under state law, such as prostitution, is still allowed to deduct its ordinary and necessary business expenses (IRC § 162). See, for example, *Richard J. Toner,* TC Memo 1990-539. Here, since the taxpayer's records had been confiscated by the police, the court allowed estimates of the business expenses, as permitted by *Cohan v. Comm,* 8 AFTR 10552 (1930).

64. *Pittsburgh Milk Co.* 26 TC 707 (1956).

65. *Comm v. Wilcox.*

66. 366 US 213 (1961).

67. IRS News Release 88-77, April 15, 1988.

68. Janice Nadler, "Flouting the Law," *Texas Law Review* 83 (2005): 1399. See also: Benoît Monin and Dale T. Miller, "Moral Credentials and the Expression of Prejudice," *Journal of Personality and Social Psychology* 81, no. 1 (2001): 33–43; Angela J. Krumm and Alexandra F. Cornin, "Who Believes Us When We Try to Conceal Our Prejudices? The Effectiveness of Moral Credentials With In-Groups Versus Out-Groups," *The Journal of Social Psychology* 148, no. 6 (2008): 689–709.

69. Monin and Miller, "Moral Credentials and the Expression of Prejudice."

70. Benoît Monin and Alexander H. Jordan, "The Dynamic Moral Self: A Social Psychological Perspective" in *Personality, Identity and Character: Explorations in Moral Psychology,* ed. Darcia Narvaez and Daniel K. Lapsley (Cambridge: Cambridge University Press, 2009), 347.

71. Ibid., 348.

72. Ignoring the "Nanny Tax" alone has caused embarrassment for Attorney General nominees Zoe Baird and Kimbra Wood. Other high-profile individuals in the news for tax indiscretions include former Senator Tom Daschle (D-SD), Rep. Charles B. Rangel (D-NY), and Treasury Secretary Timothy Geithner.

73. IRC § 6662.

74. IRC § 6662(c). The negligence penalty of § 6662 may be overcome if the reasonable cause and good faith exception of § 6664 can be demonstrated.

75. Howard Becker, *Outsiders: Studies in the Sociology of Deviance* (New York: The Free Press, 1963), 133.

76. Fuller, *The Morality of Law,* 173.

77. *John Marinzulich,* 31 TC 487 (1958).

78. Ibid.

79. IRC § 7203.

80. National Football League, *Official Rules of the NFL,* Rule 17 sec. 2 art. 1.

81. Associated Press report Dec. 30, 2010.

82. *The New York Times* report Sept. 14, 2007.

83. Senator William V. Roth Jr. and William H. Nixon, *The Power to Destroy* (New York: Atlantic Monthly Press, 1999), 10.

84. Danshera Cords, "Tax Protestors and Penalties: Ensuring Perceived Fairness and Mitigating Systemic Costs," *Brigham Young University Law Review* (2005): 1515.

85. In January 1999, in accordance with the *Internal Revenue Service (IRS) Restructuring and Reform Act of 1998,* the Treasury Inspector General for Tax Administration (TIGTA) was established, to provide independent oversight of IRS activities.

86. Holmes, *The Common Law,* 3.

87. Robert W. McGee, "Three Views on the Ethics of Tax Evasion," *Journal of Business Ethics* 67 (2006):15–35.

Chapter Seven. The Courts, Equity, and Taxes Due

1. Aristotle, *Politics,* trans. Benjamin Jowett (New York: Modern Library, 1943), bk. III, ch. 11, 1282b.

2. Paul Vinogradoff, *Common Sense in Law* (New York: Henry Holt, 1913), 209. This is a paraphrase of Aristotle's explanation of the problem of law in bk. 5 of the *Ethics*, ch.10, 1137a35-b24.

3. Aristotle, *Aristotle's Ethics: The Nicomachean Ethics*, trans. J. K. A. Thompson, revised by Hugh Tredennick (London: Penguin Books. 1953), bk. 5, ch. 10.

4. Bernard P. Dauenhauer, "On Strengthening the Law's Obligatory Character," *Georgia Law Review* 18 (1984): 821.

5. See chapter 1, note 76.

6. *Chris A. Roberts v. Comm*, TC Memo 2002-281.

7. IRC § 451(a).

8. Ronald Dworkin, *Taking Rights Seriously* (Cambridge: Harvard University Press, 1977), 28.

9. Ibid., 22.

10. Ibid., 24.

11. Blackman v. Comm, 88 TC 677 (1987).

12. Comm v. Heininger, 320 US 467 (1943).

13. *Blackman.*

14. *Heininger.*

15. Highway Farms, Inc. v. US, 89 AFTR 2d 2002-1902 (DC Iowa 2002).

16. Dworkin, *Taking Rights Seriously,* 26–27.

17. In this case, even had the petitioner appealed to his strong personal reason for setting the fire—based on a principle of justice permitting revenge against his wife who, in his absence, had allowed her boyfriend to live in the house—the court would still have denied his appeal. In conclusion, the court in *Blackman* said, "We refuse to encourage couples to settle their disputes with fire."

18. IRC § 6013(d)(3).

19. IRC § 6015(b)(1)(B) and IRS Reg. § 1.6015-1(h)(4).

20. IRS Reg. § 1.6015-1(h)(4).

21. For this purpose, IRS Form 8857, Request for Innocent Spouse Relief, is used.

22. Golden v. Comm, 548 F3d 487 (6th Cir 2008).

23. The phrase "had no reason to know" appears twice in the Code; once in § 66 and once in § 6015. The phrases, "Known or could have known," "Known or should have known," "Knew or could have known" do not appear in the Code. "Should have known" appears in three Code sections, each dealing with a penalty: IRC § 4975, § 6694, and § 6695.

24. IRS Rev. Proc. 2003-61, 2003-2 CB 296.

25. 114 TC 276 (2000).

26. Comm. v. Kowalski, 98 SCt 315 (1977).

27. Estate of Kalahasthi v. US, 630 FSupp 2d 1120 (2008).

28. IRC § 2201(b)(2) and (c). After the terrorist attacks of September 11, 2001, Congress passed the *Victims of Terrorism Tax Relief Act of 2001* ("VTTRA") to afford tax relief to victims of the attacks. See P. L. No. 107-143, § 101 et. seq., 115 Stat. 2427 (2002) (codified in various sections of the Internal Revenue Code). The act grants relief from income taxes (IRC § 692(d)(2)) and excludes certain death benefits from taxation (IRC § 101(i)) among other relief provisions.

29. IRC § 692(d)(4). According to the court, "Plaintiff argues that Kalahasthi is without question, a decedent who died as a result of wounds or injury incurred as a result of [September 11, 2001, attacks]." "The government counters that the 'plain language' of the statute excludes Kalahasthi because (1) she was never 'wounded' or 'injured' as those terms are used in the statute and (2) she

did not commit suicide 'as a result' of the attacks." This second proposition is the real question and one that an overriding principle of fairness might have reversed.

30. IRC § 692(d)(4).
31. As explained in chapter 5, the courts speak of deductions as a matter of legislative grace following *New Colonial Ice Co. v. Helvering*, 54 SCt 788 (1934).
32. Nina J. Crimm, *Tax Court Litigation Practice and Procedure* (Boston: Little, Brown, 1994), 11–12. See Woods v. Comm, 92 TC 776 (1989); Knapp v. Comm, 90 TC 430, 440 (1988), aff'd, 867 F2d 749 (2d Cir 1989); Estate of Rosenberg v. Comr, 73 TC 1014, 1017–1018 (1980). See also Comm v. McCoy, 484 US 3, 7 (1987).
33. IRC § 7442.
34. As with most tax issues, there are exceptions. Section 6664 provides a defense against taxpayer negligence based on "good faith reliance" on a tax professional's advice.
35. Crimm, *Tax Court Litigation*, 11–12. The U.S. Tax Court is a "specialized legislative court under Article I of the United States Constitution. *Tax Reform Act of 1969*, Pub. L. No 91-172, § 951, 83 Stat. 730 (1969). IRC § 7441." Crimm, 2–5.
36. Ibid., 11–12.
37. Norfolk Southern Corp, et al v. Comm, 104 TC 13 (1995), quoting Graff v. Comm, 74 TC 743, 761 (1980).
38. The Tax Court listed, "(1) A false representation or wrongful, misleading silence by the party against whom the opposing party seeks to invoke the doctrine; (2) an error in a statement of fact and not in an opinion or statement of law; (3) ignorance of the true facts; (4) reasonable reliance on the acts or statements of the one against whom estoppel is claimed; and (5) adverse effects of the acts or statement of the one against whom estoppel is claimed." *Norfolk Southern Corp, et al v. Comm.*
39. Schuster v. Comm, 312 F2d 311, 317 (9th Cir 1962), affg 32 TC 998 (1959) and rev'g 32 TC 1017 (1959).
40. Manocchio v. Comm, 78 TC 989 (1982) Aff'd 710 F2d 1400 (9th Cir 1983).
41. 312 F2d at 317.
42. 78 TC 989 (1982).
43. *Mannocchio*, 78 TC 989 (1982).
44. *Estate of George Stamos*, 55 TC 468 (1970).
45. Cohan v. Commissioner, 39 F2d 540 (2d Cir 1930).
46. *John David Zielonka*, TC Memo 1997-81.
47. A part of the following discussion was incorporated into a paper published by the author in *The Tax Adviser*, "Assessing Professional Tax Advice and Taxpayer Sophistication" (Dec. 2009).
48. IRC § 6662(d).
49. IRC § 6662(b)(2) and § 6662(b)(1), respectively.
50. IRC § 6662(c).
51. IRC § 6664.
52. The application of these criteria is laid out in IRS Reg. § 1.6664-4 Reasonable cause and good faith exception to section 6662 penalties.
53. IRC § 6664.
54. IRS Reg. § 1.6664-4.
55. IRS Reg. § 1.6664-4(b)(2).

56. According to the IRS, 59.2 percent of individuals paid to have their taxes prepared in 2006. http://www.irs.gov/taxstats/article/0,,id=102886,00.html. In Calendar Year 2009, the Internal Revenue Service processed approximately 83.1 million individual Federal income tax returns prepared by paid preparers. Report of the Treasury Inspector General for Tax Administration, Sept. 30, 2010 (Reference Number: 2010-40-127).

57. 469 US 241 (1985).

58. *Neonatology Associates, PA,* 115 TC 43, 99 (2000), aff'd 299 F3d 221 (3d Cir 2002).

59. 493 F3d 1243, 1253 (10th Cir 2006).

60. Robert R. Oliva, "When Will Reliance on a Tax Adviser Avoid an Accuracy-Related Penalty?" *The Tax Adviser* (Dec. 1997).

61. *Neonatology Associates.*

62. *Richard S. Moulton, Jr.,* TC Memo 2009-38.

63. *Neonatology Associates.*

64. *Mitchell,* TC Memo 200-145.

65. TC Memo 2008-289.

66. IRC § 104(a)(2).

67. IRC § 104(a)(2).

68. IRS Reg. § 1.664-4(b)(1).

69. IRS Reg. § 1.6664-4(b)(1).

70. Oliva, "When Will Reliance on a Tax Adviser Avoid an Accuracy-Related Penalty?"

71. IRS Reg. § 1.6664-4(b)(1).

72. Sean Murphy, "*MacMurray v. Comm.*: Distinguishing Between Reasonable Cause and Good Faith Requirements of the Section 6664 Exception to Accuracy Related Penalties," *The Tax Lawyer* 61, no. 2, (Winter 2008).

73. 96 AFTR 2d 2005-5311 (2d Cir 2005).

74. Bankruptcy Code, Title 11, § 523 Exemptions to Discharge.

75. Leo P. Martinez, "Taxes, Morals, and Legitimacy" *Brigham Young University Law Review* (1994): 521.

76. 55 F2d 396, 397 (ND Ohio 1931).

77. Bankruptcy Code, Title 11 § 523(a)(1)(B) and (C).

78. 88 AFTR 2d 2001-5686 (ED PA 2001).

79. Bankruptcy Code, Title 11 § 523(a)(1)(C).

80. 118 F3d 979, 983 (3d Cir 1997).

81. For a discussion of the view that observed physical actions are not enough to establish willfulness, see Sherrer, "The Illusion of Tax Evasion," in *The Ethics of Tax Evasion,* ed. Robert W. McGee, 114.

82. *Critzer,* 498 F2d 1160 (4th Cir 1974). Also, *Garber,* 607 F2d (5th Cir 1979).

83. In *Roger L. Tutolo v. Comm,* TC Memo 1995-186, the court listed six "badges of fraud" that were accepted by the courts—(1) large understatements of income, (2) inadequate records, (3) income from illegal sources, (4) dealing in cash, (5) implausible or inconsistent explanations, and (6) providing incomplete information to tax return preparer.

84. Cicero, *On Obligations,* trans. P. G. Walsh (Oxford: Oxford University Press, 2000), 13.

85. Jeremy Bentham, *Of Laws in General* (London: The Athlone Press, 1970), 163; italics in original.

86. Cesare Beccaria, *On Crimes and Punishments*, trans. Henry Paolucci (Upper Saddle River, NJ: Prentice-Hall, [1764] 1963), 17.
87. Ibid.
88. See note 56.
89. Adam Smith, "Of Taxes," *Wealth of Nations* (New York: Prometheus Books, [1776]1991), [bk. 5, ch. 2, pt. 2], 499.
90. Ibid.
91. Braunum v. Comm, 73 AFTR 2d 94-1675 (5th Cir 1994).
92. US v. Winthorp, 24 AFTR 2d 69-5760 (5th Cir 1969).

Chapter Eight. Compliance, Complexity, Conscience, and Fairness

1. Richard D. Schwartz and Sonya Orleans, "On Legal Sanctions," *University of Chicago Law Review* 34 (1967): 274; Robert Mason and Lyle D. Calvin, "A Study of Admitted Tax Evasion," *Law and Society Review* 13 (1978): 78; Wilbur J. Scott and Harold G. Grasmick, "Deterrence and Income Tax Cheating: Testing Interaction Hypotheses in Utilitarian Theories," *The Journal of Applied Behavioral Science* (1981): 395–408; E. F. Loftus, "To File, Perchance to Cheat," *Psychology Today* (April 1985): 35–39; Adam Forest and Steven M. Sheffrin, "Complexity and Compliance: An Empirical Investigation," *National Tax Journal* 55, no. 1 (March 2002): 75–88; Charlene Henderson and Steven E. Kaplan, "An Examination of the Role of Ethics in Tax Compliance Decisions," *Journal of the American Taxation Association* (Spring 2005); Danshera Cords, "Tax Protestors and Penalties: Ensuring Perceived Fairness and Mitigating Systemic Costs," *Brigham Young University Law Review* (2005): 1515.
2. Jeffrey A. Dubin, "Criminal Investigation Enforcement Activities and Taxpayer Noncompliance," *Public Finance Review* 35 (2007): 500; James Alm, Betty R. Jackson, and Michael McKee, "Estimating the Determinants of Taxpayer Compliance with Experimental Data," *National Tax Journal* 45, no. 1 (March, 1992): 107–14; Jeffrey A. Dubin and Louis L. Wilde, "An Empirical Analysis of Federal Income Tax Auditing and Compliance," *National Tax Journal* 41 no. 1 (1988): 61–74; Ann D. Witte and Diane F. Woodbury, "The Effect of Tax Laws and Tax Administration on Tax Compliance: The Case of the U.S. Individual Income Tax," *National Tax Journal* 38 (March 1985): 1–14.
3. Loftus, "To File, Perchance to Cheat." Feld and Frey report that "[t]ax compliance also increases with reductions in government waste." Lars P. Feld and Bruno S. Frey, "Tax Compliance as the Result of a Psychological Tax Contract: The Role of Incentives and Responsive Regulation," *Law & Policy* 29, no. 1 (Jan. 2007): 102–20.
4. Eric A. Posner, "Law and Social Norms: The Case of Tax Compliance," *Virginia Law Review* 86 (2000): 1781.
5. Joel Slemrod, "The Return to Tax Simplification: an Econometric Analysis," *Public Finance Review* 17, no. 3 (1989); Michael J. Graetz, *The U.S. Income Tax: What It Is, How it Got That Way, and Where We Go from Here* (New York: W. W. Norton, 1999).
6. Dubin and Wilde, "An Empirical Analysis of Federal Income Tax Auditing and Compliance"; Otto H. Chang, Donald R. Nichols, and Joseph J. Schultz. "Taxpayer Attitudes Toward Tax Audit Risk," *Journal of Economic Psychology* 8 (1987): 299–309.

7. Loftus, "To File, Perchance to Cheat"; Robert B. Cialdini, "Social Motivations to Comply: Norms, Values, and Principles," in *Taxpayer Compliance vol. 2: Social Science Perspectives,* ed. Jeffrey A. Roth and John T. Scholz (Philadelphia: University of Pennsylvania Press, 1989); Cords, *Tax Protestors and Penalties.*

8. Henderson and Kaplan, "An Examination of the Role of Ethics in Tax Compliance Decisions," 39–72; Feld and Frey, "Tax Compliance as the Result of a Psychological Tax Contract."

9. John T. Scholz, "Compliance Research and the Political Context of Tax Administration," in *Tax Compliance vol. 2: Social Science Perspectives,* ed. Jeffrey A. Roth and John T. Scholz (Philadelphia: University of Pennsylvania Press, 1989).

10. Graetz, *The U.S. Income Tax*; Alm et al., "Estimating the Determinants of Taxpayer Compliance with Experimental Data,"; Robert Mason and Lyle. D. Calvin, "Public Confidence and Admitted Tax Evasion," *National Tax Journal* 37, no. 4 (Dec. 1984).

11. Gideon Yaniv, "The Tax Compliance Demand Curve: A Diagrammatical Approach to Income Tax Evasion," *Journal of Economic Education* (Spring 2009).

12. Slemrod, "The Return to Tax Simplification: an Econometric Analysis."

13. Kim M. Bloomquist, "Tax Evasion, Income Inequality and Opportunity Costs of Compliance," *National Tax Association Proceedings 96th Annual Conference on Taxation,* 2003(a).

14. Feld and Frey, "Tax Compliance as the Result of a Psychological Tax Contract."

15. Harold G. Grasmick and Donald E. Green, "Legal Punishment, Social Disapproval and Internalization as Inhibitors of Illegal Behavior," *The Journal of Criminal Law & Criminology* 71 no. 3 (1980); Cords, "Tax Protestors and Penalties: Ensuring Perceived Fairness and Mitigating Systemic Costs."

16. Schwartz and Orleans, "On Legal Sanctions"; Cords, "Tax Protestors and Penalties"; Dennis M. Hanno and George R. Violette, "An Analysis of Moral and Social Influences on Taxpayer Behavior," *Behavioral Research in Accounting* 8, supp. (1996): 57–75.

17. For a comprehensive summary see Cords, "Tax Protestors and Penalties," 1522–28.

18. Henderson and Kaplan, "An Examination of the Role of Ethics in Tax Compliance Decisions."

19. Leo P. Martinez, "Taxes, Morals, and Legitimacy," *Brigham Young University Law Review* (1994): 521.

20. Philip M. Reckers, Debra L. Sanders, and Stephen J. Roark, "The Influence of Ethical Attitudes on Taxpayer Compliance," *National Tax Journal* 47, no. 4 (Dec. 1994).

21. Peggy A. Hite, "Commentary on 'An Analysis of Moral and Social Influences on Taxpayer Behavior,'" *Behavioral Research in Accounting* 8, supp. (1996).

22. Nina E. Olson, National Taxpayer Advocate, United States Senate, written statement before the Committee on the Budget, "The Causes of and Solutions to the Federal Tax Gap," Feb. 15, 2006.

23. See chapter 3, subsection, "Economic Insights."

24. "A person avoids a tax cheat because the tax cheat has shown that he has a high discount rate ['meaning that they value future payoffs relatively little compared

to current payoffs'] and is therefore a bad cooperative partner" who cannot be trusted. Posner, "Law and Social Norms."

25. Schwartz and Orleans, "On Legal Sanctions."

26. Ibid.

27. IRS Oversight Board 2009 Taxpayer Attitude Survey, Feb. 2010, table 2.

28. John O. Fox, *If Americans Really Understood the Income Tax: Uncovering Our Most Expensive Ignorance* (Boulder: Westview, 2001), 49.

29. Ibid., 39.

30. Ibid., 49. Fox provides a full explanation of this feature of our income tax system.

31. Merton used the term *Matthew Effect* in referring to the accumulation of advantages and disadvantages and in particular the tendency of scientists who were already famous to become more famous. Robert K. Merton, *On Social Structure and Science*, ed. with an intro. by Piotr Sztompka (Chicago: The University of Chicago Press, 1996), 160.

32. Matt.13:12. This is followed by, "but whosoever hath not, from him shall be taken away even that he hath."

33. Fox, *If Americans Really Understood the Income Tax*, 77.

34. Leonard E. Burman, "Is the Tax Expenditure Concept Still Relevant?" *National Tax Journal* 56, no. 3 (September, 2003): 1–20.

35. House of Representatives, testimony before the Committee on the Budget, statement of Michael Brostek, Director, Tax Issues, Strategic Issues, Government Accountability Office (GAO), "Tax Compliance: Multiple Approaches Are Needed to Reduce the Tax Gap," GAO-07-488T (Feb. 16, 2007), 11.

36. Fox, *If Americans Really Understood the Income Tax*, 12.

37. Ronald Pasquariello, *Tax Justice: Social and Moral Aspects of American Tax Policy* (Lanham, MD: University Press of America, 1985), 81.

38. Burman, "Is the Tax Expenditure Concept Still Relevant?"

39. The more a person's itemized deductions surpass the standard deduction the greater the benefit provided by the itemized deductions. This is limited to some extent for taxpayers affected by the Alternative Minimum Tax.

40. For example, an $800,000 mortgage with a 6 percent interest rate would generate $48,000 of interest expense.

41. Burman, "Is the Tax Expenditure Concept Still Relevant?" citing Christopher Howard, *The Hidden Welfare State: Tax Expenditures and Social Policy in the United States* (Princeton: Princeton University Press, 1997).

42. Government Accountability Office (GAO), *Government Performance and Accountability: Tax Expenditures Represent a Substantial Federal Commitment and Need to Be Reexamined.* GAO-05-690 (September 2005), 50.

43. Fox, *If Americans Really Understood the Income Tax*, 49.

44. Joseph R. Antos, "Is There a Right Way to Promote Health Insurance Through the Tax System?" *National Tax Journal* 59, no. 3 (Sept. 2006): 477–90, 478.

45. Ibid., 479.

46. Ibid., 482.

47. Leonard E. Burman and Amelia Gruber, "First, Do No Harm: Designing Tax Incentives for Health Insurance," *National Tax Journal* 44, no. 3 (2001): 473–93, 484.

48. Pasquariello, *Tax Justice*, 94.

49. Ibid.

50. GAO 2007, 11. The statute referred to which defines tax expenditures is cited as *The Congressional Budget and Impoundment Control Act of 1974,* Pub. L. No. 93-344, § 3, 88 Stat. 299 (July 12, 1974), codified at 2 U.S.C. § 622(3). The definition of *tax expenditure* offered there refers to "those revenue losses attributable to provisions of the Federal tax laws which allow a special exclusion, exemption, or deduction from gross income or which provide a special credit, a preferential rate of tax, or a deferral of tax liability."

51. Rossotti, *Many Unhappy Returns,* 272. Rossotti adds, "Lobbyists and members of Congress work for years waiting for the opportunity to get their special provision into whatever tax bill looks as if it is moving," 273.

52. For a thorough discussion of this problem see Fox, *If Americans Really Understood the Income Tax.*

53. Pasquariello, *Tax Justice,* 96.

54. Fox, *If Americans Really Understood the Income Tax,* 101.

55. Senate Committee on Finance, news release, March 30, 2011. Opening Statement of Senator Max Baucus (D-MT) "Regarding the Effectiveness of Tax Incentives." "These temporary tax incentives" according to Baucus, "hinder taxpayers' ability to plan. As a result, they may only benefit those people who would have acted anyway. Ultimately, the desirability of any tax incentive will depend on whether we want to encourage the activity in the first place."

56. Joel Slemrod, ed., *Why People Pay Taxes* (Ann Arbor: University of Michigan Press, 1992), 1.

57. Rossotti, *Many Unhappy Returns,* 275.

58. *Internal Revenue Cumulative Bulletin* 1976-3, vol. 2, Public Law 94-455, Dec. 29, 1976.

59. United States Senate, Committee on Finance, Report No. 94-938, *Tax Reform Act of 1976,* H.R. 10612, 94th Cong., June 10, 1976.

60. See the author's "Children and the AMT: Saved by the Kiddie Tax," *The CPA Journal* (Nov. 2011).

61. IRS SOI Tax Stats, Table 2. All Returns: Tax Liability, Tax Credits, and Tax Payments by Size of Adjusted Gross Income, Tax Year 2007.

62. This group paid $1,772,000 in AMT in 2007. IRS SOI Tax Stats, Table 2. All Returns: Tax Liability, Tax Credits, and Tax Payments, by Size of Adjusted Gross Income, Tax Year 2007.

63. Rossotti, *Many Unhappy Returns,* 270.

64. Adam Smith, "Of Taxes," in *Wealth of Nations* (New York: Prometheus Books, [1776]1991), [bk. 5, ch. 2, pt. 2] 498.

65. Carolyn Webber and Aaron Wildavsky, *A History of Taxation and Expenditure in the Western World* (New York: Simon and Schuster, 1986), 534. According to Richard Wasserstrom, "As familiar as the argument is, its plausibility is far from assured." "The Obligation to Obey the Law," *UCLA Law Review* 10, no. 4 (May 1963): 780. Reprinted in *The Duty to Obey The Law: Selected Philosophical Readings,* ed. William A. Edmundson (New York: Rowman and Littlefield, 1999), 34.

66. John Mackie, "Obligations to Obey the Law," *Virginia Law Review* 67, no. 1 (Feb. 1981): 143.

67. Scholz, "Compliance Research and the Political Context of Tax Administration," 19.

68. Mat. 6:24.
69. John Dewey and James H. Tufts, *Ethics*, 2nd ed., revised (New York: Henry Holt, 1932), 177.
70. Ibid., 178.
71. Ibid., 179.
72. Ibid., 178.
73. Robert A. Kagan, "On the Visibility of Income Tax Law Violations," in *Tax Compliance vol. 2: Social Science Perspectives*, ed. Jeffrey A. Roth and John T. Scholz (Philadelphia: University of Pennsylvania Press, 1989), 79.
74. Hans Sherrer, "The Illusion of Tax Evasion," in *The Ethics of Tax Evasion*, ed. Robert W. McGee (South Orange, NJ: The Dumont Institute for Public Policy Research, 1998), 114.
75. Martin Fishbein and Icek Ajzen, *Predicting and Changing Behavior: The Reasoned Action Approach* (New York: Psychology Press, 2010), 37–38.
76. Schwartz and Orleans, "On Legal Sanctions."
77. Martinez, "Taxes, Morals, and Legitimacy."
78. Adam Smith, *The Theory of Moral Sentiments* (Indianapolis: Liberty Fund reprint of Oxford University Press edition [1759] 1976), 45.
79. See for example, Louis Kaplow, "Accuracy, Complexity, and the Income Tax." *National Tax Journal* 49, no. 1 (March 1998): 135–50.
80. Wilbert E. Moore, "Occupational Socialization," in *Handbook of Socialization Theory and Research*, ed. David A. Goslin (Chicago: Rand McNally, 1969), 869.
81. Posner, *Law and Social Norms: The Case of Tax Compliance.*
82. Albert Bandura, *Social Learning Theory* (Upper Saddle River, NJ: Prentice-Hall, 1977), 12.
83. Ibid., 46.
84. Plato, *Laws* VII, 788 b, trans. A. E. Taylor.
85. Joseph T. Wells, *Occupational Fraud and Abuse* (Austin, TX: Obsidian, 1997), 17.
86. Barry Schwartz, *The Paradox of Choice* (New York: HarperCollins, 2004), 167–68.
87. Bernard Wand, "The Content and Function of Conscience," *The Journal of Philosophy* 58, no. 24 (Nov. 23, 1961).
88. Phillip Cary, Lecture Three, *Luther: Gospel, Law, and Reformation* (Chantilly, VA: The Teaching Company, 2004).
89. Ibid.
90. Ibid.
91. Ibid.
92. Charles E. Curran, "Conscience in the Light of the Catholic Moral Tradition," in *Conscience*, ed. Charles E. Curran (New York: Paulist Press, 2004), 3.
93. Justin Aronfreed, *Conduct and Conscience: The Socialization of Internalized Control Over Behavior* (New York: Academic Press, 1968), 2.
94. Ibid., 12.
95. Wand, "The Content and Function of Conscience."
96. Rom. 2:15.
97. William Shakespeare, *Hamlet* 3:1.
98. Leslie Stephen, *The Science of Ethics* (Honolulu: University Press of the Pacific, 2003), 250–51.

99. Sigmund Freud, *Civilization and Its Discontents*, trans. James Strachey (New York: W. W. Norton, 1961), 100.

100. Dietrich Bonhoeffer, *Ethics*, trans. Neville Horton Smith (New York: Touchstone, 1995), 28.

101. Robert Wright, *The Moral Animal* (New York: Vintage Books, 1994), 308.

102. Ibid., 218.

103. Ibid.

104. Lawrence Kohlberg, "Stage and Sequence: The Cognitive-Developmental Approach to Socialization," in *Handbook of Socialization Theory and Research*, ed. David A. Goslin (Chicago: Rand McNally, 1969), 376.

105. Ibid.

106. B. F. Skinner, *Beyond Freedom and Dignity* (New York: Knopf, 1971), 175.

107. Kohlberg, "Stage and Sequence," 399.

108. H. L. A. Hart, *The Concept of Law* (London: Oxford University Press, 1961), 88.

109. Kohlberg, "Stage and Sequence," 413.

110. Benno Torgler, *Tax Compliance and Tax Morale* (Northampton, MA: Edward Elgar, 2007), 258.

111. Aronfreed, *Conduct and Conscience*, 9.

112. B. F. Skinner, *Cumulative Record* (New York: Appleton-Century-Crofts, 1972), 10.

113. Ibid., 11.

114. John S. Carroll, "Compliance with the Law: A Decision-Making Approach to Taxpaying," *Law and Human Behavior* 11, no. 4 (1987).

115. William C. Spohn, "Conscience and Moral Development," in *Conscience*, ed. Charles E. Curran (New York: Paulist Press, 2004), 133.

116. John Dewey, "Theory of Valuation," *International Encyclopedia of Unified Science*, vol. 2, no. 4 (Chicago: University of Chicago Press, [1939] 1966), 24–25.

117. Ibid., 42–43.

118. Ayn Rand, *The Virtue of Selfishness*, 116–17.

119. Hart, *The Concept of Law*, 202.

120. George Bernard Shaw, Preface, in *Major Barbara* (New York: Penguin Books, 1957), 44.

121. U.S. House of Representatives, Hearing Before the Subcommittee on Oversight of the Committee on Ways and Means, *Taxpayers Who Fail to File Federal Income Tax Returns*, 103rd Cong., 1st sess., Oct. 26, 1993. The Church of the Brethren [http://www.brethren.org], and other organizations, expressed support for HR 2019 the U.S. Peace Tax Fund, "as a means through which members of our church who are conscientiously opposed to war may pay their entire tax obligation."

122. US v. Macintosh, 283 US 605 (1931).

123. Girouard v. US, 328 US 61 (1946).

124. Schwimmer v. US, 279 US 644, 654-55 (1929).

125. *Girouard.*

126. Hugo Adam Bedau, ed., *Civil Disobedience in Focus* (London: Routledge, 1991), 7.

127. Abraham J. Muste v. Comm, 35 TC 913.

128. Ed Hedemann, *War Tax Resistance: A Guide to Withholding Your Support from the Military*, 5th ed., edited by Ruth Benn and Ed Hedemann (New York: War Resisters League, 2003). According to this organization 49 percent of taxes are used for war and related activities.

129. Estimates of the percent of the budget that goes for war or defense range from 20 percent to 60 percent depending on what is included under the heading of defense and what items are included as part of the national budget.

130. Hedemann, *War Tax Resistance*, 11.

131. Shaw, *Major Barbara*, 70. For a discussion of the fungibility of money in Shaw's *Major Barbara*, see the author's "Tainted Money and Charity: Do 501(c)(3)s Have a Right to Refuse a Gift?," *Nonprofit and Voluntary Sector Quarterly* 38, no. 4 (2008).

132. Ibid., 25–26.

133. Ibid., 26.

134. Hedemann, *War Tax Resistance*.

135. By statute, the IRS has ten years to collect past-due taxes. IRC § 6502 Collection after assessment.

136. Citing Sherbert v. Verner, 374 US 398 (1963).

137. Oregon State Employment Division v. Smith, 494 US 872 (1990), citing United States v. Lee, 455 US 252, 258-261 (1982).

138. *Sherbert.*

139. Carl F. Taeusch, *Professional and Business Ethics* (New York: Henry Holt, 1926), 323.

140. *The Tax Relief Health Care Act of 2006* amended § 6702 to allow the imposition of a $5,000 penalty for frivolous tax returns (previously the penalty had been $500). Depending on the taxpayer's position on a tax return, a frivolous return may also indicate fraud on the part of the taxpayer, leading to the possibility of criminal prosecution.

141. See for example, John Rawls, "Legal Obligation and the Duty of Fair Play," in *Law and Philosophy: A Symposium*, ed. Sidney Hook (New York: New York University Press 1964).

142. Konvitz, Milton B., "Civil Disobedience and the Duty of Fair Play," in *Law and Philosophy: A Symposium*, ed. Sidney Hook (New York: New York University Press 1964), 28.

143. Bedau, *Civil Disobedience in Focus*, 6–7.

144. Howard Becker, *Outsiders: Studies in the Sociology of Deviance* (New York: The Free Press, 1963), 147–53.

145. Ibid., 162.

146. Stephen Pfohl, "The 'Discovery' of Child Abuse," *Social Problems* 24 (February 1997): 310.

147. Joseph A. Schumpeter, *Capitalism, Socialism, and Democracy* (New York: Harper and Row, 1976), 132.

148. Becker, *Outsiders*, 145.

149. John Rawls, *A Theory of Justice* (Cambridge: Harvard University Press, 1971), 363.

150. Ibid., 364. In presenting this definition of civil disobedience Rawls indicates he is following the definition provided by H. A. Bedau in "On Civil Disobedience," *Journal of Philosophy* 58 (1961): 653–61.

151. M. K. Gandhi, *An Autobiography or the Story of My Experiments with Truth*, trans. from the Gujarati by Mahadev Desai (Ahmedabad-380 014: Navajivan, 1927), 432–33.

152. One study found that most tax evaders tend to be dishonest in other activities. Thomas M. Porcano, "Correlates of Tax Evasion," *Journal of Economic Psychology* 9 (1988): 47–67.

153. Henry David Thoreau, *Civil Disobedience* (New York: Quill Pen, 2008), 7.

154. Ibid., 14.

155. Janice Nadler, "Flouting the Law," *Texas Law Review* 83 (2005): 1399, 1433.

156. Tom R. Tyler, *Why People Obey the Law* (Princeton: Princeton University Press, 2006), 71.

157. Alan Lewis, *The Psychology of Taxation* (New York: St. Martin's Press, 1982), 82–83.

SELECTED BIBLIOGRAPHY
EXCLUDING PUBLIC DOCUMENTS

Each of the works in this bibliography is cited in the book. Public documents, including the Internal Revenue Code (IRC), federal court cases, IRS Regulations, Congressional reports and testimonies, IRS Revenue Rulings, and reports from other governmental agencies, including the IRS Oversight Board and the General Accountability Office, are fully cited in the endnotes.

Adams, Charles. *For Good and Evil: The Impact of Taxes of the Course of Civilization.* London: Madison Books, 1993.

Alighieri, Dante. *The Divine Comedy.* Vol. 1, Inferno. Translated by Mark Musa. New York: Penguin Books, 1984.

Alm, James, Betty R. Jackson, and Michael McKee. "Estimating the Determinants of Taxpayer Compliance with Experimental Data." *National Tax Journal* 45 no. 1 (March, 1992): 107–14.

Amacher, Ryan C., and Holley H. Ulbrich. *Principles of Economics,* 5th ed. Cincinnati: SouthWestern, 1992.

Antos, Joseph R. "Is There a Right Way to Promote Health Insurance Through the Tax System?" *National Tax Journal* 59, no. 3 (Sept. 2006): 477–90.

Aquinas, Thomas. *Summa Theologica.* In *The Great Books of the Western World,* vol. 20. Translated by Fathers of the English Dominican Province. Revised by Daniel J. Sullivan. Chicago: Encyclopedia Britannica, 1952.

Aristotle. *Aristotle's Ethics: The Nicomachean Ethics.* Translated by J. K. A. Thompson. Revised by Hugh Tredennick. London: Penguin Books, 1953.

——. *Politics.* Translated by Benjamin Jowett. New York: Modern Library, 1943.

Aronfreed, Justin. *Conduct and Conscience: The Socialization of Internalized Control Over Behavior.* New York: Academic Press, 1968.

Asimow, Michael. "Civil Penalties for Inaccurate and Delinquent Tax Returns." *UCLA Law Review* 23, no. 4) (April 1976): 637.

Association of Certified Fraud Examiners. *2010 Report to the Nations on Occupational Fraud and Abuse.* Austin, TX: 2010.

Bandura, Albert. *Social Learning Theory.* Upper Saddle River, NJ: Prentice-Hall, 1977.

Bartlett, Donald L., and James B. Steele. *The Great American Tax Dodge*. Boston: Little, Brown, 2000.

Beccaria, Cesare. *On Crimes and Punishments*. Translated by Henry Paolucci. Upper Saddle River, NJ: Prentice-Hall, [1764] 1963.

Becker, Howard. *Outsiders: Studies in the Sociology of Deviance*. New York: The Free Press, 1963.

Bedau, Hugo Adam, ed. *Civil Disobedience in Focus*. London: Routledge, 1991.

Bentham, Jeremy. *The Theory of Fictions*. Patterson, NJ: Littlefield, Adams, 1959.

———. *Of Laws in General*. London: The Athlone Press, 1970.

———. *The Principles of Morals and Legislation*. Amherst, NY: Prometheus Books, 1988.

Beyleveld, Deryck, and Roger Brownsword. *Law as a Moral Judgment*, Sheffield, UK: Sheffield Academic Press, 1994.

The Bible. King James Version.

Birnbaum, Jeffrey H. "The Road to Riches Is Called K Street: Lobbying Firms Hire More, Pay More, Charge More to Influence Government." *Washington Post*, Wednesday, June 22, 2005.

———, and Alan S. Murray. *Showdown at Gucci Gulch: Lawmakers, Lobbyists, and the Unlikely Triumph of Tax Reform*. New York: Vintage Books, 1987.

Black's Law Dictionary. Abridged sixth ed. St. Paul: West, 1991.

Bloomquist, Kim M. "Tax Evasion, Income Inequality and Opportunity Costs of Compliance." *National Tax Association Proceedings, 96th Annual Conference on Taxation*, 2003(a): 91–104.

———. "Trends as Changes in Variance: The Case of Noncompliance." Working paper, presented at IRS Research Conference (June), 2003(b): 1–9.

Bobek, Donna D., and Richard C. Hatfield. "An Investigation of the Theory of Planned Behavior and the Role of Moral Obligation in Tax Compliance." *Behavioral Research in Accounting* 15 (2003): 13–38.

Bonhoeffer, Dietrich. *Ethics*. Translated by Neville Horton Smith. New York: Touchstone, 1995.

Buchholz, Todd G. *New Ideas from Dead Economists*. New York: Penguin Books, 1989.

Burman, Leonard E. "Is the Tax Expenditure Concept Still Relevant?" *National Tax Journal* 56, no. 3 (Sept. 2003): 1–20.

Burman, Leonard E., and Amelia Gruber. "First, Do No Harm: Designing Tax Incentives for Health Insurance." *National Tax Journal* 44, no. 3 (2001): 473–93.

Callahan, David. *The Cheating Culture: Why Americans are Doing Wrong to Get Ahead*. New York: Harcourt, 2004.

Calvin, John. *The Institutes of Christian Religion*. Edited by Tony Lane and Hilary Osborne. Grand Rapids: Baker Book House, 1986.

Cardozo, Benjamin N. *The Nature of the Judicial Process*. New Haven: Yale University Press, 1921.

Carroll, John S. "Compliance with the Law: A Decision-Making Approach to Taxpaying." *Law and Human Behavior* 11, no. 4 (1987): 319–35.

———. "How Taxpayers Think about Their Taxes: Frames and Values." In *Why People Pay Taxes*, ed. J. Slemrod. Ann Arbor: University of Michigan Press, 1992.

Carroll, Lewis. *Through the Looking Glass*. In *The Annotated Alice*. Introduction and notes Martin Gardner. Cleveland: World, 1960.

Cary, Phillip. Lecture Three, *Luther: Gospel, Law, and Reformation*. Chantilly, VA: The Teaching Company, 2004.

Chang, Otto H., Donald R. Nichols, and Joseph J. Schultz. "Taxpayer Attitudes Toward Tax Audit Risk." *Journal of Economic Psychology* 8 (1987): 299–309.

Christie, George C. "On the Moral Obligation to Obey the Law" *Duke Law Journal* 6 (1991): 1311.

Cialdini, Robert B. "Social Motivations to Comply: Norms, Values, and Principles." In *Taxpayer Compliance Volume 2: Social Science Perspectives,* ed. Jeffrey A. Roth and John T. Scholz. Philadelphia: University of Pennsylvania Press, 1989.

Cicero. *On Obligations.* Translated by P. G. Walsh. Oxford: Oxford University Press, 2000.

———. *The Republic and the Laws.* Translated by Niall Rudd. Oxford: Oxford University Press, 1998.

Cords, Danshera. "Tax Protestors and Penalties: Ensuring Perceived Fairness and Mitigating Systemic Costs." *Brigham Young University Law Review* (2005): 1515.

Cowell, Frank A. *Cheating the Government: The Economics of Evasion.* Cambridge: The MIT Press, 1990.

Crimm, Nina J. *Tax Court Litigation Practice and Procedure.* Boston: Little, Brown, 1994.

Crowe, Martin T. *The Moral Obligation of Paying Just Taxes.* Washington, DC: The Catholic University Press of America, 1944.

Curran, Charles E. "Conscience in the Light of the Catholic Moral Tradition." In *Conscience,* ed. Charles E. Curran. New York: Paulist Press, 2004.

Dauenhauer, Bernard P. "On Strengthening the Law's Obligatory Character." *Georgia Law Review* 18, no. 4 (1984): 821.

Deane, K. D. "Law, Morality, and Tax Evasion." *Anglo-American Law Review* 13, no. 1 (1984): 1.

d'Entrèves, A. P. *Natural Law.* 2nd ed. London: Hutchinson, 1951.

Dewey, John. *Human Nature and Conduct.* New York: Henry Holt, 1922.

———. *Logic: The Theory of Inquiry.* New York: Holt, Rinehart, and Winston, 1938.

———. "Theory of Valuation." In *International Encyclopedia of Unified Science.* Vol. 2, no. 4. Chicago: University of Chicago Press, 1939.

———. *The Quest for Certainty.* New York: G. P. Putnam's Sons, [1929] 1960.

———, and James H. Tufts. *Ethics.* 2nd edition, revised. New York: Henry Holt, 1932.

Dodge, Joseph M. *The Logic of Tax: Federal Income Tax Theory and Policy.* St. Paul: West, 1989.

Dubin, Jeffrey A. "Criminal Investigation Enforcement Activities and Taxpayer Noncompliance." *Public Finance Review* 35 (July 2007): 500–29.

———, and Louis L. Wilde. "An Empirical Analysis of Federal Income Tax Auditing and Compliance." *National Tax Journal* 41, no. 1 (1988): 61–74.

Dworkin, Ronald. *Taking Rights Seriously.* Cambridge: Harvard University Press, 1977.

Eicher, Jeffrey D., Thomas J. Stuhldreher, and Wendy L. Stuhldreher. "Taxes and Ethics: Taxpayer Attitudes Over Time." *Journal of Tax Practice & Procedure* (June-July 2007): 29–37.

Erard, B., and J. S. Feinstein. "The Role of Moral Sentiments and Audit Perceptions in Tax Compliance." *Public Finance* 49 (1994): 70–89; quoted in Benno Torgler. *Tax Compliance and Tax Morale.* Northampton, MA: Edward Elgar, 2007.

Feld, Alan L. "Congress and the Legislative Web of Trust." *Boston University Law Review* 81, no. 2 (April 2001): 350.

Feld, Lars P., and Bruno S. Frey. "Tax Compliance as the Result of a Psychological Tax Contract: The Role of Incentives and Responsive Regulation." *Law & Policy* 29, no. 1 (Jan. 2007): 102–20.

Fink, Robert S. *Tax Fraud—Audits, Investigations, Prosecutions*. New York: Matthew Bender, 1980.

Fishbein, Martin, and Icek Ajzen. *Predicting and Changing Behavior: The Reasoned Action Approach*. New York: Psychology Press, 2010.

Fisher, Richard. "Henry George Antiprotectionist Giant of American Economics," *Economic Insight*. Federal Reserve Bank of Dallas, vol. 10, no. 2 (2005).

Forest, Adam, and Steven M. Sheffrin. "Complexity and Compliance: An Empirical Investigation." *National Tax Journal* 55, no. 1 (March 2002): 75–88.

Fox, John O. *If Americans Really Understood the Income Tax: Uncovering Our Most Expensive Ignorance*. Boulder: Westview, 2001.

Frederick, Shane, George Loewenstein, and Ted O'Donoghue. "Time Discounting and Time Preference: A Critical Review." In *Time and Decision: Economic and Psychological Perspectives on Intertemporal Choice*, ed. George Loewenstein, Daniel Read, and Roy F. Baumeister. New York: Russell Sage Foundation, 2003.

Freezel, Randolph. "Baseball, Cheating, and Tradition: Would Kant Cork His Bat?" In *Baseball and Philosophy: Thinking Outside the Batter's Box*, ed. Eric Bronson. Chicago: Open Court, 2004.

Freud, Sigmund. *Civilization and Its Discontents*. Translated by James Strachey. New York: W. W. Norton, 1961.

Friedman, Milton. *Capitalism and Freedom*. Chicago: The University of Chicago Press, 2002.

Fuller, Lon L. *The Morality of Law*. New Haven: Yale University Press, 1964.

Gandhi, M. K. *An Autobiography or the Story of My Experiments with Truth*. Translated from the Gujarati by Mahadev Desai. Ahmedabad-380 014: Navajivan Publishing House, 1927.

George, Henry. *Progress and Poverty*. New York: Robert Schalkenbach Foundation, 1953.

Gleick, James. *Faster*. New York: Pantheon Books, 1999.

Goethe, J. W. von. *Faust*. Translated by Barker Fairley. In *Selected Works*. New York: Random House, 2000.

Gottfredson, Michael R., and Travis Hirschi. *A General Theory of Crime*. Stanford: Stanford University Press, 1990.

Graetz, Michael J. *The U.S. Income Tax: What It Is, How it Got That Way, and Where We Go from Here*. New York: W. W. Norton, 1999.

Grahm, Benjamin, and David Dodd. *Security Analysis*. New York: McGraw-Hill, 1934.

Grasmick, Harold G., and Robert J. Bursik Jr. "Conscience, Significant Others, and Rational Choice: Extending the Deterrence Model." *Law & Society Review* 24, no. 3 (1990): 837–61.

Grasmick, Harold G. and Donald E. Green. "Legal Punishment, Social Disapproval, and Internalization as Inhibitors of Illegal Behavior." *The Journal of Criminal Law & Criminology* 71, no. 3 (1980): 325–35.

Green, Stuart P. *Lying, Cheating, and Stealing: A Moral Theory of White-Collar Crime*. Oxford: Oxford University Press, 2006.

Greenawalt, Kent. *Conflicts of Law and Morality.* Oxford: Oxford University Press, 1987.

Groves, Harold M. *Tax Philosophers: Two Hundred Years of Thought in Great Britain and the United States.* Edited by Donald J. Curran. Madison: University of Wisconsin Press, 1974.

Gunn, Alan. "Tax Avoidance." *Michigan Law Review* 76, no. 5 (April 1978): 733.

Hall, R. E., and A. Rabushka. *The Flat Tax.* 2nd edition. Stanford, CA: Hoover Institution Press, 1995.

Hammond, N. G. L. *A History of Greece to 322 B.C.* Oxford: The Clarendon Press, 1959.

Hand, Learned, *The Bill of Rights.* New York: Atheneum, 1979.

Hanno, Denis M., and George R. Violette. "An Analysis of Moral and Social Influences on Taxpayer Behavior." *Behavioral Research in Accounting* 8, supp. (1996): 57–75.

Hare, R. M. *Moral Thinking: Its Levels, Method, and Point.* Oxford: Clarendon Press, 1981.

Hart, H. L. A. *The Concept of Law.* London: Oxford University Press, 1961.

Hawking, Stephen. "The Future of the Universe." In *Predicting the Future,* ed. Leo Howe and Alan Wain. Cambridge: Cambridge University Press, 1993.

Hayek, Friedrich A. *The Road to Serfdom.* Chicago: University of Chicago Press, 1944.

———. *Individualism and Economic Order.* Chicago: University of Chicago Press, 1948.

———. *Law Legislation and Liberty.* Vol. 3: The Political Order of a Free People. Chicago: University of Chicago Press, 1979.

Hedemann, Ed. *War Tax Resistance: A Guide to Withholding Your Support from the Military.* 5th ed. Edited by Ruth Benn and Ed Hedemann. New York: War Resisters League, 2003.

Heilbroner, Robert L. *The Worldly Philosophers: The Lives, Times, and Ideas of the Great Economic Thinkers.* 3rd ed. New York: Simon and Schuster, 1953.

Henderson, Charlene, and Steven E. Kaplan. "An Examination of the Role of Ethics in Tax Compliance Decisions." *Journal of the American Taxation Association* 27, no. 1 (Spring 2005): 39–72.

Hendrickson, Peter Eric. *Cracking the Code.* n. p., 2003.

Herrnstein, Richard J., and Charles Murray. *The Bell Curve: Intelligence and Class Structure in American Life.* New York: Simon and Schuster, 1994.

Hessing, Dick J., Henk Elffers, Henry S. J. Robben, and Paul Webley. "Does Deterrence Deter? Measuring the Effect of Deterrence on Tax Compliance in Field Studies and Experimental Studies." In *Why People Pay Taxes: Tax Compliance and Enforcement,* ed. Joel Slemrod. Ann Arbor: University of Michigan Press, 1992.

Hite, Peggy A. "Commentary on 'An Analysis of Moral and Social Influences on Taxpayer Behavior.' " *Behavioral Research in Accounting* 8, supp. (1996): 76–79.

Hobbes, Thomas. *Leviathan: Or the Matter, Forme and Power of a Commonwealth Ecclesiasticall and Civil.* Edited by Michael Oakeshott. London: Collier-Macmillan, 1962.

———. *De Corpore Politico.* Oxford: Oxford University Press, 1994.

Holmes, Oliver Wendell, Jr. *The Common Law.* Mineola, NY: Dover, 1991.

Holmes, Stephen, and Cass R. Sunstein. *The Cost of Rights: Why Liberty Depends on Taxes*. New York: W. W. Norton, 1999.

Honoré, Tony. "Must We Obey? Necessity as a Ground of Obligation." *Virginia Law Review* 67 (Feb. 1981): 39.

Hook, Sidney. "Law, Justice, and Obedience." In *Law and Philosophy: A Symposium*, ed. Sidney Hook. New York: New York University Press, 1964.

———, ed. *Law and Philosophy: A Symposium*. New York: New York University Press, 1964.

Hopkins, Bruce. *A Legal Guide to Starting and Managing a Nonprofit Organization*. New York: John Wiley and Sons, 1993.

Hume, David. *An Enquiry Concerning the Principles of Morals*. La Salle, IL: Open Court, [1777] 1966.

———. "On the Original Contract." In *Essays Moral Political and Literary*. Edited by Eugene F. Miller. Indianapolis: Liberty Fund, 1985.

———. "Of Taxes." In *Essays Moral Political and Literary*. Edited by Eugene F. Miller. Indianapolis: Liberty Fund, 1985.

Jaramillo, Christian R. "On the Use of Presumptive Income Taxes to Alleviate the Burden of Income Tax Compliance." *National Tax Association Proceedings, 96th Annual Conference on Taxation* (2003): 105–109.

Kagan, Robert A. "On the Visibility of Income Tax Law Violations." In *Tax Compliance Volume 2: Social Science Perspectives*, ed. Jeffrey A. Roth and John T. Scholz. Philadelphia: University of Pennsylvania Press, 1989.

Kahan, Dan M. "Trust, Collective Action, and Law." *Boston University Law Review* 81, no. 2 (April 2001): 333.

Kant, Immanuel. *Groundwork of the Metaphysic of Morals*. Translated by H. J. Paton. New York: Harper and Row, 1964.

———. *The Metaphysics of Morals*. In *Political Writings*. Translated by H. B. Nisbet. Cambridge: Cambridge University Press, [1797] 1991.

Kaplow, Louis. "How Tax Complexity and Enforcement Affect the Equality and Efficiency of the Income Tax." *National Tax Journal* 49, no. 1 (March 1996): 135–50.

Kelling, George L., and Catherine M. Coles. *Fixing Broken Windows*. New York: Touchstone, 1996.

Kelsen, Hans. *The Pure Theory of Law*. Translated by Max Knight. Berkeley: University of California Press, 1967.

Keynes, John Maynard. "Economic Model Construction and Econometrics." 1938. Reprinted in *The Philosophy of Economics*, 2nd ed. Edited by Daniel M. Hausman. Cambridge: Cambridge University Press, 1994.

Kidder, Robert, and Craig McEwen. "Taxpaying Behavior in Social Context: A Tentative Typology of Tax Compliance and Noncompliance." In *Tax Compliance vol. 2: Social Science Perspectives*, ed. Jeffrey A. Roth and John T. Scholz. Philadelphia: University of Pennsylvania Press, 1989.

Klepper, Steven, and Daniel Nagin. 1989. "The Anatomy of Tax Evasion." *Journal of Law, Economics, & Organization* 5, no. 1 (Spring 1989): 1–24.

Kohlberg, Lawrence. "Stage and Sequence: The Cognitive-Developmental Approach to Socialization." In *Handbook of Socialization Theory and Research*, ed. David A. Goslin. Chicago: Rand McNally, 1969.

Konvitz, Milton B. "Civil Disobedience and the Duty of Fair Play." In *Law and Philosophy: A Symposium*, ed. Sidney Hook. New York: New York University Press, 1964.

Kuhn, Thomas S. *The Structure of Scientific Revolutions.* Chicago: University of Chicago Press, 1996.

Kunreuther, H., R. Ginsberg, L. Miller, P. Sagi, P. Slovic, B. Borkan, and N. Katz. *Disaster Insurance Protection: Public Policy Lessons.* New York: Wiley, 1978.

Leiker, Bret H. "The Ethics of Tax Evasion as Analyzed through the Philosophy of Jean-Jacques Rousseau," *Journal of Accounting, Ethics & Public Policy* 1, no. 1 (1998). Reprinted in *The Ethics of Tax Evasion,* ed. Robert W. McGee. South Orange, NJ: The Dumont Institute of Public Policy Research, 1998.

Levi, Margaret. *Of Rule and Revenue.* Berkeley: University of California Press, 1988.

Lewis, Alan. *The Psychology of Taxation.* New York: St. Martin's Press, 1982.

Locke, John. *Second Treatise of Government.* Edited by C. B. Macpherson. Cambridge: Hackett, [1690] 1980.

Loftus, E. F. "To File, Perchance to Cheat." *Psychology Today* (April 1985): 35–39.

Loewenstein, George, Daniel Read, and Roy F. Baumeister. *Time and Decision: Economic and Psychological Perspectives on Intertemporal Choice.* New York: Russell Sage Foundation, 2003.

Machiavelli, Niccolò. *The Prince.* Translated by Peter Bondanella and Mark Musa. New York: Penguin Books, 1979.

Mackie, John L. *Ethics: Inventing Right and Wrong.* New York: Penguin Books, 1977.

——. "Obligations to Obey the Law." *Virginia Law Review* 67, no. 1 (Feb. 1981): 143.

Malamud, Richard B., and Richard O. Parry. "It's Time to do Something About the Tax Gap." *Houston Business and Tax Journal* 9 (2008): 1.

Martinez, Leo P. "Taxes, Morals, and Legitimacy." *Brigham Young University Law Review* (1994): 521.

Mason, Robert, and Lyle. D. Calvin. "A Study of Admitted Tax Evasion." *Law and Society Review* 13, no. 1 (Autumn 1978).

——. "Public Confidence and Admitted Tax Evasion." *National Tax Journal* 37, no. 4 (Dec. 1984): 489–96.

McGee, Robert W. "Is Tax Evasion Unethical?" *Kansas Law Review* 42 (1994): 411.

——, ed. *The Ethics of Tax Evasion.* South Orange, NJ: The Dumont Institute of Public Policy Research, 1998.

——. "An Ethical Look at Paying Your 'Fair Share' of Taxes." *Journal of Ethics, Accounting & Public Policy* 3, no. 2 (Spring 1999): 318–29.

——. *The Philosophy of Taxation and Public Finance.* Boston: Kluwer, 2004.

——. "Three Views on the Ethics of Tax Evasion." *Journal of Business Ethics* 67 (2006): 15–35.

McCaghy, Charles H., Timothy A. Capron, and J. D. Jamieson. *Deviant Behavior.* 6th ed. Boston: Pearson Education, 2003.

Merton, Robert K. *On Social Structure and Science.* Edited by Piotr Sztompka. Chicago: University of Chicago Press, 1996.

Mill, John Stuart. *Principles of Political Economy.* Abridged by J. Laurence Laughlin. New York: Appleton, 1884.

——. *On Liberty.* Chicago: Henry Regnery, 1955.

——. *A System of Logic Ratiocinative and Inductive.* Honolulu: University Press of the Pacific, 2002.

Mises, Ludwig von. *Human Action: A Treatise on Economics.* 3rd revised ed. San Francisco: Fox and Wilkes, 1949.

Monin, Benoît, and Dale T. Miller. "Moral Credentials and the Expression of Prejudice." *Journal of Personality and Social Psychology* 81, no. 1 (2001): 33–43.

Monin, Benoît, and Alexander H. Jordan. "The Dynamic Moral Self: A Social Psychological Perspective." In *Personality, Identity, and Character: Explorations in Moral Psychology,* ed. Darcia Narvaez and Daniel K. Lapsley. Cambridge: Cambridge University Press, 2009.

Montesquieu, Charles De. *The Spirit of the Laws.* Translated by Thomas Nugent and revised by J. V. Prichard. In *The Great Books of the Western World,* vol. 38. Chicago: Encyclopedia Britannica, 1952.

Moore, Wilbert E. "Occupational Socialization." In *Handbook of Socialization Theory and Research,* ed. David A. Goslin. Chicago: Rand McNally, 1969.

Murphy, Jeffrie G., and Jules L. Coleman. *Philosophy of Law,* Boulder: Westview, 1990.

Murphy, Sean. "MacMurray v. Comm.: Distinguishing Between Reasonable Cause and Good Faith Requirements of the Section 6664 Exception to Accuracy Related Penalties." *The Tax Lawyer* 61, no. 2 (Winter 2008).

Murray, Matthew N. "Would Tax Evasion and Tax Avoidance Undermine a National Retail Sales Tax?" In *Tax Policy in the Real World,* ed. Joel Slemrod. Cambridge: Cambridge University Press, 1999.

Nadler, Janice. "Flouting the Law." *Texas Law Review* 83 (2005): 1399.

National Football League. *Official Rules of the NFL.* Chicago: Triumph Books, 2008.

Netzer, Dick. "The Relevance and Feasibility of Land Value Taxation in the Rich Countries." In *Land Value Taxation: Can It and Will It Work Today?,* ed. Dick Netzer. Cambridge, MA: Lincoln Institute of Land Policy, 1998.

———, ed. *Land Value Taxation: Can It and Will It Work Today?* Cambridge, MA: Lincoln Institute of Land Policy, 1998.

Nichols, Nancy B., and Robert C. Richardson. "Criminal Investigations of Taxpayer Fraud." *Journal of Legal Tax Research* 4 (2006): 34–48.

Nietzsche, Friedrich. *The Genealogy of Morals.* Translated by Francis Golffing. New York: Doubleday, 1956.

Oliva, Robert R. "When Will Reliance on a Tax Adviser Avoid an Accuracy-Related Penalty?" *The Tax Adviser* 28, no. 12 (Dec. 1997): 772–77.

Palan, Ronen, Richard Murphy, and Christian Chavagneux. *Tax Havens: How Globalization Really Works.* Ithaca: Cornell University Press, 2010.

Pasquariello, Ronald. *Tax Justice: Social and Moral Aspects of American Tax Policy.* Lanham: MD, University Press of America, 1985.

Pfohl, Stephen. *Images of Deviance and Social Control: A Sociological History.* 2nd ed. New York: McGraw-Hill, 1994.

———. "The 'Discovery' of Child Abuse." *Social Problems* 24, no. 3 (Feb. 1997): 310–23.

Plato. *Laws,* Translated by A. E. Taylor.

———. *Republic,* Translated by Paul Shorey.

Plous, Scott. *The Psychology of Judgment and Decision Making.* New York: McGraw-Hill, 1993.

Plutarch. *Plutarch's Lives,* the Dryden trans. New York: The Modern Library, 2001.

Pollack, Sheldon D. *The Failure of U.S. Tax Policy: Revenue and Politics.* University Park: Pennsylvania State University Press, 1996.

Porcano, Thomas M. "Correlates of Tax Evasion." *Journal of Economic Psychology* 9 (1988): 47–67.

Posner, Eric A. "Law and Social Norms: The Case of Tax Compliance." *Virginia Law Review* 86 (2000): 1781.

Posner, Richard A. "Theories of Economic Regulation," *Bell Journal of Economics and Management Science* 5 (1974): 335–58.

——. *Problems of Jurisprudence.* Cambridge: Harvard University Press, 1990.

Rand, Ayn. *The Virtue of Selfishness: A New Concept of Egoism.* New York: Signet Books, 1964.

Rawls, John. "Legal Obligation and the Duty of Fair Play." In *Law and Philosophy: A Symposium,* ed. Sidney Hook. New York: New York University Press, 1964.

——. *A Theory of Justice.* Cambridge: Harvard University Press, 1971.

Raz, Joseph. *The Authority of Law: Essays on Law and Morality,* Oxford: Oxford University Press, 1979.

Reckers, Philip M., Debra L. Sanders, and Stephen J. Roark. "The Influence of Ethical Attitudes on Taxpayer Compliance." *National Tax Journal* 47, no. 4 (Dec. 1994): 825–36.

Rescher, Nicholas. *Predicting the Future: An Introduction to the Theory of Forecasting.* Albany: State University of New York Press, 1998.

Reuter, Peter, and Edwin M. Truman. *Chasing Dirty Money: The Fight Against Money Laundering.* Washington, DC: Institute for International Economics, 2004.

Rice, Eric M. "The Corporate Tax Gap: Evidence of Tax Compliance by Small Corporations." In *Why People Pay Taxes: Tax Compliance and Enforcement,* ed. Joel Slemrod. Ann Arbor: University of Michigan Press, 1992.

Richards, David A. J. "Conscience, Human Rights, and the Anarchist Challenge to the Obligation to Obey the Law." *Georgia Law Review* 18 (1984): 771.

Robinson, Paul H., and John M. Darley. "The Utility of Desert." *Northwestern University Law Review* 91, no. 2 (1997): 453.

Robinson, Richard. *Definition.* Oxford: Oxford University Press, 1954.

Rosen, Harvey S. *Public Finance.* 7th ed. Boston: McGraw-Hill Irwin, 2005.

Rossotti, Charles O. *Many Unhappy Returns: One Man's Quest to Turn Around the Most Unpopular Organization in the World.* Boston: Harvard Business School Press, 2005.

Roth, Jeffrey A., and John T. Scholz, eds. *Tax Compliance vol. 2: Social Science Perspectives.* Philadelphia: University of Pennsylvania Press, 1989.

Roth, Senator William V., Jr., and William H. Nixon. *The Power to Destroy.* New York: Atlantic Monthly Press, 1999.

Rousseau, Jean-Jacques. *Discourse on Political Economy.* Translated by Julia Conway Bondanella. In *Rousseau's Political Writings.* New York: W. W. Norton, 1988.

Rowe, David C. *Biology and Crime.* Los Angeles: Roxbury, 2002.

Rubenfield, Alan J. and Ganesh M. Pandit. "Tax 'Cheating' by Ordinary Taxpayers: Does the Underreporting of Income Contribute to the 'Tax Gap'?" *The CPA Journal* (March 25, 2009): 42–47.

Ruelle, David. *Chance and Chaos.* Princeton: Princeton University Press, 1991.

Saltzman, Michael I. *IRS Practice and Procedure.* Boston: Warren, Gorham and Lamont, 1981.

Samuelson, Paul A., and William D. Nordhaus. *Economics.* 14th ed. New York: McGraw-Hill, 1992.

Sanders, Debra L., Phillip M. J. Reckers, and Govind S. Iyer. "Influence of Accountability and Penalty Awareness on Tax Compliance." *Journal of the American Taxation Association* 30, no. 2 (Fall 2008): 1–20.

Sartorius, Rolf. "Political Authority and Political Obligation." *Virginia Law Review* 67, no. 1 (Feb. 1981): 3.

Say, Jean-Baptiste. *A Treatise on Political Economy.* Translated by C. R. Prinsep. New Brunswick, NJ: Transaction, [1836] 2001.

Schmalleger, Frank. *Criminology Today.* 3rd ed. Upper Saddle River, NJ: Prentice-Hall, 2002.

Scholz, John T. "Compliance Research and the Political Context of Tax Administration." In *Tax Compliance vol. 2: Social Science Perspectives,* ed. Jeffrey A. Roth and John T. Scholz. Philadelphia: University of Pennsylvania Press, 1989.

———. "Trust, Taxes, and Compliance." In *Trust and Governance,* ed. Valerie Braithwaite and Margaret Levi. New York: Russell Sage Foundation, 1998.

Schumpeter, Joseph A. *Capitalism, Socialism, and Democracy.* New York: Harper and Row, 1976.

Schur, Edward M. *Our Criminal Society: The Social and Legal Sources of Crime in America.* Englewood Cliffs, NJ: Prentice-Hall, 1969.

Schwartz, Barry. *The Paradox of Choice.* New York: Harper, 2004.

Schwartz, Richard D., and Sonya Orleans. "On Legal Sanctions." *University of Chicago Law Review* 34 (1966–67): 274.

Scott, Wilbur J., and Harold G. Grasmick. "Deterrence and Income Tax Cheating: Testing Interaction Hypotheses in Utilitarian Theories." *The Journal of Applied Behavioral Science* 17, no. 1 (1981): 395–408.

Seneca. *Moral Essays.* Vol. 1. Translated by John W. Basore. Loeb Classical Library. Cambridge: Harvard University Press, 1928.

———. *Moral Essays.* Vol. 2. Translated by John W. Basore. Loeb Classical Library. Cambridge: Harvard University Press, 1932.

Shakespeare, William. *Hamlet.*

Shaw, George Bernard. *Major Barbara.* New York: Penguin Books, 1957.

Sherrer, Hans. "The Illusion of Tax Evasion." In *The Ethics of Tax Evasion,* ed. Robert W. McGee. South Orange, NJ: The Dumont Institute for Public Policy Research, 1998.

Sidgwick, Henry. *Outlines of the History of Ethics.* Indianapolis: Hackett, 1988.

Siegel, Mark, with Barry Wolfson. *Tax Cheating: Hide & Seek with the IRS.* Mesa, AZ: Blue Sky Press, 1988.

Simmons, A. John. *Moral Principles and Political Obligations.* Princeton: Princeton University Press, 1979.

Singer, Marcus George. *Generalization in Ethics,* New York: Atheneum, 1971.

Skinner, B. F. *Beyond Freedom and Dignity.* New York: Knopf, 1971.

———. *Cumulative Record.* New York: Appleton-Century-Crofts, 1972.

Slemrod, Joel. "The Return to Tax Simplification: an Econometric Analysis." *Public Finance Review* 17, no. 3 (1989): 3–27.

———, ed. *Why People Pay Taxes.* Ann Arbor: University of Michigan Press, 1992.

———. "On Voluntary Compliance, Voluntary Taxes and Social Capital." *National Tax Journal* 51, no. 3 (1998): 485–91.

———, and J. Bakija. *Taxing Ourselves.* Cambridge: The MIT Press, 1996.

Smith, Adam. *The Theory of Moral Sentiments.* Indianapolis: Liberty Fund reprint of Oxford University Press edition [1759]1976 .

———. *Wealth of Nations.* New York: Prometheus Books, [1776]1991.

Smith, Carlton M. "Does the Tax Court's Use of its Golsen Rule in Unappealable Small Tax Cases Hurt the Poor?" *Journal of Tax Practice and Procedure.* Cardozo Legal Studies Research Paper No. 249 (2009).

Smith, M. B. E. "Is There a Prima Facie Obligation to Obey the Law?" *Yale Law Journal* 82 (1974): 950. Reprinted in *The Duty to Obey the Law: Selected Philosophical Readings*, ed. William A. Edmundson. New York: Roman and Littlefield, 1999.

Smith, Michael. *The Moral Problem*. Oxford: Blackwell, 1995.

Spencer, Herbert. *The Man Versus the State*, Indianapolis: The Liberty Fund, [1884] 1982.

Spohn, William C. "Conscience and Moral Development." In *Conscience*, ed. Charles E. Curran. New York: Paulist Press, 2004.

Stephen, Leslie. *The Science of Ethics*. Honolulu: University Press of the Pacific, 2003.

Stern, Philip M. *The Rape of the Taxpayer*. New York: Vintage Books, 1974.

Taeusch, Carl F. *Professional and Business Ethics*. New York: Henry Holt, 1926.

Thoreau, Henry David. *Civil Disobedience*. New York: Quill Pen, 2008.

Tittle, Charles R. *Sanctions and Social Deviance: The Question of Deterrence*. New York: Praeger, 1980.

Torgler, Benno. *Tax Compliance and Tax Morale*. Northampton, MA: Edward Elgar, 2007.

Toulmin, Stephen. *Reason in Ethics*. Cambridge: Cambridge University Press, 1968.

Tunick, Mark. "The Moral Obligation to Obey Law." *Journal of Social Philosophy* 33, no. 5 (Fall 2002): 464–82.

Tversky, Amos, and Daniel Kahneman. "Availability: A Heuristic for Judging Frequency and Probability." In *Judgment Under Uncertainty: Heuristics and Biases*, ed. Daniel Kahneman, Paul Slovic, and Amos Tversky. Cambridge: Cambridge University Press, 1982.

Twain, Mark. *Mark Twain on the Damned Human Race*. Edited by Janet Smith. New York: Hill and Wang, 1962.

Tyler, Tom R. *Why People Obey the Law*. Princeton: Princeton University Press, 2006.

Vinogradoff, Paul. *Common Sense in Law*. New York: Henry Holt, 1913.

———. *Custom and Right*. Union, NJ: The Lawbook Exchange, [1925] 2000.

Violette, George, "Effects of Communicating Sanctions on Taxpayer Compliance," *The Journal of the American Taxation Association* (Fall 1989): 92–104.

Wallace, David Foster. *The Pale King*. New York: Little Brown, 2011.

Walter, Ingo. *The Secret Money Market: Inside the Dark World of Tax Evasion, Financial Fraud, Insider Trading, Money Laundering, and Capital Flight*. New York: HarperCollins, 1990.

Wand, Bernard. "The Content and Function of Conscience." *The Journal of Philosophy* 58, no. 24 (Nov. 23, 1961): 765–72.

Wasserstrom, Richard. "The Obligation to Obey the Law." *UCLA Law Review* 10, no. 4 (May 1963): 780. Reprinted in *The Duty to Obey The Law: Selected Philosophical Readings*, ed. William A. Edmundson. New York: Rowman and Littlefield, 1999.

Weaver, Warren. "Science and Complexity." *American Scientist* 36 no. 4 (1948): 536–44.

Webber, Carolyn, and Aaron Wildavsky. *A History of Taxation and Expenditure in the Western World*. New York: Simon and Schuster, 1986.

Wellman, Christopher Heath, and John Simmons. *Is There a Duty to Obey the Law?* Cambridge: Cambridge University Press, 2005.

Wells, Joseph T. *Occupational Fraud and Abuse*. Austin, TX: Obsidian, 1997.

———. *Principles of Fraud Examination*. Hoboken: John Wiley and Sons, 2005.

Wilson, Edward O. *Consilience: The Unity of Knowledge*. New York: Vintage Books, 1998.

Wilson, James Q., and George L. Kelling. "Broken Windows." *Atlantic Monthly* 249, no. 3 (March 1982): 29–37.

Witte, Ann D., and Diane F. Woodbury. "The Effect of Tax Laws and Tax Administration on Tax Compliance: The Case of the U.S. Individual Income Tax." *National Tax Journal* 38 (March 1985): 1–14.

Wittgenstein, Ludwig. *Philosophical Investigations*. 3rd ed. Translated by G. E. M. Anscombe. Englewood Cliffs, NJ: Prentice-Hall, 1958.

Wolff, Edward N. "Distributional Consequences of a National Land Value Tax on Real Property in the United States." In *Land Value Taxation: Can It and Will It Work Today?*, ed. Dick Netzer. Cambridge, MA: Lincoln Institute of Land Policy, 1998.

Wright, Robert. *The Moral Animal*. New York: Vintage Books, 1994.

Yaniv, Gideon. "The Tax Compliance Demand Curve: A Diagrammatical Approach to Income Tax Evasion." *Journal of Economic Education* (Spring 2009).

Yankelovich, Skelly, and White, Inc. "Taxpayer Attitudes Survey: Final Report." Public Opinion Survey Prepared for the Public Affairs Division, Internal Revenue Service. New York, NY, 1984.

INDEX

Made in the USA
Lexington, KY
29 November 2013